The Convergence of Race, Ethnicity, and Gender

Multiple Identities in Counseling

Third Edition

Tracy L. Robinson-Wood
Northeastern University

Merrill
is an imprint of

Upper Saddle River, New Jersey
Columbus, Ohio

Library of Congress Cataloging in Publication Data

Robinson, Tracy L.
  The convergence of race, ethnicity, and gender : multiple identities in counseling/
Tracy L. Robinson-Wood.—3rd ed.
    p. cm.
  Includes bibliographical references and index.
  ISBN-13: 978-0-13-233716-8
  1. Cross-cultural counseling.   I. Title.

  BF637.C6R583 2009
  158'.3—dc22   2008000398

Vice President and Executive Publisher: Jeffery W. Johnston
Publisher: Kevin M. Davis
Acquisitions Editor: Meredith D. Fossel
Editorial Assistant: Maren Vigilante
Senior Managing Editor: Pamela D. Bennett
Senior Project Manager: Linda Hillis Bayma
Production Coordination: Susan A. Nodine, Elm Street Publishing Services
Design Coordinator: Diane C. Lorenzo
Cover Designer: Kristina Holmes
Cover Image: Corbis
Operations Specialist: Susan Hannahs
Director of Marketing: Quinn Perkson
Marketing Manager: Krista Clark
Marketing Coordinator: Brian Mounts

This book was set in Korinna by Integra Software Services Pvt. Ltd. It was printed and bound by R.R. Donnelley & Sons Company. The cover was printed by R.R. Donnelley & Sons Company.

Pearson® is a registered trademark of Pearson plc
Merrill® is a registered trademark of Pearson Education, Inc.

Pearson Education Ltd., London
Pearson Education Singapore, Pte. Ltd.
Pearson Education Canada, Inc.
Pearson Education–Japan
Pearson Education Australia Pty, Limited

Pearson Education North Asia Ltd., Hong Kong
Pearson Educación de Mexico, S.A. de C.V.
Pearson Education Malaysia, Pte. Ltd.
Pearson Education Upper Saddle River, New Jersey

Merrill
is an imprint of

10 9 8 7 6 5 4 3 2
ISBN-13: 978-0-13-233716-8
ISBN-10:   0-13-233716-9

> **We all know that what will transform education is not another theory, another book, or another formula but educators who are willing to see a transformed way of being in the world.**
>
> Parker Palmer, *The Grace of Great Things: Reclaiming the Sacred in Knowing, Teaching, and Learning*

Much has been invested in equipping counselors and psychologists with tools to be culturally competent in multicultural contexts. A bounty of beautifully written articles, special editions, and tomes exists on multiculturalism and cultural diversity with the collective aim of improving the quality of our clients' lives. The quality of our teaching, research, and clinical practice has been enriched, and yet there is more we must still learn and unlearn.

Historically, the multicultural counseling psychology literature has emphasized race. This is understandable considering the legacy and current reality of racism in America and the power people give to racial differences to stratify and stereotype. The initial work on multicultural psychology and counseling was written by heterosexually identified men from diverse racial backgrounds who privileged race, ethnicity, and culture. As native-born people of color, immigrants, White men and women, gay people, and people with disabilities began writing from their personal and clinical experiences, gender, sexual, and disability identities were added to the literature. Increasingly, a focus on spirituality can be found. This expanded focus on disability, spirituality, sexuality, and socioeconomic class is crucial to an inclusive cultural paradigm. Convergence requires us to honor race and ethnic identities in our clients while simultaneously incorporating other identities. Concern about injustice, regardless of the constellation of our identities and even when we have membership in privileged groups, is a reflection of our commitment to diversity.

In 1989, as a new assistant professor, I began talking about convergence. What I meant by convergence was the intersection of race, ethnicity, gender, and other primary identity constructs within the context of counseling. Each of these constructs is critical to a person's emotional and psychological development, and each intersects with other human dimensions. Fortunately, these intersecting identities have been receiving greater attention in the multicultural counseling literature. Prior to this, much of the literature focused on individual aspects of identity (most often race, culture, or ethnicity) and their subsequent influences on a cross-cultural counseling event in which the client was a person of color and the counselor was not. A consideration of how multiple identities, visible and invisible, converge simultaneously and affect development, behavior, and the counseling event itself was missing.

This new paradigm for imaging differences, both visible and invisible, allows us to engage in the never-ending process of growing in self-awareness as human beings with multiple and shifting identities. Differences are celebrated; the structural inequity that assigns power and privilege to immutable characteristics is not.

Multicultural counseling and psychology emphasize an ecological and social justice framework. As professionals, we accept our responsibility to be change agents toward reducing suffering and creating a more just and equitable world that reflects humane distribution of resources and opportunities. Multicultural counseling and psychology also recognize the way in which dominant cultural beliefs and values furnish and perpetuate feelings of inadequacy, shame, confusion, and distrust in clients in both the therapeutic process and the larger society.

The response to the first and second editions from colleagues and students has been uplifting. I am humbled by your support of my work. This third edition offers an updated format with revised and brand new chapters, case studies, and storytellings. New and existing theories and research are discussed, and greater attention is devoted to application to clinical practice. In a spirit of *Nia* (purpose), I acknowledge and celebrate the contributions of "pathshowers" who have gone before me. Our students continue to walk with us and point us in new directions.

A MESSAGE TO STUDENTS

The material presented in this book is intended to further your development as a multiculturally competent professional. Some of the information you encounter may provoke dissonance. It is hoped that you will honor your feelings and share them with your professors and classmates. Through your practica and internships, you will find that your clients will feel dissonance, confusion, anger, and a host of other emotions when exposed to a new insight or technique that will serve them long term but can be hard to take in the short term. Once the course is finished and you have your grade, it might be easy to retreat to more comfortable pre-multicultural class experiences. If you are "willing to see a transformed way of being in the world," your thoughts, actions, behaviors, and beliefs about yourself and others will undergo transformation as well. The process of transformation is part of a social justice orientation and a life-long commitment to using your power and privilege for good in the world.

I welcome you to this exploration. Please read the storytellings and case studies, and listen to other people's stories, and mine, as well as your own. Although growth cannot happen without dissonance, trust that you are being prepared to better appreciate the multiple layers and contexts that both you and your clients will bring to therapy. Your more informed sense of self will help you relate to your clients from their view of the world. This in turn will help you identify the questions to follow and avoid those that are better left unasked. As you process your own feelings and endeavor to make meaning out of new information, I hope you will have communities of support who listen, nurture, and, at the same time, challenge your positions. I also encourage you to accept that there may be individuals who will be unable to receive or support some of the new insights that you will take from this text.

A MESSAGE TO COLLEAGUES

Teaching multiculturalism is not easy. If successful, students will become aware of unearned skin color privilege and history denied and distorted. Hopefully, they will also become mindful of a dominant culture that esteems White or White-looking skin, masculinity, high-wage-earning persons, an able body, and hetero-sexuality. In coming to this awareness, there will be disillusionment, sadness, and anger—often directed toward you, the messenger. Faculty of color may be perceived as extremely well suited to teach diversity-oriented courses. Despite being well prepared and qualified to teach, White professors may be viewed suspiciously by students and faculty across race and ethnic groups. White students may fear that faculty of color are going to be punitive or make them feel guilty for being White. Students of color may feel the need to carefully weigh their words lest they offend their White professors and suffer from this power differential with an inferior grade. These matters are contextual; thus, there are White people and people of color, due to their proximity to socially constructed meanings about Whiteness, who regard White people as the most effective teachers of this material. Untenured professors of any race are naturally concerned about student evaluations, which can have positive and negative implications for promotion and tenure review. For this reason, I do not advocate junior faculty teaching this class by themselves initially—a co-teaching model with a senior colleague is recommended during the first few semesters. Senior faculty and department chairs need to understand these dynamics and act wisely, thus protecting vulnerable junior faculty. The politics are fierce and often unspoken, yet they represent the landscape of multicultural work.

With that said, the course is one where teachers are able to bear witness to students being changed at depth. This is a great gift and privilege. It does not, however, come without a price. It is important that you take care of yourselves and do the best work that you can. This is, after all, a calling. Watching students listen to other people's voices and coexist with different ways of being in the world allows us to contribute to meaningful change. At the same time, some students will receive excellent grades yet will not be significantly altered by their experiences. Be prepared to read and hear racist statements from students. However, you must be prepared to hear that which is difficult to receive when you ask students to speak from their own lived experiences. How can the rain of racism fall throughout the land and miss your house? This is a question I ask students to consider. You have to trust that for some of your students, you are nurturing growth and change that you will not see by the semester's end. I encourage new faculty members who have taken jobs away from home and other communities of support to have a ready list of people on whom to call and confide after a particularly difficult class that leaves them feeling drained and seriously questioning the decision making that led them to this place they now call home.

Finally, require your students to buy world maps. You must not assume that they know their geography. Although I have traveled the world, having a portable and laminated world map has been helpful.

OUTLINE OF CHAPTERS

The text is divided into four parts: Imaging Diversity, Valued Cultures, Converging Identities, and Reimaging Counseling. Every chapter has at least one "Storytelling" feature to honor the powerful oral tradition of storytelling that is alive in the world's cultures. To encourage the integration and application of the material, a case study that emphasizes counseling skills is presented in each chapter.

In this third edition, a separate chapter is devoted to Native Americans, Latinos, people of African descent, people of Asian descent, and people of the Middle East. The reality of bicultural, biracial, and multiracial people as the fastest-growing demographic in the United States is recognized as well throughout the book.

PART ONE: IMAGING DIVERSITY Chapter 1, Multiple Identities Defined, provides an overview of culture, race, ethnicity, gender, sexuality, disability, socioeconomic class, and religion and faith. The importance of counselors' awareness of their attitudes about sources of differences is emphasized. Examined is a dominant value structure within the United States that is touted as normal and superior to the exclusion of all others. Dominant cultural values are discussed as a way to orient the reader to core values that are not apparent, even to those of us born and reared in the United States.

Chapter 2, Multicultural Competencies and Guidelines, focuses on the knowledge, attitudes, and skills, both verbal and nonverbal, that are essential for the effective mental health professional to possess. Competencies from the American Counseling Association are discussed in depth as are American Psychological Association guidelines for teaching, research, practice, and organizational development. Information is provided on the integration of competencies in various settings, which includes the ability to know the limits of one's competence. Finally, ethical considerations are discussed within a multicultural context.

In Chapter 3, Statused Identities, gender, race, sexuality, religion, ability, disability, and class as sources of differences and status characteristics are explored. The intersections of identities and their contextual nature are discussed.

PART TWO: VALUED CULTURES Chapter 4 focuses on Native Americans and Alaskan Natives. Chapter 5 explores Latinos. Chapter 6 focuses on people of African descent. Chapter 7 is dedicated to people of Asian descent, Native Hawaiians, and Pacific Islanders. Chapter 8, new to this edition, focuses on Arab Americans and people of the Middle East. A succinct overview of demographic characteristics, historical information, migratory patterns (where applicable), and cultural values is explored. The terms "people of Asian descent," "people of African descent," "Latinos," "Native Americans and Alaskan Natives," and "people of the Middle East" are used for three reasons: to reflect the biracial and multiracial heritages reflected within and across racial categories; to respect the reality that people may live in America but hail from other parts of the world, such as the Caribbean or the continents of Asia and Africa; and to honor the reality that many whose people have resided in America for many generations may not choose to self-identify as Asian American, Arab American, Latino American, or African American but by a particular ethnicity, such as Korean, Jamaican, Lebanese, Guatemalan, Cherokee, or Ghanaian.

In 1978, the Office of Management and Budget (OMB) adopted the term *Hispanic* to describe people who were perceived to have a similar ethnic background. Instead of Hispanic, *Latino* is used throughout this text because it is a self-defined term. Latinos can be of any race.

PART THREE: CONVERGING IDENTITIES   Chapter 9, Converging Race, explores race from sociopolitical perspectives. Primary stage models of racial identity development and relevant research are presented. Via the case study, race, gender, acculturation, and assimilation are explored.

Chapter 10, Converging Biracial and Multiracial Identities, provides important definitions. Research is summarized that speaks to identity development. Clinical issues related to multiple racial and/or cultural identities are also presented by way of the case study that examines group affiliation and belonging.

Chapter 11, Converging Gender, discusses gender roles and gender identity and examines gender development from a biological perspective. Sex and sex role typing are explored, and distinctions are made among terms. Female and male models of gender identity are discussed. Attention is given to gender socialization, the construct of physical beauty, emotion, and their influence on power and status.

Chapter 12, Converging Socioeconomic Class, focuses on class as a status variable both in society and within the therapeutic encounter. Class is inextricably linked to self-worth and income. The limited training that graduate students in counseling programs receive is discussed within the context of culture. Questions are provided to help students unravel the role of class in their own development and with respect to their perceptions of others. The intersections of power, powerlessness, gender, and race are considered.

Chapter 13 is titled Converging Sexuality. Often counselors and psychologists do not receive adequate training in sexuality, with respect to their own lives and those of their clients. The goal of this chapter is to expose readers to the heterosexual bias that exists in American culture and to increase sensitivity about the inherent danger to lesbian, gay, bisexual, and transgender clients in a climate of heterosexism. Greater attention is focused on transgender and intersexuality issues.

Chapter 14, Converging Disability, is a focused look at the able-bodied culture and its impact on perceptions of normalcy, beauty, and well-being. Counseling individuals with disabilities is emphasized, and demographic data are provided with respect to numbers, type of disability, poverty, housing status, and occupational participation.

PART FOUR: REIMAGING COUNSELING   Chapter 15, Diversity in Relationships, focuses on a variety of interpersonal and intimate relationships, including traditional marriages between women and men, same-gender couples, extended families, and close friendships that function as families even though the participants are not related by blood. Family structure, marital status, and diverse family patterns, such as father-headed households and the extended family, are discussed. Strategies for counselors to work effectively with a diversity of relationships are emphasized.

The therapeutic process can foster greater self-understanding and be a place where people experience the advocacy and social justice orientation of their counselor or psychologist. This is the message of Chapter 16, Advocacy and Social Justice, a new chapter. Advocacy is one of the goals of psychotherapy. Those forces that leave people bereft of power are discussed. Empathy is defined as critical to effective counseling, and empowerment is discussed as an outcome.

Finally, Chapter 17, Converging Spirituality, is a new chapter that defines religion and spirituality and provides the helping professional with insight on how to integrate spirituality into the therapeutic event competently and comfortably. A case study illustrates a therapist's skill at attending to a client grappling with a crisis of faith.

An epilogue concludes this work.

ACKNOWLEDGMENTS

Fifteen years ago, Mary Howard-Hamilton and I approached a publisher in the exhibition hall at an American Counseling Association convention. We told her of our desire and our dream: to write a book on multicultural issues in counseling that incorporated race, ethnicity, and culture as well as the muted topics of gender, socioeconomic class, and sexual orientation. We asked the editor if we could buy her a cup of coffee. She graciously accepted. Out of that conversation, her scrutiny of us, and our scrutiny of multicultural counseling and of ourselves as women, Black Americans, and academicians, an invitation was extended to us to develop a book prospectus. Linda Sullivan had coffee with Mary and me at the ACA in Maryland and eventually moved us forward to a signed contract for the first edition.

More than 14 years later, I offer this third edition. I thank Mary for her invaluable contributions to the first edition of this text. I am indebted to Mary for her scholarship and creativity. Her friendship, sisterhood, and collegiality are the staff of life.

I also want to thank my husband, friends, students, graduate assistants, and colleagues for inspiration, encouragement, welcome distractions, help, prayers, and love. Everett Dickerson and Jennifer Tang, my graduate assistants, did an exceptional job of finding and organizing resources—census data, books, and research articles—for this third edition. In the academy, our students are our greatest gifts.

Anybody can show up at the celebration party, but not everyone can walk with you on the journey when there is no clear end in view. Geoffrey, Rita, Caren, Sherry, Ro, Karen C., Barbara, Jess, Rob, Ms. Fay, Marilyn, Betsy, Janie, and Brookins have had their walking, dancing, marking-time, and "I'm with you" shoes on forever. Your support gives me strength and direction. My angel mother has never left my side. Geoffrey's love has anchored and elevated me.

I want to thank the following reviewers: Lisa Hawley, Oakland University; Marty Jencius, Kent State University; Jill C. Jurgens, Old Dominion University; and Huijun Li, Florida State University. I also want to thank Sue Nodine, project editor at Elm Street Publishing Services, for her scrupulous attention to detail and her efficiency. Books do not get to press without good editors. I also want to thank Pearson/Merrill project manager Linda Bayma and editorial assistant Maren Vigilante for all of their production assistance. Both of you have been consistently available to me—thank you.

Tracy L. Robinson-Wood

BRIEF CONTENTS

CONTENTS

Chapter 3
Statused Identities 38

Part Two
Valued Cultures

Chapter 4
Native Americans and Alaskan Natives 58

Chapter 5
Latinos 74

Part Three
Converging Identities

Chapter 9
Converging Race

Chapter 10
Converging Biracial and Multicultural Identities

Chapter 11
Converging Gender   182

Chapter 12
Converging Socioeconomic Class   208

Chapter 13
Converging Sexuality

Chapter 14
Converging Disability

Part Four
Reimaging Counseling

Chapter 15
Diversity in Relationships

Chapter 16
Advocacy and Social Justice

Chapter 17
Converging Spirituality

NOTE: Every effort has been made to provide accurate and current Internet information in this book. However, the Internet and information posted on it are constantly changing, and it is inevitable that some of the Internet addresses listed in this textbook will change.

The Convergence of Race, Ethnicity, and Gender

Part One
Imaging Diversity

Chapter 1

Multiple Identities Defined

**MULTICULTURAL COUNSELING
AND PSYCHOLOGY DEFINED**

DIVERSITY: AN OVERVIEW

A, B, AND C DIMENSIONS

CONCEPTUALIZATION OF THE SELF

IMAGES OF DIVERSITY

**IMPLICATIONS FOR COUNSELORS
AND PSYCHOLOGISTS**

CASE STUDY

SUMMARY

Trying to avoid our problems or simply
not thinking about them may provide
temporary relief, but I think that there
is a better approach. If you directly
confront your suffering, you will be in
a better position to appreciate the
depth and nature of the problem.

His Holiness, The Dalai Lama, *The Art of Happiness*

Race, ethnicity, culture, gender, sexuality, mental and physical ability, socioeconomic class, age, and religion refer to identity constructs and are sources of difference. Identities are multiple, simultaneous, and ever-shifting, and they refer to a person's sense of themselves and their view of themselves within the context of other people. Depending on the context, certain identities have more power than do others and can take on different meanings. Within the therapeutic event, identity affects both a client's problem orientation and the relationship between therapist and client.

A primary tenet of this text is that effective clinicians acknowledge sources of differences among people, are mindful of their proximity to discourses about differences, and seek to improve their multicultural competence with a diversity of people. Age, ethnicity, ability, disability, gender, race, religion, sexuality, and socioeconomic class diversity are indications of a heterogeneous culture at its best. A distinction, however, exists between sources of difference among people and the socially constructed meanings about these differences.

This chapter explores the implications for clinicians, counselors, psychologists, and other mental health professionals practicing within a culturally diverse nation historically challenged by the concept of *equity for all*. Numerous movements and laws—such as the Asian rights movement, the Chicano moratorium, the civil rights movement, the women's movement, the gay rights movement, immigrant rights movement, Section 504 of the 1973 Rehabilitation Act, and the Americans with Disabilities Act (ADA)—are evidence of the ongoing struggle for human rights, social justice, access, and inclusion.

Historically, the focus of multicultural counseling was primarily on race and culture. Increasingly over the past 15 years, scholars in multicultural counseling and psychology have been privileging the discussion of other components of identity, those visible and invisible, such as gender, disability, sexuality, class, and religion. It is important to remember that invisible aspects of the self can be just as powerful if not more influential in the construction of one's identity than visible identities. Even among people of color, aspects of the self, such as sexuality or gender, may be the clinical point of focus or represent a dominant identity (Robinson, 1999b). Although race and gender have been socially constructed to function as primary status or master traits (Robinson, 1993), race has grand-master status, often having the power to eclipse the significance and presence of other identities (Robinson-Wood, in press). Cose (1993) argued that race is never not relevant, particularly for Black people, but this observation rings true for other people of color as well.

At the same time, a primary tenet of this work is that although gender and race are characteristics into which people are born and are often visible, they are not always available to the naked eye. A client, then, is done a disservice when the most visible aspect of the self is privileged over other identities historically dominated by those visible. In this work, neither race nor the other dimensions of identity are essentialized. Essentialism boxes people into limiting and restricting behaviors based on preexisting and predetermined definitions regarded as natural. Rosenblum and Travis (2006) said,

> for essentialists, the categories of race, sex, and sexuality orientation, and
> social class identify significant, empirically verifiable differences among

people. From the essentialist perspective, racial categories exist apart from any social processes; they are objective categories of real difference among people. (p. 3)

Separating people into mutually exclusive racial and gender categories is not what this text is meant to communicate. This text celebrates and recognizes that each of us has multiple identities that are shifting, fluid, and substantial to personal identity construction.

Within a color-conscious society, people are judged initially by the color of their skin, an immutable characteristic, and often by their gender, more so than by acquired traits. Discourses associated with race, gender, and other sources of difference have far-reaching implications for one's livelihood, place of residence, employment opportunity, educational quality and access. The process of judging by appearances is largely unconscious, yet it occurs both outside and within therapy and other professional contexts. (See Storytelling: "The Insensitive Professional.")

STORYTELLING: The Insensitive Professional

A woman in her 50s had been receiving medication to treat her bipolar condition. She had been suffering with this condition for decades, but the medications had only been working for a few years to help her manage her symptoms. She had also stopped working because she discovered that working exacerbated her mood swings. The woman also struggled with short-term memory loss. The demands of work increased her stress levels and contributed to her forgetfulness at work—consequently, her work performance suffered. The woman was a single parent, and she had two adult children, one who resided with her and had special needs. Providing care to this adult child while managing her own illness was exhausting. Not working was a relief, and although money was tight, she was grateful not to have the stress of a full-time job. During a scheduled appointment with a new psychiatrist, she mentioned she was not working. The psychiatrist leaned back in his chair and with a huge smile on his face asked, "So, are you enjoying your vacation?" The woman was so offended by the comment that she could not respond to his offensive question. At the same time, the power differential was operating—this woman was out of one of her medications and she was depending on the psychiatrist to write her a prescription for a refill. She knew how miserable she felt without this medication.

Confronting clients can be an effective therapeutic technique, but that does not appear to be the issue here. The psychiatrist missed the mark and made a mistake. It appears that the psychiatrist was influenced by the stigma of his clients' identities: having bipolar, depression, being a middle age, single, and overweight woman in her 50s. Being genuine means that as mental health professionals, we have enough respect for our clients to apologize when necessary, admit to our mistakes, and communicate honestly and respectfully. I shared this story with another mental health professional who said "with behavior like that, this psychiatrist will continue to keep us (psychologists and counselors) in business."

MULTICULTURAL COUNSELING AND PSYCHOLOGY DEFINED

Multicultural counseling and psychology are not new forces. Often used interchangeably with diversity, "multiculturalism recognizes the broad scope of dimensions of race, ethnicity, language, sexual orientation, gender, age, disability, class status, education, religious/spiritual orientation, and other cultural dimensions" (American Psychological Association [APA], 2003). Dramatic demographic changes within the United States such as the "browning of America," a term used back in the late 1980s, alert the profession to the need to rethink assumptions about minority and majority status shaped largely by cultural discourses about power and powerlessness.

Weedon (1987) defined *discourses* "as ways of constituting knowledge, together with the social practices, forms of subjectivity and power relations which inhere in such knowledges and relations between them. Discourses are more than ways of thinking and producing meaning. They constitute the 'nature' of the body, unconscious and conscious mind and emotional life of the subjects they seek to govern" (p. 105).

As mental health professionals and students, we need to ask: What are the unconscious and/or unspoken discourses that frame or lie beneath socially constructed categories of difference? What do unspoken discourses mean in therapeutic contexts and in the classrooms where our students learn? Discourses may be unconscious in that people may not be aware of where they are located within and positioned by certain discourses. Location means "identifying where one resides in this society on a continuum from privilege to oppression in relation to various contextual aspects of the self, such as ethnicity, gender, sexual orientation, religion, and class status" (Vasquez & Magraw, 2005, pp. 66–67). Discourses can be subtle and still be pervasive throughout society, holding enormous power.

Within the framework of multicultural counseling and psychology (which emphasizes diversity), discourses about privilege, oppression, and difference often reflect confusion about what is meant and for whom. One of the discourses of cultural diversity is that it refers to people who are categorized as *other*: non-White, non-male, and non-mainstream. The disadvantage of this discourse is that it does not encourage people, regardless of group membership, to think about themselves as racial, cultural, sexual beings. White people exist as persons who are not defined as racial beings, thus remaining invisible while defining and interpreting people of color.

Another challenge with the current state of multicultural studies is that the distinction between stigmatized/marginalized identities and internalized oppression is often not clear at all. In addition, the dialectic or the reality that people often possess both privileged and stigmatized identities simultaneously and across dynamic contexts is not presented. Each of us occupies a variety of statuses at any given moment. We may feel that one status is just as or more important than another, yet we do not always get to select which status is most important to others (Ore, 2006).

Multicultural counseling and psychology are respectful of multiple epistemological and philosophical perspectives and is to be contrasted with ethnocentrism, which is a belief that one's own culture and belief systems are superior to those who are culturally different from oneself. Ethnocentrism is in direct contradiction to the goals and aims of multiculturally competent counseling and psychology. Single-system or monoculturalism assumes that all people come from the same cultural plane and desire the values of the dominant culture dictated by those with the most racial and ethnic power (McIntosh, 1990). Multicultural counseling and psychology reaffirm comfort with and not just tolerance of people from various cultures (Hoopes, 1979). Differences are viewed as indispensable to a healthy society. Multiculturally competent counselors and psychologists strive to coexist with similarities and differences without defensiveness or denial. A dialectical, or both/and, approach to multicultural counseling and psychology allows for complexity and strives for balance (Pedersen, 1990).

Embedded deeply in the fabric of daily life, culture is often rendered invisible, largely because of its pervasiveness. Dominant American cultural values include assertiveness, competition, convenience, Christianity, conformity, democracy, educational attainment, equality, heterosexuality, individualism, materialism, meritocracy, productivity, Protestant Work Ethic, Whiteness, and youth. Many people are not conscious of the impact of their culture on their situation or problem in therapy. For some people, culture is a dominant identity. Others are seemingly oblivious to it. Clinicians need to be sensitive and respectful of the role that culture and conceptualization of the self as a function of culture plays in people's lives.

Despite espoused values of democracy and equality as taught by schools, church, political structures, and the family, Americans are socialized to develop an ethnocentric ideology. Ethnocentrism leads to misinformation about people who are not legitimized by the culture. Students, regardless of race, admit their ignorance of the enormous contributions from people of color to the United States and to the world. As racial and cultural awareness increases, students might appear confused and/or agitated, asking, "How could I have earned a bachelor's degree from a reputable institution and have such limited and inaccurate knowledge about people who do not look like me or who do?" Just as curriculum materials are a reflection of what is valued throughout society, U.S. history, too, is an institutionalized narrative. Loewen (1995) put it this way: "we are told that White plantation owners furnished food and medical care for their slaves, yet every shred of food, shelter, and clothing on the plantation was raised, built, woven, or paid for by black labor" (p. 95). Most of us also did not hear "America . . . derived its wealth, its values, its food, much of its medicine, and a large part of its 'dream' from Native America" (Gunn Allen, 1994, p. 193).

DIVERSITY: AN OVERVIEW

Since its beginning in 1776, the United States has been home to a diverse population. There are more than 303 million documented people living in the United States. Of course, persons are also here illegally and are not among this count.

If you are not one of the 4 million Native Americans, then your people came here from somewhere else at some point in time by boat, by plane, by train, by car, or on foot. Some of us or our ancestors came legally; some illegally, without a government-issued visa, passport, or other document granting entry. Others came voluntarily and others came against their wills.

Sources of diversity include race, ethnicity, gender, sexuality, nationality, physical ability, mental ability, disability, socioeconomic status (SES), and religion. Of all Americans, about 30% are persons of color. The designation "people of color" refers to individuals who are African American, Native American Indian/Alaskan Native (Indian/Native), Asian American, Latinos (who can be of any race), biracial, and multiracial. Nearly 7 million people in the 2000 census described themselves as being a member of two or more races (U.S. Census Bureau, 2002).*

The latest figures from the American Community Survey indicate that European Americans are approximately 73.9% of the population (they were 75% just 3 years ago). Latinos are 14.8% of the population; African Americans are 12.4% of the population. Since the 2000 census, Latinos surpassed African Americans as the largest group of color sometime during the early part of the 21st century. Much of the racial and ethnic diversity in U.S. society has been influenced by persons from Latin America and Asia, the areas from which the majority of current immigrants originate. Asians are 4.4% of the population. Native Americans are 1.4% of the population (U.S. Census Bureau, 2007).

Since the start of the 21st century, the workplace has undergone many changes. It is becoming the most highly educated workplace ever, with 38% having a 2-year, 4-year, or advanced college degree. Women under 25 now have labor force participation on par with men, and women in their 30s and 40s are approaching 85% of the male participation rates. The proportion of Black people in management and professional occupations has doubled over the past 30 years. The proportion of Latinos has nearly tripled and the proportion of Asians has increased by more than four times.[†]

In addition to changes in the workplace, U.S. schools will also undergo demographic shifts. Currently, nearly 33% of all children under age 18 are children of color. By 2010, children of color will represent the majority of young people in California, Florida, New York, and Texas—states that will account for a third of the nation's youth (The Children's Partnership, 2000).

Gender and sexuality are two other components of the diversity in the United States. Approximately 51% of the population is female and 49% are male—the male–female ratio is dictated, however, by race and age. This topic will be discussed in greater detail in subsequent chapters. Human sexuality exists on a continuum and includes heterosexuality, bisexuality, and homosexuality (Robinson & Watt, 2001). The incidence of exclusive homosexuality is estimated to

---

* Projections of the total resident population by 5-year age groups, race, and Hispanic origin with special age categories: Middle Series, 2006 to 2010. Population Projections Program, Population Division.

[†] www.epf.org/research/labordayreports/2002/LDRsummary2002.asp, Challenges facing the American workplace. The seventh annual workplace report challenges facing the American workplace. The state of the American workplace in 2002.

range from 2% to 10% for men and slightly less for women. It is clear that this is not an exact number. People who identify as transgender do not subscribe to a bifurcated male/female dichotomy. A person can be a biological female yet identify as male with respect to gender and sexual identities. The term *transgender* refers to the full spectrum of persons with nontraditional gender identities including pre- and post-transsexuals, transvestites, and intersex persons. Intersex persons are often, but not always, born with ambiguous genitalia and are assigned a gender by physicians and family members after surgical intervention (Carroll & Gilroy, 2002). Such surgical interventions are highly contested, particularly if there are no health risks involved. A large clitoris and a small penis are not life-threatening conditions.

Ours is an aging population, but such demographic trends are affected by race. The majority of the population, or 75.4%, is 18 years of age and older. More than 12% of the population is 65 years and older. African Americans and Native Americans have shorter life spans than do European Americans. Latinos and Native Americans have lower median years than Whites.

A, B, AND C DIMENSIONS

As a means of conceptualizing human differences, Arredondo et al (1992b) referred to the characteristics into which people are born as *A dimensions* of personal identity. These include age, culture, sex, sexual orientation, language, social class, and physical disability. *C dimensions* are historical events that affect people's present and future lives and are grounded in historical, political, sociocultural, and economic contexts. Arredondo indicated that the C dimension "suggests there are many factors that surround us over which we have no control as individuals, but which will, nevertheless, affect us both positively and negatively" (p. 51). For immigrants, historical events can refer to political events that prompted departure from their home countries. The outbreak of diseases (such as polio, SARS, HIV), as well as terrorist events are examples of historical events that intersect with A and B dimensions. *B dimensions* are characteristics not necessarily visible to others but influenced by individual achievement; these include educational background, geographic location, income, marital status, religion, work experience, citizenship status, and hobbies. The B dimensions may represent the "consequences" of A and C dimensions. Arredondo et al. (1996) said, "What occurs to individuals relative to their B Dimensions are influenced by some of the immutable characteristics of the A Dimension and the major historical, political, sociocultural, and economic legacies of the C Dimension" (p. 52).

Understanding the convergence of multiple-identity constructs (A, B, and C dimensions) in people's lives is crucial to viewing clients holistically. Throughout this text, the intersections of race, gender, class, spirituality, disability, and sexuality (A and B dimensions) with historical events (C dimensions) and the social construction of difference are given primary focus.

CONCEPTUALIZATION OF THE SELF

The primary focus on the individual is not standard in every culture. In many societies throughout the world, the self is conceptualized within the context of the collective or the community, not as a separate entity. The internalization of cultural values is influenced by acculturation, migration status, income, education, generational status, and racial/ethnic identity development.

Individualism and collectivism have roots in political and economic history, religion, and philosophy (Kagitcibasi, 1997). In **individualism,** the person is regarded as discrete from other beings and is considered the essential cornerstone of society (Kagitcibasi, 1997). Myers (1991) maintained that because Western society is philosophically oriented to individualism, individuals are the primary referent point and are separate from others. She saw fragmentation between spirit and matter (or *bifurcation of the self*) as an outcome of an individualistic frame of reference.

Enns (1994) stated, "consistent with individualistic cultural values, the separate self values personal initiative, self-reliance, and achievement as coping mechanism and tends to take internal responsibility for both success and failure. In contrast, the collectivist is more likely to value making a contribution to a group effort, more likely to express modesty or self-effacement in the face of success and less likely than the individualist to make internal attributions for either success or failure" (p. 207).

Individualism influences and is associated with other core U.S. cultural values such as empiricism. The scientific tradition in academia emerged from a positivistic-empirical model that emphasizes quantification, statistical measurement, and validation of reality by use of the five senses. In Western ideology, individualism, measurement, and control are cultural values, exerting powerful influence on the policies, programs, and politics of the United States, both past and present. The visible is legitimate and the invisible is suspect because it cannot be proven and counted. Yet Albert Einstein knew that "not everything that counts can be counted, and not everything that can be counted counts" (Harris, 1995).

Strangely enough, individualism may suppress individual expression. For example, external conformity and individualism appear to be in contradiction, yet these are two cultural values in the United States. Americans are encouraged to be autonomous, to be their own persons, and to do their own thing. They are also told to maintain the status quo and "not rock the boat." There is almost an unwritten edict against extreme levels of individuality because this tends to be indicative of nonconventionality. U.S. society espouses, "be all you can be," but conflicting messages are also given: "Do not cross the border of what is acceptable thinking and behavior." "Color within the lines and stay within the box!"

By not knowing the self or being able to ask and answer questions—"Who am I?" "What do I want to be?" "What and whom do I want?"—one is vulnerable to adopting others' answers to these questions. Although excessive forms of individualism can interfere with one's ability to live collectively and ask for help, as well as receive help from others, individuality can play a critical role in forming an identity.

In addition to socialization factors, structural and economic structures mediate individualism. For example, when the United States's economy was agrarian-based and people were less mobile, interdependence was greater than it is in today's highly technological and mobile society in which people are often physically removed from extended family and community support.

IMAGES OF DIVERSITY

CULTURE

Culture is ubiquitous, central to each of our lives, and shapes the way we see the world. It has been defined as the myriad ways of people to preserve society and meet a range of human needs. Belief systems, behaviors, and traditions make up the essence of culture (Pinderhughes, 1989) as do people's relationships with time, nature, other people, and mode of activity (Kluckhohn & Strodtbeck, 1961). As pervasive as culture is, people are often oblivious to its impact on their and others' lives because of unstated assumptions and shared values that go unrecognized (Bronstein & Quina, 1988).

Enculturation refers to immersion in our own culture to the point where we assume that our way of life is "natural" or "normal" (Ore, 2006, p. 3). Enculturation is an impediment to effective multicultural work. Clinicians need to recognize and be willing to address their cultural biases. Dana (1993) identified an **emic perspective** as one that is respectful of, and sensitive to, the native culture's meanings for phenomena and native language, and encourages recognition of persons on their own terms. It holds that the best place from which to help people of color is from their own perspective (Vontress, 1986). In contrast, an **etic perspective** emphasizes the observer's culturally driven meanings that are referenced as the standard for interpretation. Here, the focus is on similarities instead of cultural differences since a global view of humanity is taken (Vontress, 1986).

Acculturation appears to be a process of socialization into accepting and adapting to the cultural values of the larger society. Berry and Sam (1997) provided a definition of acculturation from Redfield, Linton, and Herskovits's (1936) definition: "Acculturation comprehends those phenomena which result when groups of individuals having different cultures come into continuous first-hand contact with subsequent changes in the original culture patterns of either or both groups" (pp. 293–294). Acculturation can take place at the expense of one's original cultural values as one internalizes the dominant society's values and traditions. Berry and Sam stated that *acculturation* is a neutral term in that changes may happen in both groups. Acculturation tends to bring about change in one group, which is referred to as the acculturating group. Two questions clarify the outcome of acculturation strategies:

1. Is it considered to be of value to maintain relationships with the dominant society?
2. Is it considered to be of value to maintain cultural identity characteristics?
   (Berry & Sam, 1997, p. 296)

Acculturation is not so much identification as it is internalization. Because this process is not always conscious (Sue, 1989), the possibility of cultural alienation from one's traditional culture is high.

Berry and Sam (1997) discussed four acculturation strategies: assimilation, traditionality, integration, and marginality. Although a dimension of acculturation, **assimilation** is different and describes those persons who do not desire to maintain their cultural identities and thus seek sustained interaction with other cultures outside their own. Sue (1989) discussed a similar phenomenon when describing assimilation. He said it refers to a conscious process in which the person desires to identify with the traditional society because its art, language, and culture are perceived to be more valuable than the person's own. Persons who are acculturated are viewed as being low in a knowledge of and appreciation for their own cultures while holding the dominant culture in high regard. The original cultures have been lost or relinquished, and persons have given up most cultural traits of their cultures of origin and assumed the traits of the dominant culture (Berry & Kim, 1988).

Traditionality describes persons who choose to hold on to their cultural connections and avoid interaction with others. Here, people have knowledge of, and appreciation for, their own cultures while holding the dominant culture in lower regard. When the dominant culture engages in these practices, the term is *segregation* (Berry & Sam, 1997).

Integration describes an interest in maintaining one's original culture while simultaneously seeking interactions with the other culture. According to Berry and Kim (1988), these persons are characterized as being *bicultural*. They are high in knowledge of, and appreciation for, their own cultures while esteeming the dominant culture as well. An integration of both an original culture and the dominant culture has transpired. Mental health and acculturation modality are related. Berry and Kim (as cited in Dana, 1993) stated that "mental health problems will be least intense with biculturality and progressively increase in severity with assimilation, traditionality, and marginality outcomes of acculturation" (p. 112).

Little interest in cultural maintenance and limited desire to interact with others from different cultures is defined as **marginality.** According to Dana (1993), "marginality will often occur when the traditional culture is not retained and the dominant society culture is not accepted" (p. 112). Emotional and psychological stress is associated with seeking to become acculturated within a given culture. Gloria and Peregoy (1996) discussed how alcohol and other drug abuse may be by-products of acculturation stress among some Latino populations. This connection between substance abuse and acculturation stress also seems to apply to Native Americans and other ethnic and racial groups in their attempts to contend with historical cultural devastation and the modern, ubiquitous, and subtle effects of institutionalized racism (Herring, 1992).

RACE

Every human being is a member of the human race, of the species of *Homo sapiens*. Typical conceptions of race often refer to people of color (Christian, 1989); nonetheless, *race* refers to White people as well. Race is an extremely volatile and

STORYTELLING: New York City?

I participated in an Asian American literature book club some years ago. One of the men in the group, a native New Yorker, talked about how on a regular basis, people ask him where he is from. He tells them New York—they then ask, "no, where are you really from?" He says, "New York City." "Which country were you born in," they continue. He responds, "that would be America." People then ask him where his family is from and he says, "New York." This man's English sounds like mine and yet many people, based on the fact the he is Asian and looks Asian, assume he is foreign-born and not from here—not American.

divisive force in this nation despite the heroic efforts of various movements (e.g., the Asian, Latino, and civil rights movements) that coalesced to create greater racial equity. Huge variations in income, occupational distribution, educational levels, quality of and access to education, health care, and longevity can be seen between and within racial groups (Anderson, 2003). Race and skin color affect perceptions of nationality and citizenship. (See Storytelling: "New York City?")

What is race? To begin, there is no consensual definition of the term. According to some biologists, **race** (or subspecies) "is an inbreeding, geographically isolated population that differs in distinguishable physical traits from members of the species" (Zuckerman, 1990, p. 1297). Healey (1997) said that race was "an isolated inbreeding population with a distinctive genetic heritage. Socially, the term is used loosely and reflects patterns of inequality and power" (p. 309).

The biology of race is heavily debated (Cornell & Hartmann, 1997; Healey, 1997). In fact, most biologists regard race as a social construct only. Even persons who appear very different from one another by virtue of skin color, facial features, body type, and hair texture are very similar genetically. The Human Genome Project discovered that 99.9% of our 30,000 human genes are shared by everyone (Anderson, 2003). Yet, properties such as hair texture and the amount of melanin in the skin are typically the dimensions commonly associated with race (Lee, 2001). "Biological racial categories have more within group variation than between group variation" (APA, 2003, p. 1). Melanin is responsible for darker skin color hue and represents "an adaptation to a particular ecology" (Healey, 1997, p. 11). Although race is based on phenotypic variables, these variables do not accurately reflect one's race but rather represent a basis for assigning people to a particular racial group. This issue is explored in greater depth in Chapter 9. This text recognizes that race is a social construction and not biologically determined (APA, 2003).

ETHNICITY

Race and *ethnicity* are used interchangeably by some authors and researchers; however, these terms are not synonymous. According to Pinderhughes (1989), **ethnicity** refers to a connectedness based on commonalities (e.g., religion, nationality, regions) in which specific aspects of cultural patterns are shared and transmission over time creates a common history and ancestry.

Ethnicity refers to commonality in which unique cultural aspects are shared and transmitted. Among some racial groups, *ethnicity* refers more to nationality and country of origin. For others, religion describes ethnicity or values and lifestyle (Lee, 2001). Ethnicity has been defined as the acceptance of the group mores and practices of one's culture of origin and having a sense of belonging (APA, 2003). Persons can be of the same ethnicity (e.g., Latino) but represent different racial backgrounds (e.g., White, Black, biracial, Asian). Persons can also be of the same racial group (Asian) but of differing ethnicities (e.g., Chinese, Southeast Asian Indian, Cuban, Filipino). When transmitted intergenerationally within the culture, language, dancing, dressing, singing, storytelling, ways of worship and mourning, quilt making, weaving, and cooking, for example, are ethnic behaviors (Alba, 1990).

Common discussions of ethnicity in the United States tend to include the "melting pot." This pot has been brewing and bubbling over for generations. Originating in 1910 at the University of Chicago (Steinberg, 1989), the term described the assimilating tendencies of the more than 1 million European immigrants who were entering the United States each year. Sociologists were interested in knowing how the more than 20 nationalities managed conflict. The melting pot theory differed from the theory of *ethnic pluralists,* who maintained that ethnicity was an enduring factor throughout American life. Yet, the loss of native tongues, the decline of ethnic cultures, the dispersion of ethnic communities, the increase in ethnic and religious intermarriage, and the transformation of ethnic-sounding names to White Anglo Saxon Protestant sounding names were and continue to be examples of Americanization (Steinberg, 1989). In addition, the melting pot assailed the preservation of individual differences in that the pot was dominated by the ingredient in the majority with the most power.

The process of assimilation among White ethnic microcultures differs greatly from that among people of color. Race often makes people of color easy targets for discriminatory treatment. (See Storytelling: "New York City?") Historical differences exist between race and ethnicity as a function of U.S. policy. The 1790 Naturalization Law, which was in effect for 162 years, stated that only free "White" immigrants would be eligible for naturalized citizenship. This meant that general citizenship was denied Asians until 1952, with the Walter-McCarran Act, and even Native American Indians until 1924 (Takaki, 1994).

When people lack an understanding of history, and this misunderstanding is the basis for ignorance about race and the perpetuation of racism. For example, Loewen (1995) informs us that Pilgrims did not introduce Thanksgiving; the Eastern Indians had been observing autumn harvest celebrations for not just years but centuries. Abraham Lincoln, in a move to bolster patriotism, proclaimed Thanksgiving a national holiday in 1863. Alba (1990) also referred to persons from Latin America as "new immigrant groups" (p. 1). During the late 19th and early 20th centuries Europeans represented the largest group of immigrants to this nation. Mexico lost half of its national territory, which included Texas, New Mexico, California, Arizona, Nevada, Utah, and half of Colorado, in the Treaty of Guadalupe Hidalgo (Novas, 1994). Awareness of historical inaccuracy is helpful; otherwise, it has the potential of misinforming and distorting our perceptions of people.

GENDER

Traditional notions of gender reference non-males (Christian, 1989), yet *gender* refers to males, females, and to transgendered individuals. Gender has socially constructed categories in terms of roles and behaviors based on a biological given of sex (Renzetti & Curran, 1992). **Gender** refers to the roles, behaviors, and attitudes that come to be expected of persons on the basis of their biological sex. Despite the advent of the women's and men's movements, in U.S. society, men continue to be socialized to restrict emotionally; function independently; value assertiveness and power; and equate sexuality with intimacy, manhood, and self-worth. On the other hand, women are socialized to be emotional and to nurture and are groomed to direct their achievement through affiliation with others, particularly men (Mintz & O'Neil, 1990). In truth, men are emotional beings who rely on others, do not always feel strong, and desire to express a full range of emotions including vulnerability. Women are leaders, are strong, are providers, and can be extremely competitive and harsh.

Biological sex refers to the possession of an XY chromosome pair for a genetically healthy male and an XX chromosome pair for a genetically healthy female, along with the corresponding anatomical, hormonal, and physiological parts (Atkinson & Hackett, 1995). Some people are born with a variety of chomosomal configurations, such as Klinefelter's, in which a male person has an extra X chromosome or XXY. Sensitivity to this reality is critical, particularly within the context of counseling and therapy. Support for the client's exploration of the ways in which one's life has been affected by their biology and social constructions about normalcy displays multicultural competence.

Although not often related to chromosomal abnormalities, there are persons who are born with ambiguous genitalia. Physicians, in conjunction with results from appropriate endocrine tests and parental consent, affix a child's gender that corresponds with sexual reassignment. The ethics of this issue are hotly debated by the Intersexual Society of North America.

Sex and *gender* are terms that are easily confused. For instance, lactation and penile ejaculation are sex roles that are not biologically interchangeable for men and women, respectively. Diaper changing and car repair are not sex roles. They are socially constructed gender roles. There are no isolated genes for putting up sheet rock or planting flowers, yet the arbitrary divisions of labor that society has constructed based on biological sex are stringent and far too often attributed to biology.

Psychological masculinity is not a biological phenomenon, yet it is often equated with characteristics of the U.S. culture, such as rugged self-reliance, competition, and fierce individualism (Robinson & Watt, 2001). The characteristics often attributed to femininity, such as loving children, yielding, and nurturing, are not exclusive to the female sex or to heterosexuals of any gender.

Androcentrism is a traditional systematic construct in which the worldview of men is used as the central premise of development for all individuals, including women (Worell & Remer, 1992). The central image underlying this concept is "males at the center of the universe looking out at reality from behind their own eyes and describing what they see from an egocentric or androcentric point of view" (Bem, 1993, p. 42). The many benefits associated with unearned privilege can distort one's vision of the disadvantages that accompany privilege. Both men and women alike suffer from the constricting consequences of socially constructed gender roles.

SEXUALITY

Sexuality exists on a continuum and encompasses homosexuality, bisexuality, and heterosexuality. There are different expressions of sexuality within and across the sexuality continuum.

All major mental health associations have affirmed that homosexuality is not a mental illness. There was a time when the American Psychiatric Association, the publishers of the *Diagnostic Statistical Manual,* viewed homosexuality as an indication of mental illness. Even today, the United States values heterosexuality and assumes it is normal. **Heterosexism** is the ideological system that denies, denigrates, and stigmatizes any nonheterosexual form of behavior, identity, relationship or community (APA, 2006). Heterosexism is institutionalized through law, religion, education, and the media and leads to homophobia (Pharr, 1988). Heterosexism has implications for the client–therapist dyad. Heterosexism could limit the type of advocacy a heterosexual therapist might engage in with a gay, transgendered, or bisexual client. This is particularly true if the professional is extremely self-conscious about being labeled as gay because of affiliation with, or advocacy for, gay men and lesbians.

Related to heterosexism, **homophobia** is the irrational and unreasonable fear of same-sex attractions and "persons whose affectional and erotic orientations are toward the same sex" (King, 1988, p. 168). It also applies to persons perceived to be gay or lesbian and emanates from the perception of homosexuality as an aberration of the correct social order. The term **homosexual** defines attraction to the same sex for physical and emotional nurturance and is one orientation on the sexual orientation continuum. The terms *gay* and *lesbian* are preferred and used throughout this work. *Homophobia* comes from the Latin *homo,* meaning "same" (in this case, referring to same-gender attraction), and *phobia,* meaning "fear of."

As a reflection of changing times and sentiments regarding sexuality, some corporations and universities provide same-sex partner benefits (such as Northeastern University) for committed couples who are not married yet live together. Vermont and New Hampshire recognize same-sex partnerships as legal within civil unions. The Commonwealth of Massachusetts recognizes same-sex marriages.

DISABILITY

Section 504 of the Rehabilitation Act of 1973 and the Americans with Disabilities Act of 1990 (ADA) prohibit discrimination against individuals with disabilities. According to these laws, no otherwise qualified individual with a disability shall, solely by reason of his disability, be excluded from the participation in, be denied the benefits of, or be subjected to discrimination under any program or activity of a public entity. Disabilities can be physical, mental, psychological, and the result of injury, accident, illness, congenital, or organic.

According to the *Americans with Disabilities Act Handbook* (Equal Employment Opportunity Commission [EEOC], 1991), an individual with a disability is a person who has a physical or mental impairment that substantially limits one or more "major life activities," or has a record of such an impairment, or is regarded as having such an impairment. Examples of physical or mental impairments include, but are not limited to, contagious and noncontagious diseases and conditions such as orthopedic, visual, speech, and hearing impairments; cerebral palsy; epilepsy; muscular dystrophy; multiple sclerosis; cancer; heart disease; diabetes; mental retardation; emotional illness; specific learning disabilities; HIV disease (whether symptomatic or asymptomatic); tuberculosis; drug addiction; and alcoholism. According to the U.S. Census Bureau (2006), there are 51.2 million people, or 18%, of the population age 5 and over with a disability.

The nature of disabilities among people varies, and the term itself is dynamic given the open membership of this identity as a function of injury, disease, or the natural aging process. Numerous categories exist in describing persons with disabilities, from mild to moderate to severe. People need not be born into a disability, but whether it exists at birth or occurs at some juncture in life, it is a biological reality nonetheless. Disability is a lived experience for millions of Americans, yet persons with physical and mental disabilities continue to face obstacles to access and experience discriminatory attitudes. How many of us have gone to a restaurant with a friend who had a visible disability to find that you cannot get into the place because there is no ramp or the waiter or waitress completely ignored the person in the wheelchair and instead asked you what the person with the disability wanted to eat? Such attitudes are fueled by a societal perception that persons with disabilities are dependent, helpless, childlike, and incomplete. When people who are able-bodied disrupt this exchange and say, "please ask him or her," the discourse that disabled people are not just childlike but infantlike will be challenged and hopefully extinguished.

Disability has tremendous class implications. Nearly 80% of people with a severe disability had personal incomes below $20,000 in 2004 compared with 39% among people with no disability. Median earnings for people with no disability was $25,000 in comparison with $22,000 for persons with a nonsevere disability and $12,800 for those with a severe disability. In addition, the poverty rate among the population 25 to 64 years of age with no disability was 8% compared with 11% for people with a nonsevere disability and 26% for people with a severe disability (U.S. Census Bureau, 2006).

Disability is one component of a person's overall identity, yet Fowler, O'Rourke, Wadsworth, and Harper (1992) noted that the term *disabled* "conveys a message of inability which overshadows other identity descriptors of the person and becomes the exclusive role for persons who are disabled" (p. 102). Disability can function as a primary status trait when it is visible and regarded as the most salient component of a person's existence. For instance, a therapist who associates the experience of being able-bodied and middle class with feelings of power may perceive an unemployed client with a disability as helpless and pitiable. Actually, the client may feel psychologically empowered and have access to an abundance of emotional and spiritual resources that enable her to feel powerful about her life (Robinson, 1999a) and see unemployment as a transition and a chance to rest and regroup.

SOCIOECONOMIC CLASS

Socioeconomic class has traditionally referred to a person's or group's social and financial position relative to rank. Factors that affect one's socioeconomic ranking include educational level, employment stability, wages, marital status, income of spouse and/or other persons in the home, size of household, citizenship, and access to medical benefits. Exceptions exist, but increased education tends to be associated with higher incomes (Hacker, 1992). According to the U.S. Census Bureau in 2006, the poverty rate for non-Hispanic Whites was 8.2%; 10.3% for Asians, 18% for Pacific Islanders, 20.6% for Latinos, 24.3% for Blacks, and 24.6% for American Indians and Alaskan Natives (DeNavas-Walt, Proctor, & Smith, 2007; U.S. Census Bureau, 2007). (See Table 1.1.)

In rehabilitation and vocational counseling, emphasis has been placed on career and vocational development and assessment with less attention devoted to socioeconomic class as a personal identity construct. Class intersects with gender and race. Black, Latino, Pacific Island, and Native American women have higher rates of poverty than Asian and White women. Socioeconomic class affects other dimensions of one's life, including sense of worth, access to health care, exposure to violence, a sense of personal power and agency, and access to clear air and water. Schliebner and Peregoy (1994) described its impact on the family:

> The family unit . . . derives its routine and ordering of time, place in a social
> network, status, and economic well-being from the labor force participation
> of its parental members . . . When productivity is halted, profound feelings
> of loss, inadequacy, guilt, and lowered self-esteem can result. (p. 368)

Self-construct and feelings of self-worth are affected by employment and socioeconomic class. It is not surprising that child-rearing practices would also be affected. Storck (1998) suggested that class has to be expanded to include psychosocial characteristics such as a sense of well-being. In their study of working parents, McLoyd and Wilson (1992) found that parents with fewer economic resources, in comparison to parents who were considered middle class, placed less emphasis on happiness as a goal while they were rearing their children. These parents were less likely to believe that childhood was a protected, carefree, and happy-go-lucky space, or that it was their responsibility as parents to create such a climate for their children.

TABLE 1.1   2006 Poverty Rates by Race and Ethnicity

Group	Poverty Rate
Asians	10.3%
Blacks	24.3
Latinos	20.6
Native Americans	24.6
Whites	8.2

The research presented by McLoyd and Wilson plus Storck's call for an expansion of the concept of social class suggest that class is not independent of other dimensions of one's personhood, such as psychological well-being and attention to happiness. Socioeconomic status is also a major driver of health behaviors and health-related psychological processes, including physical activity, smoking, healthy eating habits, sleep quality, depression, cynical hostility, obesity, and chronic stress (Anderson, 2003). A loaf of quality multigrain bread is $3.50. The more nutritious bread is less accessible.

Wilson (1994) argued that to understand the economic plight of people in society, work needs to be examined in conjunction with race and structural and infrastructure issues such as technology and illegal immigration. Illegal migrant and/or undocumented laborers work for depressed wages in jobs that some U.S.-born workers are less willing to take, particularly if the jobs are regarded as dead-end or poorly paid.

Regardless of race, the last few years have not been favorable for many Americans and during the writing of this text, a recession appears to be on the horizon. Also, at the time of the writing of this third edition, housing sales are depressed and foreclosure rates are sharply up as a function of adjustable rate mortgages and the subprime mortgage mess, where borrowers were given loans by banks and mortgage companies without the income to afford the payments that were guaranteed to rise over time.

SPIRITUALITY

Across all age, race, and ethnic groups, religion and/or spirituality plays a part in many people's lives. The United States was founded on Christian principles. There exists much religious and faith diversity within and between religious and spiritual groups. Christianity is clearly the largest religion worldwide and is purported to have 2.1 billion members, or one third of the world's inhabitants. Islam has approximately 1.5 billion members, or 21% of the planet's population. Persons who are secular, nonreligious, agnostic, or atheist number 1.1 billion and are now the third largest group, instead of fourth as was the case 3 years ago. They represent 16% of the world's religious population. Hinduism is fourth with 900 million followers and 14% of religious followers. Chinese traditional religion is fifth with 394 million people, and Buddhism is sixth with 376 million people, each representing 6% of the world's religious population (Adherents.com, 2007).

Other world religions include African traditionalism, Sikhism, Judaism, Bahai, Shinto, and spiritism. Religion, spirituality, and their various expressions are all affected by the identity dimensions of race, ethnicity, gender, sexual orientation, class, and culture.

Religion and spirituality are conceptualized differently. **Religion** may be measured by denominational affiliations (e.g., Baptist, Methodist), as well as by empirical, behavioral, or public indicators, such as churchgoing and avoidance of denounced (sinful) behaviors (e.g., alcohol consumption; cigarette smoking; foul language; the revealing of one's face or body; disobedience to one's family, culture, or husband;

sexual intercourse outside marriage). **Spirituality** is often private and/or internally defined, transcends the tangible, and serves to connect one to the whole (other living organisms and the universe). Spirituality gives life direction and can help people maintain mental health (McDonald, 1990; Swinton, 2001). It is possible to define oneself as spiritual without being religious and to be religious but not spiritual (Burke & Miranti, 2001). Faith was defined by Fowler and Keen (1978) as being connected to but not the same as religion. It is "a person's or a community's way-of-being-in-relation to other persons and groups, and to the values, causes, and institutions that give form and pattern to life" (pp. 23–24).

IMPLICATIONS FOR COUNSELORS AND PSYCHOLOGISTS

Multicultural counseling and psychology recognize differences exist among people. It views the assessment and understanding of one's proximity to discourses as critical and holds as a core value the development of multicultural competence among mental health professionals. An unwillingness for clinicians to look at themselves suggests a rigidity and fear that does not in the end serve clients well. Clinicians are encouraged to acknowledge where they are in their own cultural and ethnic/racial development since attitudes and beliefs about differences affect the creation of a therapeutic encounter that feels either respectful or dismissive. Clinicians need to learn to communicate effectively with their clients about the full range of the clients' values towards assisting the client in seeing the connection among these values and how they view their situations and think about problem resolution. Clinicians need to honestly gauge their knowledge and feelings about various sources of difference. It is all right not to know; what one does with not knowing makes the difference. (See Case Study: "Not My First Choice.")

To assist readers with the integration and application of the material to actual situations, a case study is included in each chapter.

CASE STUDY
Not My First Choice

Maria is a 41-year-old, physically healthy White woman living in a medium-sized city in Georgia with her husband, Timothy. He is also White. They have been married for 17 years and have lived in Georgia for 10 years. They have two sons, 13 and 15. Timothy recently admitted to Maria that that he is bisexual and has been interested in men for as long as he can remember being interested in women. Timothy also told Maria that she should get tested for HIV. While he assures her he is HIV negative, he has had unprotected sex with a gay man within the last few months and wants her to be safe. Upon hearing

Timothy come out, Maria went into a rage. She picked up a lamp and threw it at him. The lamp hit him on the side of the face and cut him. Their oldest son was home at the time. After picking up a few items of clothing, Timothy drove himself to the hospital to get treatment. Timothy chose not to call the police. After leaving the hospital (his jaw was broken), Timothy went to a hotel. The next morning, Maria was tested for HIV. She was soon told her test was negative but to follow up in a few months. Her doctor recommended she seek counseling for her anger and anxiety—she was having heart palpitations, feeling dizzy, and experiencing panic attacks and diarrhea. Maria is enraged. She does not know what to tell her children, and she feels sad all at the same time. After taking several days to call a private agency that provides psychological counseling, Maria is told that she is scheduled to meet with a male clinician. She then asks if there is a female available. Although there is one available, Maria would have to wait a few weeks for an appointment with her. Maria reluctantly accepts an appointment to see Dr. Rudolf.

QUESTIONS

1. What are the dominant discourses regarding Timothy's sexuality?
2. Where is a good place for the clinician to begin with Maria?
3. How might transference with a male clinician help Maria deal with her feelings about her husband?

DISCUSSION AND INTEGRATION
The Client, Maria and the Therapist, Dr. Rudolf

Upon meeting Dr. Rudolf, or Bob, Maria has many feelings. He is not her first choice, but she does not know why. She is uncomfortable and embarrassed about having to see a therapist, yet hopeful that she can receive help.

As a therapist influenced by a psychodynamic perspective, Bob attends to the overt information that Maria expresses to him but also wonders what unspoken and/or unconscious forces might be having an

influence on her life. After completing an intake, Bob looks at Maria and asks, "What would you like to talk about?" Maria's body language tells Bob that she is not just uncomfortable, she is hostile. Bob understands Maria's initial reluctance to see him from information he has gathered during the intake—Timothy's infidelity and high-risk behaviors have contributed to Maria's distrust and suspicion. At the same time, Bob knows that transference can help Maria. Transference is "the unconscious process by which early unresolved relational dynamics or conflicts are unwittingly displaced or 'transferred' onto the current relationship with the clinician and then reenacted or expressed as though appropriate or 'real' in the moment" (Murphy & Dillon, 2008, p. 313).

Research supports the principle that transference strengthens the therapeutic relationship. In grounded theory research with 26 clients, it was discovered that the "transferential" process was described as positive and appeared to aid alliance building (Levitt, Butler, & Travis, 2006).

Bob says to Maria, "Let's try this first session and see how it goes. If after our time is up you would like a different therapist, I will do what I can to get you an appointment sooner." After a hesitant start, Maria begins to talk. Bob listens and communicates to Maria that her experience is akin to an emotional roller coaster. He validates her emotions and says she feels an alphabet of emotions: anxious, angry, ashamed, betrayed, conflicted, confused, depressed, defeated, disappointed, enraged, embarrassed, fearful, guilty, humiliated, isolated, jealous, lonely, etc. He tells her that feeling crazy is part of the confusion and that it is helpful to have the opportunity to emote, to release the emotions—without an effort to gain insight or to think about her thinking, just unload for now. Slumped in her chair, Maria cries and begins to curse and rail against men who are "entitled and always use women." Fearing she has hurt Bob's feelings, Maria apologizes for her profanity and her remarks about men. Bob refuses to accept the apology and says, "In this space, you say what you want. I don't need to be protected." He is quiet as she wails—and available to her. He does not divert his gaze when she cries with such force that she nearly chokes. He attends—not feeling embarrassment or discomfort but compassion and empathy for his client. A theme that has emerged with clients in therapy is that psychologists and counselors should explain to clients that therapy is a place where painful experiences are discussed and that they, the clinicians, do not need to be protected (Levitt et al., 2006).

In addition to creating a safe place for Maria, Bob encourages her to find a good lawyer who can help her with legal aspects of her situation, even if she has not yet decided to terminate the relationship. Knowing what one's options are can be empowering. Bibliotherapy, or reading the stories of other women who have had their husbands come out, can have a universalizing experience—lessen her feelings of isolation or feeling so different from others. A support group may also be helpful. Family counseling is also highly recommended given that her children need a place to go with their questions, fears, anger, and other emotions.

After a few sessions, Bob brings to Maria's attention his observation that she seems to secretly hope that Timothy is going through a phase and will return home permanently, cured of his desires for men. She denies this initially but concedes that he is right—after all they have been married for nearly 20 years, have two children, and have built a life together. Discourses to which Maria has close proximity include these: marital longevity is more powerful than bisexual feelings; bisexual feelings can be cured; and heterosexual marriage is inconsistent with bisexual feelings. Bob agrees that a person's sexual identity is not solely determined by sexual behavior or the lack thereof and that sexuality may be an evolving part of identity; however, the longevity of Timothy's sexual feelings for and attraction to other men is a strong indication that he may not be just experimenting sexually with a male partner as Maria is hoping. Bob confronts Maria's denial, not judgmentally, but he gently presents the evidence to her so that she may attend to it and make responsible decisions, not only for herself but for her children. They need her to be an adult, use wisdom, and pay attention to the data.

With the support of her therapist, Maria is not alone in walking the path of her life. Bob can help Maria confront a number of pressing issues such as the social stigma associated with her husband's bisexuality and possible divorce. Existential concerns, such as loneliness, meaning-making, and living life with purpose are issues that Maria will need to reflect upon and are part of her evolution and change. Maria's losses are multiple and need to be mourned. In terms of taking care of herself, she will need to engage in safe-sex practices.

SUMMARY

The various faces of diversity were discussed in this chapter. Included were culture, race, ethnicity, gender, sexuality, disability, socioeconomic class, and spirituality. The multiple identities in shaping psychosocial development were highlighted. A case study was presented to illustrate the textured lives of a client in crisis and skills that therapists can use to join with clients and help alleviate their suffering.

Chapter 2

Multicultural Competencies and Guidelines

I generally tell my clients to start with those relaxing/soothing skills that have worked for them in the past. If they typically use jogging, hot baths, and TV shows to relax or take care of themselves, I encourage them to do that rather than take up a new skill or activity. When faced with the stress of a crisis, clients don't need the added stress of learning a new activity. On the other hand, for some clients, focusing on a new skill may help to distract them from perseverating on the crisis. It depends on the individual client.

Bianca Cody Murphy and Carolyn Dillon,
Interviewing in Action in a Multicultural World

This chapter explores the development of multicultural competencies in counseling and the guidelines on multicultural education, training, research, practice, and organizational change for psychologists. Strategies for becoming a multiculturally competent counselor and guidelines on monitoring dissonance and measuring multicultural effectiveness are reviewed. A case study activity allows for an integration of the material presented.

Prior to a discussion of competencies and guidelines, a distinction is made between cultural competence and multicultural competencies. According to Chin (2003), cultural competence arose from a systems perspective to evaluate the quality of mental health service delivery programs for children of color. Multicultural competence emerged from a need to move beyond the traditional focus in psychology and mental health, which emphasized a Eurocentric and Western paradigm. The limitations of this paradigm were particularly apparent with clients of color.

MULTICULTURAL COMPETENCIES

Multicultural competencies (MCCs) have a 25-year history (Sue et al., 1982; Sue, Arredondo, & McDavis, 1992; Sue, Ivoy, & Pedersen, 1996; Sue et al., 1998; Worthington, Soth-McNett, & Moreno, 2007). What is best said is that there are three competencies recognized by the American Counseling Association (ACA), appearing in bold in this section. Each competency is followed by italicized statements about the parallel components: (1) attitudes and beliefs, (2) knowledge, and (3) skills.*

COMPETENCY ONE: COUNSELOR AWARENESS OF OWN CULTURAL VALUES AND BIASES

ATTITUDES AND BELIEFS   The first competency is **counselor awareness of own cultural values and biases**.

1. *Culturally skilled counselors believe that cultural self-awareness and sensitivity to one's own cultural heritage are essential.* They understand the importance of their own cultural heritage and are able to identify their own cultural groups and the associated values and beliefs of these groups. In addition, counselors understand the impact of their cultural groups on their personal lives.

---

* Competencies and explanatory statements on pp. 24–28 of this text are from "Operationalization of the Multicultural Competencies," by P. Arredondo, R. Toporek, S. P. Brown, J. Jones, D. C. Locke, J. Sanchez, and H. Stadler, 1996, *Journal of Multicultural Counseling and Development, 24*, pp. 57–73. Copyright 1996 by The American Counseling Association. Used with permission. No further reproduction authorized without written permission of the American Counseling Association.

2. *Culturally skilled counselors are aware of how their own cultural backgrounds and experiences have influenced attitudes, values, and biases about psychological processes.* Counselors are able to identify cultural influences on cognitive development, problem solving, and decision making. Counselors are also able to express the beliefs of their particular religions and cultural groups and relate them to dimensions of identity, including class, disability, and sexual orientation.

3. *Culturally skilled counselors are able to recognize the limits of their multicultural competency and expertise.* More specifically, counselors can identify how their cultural attitudes, beliefs, and values may interfere with best service delivery to clients. Counselors are also aware of their clients' characteristics and identities that might challenge their values.

4. *Culturally skilled counselors recognize their sources of discomfort with differences that exist between themselves and clients in terms of race, ethnicity, and culture.* Such differences are acknowledged, ways to handle these differences are understood within the counseling relationship, and the solutions are responsibly implemented. (See Case Study: "Client Identities" at the end of this chapter.)

KNOWLEDGE

1. *Culturally skilled counselors have specific knowledge about their racial and cultural heritage and how it personally and professionally affects their definitions of, and biases about, normality/abnormality and the process of counseling.*

2. *Culturally skilled counselors possess knowledge and understanding about how oppression, racism, discrimination, and stereotyping affect them personally and their work.* Counselors are aware of privileges associated with a variety of identities, such as light skin color, the absence of physical disfigurements, gender-conforming behavior, wealth, and heterosexuality. They are also knowledgeable of the recent research on racism, ways to combat racism, racial identity development and measurement (Helms, 2007) and the relationship of these themes to counselors' professional development.

3. *Culturally skilled counselors possess knowledge about their social impact on others.* More specifically, counselors are aware of the various dimensions of difference and how power dynamics interact with dimensions of difference, across contexts and situations. Counselors are also clear about nonverbal communication styles within and among cultures.

SKILLS

1. *Culturally skilled counselors seek out educational, consultative, and training experiences to improve their understanding and effectiveness in working with culturally different populations.* Essentially, effective counselors know when they need to refer clients to other helpers and maintain an active list of potential referrals.

2. *Culturally skilled counselors are constantly seeking to understand themselves as racial and cultural beings and are actively seeking a nonracist identity.*

COMPETENCY TWO: COUNSELOR AWARENESS OF CLIENT'S WORLDVIEW

ATTITUDES AND BELIEFS   The second competency is **counselor awareness of client's worldview**.

1. *Culturally skilled counselors are aware of their negative and positive emotional reactions toward other racial and ethnic groups that may prove detrimental to the counseling relationship.* Counselors are honest about their biases relevant to certain racial, gender, class, ability, and ethnic groups.
2. *Culturally skilled counselors are aware of their stereotypes, preconceived notions and proximity to discourses that they may hold toward people due to their race, class, gender, sexuality, and other identities.*

KNOWLEDGE

1. *Culturally skilled counselors possess specific knowledge and information about the particular group with which they are working.* Effective counselors know about their clients' cultural values, history, and the ways in which histories have been obscured and/or lied about.
2. *Culturally skilled counselors understand how race, culture, and ethnicity may affect personality formation, vocational choices, manifestation of psychological disorders, help-seeking behavior, and the appropriateness or inappropriateness of counseling approaches.* Counselors are clear about how societal oppression affects groups and can interpret traditional systems (e.g., regarding personality development) and interrogate how such a system may or may not relate to particular groups.
3. *Culturally skilled counselors understand and have knowledge about sociopolitical influences that impinge on the lives of racial and ethnic minorities.* Counselors are knowledgeable about institutionalized racism, internalized oppression, poverty, and other forces that press down on their clients and the communities in which these clients live. In addition, they are aware of how the media, written and visual, along with certain policies (e.g., affirmative action setbacks), influence the perceptions of people of color and other stigmatized groups.

SKILLS

1. *Culturally skilled counselors should familiarize themselves with relevant research and the latest findings regarding mental health and mental disorders that affect various racial and ethnic groups.* Counselors are mindful of the research in mental health and career issues that affect different cultural groups and are able to identify a variety of multicultural experiences in which they have been involved.
2. *Culturally skilled counselors become actively involved with persons of color and other groups outside the counseling setting.* Counselors seek to engage in activities that both challenge preconceived stereotypes and encourage comfort with people across differences.

COMPETENCY THREE: CULTURALLY APPROPRIATE INTERVENTION STRATEGIES

ATTITUDES AND BELIEFS   The third competency is **culturally appropriate intervention strategies.**

1. *Culturally skilled counselors respect clients' religious and spiritual beliefs and values.* In doing so, they are able to identify aspects of spirituality relevant to wellness and healing.
2. *Culturally skilled counselors respect indigenous helping practices and respect help-giving networks among communities of color.* Counselors are also able to integrate their efforts with indigenous helpers where appropriate.
3. *Culturally skilled counselors value bilingualism and do not view another language as an impediment to counseling.* Monolingualism is recognized as limiting in itself.

KNOWLEDGE

1. *Culturally skilled counselors have a clear and explicit knowledge and under-standing of the generic characteristics of counseling and therapy (culture bound, class bound, and monolingual) and how they may clash with the cultural values of various cultural groups.* Counselors understand the context in which theories and the current counseling knowledge base have arisen.
2. *Culturally skilled counselors are aware of institutional barriers that prevent some people of color; women; persons with disabilities; people from low-income groups; and gay, lesbian, and transgender clients from using mental health services.* By doing so, counselors can also suggest alternatives to tradi-tional systems of helping and communicate effectively with others about how to intervene appropriately.
3. *Culturally skilled counselors have knowledge of the potential bias in assess-ment instruments and use procedures and interpret findings in a way that recognizes the cultural and linguistic characteristics of the clients.* Counselors are able to interpret assessment instruments in the context of a client's culture and are also aware of existing bias in traditional systems of diagnosis, including the *DSM–IV–TR (Diagnostic and Statistical Manual of Mental Disorders,* 4th ed., Revised).
4. *Culturally skilled counselors have knowledge of family structures, hierarchies, values, and beliefs from various cultural perspectives.* Counselors are aware of various resources within the community that can assist their clients with a host of concerns while recognizing that culture can contribute to clients' decisions that are not culturally consistent with that of the counselor. Some feminist-oriented counselors may perceive certain traditional gender roles to be oppressive when, according to the client, they represent normative ways of being in the world.
5. *Culturally skilled counselors should be aware of relevant discriminatory practices at the social and community levels that may be affecting the*

psychological welfare of the population being served. This would include knowledge of both state and national policies (e.g., repeals of affirmative action in California or Ohio's declaration that marriage is between a man and a woman only).

SKILLS

1. *Culturally skilled counselors are able to engage in a variety of verbal and nonverbal helping responses.* They are able to send and receive both verbal and nonverbal messages accurately and appropriately. Counselors are aware of why they use particular communication styles at a given time and are able to modify techniques for a variety of contexts.
2. *Culturally skilled counselors are able to exercise institutional intervention skills on behalf of their clients.* Counselors can help equip clients with coping and resistance strategies and effective skills to deal with institutional discrimination.
3. *Culturally skilled counselors are not averse to seeking consultation with traditional healers or religious and spiritual leaders and practitioners in the treatment of culturally different clients when appropriate.* If necessary, counselors are aware of appropriate referrals within indigenous communities.
4. *Culturally skilled counselors take responsibility for interacting in the language requested by the client and, if not feasible, make appropriate referrals.* Counselors are able to seek out the services of translators and are familiar with resources that provide appropriate language services to clients.
5. *Culturally skilled counselors have training and expertise in the use of traditional assessment and testing instruments.* Counselors understand the cultural context in which traditional assessment tools have developed.
6. *Culturally skilled counselors should attend to, as well as work to eliminate, biases, prejudices, and discriminatory contexts in conducting evaluations and providing interventions and should develop sensitivity to the intersections of oppression: sexism, discrimination against people with disabilities, heterosexism, class elitism, and racism.* Counselors are able to address the need for change, regarding discrimination, on an organizational level. Advocacy and social justice are core to multicultural competence.
7. *Culturally skilled counselors take responsibility for educating their clients to the processes of psychological intervention, such as goals, expectations, legal rights, and the counselor's orientation.* Clients are encouraged and, in some cases, empowered by their counselors to advocate for themselves through an educational process.

Arredondo and Arciniega (2001) added grounding principles to these competencies, which place the competencies within an ecological framework. The first principle is of the learning organization. Namely, such an organization is teachable and open to change by questioning and challenging itself. The lone cross-cultural class that characterizes most graduate counseling training programs was criticized as not being representative of a learning organization or responsive to the research available on the significance of multicultural competence.

The second principle is a competency rationale, which provides the profession with guidelines as well as developmental benchmarks for attributes and characteristics that distinguish competent counselors from those who are not. Despite the greater attention given to multicultural counseling competence and research suggesting that multicultural education produces positive outcomes with respect to MCCs (Worthington et al., 2007), how to teach MCCs to graduate students in the most effective way possible continues to be explored (Kim & Lyons, 2003). (See Storytelling: "I Fear.")

STORYTELLING: I Fear

A few years ago, my students and I watched the video by Mun Wah, *The Color of Fear*. When it was over, I asked them to answer this question on a piece of paper, without giving their names: "Within the context of multicultural counseling, what are you afraid of?" These were some of the answers I received.

1. I am afraid of people thinking that I am ignorant and don't know anything.
2. I am afraid of saying something insensitive to a person of color.
3. I am afraid that people of color will think I am racist.
4. I am afraid of not knowing what to say or do.
5. I am afraid that I won't be able to help someone.
6. I am afraid that I am racist.
7. I am afraid that people think I won't have anything to offer them.
8. I am afraid that people will think I am the enemy because of the color of my skin.
9. I am afraid that I'm more like David (the middle-age man that the whole group spent an inordinate amount of time helping) than I dare to think.
10. I am afraid of people's anger.
11. I am afraid of not knowing how to help problems that I've never encountered or have not heard about.
12. I am afraid that people will think, not only am I young but I am dumb.

Students in training as well as seasoned clinicians will omit information deemed as fugitive or risky or avoid asking particular questions out of fear of being perceived as ignorant, racist, insensitive, or discriminatory. This fear can paralyze the therapeutic event and interfere with the client's growth. Clients depend on the clinicians' awareness and initiative to bring difficult conversations into the room. It is impossible to help clients explore complex issues concerning sexuality, class, race, and cultural differences if clinicians are not actively engaged in this important work themselves. It is also a component of multicultural competence to participate in personal introspection. Bringing students face to face with their own stories and feelings is essential to multicultural education. Creating the space for the unspeakable to be spoken is empowering. Checking in with students and asking how they are doing, acknowledging the hard work they are doing, and honoring the emotions, including uncertainty, is important to training. Initially, such awareness can usher in feelings of powerlessness, yet powerlessness is what many clients feel by the time they arrive to therapy.

GUIDELINES

Six guidelines have been articulated by the American Psychological Association to provide psychologists with the rationale and needs for addressing multiculturalism and diversity in education, training, research, and practice; basic information, relevant terminology, and empirical research that support these guidelines; references to enhance ongoing education training, research, practice, and organizational change; and paradigms that broaden the purview of psychology as a profession.

Guideline 1: Psychologists are encouraged to recognize that they are cultural beings and as a result may hold attitudes and beliefs that can have an adverse impact on their perceptions of and interactions with individuals who are ethnically and racially different. Psychologists are encouraged to learn how cultures differ in basic ideologies.

Guideline 2: Psychologists are encouraged to recognize the importance of multicultural sensitivity/responsiveness to, knowledge of, and understanding about ethnically and racially diverse individuals. Multicultural competencies have evolved into a framework to be used as a guide for the training and practice of counselors. Psychologists are encouraged to understand stigma and its relationship to marginalized identities.

Guideline 3: As educators, psychologists are encouraged to employ the constructs of multiculturalism and diversity in psychological education. Psychologists are encouraged to become knowledgeable of different learning models and approaches to teaching from multicultural perspectives.

Guideline 4: Culturally sensitive psychological researchers are encouraged to recognize the importance of conducting culture-centered and ethical psychological research among persons from ethnic, linguistic, and racial minority backgrounds. Psychologists need to become knowledgeable of the way in which culture affects assumptions made about variables under investigation as well as the research instruments used to measure certain constructs.

Guideline 5: Psychologists are encouraged to apply culturally appropriate skills in clinical and other applied psychological practices. Psychologists are open to the reality that culture-centered interventions may be more effective in certain contexts.

Guideline 6: Psychologists are encouraged to use organizational change processes to support culturally informed organizational policy development and practices. A variety of contexts—schools, organizations, and communities—can benefit from psychologists' skills to facilitate culturally informed organizational development of policies and practices.*

*Adapted from "Guidelines on multicultural education, training, research, practice, and organizational change for psychologists," 2003, *American Psychologist*, *58*(3), 377–402. Copyright 2003 by the American Psychological Association.

DIVERSITY TRAINING

Controversy surrounds which training model methods are the most appropriate for training counselors. Dinsmore and England (1996) stated that there is "no general consensus regarding what set of program characteristics constitutes a standard for multicultural program competence" (p. 59). There is considerable variety in counselor diversity training programs. Although exposure to race and culture is standard in most courses on diversity, regardless of whether issues of power and privilege are discussed, not all programs expose students to spirituality, class, and disability issues (APA, 2003). Despite greater emphasis on spirituality, gender, and sexuality, a focus is needed on transgender issues, intersexuality, and biracial/multiracial populations. Students also tend not to have exposure to gerontology themes.

Faculty grapple with how to best teach multicultural counseling and psychology. Bowman (1996) concluded that "multicultural instruction should not be limited to one course but should be infused in all aspects of the training" (p. 16). A separate course on multicultural counseling does not allow the material to be incorporated into other core courses such as history and systems of psychology, psychopathology, and cognitive-affective basis of behavior. Mio (2005) suggests that courses build on each other in a heuristic fashion: for example, an introductory multicultural course, a second course on testing in multicultural issues, a third course on research, and a fourth course on clinical interventions.

Because society is very much segregated along racial lines, people continue to need to be made aware that racism exists (MIO, 2005). It is likely that many graduate students and their faculty do not have intimate friendships outside of their racial, sexual, and class groups. Bowman (1996) stated that "trainees need opportunities to examine the dynamics of establishing relationships with culturally diverse populations and to question how they apply what they know about self and others to successful cross-cultural interactions" (p. 23). To promote self-awareness and empathy, laboratory experiences may be helpful. As students encounter dissonance, they need safe places where they can ask questions and process newly encountered information. Faculty need to support students in their efforts at risk-taking while encouraging all students to be receptive to new, conflicting, and, in some cases, dissonant-provoking ideas from classmates, professors, course readings, and videos.

There are exercises that can facilitate student introspection and application of multicultural theory. Drawing one's culture with crayons and constructing a genogram to outline family history are two examples. Reading McIntosh's (1989) article "White Privilege: Unpacking the Invisible Knapsack" can be very thought-provoking. The unearned privileges associated with ability, gender, and sexual orientation can also be investigated as well as how White people who are gay, disabled, or low-wage earning receive privileges because of their skin color yet have stigmatized identities as well. Journals, personal narratives, participation in cross-cultural activities as a racial minority, and reading about power and oppression are critical aspects of multicultural training. Reading the text *Explorations in Privilege, Oppression, and Diversity* by Anderson and Middleton (2004) is an excellent way for students to gain exposure to personal narratives as they think about their own stories. One instructor encourages her students to write a comprehensive racial psychohistory, allowing them to document the role that race has played in shaping their life philosophies, personalities, and coping patterns (Kogan, 2000).

A variety of experiential activities, such as role-play, games, and films, are recognized as a means of educating counseling students about the counseling process. According to Kim and Lyons (2003), games, in particular, offer "optimal opportunities to gain multicultural counseling competence across attitudes, beliefs, knowledge, and skills" (p. 402).

To guide counselor education and counseling psychology departments in their training efforts, Ponterotto, Alexander, and Grieger (1995) developed a multicultural competency checklist. There are six themes, each with several items:

1. Minority representation.
2. Curriculum issues.
3. Counseling practice and supervision.
4. Research considerations.
5. Student and faculty competency evaluation.
6. Physical environment.

The first four items on the checklist seek to ascertain *minority representation*—whether 30% of faculty, students, and program support staff are visibly racially/ethnically diverse. Bilingual skills are also important. The second theme, *curriculum issues,* is covered across five items that reflect course work, pedagogy, and student assessment. For example, multicultural issues are integrated into all course work. All program faculty can specify how this is done in their courses. Furthermore, syllabi clearly reflect multicultural inclusion. *Counseling practice and supervision* is the third area and contains three questions. The focus here is on students' practicum, supervision quality, and the "Multicultural Affairs Committee," which is recommended as a way to monitor multicultural activities. *Research considerations* has four questions concerned with a multicultural research presence in the program. Statement 14 of the checklist asks if there is clear faculty research productivity in multicultural issues as is evidenced by journal publications and conference presentations on multicultural topics. The four items in *student and faculty competency evaluation* emphasize proficiency in multicultural issues. Statement 19 asks whether students' "comprehensive exams reflect Multicultural issues." The final two items concern the *physical environment* and whether it reflects diversity in the faculty offices, reception area, and clinic area. The authors of this checklist recognize that very few programs will meet all the competencies in the checklist and suggest the development of 1-, 3-, and 5-year action plans.

ASSESSMENT AND RESEARCH

One of the guidelines for counselors and psychologists affirmed earlier was the importance of conducting culture-centered and ethical psychological research among persons from ethnic, linguistic, and racial minority backgrounds. Multicultural research is defined as the empirical examination of or inquiry into the experiences of individuals from diverse cultural backgrounds" (Utsey, Walker, & Kwate, 2005, p. 249). Not only are psychometric properties of instruments important to consider, but also flaws in methodological approaches, such as the tendency to aggregate groups instead of disaggregate them. An example is looking at Asian and Pacific Islanders together (see Chapter 7). Their experiences are extremely different with respect to poverty, educational attainment, and income. Including people from the very cultures being investigated but who are outside of the academy would add to the multicultural variety and authenticity (Chang & Sue, 2005).

In a recent study, Worthington, Soth-McNett, and Moreno (2007) reviewed and evaluated the content of the 75 articles and 81 studies done on multicultural competencies (MCCs). Their findings showed that (1) empirial research on MCCs has increased over the past 20 years; (2) a small number of researchers are producing the majority of research, and (3) the methods used in producing empirical research are narrow: 73% are from descriptive field studies and 25% from analogue research. In addition, most of the samples were convenience samples, which has implications for external validity.

Many traditional psychoeducational measures used for assessment and research purposes were not initially validated with diverse populations in their original sample groups and are based on individual performance or self-report or both. The appropriateness and validity of commonly used psychological and psychoeducational assessment instruments, when used with individuals and diverse populations, may be questionable. The American Psychological Association (2003) stated, "culturally sensitive psychological researchers should strive to be knowledgeable about a broad range of assessment techniques, data-gathering procedures, and standardized instruments whose validity, reliability, and measurement equivalence have been investigated across culturally diverse samples" (p. 389).

The validity and reliability of assessment tools have implications for research and practice. Culturally insensitive research accommodates and further perpetuates inadequate training models and subsequent counseling services. According to Ponterotto and Casas (1991), one criticism of current research on people of color is that important intrapersonal and extrapersonal factors, such as client attitudes, client–counselor racial similarity, communication styles, acculturation, and discrimination and poverty, have virtually been ignored. Furthermore, the research has not considered or studied the tremendous heterogeneity in multicultural populations, which has affected, fostered, and perpetuated ethnic stereotypes and global categorizations. Last, easily accessible subject populations (e.g., White psychology college students from large midwestern universities) who tend not to be representative of the larger community have typically been selected as research populations. Overreliance on research using analogue designs, "whereby the subject pools have consisted of pseudo-clients (e.g., students) and pseudo-counselors (e.g., graduate students in counseling) instead of 'real' clients and counselors" (Ponterotto & Casas, 1991, p. 78), limits generalizability to actual client and counselor populations.

Researchers such as Ruelas (2003) and Worthington, Soth-McNett, and Moreno (2007) note limitations with multicultural competency measures, namely, their tendency to be self-report instruments, which tend not to be related to observer-rated MCCs. Several instruments have been created to measure multicultural competencies. In a study by Kocarek, Talbot, Batka, and Anderson (2001), they explored the reliability and validity of three instruments: the Multicultural Counselor Awareness Scale (MCAS), the Multicultural Awareness of Knowledge and Skills Survey (MAKSS), and the Survey of Graduate Students' Experience with Diversity (GSEDS). With a sample size of 120 master's degree students from seven programs across the country, the reliability and validity of these instruments varied but for the most part held up, except for the awareness subscale of the MAKSS. The authors argue that a lack of consistency exists "between same-named subscales and high correlations between the Knowledge and Skills subscales" (p. 494). Subsequently, questions are raised about the development and meaning of the very constructs being measured.

Concern has also been raised over the validity and applied pragmatic utility of the many research findings appearing in the multicultural literature (Ponterotto & Casas, 1991). Simplistic client–counselor process variables have been overemphasized, and significant cultural as well as psychosocial variables that might affect counseling have been disregarded. In other words, important psychosocial variables (e.g., learning styles, communication patterns, racism, oppression, poverty), which may be more difficult to study but are vital to understanding the role of counseling with real clients, have been overlooked. A high degree of heterogeneity, such as demographic characteristics, class, and attitudes, exists within multicultural populations, yet these intracultural differences tend not to be noted in the research literature.

Qualitative research is also becoming increasingly popular, particularly as it relates to allowing voices to be heard that have traditionally been overlooked or silenced. In doing so, the researcher is not an objective entity but is actively engaged in the research through an ongoing examination of oneself across multiple contexts (Choudhuri, 2005).

To demonstrate competence in multicultural assessment, conceptualization of presenting problems, establishment of appropriate interventions, development of client treatment goals, and the formulation of multiculturally sensitive research, psychological service providers and academicians will need to acquire cultural knowledge, information, and skills.

IMPLICATIONS FOR COUNSELORS AND PSYCHOLOGISTS

Both the American Counseling Association and American Psychological Association have voiced a commitment to diversity. These professional organizations, to which the majority of counselors and psychologists belong, have great power—as do the boards affiliated with them that approve graduate counseling and psychology programs according to their adherence to program standards. An elephant in the room, but how do APA-affiliated graduate programs with 100% White faculty receive a stamp of approval cycle after cycle from the APA if racial diversity is more than an espoused value? One of the risks associated with expanding diversity to include other dimensions is that some see this as an opportunity to avoid or minimize a focus on race and instead bend diversity to mean gender and sexuality diversity while maintaining whiteness as a non-negotiable construct or territory.

Unlearning oppressive practices that distance mental health professionals from themselves and their clients and students is lifelong work and an ongoing process. Willingness to be open and to be changed are crucial to this process of developing not only a nonracist identity but nonsexist, nonclassist, and non-homonegative identities. Being honest about the various emotions that are understandably within us as counselors and psychologists, even during the cross-cultural therapeutic event is essential. Abernathy (1995) said that "minimal attention has been devoted to addressing the anger that frequently emerges in cross-racial work" (p. 96). (See Case Study: "Client Identities.")

Numerous books, articles, conferences, and associations are in the service of fostering a climate of multiculturalism and equity for all people. The ACA and the APA provide excellent resources for students, professionals, and practitioners who want to develop themselves and to connect with others who are like-minded in their focus on multicultural competence. Hartung (1996) noted the difficulty in developing cultural competencies among both faculty and students.

Knowledge of available resources does not replace genuine and authentic relationships—not just with colleagues who we may step out with for a coffee or lunch but with friends who are invited to each other's homes where honest talk can occur about our lives as racial, cultural, and gendered beings. This type of sharing and being together allows us to discuss, understand, and ultimately transcend the scourge of race oppression. At the same time, acknowledging the shame experienced by many clinicians-in-training is a crucial beginning to understanding oppression and inequity. Such feelings are important and should be worked through as part of the multicultural training process (Parker & Schwartz, 2002).

CASE STUDY
Client Identities

I routinely ask my students, during their psychosocial narrative assignment, to discuss any client identities that would present a challenge for them within a therapeutic encounter. I get a minority of students who admit to anticipating some difficulty working with someone who is mentally retarded, a sexual predator, or an elderly person. A few students have discussed their reluctance to work with someone who is a Nazi (blatantly racist) or who does not support women's egalitarianism (blatantly sexist or a traditional gender-conforming man or woman). For the most part, students indicate their willingness to essentially work with anyone, despite their characteristics. Part of this may be a desire to be open and accepting of all of God's people. At the same time, not building an awareness of oneself as a gendered, racial, and cultural being shaped by dominant race, gender, and sexuality discourses does not encourage multicultural competence. The maxim, mental health professional know thyself, is still relevant.

QUESTIONS AND DISCUSSION

The following is a list of client identities. Take the role of therapist. Ask yourself the questions indicated. Then review the guidelines and competencies at the end of the chapter and, in small groups, add any others that apply.

1. **A person actively committing adultery on his or her spouse and expressing no guilt or remorse.**
   First, identify your feelings, then ask:

   a. If the client wept in therapy from feelings of guilt, would my feelings about working with the client change?

   b. If the cheating spouse had been cheated on initially by the spouse, would my feelings about working with the client change?

   c. If the cheated-on spouse had terminal cancer and had been given 6 months to live, would my feelings about working with the client change?

2. **A proud and out lesbian who is very masculine in dress and mannerisms.**
   First, identify your feelings, then ask:

   a. If the client was more feminine (e.g., gender conforming) in appearance, would my attitude about working with her change?

   b. If the client was conflicted about her sexuality and wanted exposure to conversion therapy to move away from her homosexuality, would my attitude change?

3. **A man who will not allow his wife to work or leave the house without accompanying her.**
   First, identify your feelings, then ask:

   a. If the wife supported her husband's position, would my feelings about working with him change?

   b. If the wife had incurred tremendous shopping debt when she was out of the house, would my feelings change?

4. **A pregnant mother who is abusing heroin.**
   First, identify your feelings, then ask:

   a. If the client was in the last trimester as opposed to the first trimester, which is when critical systems are developing, would my feelings about working with her change?

   b. If the client knew her baby had a genetic disorder and the child was most likely not to survive after the first few days of life, would my attitude change?

   c. If the woman planned to give her child up for adoption to a loving family who did not care how extensive the child's disabilities were, would my attitude about working with her change?

5. **A man on the *down-low* (is in a heterosexual marriage but is secretly having sex with men).**
   First, identify your feelings, then ask:

   a. If the client's wife had multiple sclerosis and was unable to be sexual with her husband, would my feelings about working with him change?

   b. If the client used condoms faithfully during sexual intercourse with men, would my attitude about working with him change?

   c. If the client's wife was super-morbidly obese, would my feelings about his behavior change?

6. **A woman who is planning to leave her husband and two dependent children for another man.**
   First, identify your feelings, then ask:

   a. If the client's husband had been beating her, would my feelings about her decision to leave her husband and children change?

   b. If the children were her stepchildren, would my attitude about her decision change?

7. **A man who announces he does not want to work with you because of your race.**

   a. If I knew the client had a negative experience in therapy with someone from my same racial group, would my attitude about working with him change?

b. If the client were of minimal intelligence, would my attitude about working with him change?

8. **A woman wants her school-age, biracial child, who is foreign-born, tested for learning disabilities prior to finalizing the adoption.**

   a. If I knew the client had already adopted a child with servere learning disabilities, would my attitude about her choice to do testing prior to the adoption change?

   b. If the child's biological mother had a low IQ, would my attitude about working with her change?

Recommendations from *Guidelines and Competencies for Practice, Research, and Education* (APA, 2003)

1. Acknowledge your racial and/or cultural group's history in the oppression of other peoples.
2. Be able to recognize how your religious values affect your views about sex, drugs, death, marriage, and divorce.
3. Be aware of unearned able-body privilege and how this affects everything from driving, sexual activity, accessing buildings and mobility, and people's perceptions of another's attractiveness, intelligence, and moral character.
4. Know the limits of your multicultural expertise, and seek help when needed.
5. Acknowledge who is in your circle of friends, and if racial, sexual, and class diversity is lacking, ask yourself why you have been reluctant to develop friendships with people who are not like yourself.
6. Acknowledge feelings of guilt, shame, or resentment that arise as a function of your exposure to different types of diversity.
7. Realize that there are cultures that do not accept your attitudes about individuality, freedom, and women's rights—and they are not necessarily wrong or worse off.
8. Ask yourself what the impact of your culture and ethnicity have been on your education, career, and/or mate choice.
9. Consider how much value you attach to consulting with healers who have not graduated from high school or did not go through a practicum or internship like you did.
10. Understand the potential bias of instruments and the cultural context in which they are normed.

SUMMARY

This chapter offered an overview of multicultural competencies and skills. A brief review of diversity training programs for counselors in training was provided, as well as strategies for becoming a multiculturally competent counselor. The importance of attending to students' dissonance about their future multicultural effectiveness was discussed through Storytelling. The case study activity dealt with a variety of client scenarios. The message was sent that identity profiles of our clients can be challenging and our feelings about these identities must not be ignored. Acknowledging this is not an assault to our professional identities but an opportunity to develop competence and not be afraid of difference.

Chapter 3

Statused Identities

Be patient toward all that is unsolved in your heart and try to love the questions themselves . . . Live the questions now. Perhaps you will then gradually, without noticing it, live along some distant day into the answer.

Rainer Maria Rilke

The therapeutic event is affected by the perceptions that clients and mental health professionals have about identity constructs, particularly those that are visible. Attitudes about sources of difference have to be examined, and the impact of these attitudes on the therapeutic event must be assessed. This chapter explores sources of human differences. The social construction of identities within U.S. society is conveyed via the Contextual and Social Construction of Differences Model. Implications for mental health professionals and their client populations are emphasized throughout.

IDENTITIES AS STATUS: THE CONTEXTUAL AND SOCIAL CONSTRUCTION OF DIFFERENCES MODEL

More than 60 years ago, Hughes (1945), a sociologist, addressed dilemmas of occupational and ascribed status. He stated that occupational or vocational status has a complex set of supplementary characteristics that come to be expected of its incumbents. For example, it is anticipated that a kindergarten teacher will be a female. Such expectations are largely unconscious because people do not systematically expect that certain people will occupy given positions. Through a process of cultural socialization from the media, educational systems, clergy, and family, people "carry in their minds" the auxiliary traits associated with most positions in society. Persons who newly occupy prestigious positions contend with ongoing suspicions from those who have historically maintained these positions and from those who have observed such people occupying these positions. Democratic presidential candidates Barack Obama and Hillary Clinton contend with this very dynamic, albeit differently due to their race and gender statuses.

At the base of people's thinking is the perception that new incumbents may not be as qualified or worthy as others preceding them and that their incumbency is due primarily to affirmative action or other political processes, and not as a result of hard work or merit. As new groups occupy positions that have been held almost exclusively by one racial and/or gender group, discourses do not completely disappear. It is possible to have close proximity to dominant discourses and to embody the belief that luck, injustice, and/or quotas, not merit, equity, and/or skill, are responsible for occupational success, particularly for people regarded as "other" due to their stigmatized identities.

In the society about which Hughes spoke, race membership was a status-determining trait. Race tended to overpower any other variable that might run counter to it such as occupational success, a component of social class. Because racism, sexism, and homophobia are interlocking systems of oppression, membership in groups that are marginalized is associated with stigma. *Stigma* refers to "a bodily sign designed to expose something unusual and bad about the moral status of an individual" (Rosenblum & Travis, 2005, p. 27). Hughes's decades-old observations have contemporary relevance.

The **Model of Socially Constructed Discourses** suggests that human characteristics operate as status variables in society. (See Table 3.1.) The model maintains

TABLE 3.1   Model of Socially Constructed Discourses

Visible and Invisible Sources of Difference	Dominant Discourses	Consequences of Socially Constructed Meanings About Difference
Race	Whiteness is unexplored and yet exists as the basis by which people of color are evaluated.	Racism; obliviousness about one's status as a racial being, particularly among Whites
Skin color	White and white-looking skin are normative in ways that dark skin is not.	Colorism
Sex	The male experience and masculinity are valued in ways that women are not.	Sexism; unrealistic gendered expectations for women and men
Sexuality	Heterosexuality is valued over being gay, bisexual, lesbian, or transgendered.	Homonegativity
Ability	Physical and mental ability are esteemed and rewarded. Disability is an eventual reality for all people who are fortunate enough to grow old.	Able-ism
Class	Upper-middle-class status is glamorized. Being middle class or poor is less valued.	Class elitism
Religion	Christianity is normative and privileged. Not having a religious orientation is devalued over non-Christian religions.	Religious bigotry

that in the United States race, gender, and class are socially constructed. From a constructionist perspective, these identities matter because society wants them to—not that this is right, but it is so. Contextual and socially constructed discourses maintain, in both subtle and blatant ways, that persons who hold membership in particular groups have status within society and that this means something different from persons who do not hold membership in these same groups. This stratification of race and other identities is a social construction—and not a given like the rising of the sun each day. (See Storytelling: "Transcending Discourses" on page 49.)

Visible and invisible identities (e.g., race, gender, sexuality, religion, ability, and disability) are not oppressive. Racism, colorism, sexism, homonegativity, able-body-ism, class elitism, and religious bigotry, however, are oppressive and discriminatory (Robinson, 1999). A distinction exists between having an identity that is stigmatized (e.g., being a quadriplegic) and being a problem or internalizing a sense of inadequacy or inferiority. The problem is discrimination against the disabled, not being disabled.

According to Reynolds and Pope (1991), a customary norm by which people are evaluated in the United States is based on proximity to being American. A discourse associated with being American is that being American is associated with Whiteness. Maleness, gender-conforming femininity, upper middle class, status, Christianity, heterosexuality, English-speaking, youthfulness, and mental/physical ability have been constructed to mean normativity. Economic exploitation, religious bias, homophobia, racism, able-body-ism, and other sources of discrimination emanate from this narrow and limiting construction of normalcy. The "other" refers to persons who are perceived to be not only different from the norm but less than the norm.

ASSUMPTIONS OF HIERARCHICAL SOCIALIZATION PATTERNS

The Model of Socially Constructed Discourses presents sources of differences as social constructions. The consequences of these social constructions are also detailed.

Sources of differences between and among people possess rank, have value, and function as primary status-determining traits. Characteristics perceived as normal are thought to be desired by and representative of all. For instance, students often have a difficult time understanding why a woman with a disability would not want to be able-bodied. It is believed that life would be so much easier not having to deal with a scooter, walker, or wheelchair. Characteristics with less rank (such as being old, or short, or fat), are held in lower esteem, are not regarded as desirable, and have less social power. Within this hierarchical framework, the most valued aspect of a person is not an achieved or acquired trait, such as perseverance or openness to new experiences, but an immutable quality, such as White skin.

Although human beings are more similar than they are different, a hierarchical framework, where differences have rank, inflates and distorts differences among people. In contrast, a system where people are worthy because they are here and exist with "unique expressions of spiritual energy" (Myers et al., 1991, p. 56) honors our humanity.

RACISM

Racism involves the total social structure in which one group has conferred advantage over another through institutional policies. **Racism** is a social construction based on sociopolitical attitudes that demean specific racial characteristics, as Pinderhughes (1989) makes clear:

> Racism raises to the level of social structure the tendency to use superiority as a solution to discomfort about difference. Belief in the superiority of Whites and the inferiority of people-of-color based on racial difference is

legitimized by societal arrangements that exclude the latter from resources
and power and then blame them for their failures, which are due to lack of
access. (p. 89)

Discussing racism is unsettling and dissonant-provoking. People are often reluctant
to engage in dialogue about racism, yet racism is a major part of this country's origins.
Other terms may be used instead of racism, such as *manifest destiny, progress,* or
ambition, but let us not put lipstick on a pig and delude ourselves. It is imperative that
we call things as they are. Part of being committed to the process of transformation
and social justice is to not turn away from the truth. Ambition and racial exploitation
should not be confused. Christopher Columbus was an ambitious explorer. He also
racially exploited the Arawaks.

It has been said that America was built by taking land from a people and people
from a land. Racially discriminatory practices were under way when Africans built the
infrastructure for major cities in the South and were not remunerated. Americans
behaved arrogantly and perceived themselves as superior to Native American Indians
when, for centuries, they stole (there is no other, more appropriate term) the
American Indians' land and destroyed their way of life. Americans behaved in a racist
manner when scores of first- and second-generation Japanese Americans were
interred in U.S. concentration camps during World War II. Small numbers of German
and Italian Americans were interred also, but not to the same extent as were the
Japanese. A racist ideology existed when the Southwest, which was once Mexico, was
ceded to the United States by the Treaty of Guadalupe Hidalgo in 1848. People
became "foreigners in their native land," which they had inhabited for centuries. A
racist ideology existed when laws, such as the 1882 Exclusion Act, restricted Chinese
from this country while white-skinned European immigrants flooded in. Racism was
practiced when the 1790 Naturalization Law was in effect for 162 years; this policy
reserved naturalized citizenship for Whites only (Avakian, 2002). There are current
acts of violence and racism in countries we currently occupy, where children—who
should never be held responsible for the actions and choices of adults—are made
more vulnerable. At various junctures in U.S. history, laws forbade women across
racial groups and men of color from voting, becoming literate, marrying White
people, becoming educated at all-White institutions, owning property, working, and
drinking water from public facilities. Such policies attested to the institutionalization
of racism and sexism as blatant devaluations of women and non-White people. "The
rationale of segregation implies that the oppressed are a pariah people. Unclean was
the caste message of every colored water fountain, waiting room, and courtroom
Bible" (Loewen, 1995, p. 163).

Racist attitudes portrayed in sentiments against racial intermixing were not
simply between races but within ethnic groups as well. In the Nazi publication
Neues Volk, it was written, "Every German and every German woman has the duty
to avoid association with other races, especially Slavs. Each intimacy with a people
of inferior race means sinning against the future of our own people" (cited in
Rogers, 1967, p. 19).

Scientific notions about intelligence were developed against a biological and
sociopolitical backdrop of racism. Herrnstein and Murray (1994), in their controversial

work *The Bell Curve,* examined ethnic differences on intelligence tests. They concluded that "for every known test of cognitive ability that meets basic psychometric standards of reliability and validity, Blacks and Whites score differently" (p. 276). These authors indicated that the differences are reduced once the testing is done outside the South, after age 6, and after 1940. Herrnstein and Murray argued that even once socioeconomic differences are controlled for, the differences do not disappear, but class may reduce the overall differences in intelligence testing by about one third.

Grubb (1992) investigated the claim that Blacks are genetically inferior to Whites on intelligence testing. As a clinical psychologist specializing in the treatment of childhood and adolescent disorders, he examined 6,742 persons with developmental disabilities from three western states. If this argument that Blacks were genetically inferior to Whites was true, then he could expect to see a higher proportion of Blacks identified as having mental retardation, in comparison with Whites. Grubb found that, of the total population included in this project, 0.03% had developmental disabilities. This figure was consistent across racial groups. He concluded that the assumptions regarding heredity among the Black race were not upheld in this study, leading him to reject this line of reasoning.

Nisbett (1995) also challenged Herrnstein and Murray (1994). Nisbett argued that comparing Blacks at high socioeconomic status (SES) with high-SES Whites is inherently flawed, given the higher income levels of Whites in comparison with Blacks. In addition, Nisbett stated that socialization and social factors affect ability levels. Claims by Jensen and other authors stating that "g-loaded" tests differed between the races, with Whites having faster reaction times on complex maneuvers, was subjectively interpreted. According to Nisbett, "For skills such as spatial reasoning and form perception, the g-loading was relatively low and B/W gap relatively low" (p. 44).

During slavery, two forms of psychopathology were common among slaves. The first, "drapetomania," consisted of a single symptom of slaves running away. The second, "dysathesia aethiopica," consisted of numerous conditions such as destroying plantation property, showing defiance, and attacking the slave masters. This second condition was also known as "rascality," and both were nerve disorders coined by reputable physicians (Bronstein & Quina, 1988). Liberty and the pursuit of happiness are explicit in this nation's charter, yet the desire for these entitlements among Blacks during this time in history was appraised as pathological. Black people took care of White people, yet they were perceived of and depicted as childlike, incapable of providing for themselves, and dependent on their benevolent White masters. Clinicians of the day interpreted 1840 census data that reported higher rates of psychopathology among Blacks to support the belief that "the care, supervision, and control provided by slavery were essential to the mental health of Blacks" (Bronstein & Quina, 1988, p. 39). This paradigm supported a false belief that Blacks were not only different but inferior. It was not possible to be diagnosed accurately when the psychological community perceived Black people to be chattel and inherently flawed. The current distrust of the mental health community in many communities of color cannot be adequately appreciated without an understanding of this history.

CONSEQUENCES OF RACISM FOR EUROPEAN AMERICANS There are consequences of racism for people of color (e.g., stress, high blood pressure, disparities in access to health care). There are also consequences for Whites (Pinderhughes, 1989). How can there not be consequences, given the pernicious nature of racism that affects all people? The untruth about racism is that White people are not affected, only the "other."

White people lack understanding about the effects and consequences of race and racism on their own lives, due largely to "race," typically referring to non-White people. Not having an identity as a racial being contributes to misperceptions among Whites about the reality of racism, racial inequities, and discrimination against people of color. More White Americans than people of color believe there is equity for Blacks and Whites in this country and that Blacks are as well off as Whites in terms of jobs, incomes, health care, and schooling (Institute of Medicine, 2003). (See Storytelling: "They're Sitting Right Next to Us.")

One way to facilitate a discussion of racism is through an examination of unearned White skin color privilege. McIntosh (1989) maintained that privilege is an invisible knapsack of assets an entitled group can refer to on a regular basis to negotiate their daily lives more effectively. Unearned skin-color privilege is a fugitive subject for two reasons: privilige is something people are meant to be oblivious about and non-Whites do not share in the privileges Whites take for granted. Unpacking privilege produces dissonance among many Whites because it assails fundamental Western beliefs of meritocracy and creates confusion about the meaning of being White.

One consequence of racism for European Americans is that it limits emotional and intellectual development (Pinderhughes, 1989). Zetzer (2005) discussed her desire not to be a WMWP or a well-meaning White person—defined as a White person who does not understand the social construction of race, the impact of daily racism on people of color, and their role in the perpetuation of inequity.

STORYTELLING: They're Sitting Right Next to Us

There was a recent article in the *Boston Globe* about students' experiences with racism at Boston-area campuses. Asian, Black, and Latino students discussed some of their White peers' perceptions regarding their acceptance into the universities. Affirmative Action was viewed as the only reason certain students of color had been admitted.

Some students stayed in their rooms during parties due to concerns that alcohol contributed to racist comments from Whites. Parties where White students had to climb under a fence in order to be admitted (mocking the harrowing experiences of Mexican immigrants) were mentioned as contributing to a hostile atmosphere on campus. In a class discussion about this article, some White students admitted that they were not aware of this situation—that they did not know life was like this for many college students of color in Boston and throughout the country.

Self-conception is adversely affected when race as a core component of the self is ignored.

A growing area of research deals with the psychosocial costs of racism to Whites. Spanierman, Poteat, Beer, and Armstrong (2007) conducted research with 230 White undergraduate students using the Psychosocial Costs of Racism to Whites (PCRW) scale, with three subscales: 1. White Empathic Reactions toward Racism, such as sadness and anger. 2. White Guilt. 3. White Fear of Others.

Five distinct cluster groups were also identified: A. Unempathic and unaware. B. Empathic but unaccountable. C. Informed empathy and guilt. D. Fearful guilt. E. Insensitive and afraid. Spanierman et al. (2007) regard cluster C at the most desirable in that the participants had the greatest levels of racial awareness (lowest scores on color-blind measures from the CoBRAs), which was interpreted to reflect an understanding of institutionalized racism. Furthermore, these researchers see guilt as "not necessarily undesirable" (p. 439). In fact, accountable guilt coexists with empathy and might predict antiracist activism.

The consequences of racism in people's lives may be invisible, as are skin-color privileges. Two conditions might intensify obliviousness to unearned privilege. The lack of awareness about the circumstances that entitle groups to privileges as well as not grasping how others who do not share group membership also do not share privileges. This *non-seeing* can translate into reduced empathy during the therapeutic encounter. As the quintessential tool in counseling, mental health professionals are severely limited in their effectiveness when they are unable to empathize.

All of us have membership in groups that we have chosen: the gym, university, professional organizations, families, etc. Each of us also has memberships that, although unchosen, are nonetheless desired. A social justice paradigm recognizes that people choose how to respond to earned and unearned privileges by using privilege in their various forms to empower and equalize systems of injustice.

McIntosh (1989) identified several privileges that enabled her to negotiate her daily existence more effectively. She could choose not to teach her children about race or racism if teaching it would cause them some discomfort. The growing numbers of White women who are mothering non-White children are finding that this privilege is not afforded to them (Robinson, 2001). She could move to most any neighborhood, confident that she would be treated well and welcomed (low-wage earning White people do not have this choice). She also knew that her children would be given school curricular materials that testified to the existence of their race.

Despite the benefits of privilege, not having skin-color privilege does not leave a person bereft of invaluable resources. In and of itself, unearned skin-color privilege does not supply moral fiber or self-knowledge. This point is illuminated in the docudrama *Yesterday*. The primary character is a South African woman who was HIV-positive. Her husband had given her the virus. She traveled to Johannesburg to tell him that she was ill and that he must be as well. He beat her in front of his supervisor—and nothing was said. Upon returning to the village with her health failing, she continued to care for her child. Evenutally, her husband returned home, unable to work because his virus was in its advanced stages. She tended to her husband and even built him a final resting place with her bare hands outside of town (the village people knew he was ill and were frightened by his presence). This woman's commitment to live, even in the midst of death, was superior to the death that was quickly coming to her. Her power to love, persevere, and stand in her own convictions were obvious and a reflection of her sense of identity. This act of resistance—of confronting messages that seek to demean and replacing them with knowledge that empowers and informs— enables marginalized groups to thrive in the face of oppression.

PATRIARCHY

Patriarchy comes from a hegemonic or a ruling ideology (Rosenblum & Travis, 2005), wherein men have advantage conferred on them because of their prescribed rank or societal status. During the more than three decades of the women's movement, there have been increases in the college attainment rates of women and dramatic increases among women in the workforce. In fact, women under 25 are on par with men in labor participation. Amid these and other advances, gender inequity continues. In the United States, women earn $0.80 to men's $1.00 after 1 year out of college. Ten years later, it is said to fall to $0.69 (Dey & Hill, 2007). Compared with men, women pay more for dry cleaning and automobiles.

Patriarchy is intertwined with power and privilege. The ascribed status of sex is elevated as a primary status trait over achieved status. This system is inherently unjust because biological sex is not chosen; nonetheless, it is an extremely powerful determinant of how people are treated. Both women and men are necessary to society's maintenance; yet through an elaborate gender socialization process, expectations and behaviors are disseminated and internalized. These socialization practices, both blatant and subtle, maintain a system not only in the United States but also in other countries throughout the world, where women are not as advantaged because of their less prominent status as females. Haider (1995) discussed this phenomenon from both global and historical perspectives:

> In many cultures, the notion of male dominance—of man as woman's "god," protector and provider—and the notion of women as passive, submissive, and chaste have been the predominant images for centuries. In many cases, customary practices have been based on a pecking order that has not always been conducive to the well-being and personal development of those lower down the status line. (p. 53)

One consequence of patriarchy for men is that it contributes to a skewed emotional existence. Difficulty with experiencing and expressing a full range of emotions, such as fear, vulnerability, and uncertainty, is an outcome of patriarchy and a dichotomizing system that is polarizing. Patriarchy is a system of wide-scale inequity to which many people, including women, are oblivious.

Given the potential disadvantages of patriarchy for men, are there possible benefits of patriarchy for women? Patriarchy has its genesis in injustice. If any presumable benefits of patriarchy result for women, they are temporary and elusive, primarily because the benefits would be dictated by women's adherence to the parameters of patriarchy and their compliance with subscribed gender roles. Does equality for women apply primarily to those women who subscribe to at least some but not to too many of the characteristics associated with masculinity (e.g., self-sufficiency, assertiveness, competition)? According to Bem (1993), any such benefits accorded to women are most likely a by-product of androcentrism, or male-centeredness, in which the male standard prevails. For the most part, ours is a society in which men benefit over women. Yet male privileges do not bestow power on all men and ultimately deny all women. In fact, one benefit of the men's movement is that it has called attention to the myth that women's powerlessness translates into men's power. Individual men may feel powerful, but not all men do. Swanson (1993) recognized this as the "new sexism" and noted, "Some men, rather than feeling like patriarchs, often feel like workhorses, harnessed with the burden of being family provider, trying to pull the family wagon up a muddy hill of financial debt" (p. 12). Men are conditioned to be providers, protectors, and ready for combat, yet they experience pressure from women to be nurturing, soft, and intimate (Skovholt, 1993). These messages are conflicting. Part of being a protector is not asking for help or appearing to be vulnerable, which is what intimacy and nurturance entail.

Many White men; men of color; or poor, disabled, old, and/or gay men do not share the same privileges that some economically privileged, able-bodied, and/or heterosexual men do. Thus, all men do not perceive a sense of personal power in that they do not possess crucial markers that society deems normative and valued. The presence of these critical markers, does not ensure that individual men will automatically feel powerful. Because of the underlying assumption that persons who share gender are monolithic, use of the phrase *men in general* is problematic (Carrigan, Connell, & Lee, 1987). Making inappropriate attributions regarding clients' identity constructs is called a *miss*—for example, assuming a person without a visible disability is not disabled or in pain.

SEXISM

The women's movement challenged many traditional stereotypes about women, their work, and their place in society. That women wanted equal pay for equal work, respect in a society that too often reduced them to sexual objects, and denied them choice about their bodies and minds was the message echoed across numerous platforms. Another part of these platforms encouraged women to consider seriously the socialization experiences that contributed to their reliance on others for their emotional and financial well-being. **Sexism**, an institutionalized system of inequity based on biological sex, was brought to the nation's attention.

Bem (1993), author of the Bem Sex Role Inventory, maintained that androcentrism responds to men as human and to women as other. Given this perspective, it is easy to understand that men enjoy certain privileges that women do not. Privilege, despite the assets and benefits associated with it, does not dictate real power.

Another identity construct that can mitigate the privileges that certain groups have is sexuality. Some of the privilege associated with maleness has a qualifier of heterosexuality. Gay men who are "out" experience violence from a homophobic society in the form of ostracism, discrimination, and in some instances physical aggression. Despite these clear disadvantages, being gay does not cancel all privileges associated with being male or being White. Within a society where White skin is associated with unearned privilege, gay White men mediate the effects of homophobia with their White skin. Gay men of color receive male privilege yet contend with both racism and homophobia (Loicano, 1989).

CONSEQUENCES OF SEXISM FOR MEN   Racism contributes to a dehumanizing stance and limits human development for people regardless of their race and ethnicity (Pinderhughes, 1989). Sexism adversely affects all people, men and transgender people included. The male gender role often results in men being restricted in their emotional expressiveness and promotes a limited range of behaviors available to them. "Restrictive emotionality involves the reluctance and/or difficulty men have in expressing their feelings to other people and may be related to their hesitancy to seek help from others" (Good, Dell, & Mintz, 1989, p. 295). Men are gendered beings and are influenced by rigid and sexist discourses whereby they are oriented toward success, competition, and the need to be in control (Robinson, 1999). The danger in the male role is that it has been connected to "Type A" behavior patterns and to depression (Good & Mintz, 1990).

HOMOPHOBIA

Homophobia emanates from the perception of homosexuality as an aberration of the correct social order. Discourses about gay people are that they are promiscuous, can be marked according to mannerisms and dress, are sexually aberrant, and are not to be trusted around young children.

STORYTELLING: Transcending Discourses

I was in New Zealand presenting my research on White Mothers of Non-White Children—half of my sample is located in New Zealand. I reviewed dominant discourses about Black people: great athletes; fine entertainers; wonderful dancers; women as spiritual, men as dangerous; loud; not as intelligent as Whites or Asians. I then asked if any of these discourses referred to Maori. The audience chuckled, and the majority of the Maori in attendance nodded their heads. What are the similar historical events and colonizing realities that result in most of the discourses about one group of color having relevance to another group of color?

CONSEQUENCES OF HOMOPHOBIA FOR HETEROSEXUALS   Men who engage in behaviors deemed "feminine" are suspected of being gay by other men and by women as well. One of the teachings of traditional masculinity is that anything associated with femininity is anathema. Within this restrictive context, heterosexual men may feel real fear in expressing physical affection with another man because of connotations of homosexuality. This concern may explain why American men, often, upon greeting one another, engage in roughhousing, evidenced by vigorous slaps on the back. Such behavior, however, is culturally dictated. In Ghana, West Africa, or in Cairo, Egypt, for example, it is quite natural to see men holding hands while walking together. European men are often more demonstrative in their affectionate behavior. Affection and endearment, and their cultural expressions, support this behavior. In the United States, similar behavior might be interpreted as an indication of homosexuality.

Homophobia also interferes with the formation of cross-sexual orientation friendships out of fear that such interaction and proximity would be misinterpreted by others. In this context, heterosexual counselors can be inhibited in their ability to be allies to gay, lesbian, bisexual, transgender, intersexual, and questioning (GLBTIQ) clients.

ABLE-BODY-ISM

People with disabilities have a long history of being discriminated against. An understanding of this type of discrimination is enhanced by an assessment of the "mastery-over-fate" orientation descriptive of American society. The U.S. culture places inordinate emphasis on youth and fitness and demonstrates a marked preoccupation with the body beautiful. A disability is seen as an imperfection, which is contrary to the culturally sanctioned values of control and domination.

Smart and Smart (2006) argue that the conceptualization of disability as "an attribute located solely within an individual is changing to a paradigm in which disability is thought to be an interaction among the individual, the disability, and the environment (both social and physical)" (p. 29). Despite this observation, a clear bias for the able-bodied exists. Because most buildings have been constructed for able-bodied persons, persons without disabilities are often oblivious to their unearned privileges. How much thought do most able-bodied people give to the accessibility of a house or other building? Having disabled people in our lives or being temporarily disabled (e.g., after foot surgery) increases our awareness. Architectural space and design are outgrowths of cultural attitudes and assumptions that are biased against persons, and in particular, women with disabilities. As Weisman (1992) pointed out:

> Placement in barrier-free housing and rehabilitation services favors men . . .
> Disabled women are not usually thought of as wives and mothers who often
> manage households with children and husbands. The wheelchair-accessible
> two- and three-bedroom unit is a rarity. (p. 118)

The myth that people with disabilities are childlike, dependent, and depressed contributes to ignorance from the larger society and denial about the fact that, at any time, able-bodied people can and most likely will become disabled if they live long enough. Multiculturally competent professionals have the ability to regard clients with disabilities as whole human beings wherein the disability is understood as a component of identity and not the entire focus of the counseling event or an exhaustive account of the client's essence (Fowler, O'Rourke, Wadsworth, & Harper, 1992). Facility at holding the client's multiple spiritual, occupational, sexual, and social identities is commentary about the professional's moral and ego development.

CONSEQUENCES OF ABLE-BODY-ISM AMONG THE ABLE-BODIED   Society was cre-ated for persons who are able-bodied. Our society of concrete sidewalks and curbs is uninviting to persons with temporary and permanent disabilities.

Discourses abound regarding people with disabilities. One of the most perni-cious is that persons with disabilities desire to be able-bodied. This mistaken belief is similar to the belief that people of color desire to be White or that women desire to be men. Equating the experience of having a disability with living a lesser life is problematic for two reasons in counseling and psychology. Such an attitude does not embody the spirit of multicultural competence. Second, this atti-tude is psychologically restrictive for able-bodied persons. Clearly, having a disabil-ity in an able-bodied world can deflate a sense of self and depress self-esteem (Livneh & Sherwood, 1991), yet this is not the experience of all persons with disabilities.

CLASS ELITISM

Much of the formal training counselors receive in traditional counselor educa-tion programs emanates from a middle-class bias. This bias is characterized by emphasis on meritocracy, the Protestant work ethic, Standard English, and adher-ence to 50-minute sessions (Sue & Sue, 1990). The difficulty with this type of partiality is that it can alienate counselors from poor clients. Persons who have lim-ited access to material wealth in a materialistic culture are not perceived as being as viable as those with greater resources. A dangerously close relationship exists between self-worth and income in our capitalistic culture. Thus, the poor, regard-less of their work ethic, tend to be perceived as being lazy and even immoral (Gans, 1992). Conversely, the rich are esteemed and admired, often independent of their moral or immoral conduct.

The relationship between class and power is dubious. Low-income status (despite being hard working) is not valued in a consumeristic society, and having membership in this devalued group can provoke feelings of powerlessness and depression (Pinderhughes, 1989).

CONSEQUENCES OF CLASS ELITISM   Because socioeconomic class converges with gender, race, ability, and personal power, as well as other identity constructs, it is simplistic to conclude that being able-bodied or male or having a high income is automatically associated with feelings of safety and security, a lesser tendency toward depression, and less pain. (See Storytelling: "Health Care Access.") Counselors and psychologists in particular are mistaken in assuming that not having high status is related to feelings of less power, thus ascribing low status to non-White persons, ethnic group members, and persons who have low income (Gibbs, Huang, & Associates, 1989).

AGEISM

Ageism refers to discrimination against people because of their age. This discrimination is often aimed at the middle-aged or the elderly. Ageist terms vary and include primarily negative expressions. Examples are *crotchety, fuddy-duddy, fart, senility, golden-ager, graybeard,* and admittedly dated, *Lawrence Welk generation* (Nuessel, 1982). Atkinson and Hackett (1995) stated that "delineating the elderly as being 65 and over is a purely arbitrary separation" (p. 192). Its genesis is in the decades-old Social Security system, which was instituted when people did not live as long as they now do.

Ageism is compounded with other layers of discrimination. Until very recently, limited attention had been devoted to the study of breast cancer. On the surface, this lack of focus could be attributed to sexism; however, ageism is also at fault. Does the fact that the majority of women survivors of breast cancer are not in their 20s or 30s, but rather in their 40s and 50s, contribute to the limited (but thankfully growing) research on this disease? Is there a different consequence for a middle-aged woman

STORYTELLING: Health Care Access

My husband and I had traveled to Ireland. I had always wanted to go and one of the airlines was offering a great deal. Geoffrey began feeling poorly upon our arrival. We figured it was jet lag but it turned out not to be. He had a sore threat, headache, fatigue, and no appetite. It turned out that Geoffrey was sick. Our destination was Sligo but we stopped in a little town called Westport. On the fourth day of our Ireland holiday, upon awakening Geoffrey said, "I need to see a doctor." We got into our little Toyota and off we drove down the left side of the street. The hotel staff told us where the clinic was. We went in and sat down along with everybody else. After about an hour's wait, the doctor called us in. Her bedside manner was lovely. She listened to Geoffrey's lungs and without missing a beat said, "You have pneumonia." She then prescribed two antibiotics and said he should be feeling better in a few days. On our way out, we met the receptionist to settle our bill. She said, "That will be 50 Euros, if you have it." I was curious so I asked, "So what would you say to us if we didn't have the money?" She said, "I would say, good day to you." Geoffrey and I looked at each other incredulously and said, "We are not at home." We happily paid the money which was a little over 60 American dollars, feeling grateful for having received affordable and quality care. Given that we were not home, we were also relieved to know what the problem was. Can you imagine being sick and not being able to get well? This is the experience of the more than 47 million Americans who do not have health care insurance.

who loses the commodity of beauty and thus sexuality? This is an unsettling question, yet counselors and psychologists need to know how adversely affected they might be by the intersecting layers of discrimination.

Elders ought not be treated as monoliths. Doing so greatly impedes the delivery of effective services. Differences exist between a 65-year-old healthy person and a 90-year-old elder whose health has begun to decline. Atkinson and Hackett (1995) described the "young-old" and the "old-old" (p. 14). The young-old is in fairly good health with stable financial supports. The old-old is experiencing deficits in several psychological, physical, social, and financial resources.

Mental health professionals need to be mindful of the social supports available to the elderly client. Sturdy social supports with both friends and family results in less dependency on formal psychological help (Phillips & Murrell, 1994). Part of a counselor's assessment, then, should be an examination of an elder's level of involvement in meaningful and purposeful social activity. The elder's sense of personal autonomy or control over life is also an important component of overall wellness. Some illnesses, such as Alzheimer's disease, will require working in sync with other caregivers to maximize the quality of living during a stressful, disquieting, and potentially chaotic time. Age biases contribute to some counselors seeing little merit in providing psychotherapy to aging persons. For example, one weakness of psychoanalytic theory is that it is not generally regarded as viable when started with persons age 50 or older or for low-wage-earning people. Identifying a client's strengths, regardless of the presenting problem, is a crucial step in facilitating growth or bolstering coping abilities.

CONSEQUENCES OF AGEISM FOR THE NON-ELDERLY Unlike most traditional cultures in which the elderly tend to be respected and valued, in the U.S. culture, inordinate emphasis is placed on youthfulness. The societal significance attached to doing, productivity, and maintaining mastery over nature may explain this cultural preoccupation with youth and the herculean effort to defy and, in some instances, deny or defeat aging. Aging appears to be viewed as a loss of control and of diminishing power and beauty. Discrimination against a segment of the population that is composing a higher percentage of the total and of which all will be members, if they are fortunate, culminates in fear-based discourses about the experience of being an elder. It is heartening to see how a culture of menopausal women is redefining hot flashes as power surges and recognizing the "change" in life as a time of ascendancy and coming into one's own.

IMPLICATIONS FOR COUNSELORS AND PSYCHOLOGISTS

Not acknowledging the meaning of race can restrict the development of a racial self. This lack of clarity about a core identity construct adversely affects clinician's empathy toward their clients. Counselors must also ascertain whether they are able to work effectively with a variety of clients. (See Case Study: "The Difference Race Makes.") Despite a value of diversity, American society socializes people into attitudes that are not honoring of difference. Professionals need to recognize these and other biases within themselves and not allow shame or guilt to fan denial. The process of unlearning these attitudes is ongoing, but it is possible.

Although professionals have an ethical obligation to refer clients to other professionals when they are unable to provide necessary assistance, the counselor who is highly judgmental of a White woman involved in an interracial relationship needs to be concerned if intolerance in one area of her life extends to persons who, for example, do not practice her same religious affiliation.

CASE STUDY
The Difference Race Makes

Jade is a 25 year-old White American female. She is at the end of her second year in a sociology PhD program at a large Denver university. Her mother is a voice teacher and her father an electrician. Jade grew up and went to school in a predominantly White neighborhood in Indianapolis. She and her parents went to church regularly, and they taught her that people are people and to be nice to everyone. For 6 months, Jade has been dating Matt, a Black American student from Chicago. When she told her mother over the phone she wanted to bring Matt home for Thanksgiving, her mother said this was fine. Jade told Matt her parents were looking forward to meeting him. When he asked if she told them he was Black, she said that she had not and questioned why he was so focused on race. Matt asked why after 6 months of dating he hadn't met her parents, although they had been to campus twice to visit. Matt told Jade that he wanted to spend the holidays with her but requested Jade's family know his race. Jade told Matt her parents were Christians and didn't care about his race but his character. Jade promised Matt she would tell her parents his race but had not done so after a month. Matt ended the relationship because he felt Jade was afraid to talk about race and was not as far along as he thought. Jade was distressed over the breakup and the stress of preparing for comps. What follows is a conversation between Jade and Rita, a Black female Counselor Educator.

JADE: My ex-boyfriend recently broke up with me—he thinks I am afraid to tell my parents he is Black, but I'm not.

RITA: Why haven't you told your parents he is Black?

JADE: Matt is smart; he's kind, and he really cares about me. His parents were at first a little stand-offish with me, but Matt said he wouldn't have brought me home without first, you know, telling his parents that I am White. What is the big deal?

RITA: Why haven't you told your parents that Matt is Black?

JADE: I just think, I just don't think it's all that important. I think Matt places too much importance on people's race.

RITA: Would Matt's race matter to your parents?

JADE: I once heard my father say when watching a news story about an interracial couple that it was really important that his grandkids look like him.

RITA: What did your father's words mean to you?

JADE: I'm not really sure. I never asked him.

RITA: Do you think your father would like Matt?

JADE: I know he would—they both like to golf and tinker with engines.

RITA: Do you think your father would care that Matt is Black?

JADE: Why should he? He's much nicer to me than my last boyfriend.

RITA: It is hard for you to talk about these issues concerning race, isn't it?

JADE: Pause and sigh . . . It *is* hard. I don't care that Matt is Black.

RITA: Then why haven't you told your parents he is Black?

JADE: Why should I have to tell my parents that Matt is Black?

RITA: How would Matt answer your question?

JADE: He would say that in America a person's skin color takes on greater importance than it should.

RITA: Do you agree with Matt?

JADE: I get really confused about all of this race stuff. My parents taught me to treat everybody the same. I know my parents would think Matt is a nice person and would be very kind to him.

RITA: Would they care that Matt is not White?

JADE: My parents would not want me dating Matt because he is Black. I hate saying that, but it's true. But that does not make them bad people. I love my parents; I don't want to disrespect them, but I feel badly because Matt is good to me. He loves me and I love him.

RITA: It is hard to say what you have said. Ambivalence is hard, but becoming aware of the source of your conflict will help you behave differently.

JADE: Thank you. I feel relieved looking at what I've said, although it was the hardest thing.

RITA: I've struggled a lot in my life—I grew up very poor and without a dad. It is not easy to look at the probability that I struggled more as a person of color.

QUESTIONS

1. What do Rita's questions and responses to Jade say about Rita's racial identity development?
2. How might the counseling situation been affected if Rita were at a similar place in her racial identity development as Jade, her client?
3. Was Rita effective at attending to the slow process of Jade's growing insight while mining any feelings of fatigue and/or frustration?

DISCUSSION AND INTEGRATION
The Counselor, Rita

Rita demonstrates wonderful counseling skills. She listens, confronts, is genuine, and shares appropriate personal information about herself as a means of helping her client develop insight. It is also important to note that Rita's level of racial identity development is very developed. She is aware of the construct of race and its personal relevance in her own life—because of this, she is able to recognize the conflict and dissonance that is descriptive of her client, Jade. On one hand, Jade wants to do the right thing, which is to accept Matt for the kind and decent man he is. On the other hand, Jade realizes that her parents would not want Matt as their daughter's boyfriend because of his race. This is an indication of the weight or status that race has, and it is quite a dilemma for Jade.

One of the skills that Rita possesses is her ability to assist Jade in thinking about things differently and doing them differently—but before this happens she has to increase her awareness. Murphy and Dillon (2008) said, "As behaviors change, so do relationships. Doing things differently affects not only one's own behavior, but also the behaviors of others with whom the client relates" (p. 261). A technique that might be helpful for Jade is for her to think about what she wants. Therapy could be a way for her to explore how to narrow the gap between where she is and where she wants to be.

It is important that Rita unravel any feelings of discomfort that she may have in working with a client who is as naïve as Jade is about race. Fortunately, Rita looks at Jade's situation from a perspective of change and power. Rita understands that personal power does not come from denying injustice or oppression, but rather from recognizing these forces while appreciating your own vulnerabilities (Pinderhughes, 1989). Rita sees that Jade is in a state of crisis and is experiencing confusion, fear, and shame.

Rita also has to deal with her reaction to Jade's feelings. Rita feels proud of Jade for her willingness to stay with her skillful questioning. At the same time, Rita is tired after her session and asks herself why. She realizes the impact of Jade's story on her own life as a single woman. Although she genuinely cares for her client, she sees Jade "as a privileged White woman dating a well-educated Black man in limited supply." *Congruence* refers to the clinician's ability to express persistent feelings that exist in the therapeutic relationship and committing not to hide behind a professional mask (Murphy & Dillon, 2008), and yet it might be damaging to the session to reveal this, particularly given where Jade is in her emotional and racial identity development. Providing empathy and support is important work but takes energy. Murphy and Dillon caution clinicians against exploring too quickly and too much. It is also important to acknowledge clients' small growths as they identify and express feelings. If these issues continue for Rita, she may need to seek supervision or her own personal therapy.

The Client, Jade

In many ways, Jade is typical of many White people. She was raised with the values of democracy and meritocracy, of treating everyone the same. She did not develop a consciousness of the numerous inequities on the basis of money, skin color, gender, body size, age, and more. Part of privilege is to keep people oblivious to the ways in which immutable characteristics are rewarded. Zetzer (2005) would refer to Jade as a well-meaning White person (WMWP). She means well but is clueless regarding herself as a racial being. Jade is also unable to live authentically in the world with racially diverse people because her understanding of race as a core component of identity, for herself and others, is unexplored. Matt appears to be at a more advanced place in his own consciousness about race as a status variable and a personal identity construct. Given the difference in where each of them is developmentally, the conflict was hard to manage and led to the dissolution of their relationship.

Jade begins to realize that staying guilty or confused will not advance her position. She feels encouraged to go on as a function of Rita's probing. She is not even conscious enough of race to wonder how her Black therapist might perceive her story! Although it is not Jade's job to protect Rita, clients will sometimes restrict information if they are concerned how it might affect the therapist.

Jade perceives Rita to be available to her. She trusts her and does not experience Rita to be judgmental or critical. Being challenged by a therapist has been identified in research as helpful to clients in therapy. "Confrontation was thought to disrupt trust and compromise the therapy in most cases, with the exception of when the client was being manipulative or avoidant of difficult material, and then it was desirable" (Levitt, Butler, & Travis, 2006, p. 320).

In time, Rita acknowledges the elephant in the room and asks Jade her feelings about working with her (Rita) as a Black therapist given the nature of Jade's issues.

SUMMARY

In this chapter, the presentation of human differences as status variables was explored through an examination of the Contextual and Social Construction of Differences Model. Hughes's (1945) work on the dilemmas and contradictions of status was also useful. The consequences of hierarchical socialization were presented, and the advantages of a model based on cultural pluralism were envisioned. The importance of counselors recognizing systems of inequity was articulated, and a case study allowed readers to synthesize the ideas presented.

Part Two
Valued Cultures

Chapter 4

Native Americans and Alaskan Natives

HISTORY

DEMOGRAPHY

SOCIAL, PSYCHOLOGICAL, AND PHYSICAL HEALTH ISSUES

CULTURAL PHILOSOPHIES AND VALUES

ACCULTURATION

CASE STUDY

IMPLICATIONS FOR COUNSELORS AND PSYCHOLOGISTS

SUMMARY

The Circle of Life is believed to consist of spirit, nature, body, and mind, referred to as the Four Winds of Life or the Four Directions . . . When we honor the Circle, we honor all that is, all that has ever been, and all that ever will be. When we remember those who have walked before us, we honor the Circle.

Michael Tlanusta Garrett, *Walking on the Wind: Cherokee Teachings for Harmony and Balance*

American Indian and *Alaskan Native* refer to people having origins in any of the original peoples of North and South America (including Central America) and who maintain tribal affiliation or community attachment (U.S. Census Bureau, 2000). The origins of Native American/Alaskan Native people have been greatly debated. One of the most insightful theories regarding the people who occupied the New World was proposed by José de Acosta, a Jesuit missionary. He theorized that North America, which was a continent clearly separate from Asia, had been settled before the birth of Christ by a group of hunters and their families who, in following animal herds, passed overland from Asia to the Americas (cited in Hoxie, 1996). Many anthropologists agree with de Acosta's theory. The debate rages over timing issues, whether the first people arrived in America more than or less than 15,000 years ago. DNA studies comparing Native Americans with other population groups found three distinct genetic mutations in Mongolia and Siberia, which suggests a separation as early as 30,000 years ago. It is widely accepted that the first Americans arrived in North America by way of the Bering Strait Land Bridge, or Beringia. Temporary ice melts for several thousand years most likely created natural passageways for large game and their human, spear-wielding, predator (Waldman, 2000).

Native American Creation stories tell of being brought into existence by the Great Spirit or having come from the womb of Mother Earth. In writing of these origins, Gunn Allen (1994) honored Woman:

> There is a spirit that pervades everything, that is capable of powerful song
> and radiant movement, and that moves in and out of the mind. The colors
> of this spirit are multitudinous, a glowing, pulsing rainbow. Old Spider
> Woman is one name for this quintessential spirit, and Earth Woman is
> another, and what they together have made is called Creation, Earth,
> creatures, plants, and light. (p. 13)

HISTORY

It is estimated that in 1492 when Christopher Columbus arrived in the New World, there were approximately 1 million inhabitants within the continental United States (Russell, 1994). Because Columbus mistakenly thought he had landed in India, he referred to the Native people as Indios. The different European dialects represented pronounced the word as Indien or Indianer (Brown, 1981).

The treatment of Native Americans and Alaskan Natives in the United States has been disgraceful. Within 400 years after the Europeans' arrival, the Native population had been decimated by wars, starvation, slavery, genocide, and disease, with typhus, small-pox, and measles being the greatest killers (Vernon, 2002). In 1790, the enactment of federal policies began with the goal of displacing Indian people. The Bureau of Indian Affairs (BIA), which today is responsible for the United States's relationship with the 562 federally recognized tribes and Alaskan communities, was created in 1824. The job of

Thomas McKenney, the first director of the BIA, was to manage Indian schools, administer Indian trade, and handle the various negotiations associated with Indian trade. For many tribes, the BIA represented betrayal and broken promises. One Native person remarked, "They made us many promises, more than I can remember, but they never kept but one; they promised to take our land, and they took it" (Brown, 1981).

The Indian Removal Act of 1830, under the leadership of President Andrew Jackson, who was known as "Sharp Knife" among some of the Native people, was intended to relocate Indians to Indian country west of the Mississippi, not to include Missouri, Louisiana, or the territory of Arkansas (Hoxie, 1996; Russell, 1994). America's defeat of the British during the War of 1812 prompted little concern for European alliances. The annexation of Spanish Florida contributed to America's perception of Indians as hindrances to the interests of expansionism from the millions of White Europeans who were coming to America. The cultural and psychological violence is evident in Jackson's Second Annual Message to Congress, given shortly after he became the president of the United States (1908):

> It gives me pleasure to announce to Congress that the benevolent policy of
> the government, steadily pursued for nearly thirty years, in relation to the
> removal of the Indians beyond the white settlements is approaching to a
> happy consummation . . . It will relieve the whole state of Mississippi and
> the western part of Alabama of Indian occupancy, and enable those states
> to advance rapidly in population, wealth, and power. It will separate the
> Indians from the power of the States; enable them to pursue happiness in
> their own way and under their own rude institutions; will retard the progress
> of decay, which is lessening their numbers, and perhaps cause them grad-
> ually under the protection of the Government and through the influence of
> good counsels, to cast off their savage habits and become an interesting,
> civilized, and Christian community.

Jackson considered this act of removal to be benevolent because the government was funding the relocation. To the Native people, it was their "trail of tears" or the westward herding of the "Five Civilized Tribes" (Cherokees, Chickasaws, Choctaws, Creeks, and Seminoles) to Oklahoma. During the cold and brutal winter, people traveled by foot, horseback, wagon, and steamboat. They were hungry, cold, and sick, and hundreds died from starvation, exhaustion, disease, exposure, and accidents (Brown, 1981; Hoxie, 1996). Native resistance to removal was fierce, but their oppressors were opportunistic and destructive. For example, the Georgia militia in Echota destroyed the printing press of the *Cherokee Phoenix*, a newspaper written in Cherokee syllabary created by Sequoyah (Waldman, 2000).

In 1934, the Indian Reorganization Act was passed, with a goal of ending restrictions against Native religions. Albeit shortlived, during this time there was greater understanding and acceptance of Indian culture. World War II ushered in a period of greater restriction and attempts by the government to integrate Native people into American society. But as was characteristic of the past, more sacred lands were lost during this time and cultures were destroyed. During the 1970s, many traditional Indians found themselves arrested for possessing sacred objects such as eagle feathers or for the use of peyote. Protests against this interference contributed to the 1978 passage of the American Indian Religious Freedom Act. Congress concluded that Native ways of worship were an essential part of Native life, and this law sought to protect and preserve such religious liberties (Hoxie, 1996).

Today, Native American and Alaskan Natives are a heterogeneous group, with 252 tribal languages and 562 federally recognized Indian tribes in the United States and in Alaska (U.S. Department of the Interior, 2002). There are nearly 90,000 Alaskan Native tribes, which include Alaska Athabascan, Aleut, Eskimo, Tlingit-Haida, and other Alaskan Native tribes (U.S. Census Bureau, 2007).

Among the tribes is tremendous diversity across custom, language, and family structure (Hoxie, 1996). Apache, Arapahoe, Arikara, Blackfoot, Catawba, Cherokee, Cheyenne, Chickasaw, Chippewa, Choctaw, Comanche, Coushatta, Cree, Creek, Crow, Erie, Eskimo, Haida, Hopi, Hupa, Iroquois, Lumbee, Osage, Mi'kmaq, Mohave, Narragansett, Navajo, Ottawa, Paiute, Pima, Potawatomi, Seminole, Seneca, Shawnee, Shoshone, Sioux, Tlingit, Tununak, Ute, Winnebago, Yaqui, and the Zuni represent only a fraction of Native American and Alaska Native tribal groups. The 10 largest Native American tribes in the United States are Cherokee, Navajo, Chippewa, Apache, Lumbee, Choctaw, Iroquois, Pima, Pueblo, and Blackfoot.

DEMOGRAPHY

The increase in numbers among Native people is a reflection of better census methods and people's acknowledgement of mixed ancestry. According to the 2004 American Community Survey, American Indian and Alaskan Natives who reported this as their only race was estimated to be about 2.2 million, or 0.8% of the population. Another 1.9 million reported their race as American Indian and Alaskan Native and one or more other race. Of these, 1.4 million reported being American Indian and White. More than 550,000 Latinos are included in the number for American Indian and Alaskan Native alone or in combination. During the 2000 census, nearly 183,000 people indicated that they were both Native and Black or African American (U.S. Census Bureau, 2000). Clearly, the majority of American Indian and Alaskan Natives have mixed backgrounds as biracial and multiracial people. Consequently, a variety of phenotypic characteristics are found among Native American Indians.

One third of Native Americans and Alaskan Natives live in one of three states: Arizona, representing about 13% (12.6) of the population; Oklahoma, 12.4%; and California, 12.2%. New Mexico, Texas, North Carolina, Alaska, Washington, New York, and Montana are other states with high numbers of Native Americans and Alaskan Natives (U.S. Census Bureau, 2007). Alaska alone had the largest proportion of single-race American Indians and Alaskan Natives in its population: 13%. Wyoming and South Dakota had 3.4% and 3.2%, respectively, of Native Americans and Alaskan Natives in their populations. All other states combined represented 34% of the Native American and Alaskan Native population.

In 2004, 42.3% of the Native American/Alaskan Native population over the age of 15 had married, compared with 57.3% among Whites. Rates of separation are slightly higher than the general population, 3.0% compared to 2.1% for the total (U.S. Census Bureau, 2007). Overall, about 68% of Native Americans and Alaskan Natives live in family households. Twenty percent of these families are maintained by a woman only with no husband present; 7% of family households were male only with no wife present. Nonfamily households comprised 31.8%. A *nonfamily household* is defined as people who live alone or people living with unrelated individuals.

In 2004, Native American/Alaskan Native women had higher rates of fertility than non-Hispanic White women. Forty-six percent of women in this group who gave birth in 2004 were unmarried, compared with 20.5% of White women. The greatest percentage of Native American/Alaskan Native adults were married, at 40.1%. Similar to Blacks, Native American/Alaskan Natives are also more likely than non-Hispanic Whites to live with and care for grandchildren. About 7% of Native American/Alaskan Natives aged 30 and older were grandparents living in the same household with their co-resident grandchildren under the age of 18. More than half of grandparents (58%) were also responsible for the care of their grandchildren.

About 75% of Native Americans/Alaskan Natives aged 5 and older spoke only English at home compared with 94% among non-Hispanic Whites. Roughly 18% of Native Americans/Alaskan Natives spoke a language other than English at home and spoke English very well. Approximately 280,000 Native American and Alaskan Natives speak a language other than English at home, and more than half of Alaskan Natives who are Eskimos speak either Inuit or Yup'ik (U.S. Department of Health and Human Services [DHHS], 2001).

About one quarter of Native American and Alaskan Native elderly live on Native American Indian reservations or in Alaskan Native villages. In addition to earlier federal laws that played a role in the populating of urban areas with Native people, high unemployment on the reservations has contributed to the move of Native people to urban areas. Horse (2001) maintains that Native people are geographically dislocated from their homeland within a culture bombarded by the Internet, the U.S. school system, peer pressure, and the mass media. Despite the reality of cultural discontinuity for some Native people, which refers to the gulf between mainstream expectations and Native people's cultural values, many Native people have learned to survive by becoming bicultural (Garrett & Pichette, 2000).

SOCIAL, PSYCHOLOGICAL, AND PHYSICAL HEALTH ISSUES

Compared with the non-Hispanic White population, Native Americans and Alaskan Natives had a larger proportion of younger people and a smaller proportion of older people in 2004. Nearly 30% of this group is younger than age 18, whereas only 6.5%

are 65 years or older. The median age is 31.9 years, which is more than 8 years younger than the median age for the non-Hispanic White population.

In 2004, the poverty rate for American Indians and Alaskan Natives was 24.6%. This rate was higher than the poverty rates for non-Hispanic Whites, Asians, Pacific Islanders, and equal to that of Blacks (U.S. Census Bureau, 2000). Among children under the age of 18, the poverty rate is 30.7%; that is, nearly one in three Native American children lives in poverty (U.S. Census Bureau, 2007).

In 2004, the median household income for Native American and Alaskan Natives was $31,605, or nearly $14,000 less than the median income for the general population. Income is related to status of housing. Although the majority of Native Americans and Alaskan Natives lived in owner-occupied homes, the percentage of renters is more than 11% higher than the general population, or 44.5% compared with 32.9%. Overall, Native Americans and Alaska Natives tend to have lower rates of home ownership at 55.5% compared with 67% and 74% for the total nation and among non-Hispanic Whites, respectively (U.S. Census Bureau, 2007). Among Native Americans and Alaska Natives who own their homes, the median value is $95,000, which is $60,000 less than the median value of $154,000 for White owner-occupied homes.

Nationally, one third (32.8%) of American Indians and Alaskan Natives do not have a usual or normal source of health care where they are regularly seen by a doctor or a clinic that can provide preventive care (U.S. DHHS, 2001; Institute of Medicine, 2003). The lack of health insurance among the general population is 17.5%. As a result of treaty obligations, Native Americans receive their health services largely through the federal government and the Indian Health Service. Since 1955, a part of the U.S. Public Health Service was to provide health care to all Native Americans/Alaskan Natives who belonged to federally recognized tribes and lived on or near the reservations throughout 12 service areas (Byrd & Clayton, 2003).

More than half of the total Native American Indian population resides in urban areas. Only 38% of Native Americans reside on federal trust lands, and although the federal government has played a key role in health care delivery for Natives, unlike other groups of color, the quality of and access to such care has been adversely affected by the way in which Native people are scattered throughout the country (Joe, 2003). In light of these and other data that reveal the poor quality of life for unacceptably high numbers of American Indian and Alaskan Native people, many American Indians and Alaskan Natives feel a distrust for the dominant culture (Heinrich, Corbine, & Thomas, 1990).

Partly as a result of this legacy and continuing cultural conflict, alcoholism presents social problems for many Native Americans, affecting their family life, the health of newborns, and the sustainability of employment. Co-morbidity is evident given the relationship between substance addictions and mental health problems. Alcohol abuse is a substantial problem, with an estimated rate of alcohol-related deaths for Indian men of 27% and 13% for Indian women (U.S. DHHS, 2001). The research is inconclusive regarding cultural identity and substance problems. Venner, Wall, Lau, and Ehlers (2006) report conflicting findings about the protections against substance abuse that a bicultural identity offers. In addition to the adverse health effects of alcohol abuse on the body, alcoholism is linked to high-risk behaviors such as unprotected sex because it decreases inhibition. The introduction of black tar heroin on many reservations has contributed to an increase in substance dependency.

The number of reported Native American AIDS cases as of December 1999 was 2,132. Although this number seems low, AIDS is the eighth leading cause of mortality among Native Americans between ages 15 and 34 living on or near reservations (Vernon, 2002). Related to poor diet, diabetes ranges from 5% to 50% among tribes and Native communities, and colon and rectal cancer rates are the highest among any racial or ethnic group in the country (Institute of Medicine, 2003). As major causes of morbidity and premature death, these and other poor health outcomes contribute to nearly one in three Native people's death before the age of 45 (Vernon, 2002).

Many alcoholism treatment programs exist that have special programs for Native Americans, however, there are no empirical, research-based findings on the efficacy of various treatments for alcohol problems in Native Americans (Thomason, 2000). The term *nativized treatments* refers to standard treatments that have been adapted to be more culturally appropriate for Native populations. These nativized treatments would include, for example, Native American cultural values and traditional healing techniques and ceremonies. A comprehensive program may be the best approach to treating Native clients with alcohol abuse issues. Such a program is descriptive, includes medical care, self-help groups, and purification ceremonies (Thomason, 2000).

Educationally, there have been increases in the high school graduation level, now at 76.6% among Native American/Alaskan Natives 25 years of age and older. This compares with 83.9% for the general population (U.S. Census Bureau, 2007). Just over 14% had completed a bachelor's degree compared with 27% of the general population (U.S. Census Bureau, 2007). Nearly 31 different tribal groups have established their own tribal colleges (Horse, 2001). Among Native American people who are more traditional and are not interested in leaving their reservations, lack of educational attainment may be a conscious decision, particularly in light of limited access and economic challenges (Rayle, Chee, & Sand, 2006).

About one quarter of Native American/Alaskan Native workers are employed in management or professional occupations compared with 38% among non-Hispanic Whites. Nearly 23% of Native Americans work in sales and office occupations which is similar to non-Hispanic Whites (27%). Higher percentages of Native Americans and Alaskan Natives work in service occupations at 21.5% and in construction at 15%. Among non-Hispanic Whites, 14% are in service and 10% work in construction jobs.

Despite chronic and contemporary challenges, commitment to peoplehood, a spirit of resilience, and a strong sense of identity are evident. American Indian people have been overlooked for their inestimable contributions to the Western world:

> In various parts of the Americas, Indians invented items as varied as the ham-
> mock, snowshoes, the bulb syringe, kayaks, and the process of using acid to

etch designs onto shell. Indians invented the blowgun, developed animal and bird decoys for use in hunting, wove cloth from feathers, made rubber boots, and invented various musical instruments. (Hoxie, 1996, p. 270)

Gunn Allen (1994) reminds us of the irrefutable influence of American Indian and Alaskan Native people. Elaborate systems of thought and governments based on egalitarianism, service, pacifism, and freedom characterized many tribal societies prior to the presence of patriarchy. Portman and Herring (2001) stated:

> Native American Indian women were integral to the economic and social survival of their nations and tribes. They also held positions of political importance. Native American Indians provided guidance and influenced governance decisions and served as leaders and advisers in many Native American Indian tribes and nations. (p. 187)

Among Native American Indians, a leader's influence was based on personal qualities. Authority within a group was derived from the ability to make useful suggestions and a knowledge of traditional ways and tribal love (Waldman, 2000).

CULTURAL PHILOSOPHIES AND VALUES

Tribe is a source of belonging and security for Native American and Alaskan Native people. Personal accomplishments are honored and supported if they serve to benefit the entire tribe or collective. Competition, the hallmark of the educational school system and a dominant cultural value rooted in individualism, is at odds with collectivism, a spirit of cooperation, and sharing of resources that belong to everyone.

Although values vary from tribe to tribe, American Indian and Alaskan Native people believe in a Supreme Creator that is considered both male and female and is in command of all the elements of existence. Gunn Allen (1994) said, "There are many female gods recognized and honored by the Nations. Females were highly valued, both respected and feared and all social institutions reflected this attitude" (p. 193). Indians/Alaskans also believe that all things in the universe are connected, have purpose, and exemplify personhood (Garrett & Garrett, 1994, 1996), "including plants (e.g., 'tree people'), animals ('our four-legged brothers and sisters'), rocks and minerals ('rock people'), the land ('Mother Earth'), the winds ('the Four Powers'), 'Father Sky,' 'Grandfather Sun,' 'Grandmother Moon,' 'The Red Thunder Boys'" (p. 138).

Honoring the Creator is sacred to Native American and Alaskan Native people and is central to Indians'/Alaskans' harmonious relationships with nature and all things. Garrett (1998) said that "the wellness of the mind, body, spirit, and

STORYTELLING: Wrong Note

Several years ago I went to the concert of a very famous Native American flutist. I was really excited as I so enjoyed his music. The audience was full of people, and we were eagerly waiting for the concert to begin. The flutist came out and greeted his audience warmly. He then said, and I paraphrase, that "anybody whose people were born in this country within the last two generations is a Native American." The audience erupted with applause and felt embraced by this Native American's recognition of a sense of universal brother/sisterhood. I did not resonate with this sentiment and left shortly after a few selections. While I am native to the United States, I am not one of the Native daughters and to suggest that I am is to blur and even minimize Native people's experiences and suffering with the rest of us who came later, voluntarily or involuntarily. I questioned this artist's motives. I wondered if he surveyed the audience and upon seeing 99% of the audience who looked White, irrespective of whether they identified as such, felt this sentiment was appropriate. Would he have shared this belief at an Indian Pow-Wow?

natural environment is an extension of the proper balance in the relationship of all things" (p. 78). In these cultures, sharing is valued over materialism because all things belong to Earth.

Elders are valued among Native American and Alaskan Natives "because of the lifetime's worth of wisdom they have acquired" (Garrett & Garrett, 1994, p. 137). Elders are accorded respect, and as they age, there is an increase in sacred responsibility for the tribe and family. They understand that their purpose is to care for and guide young people, yet a spirit of curiosity and openness to life's lessons prevails (Garrett & Herring, 2001).

Native American cultural values emanate from a spiritual center that emphasizes coexisting in harmony with nature. (See Table 4.1.) This entails a respect for Earth as natural medicine (Peregoy, 1993). Native people have always depended on the land, because it was life and medicine. The Paiute boiled sagebrush to relieve headaches and rheumatism. Even dandruff was cured by rubbing boiled willow leaves into the hair and scalp (Ballentine & Ballentine, 1993). "This harmony entails a holistic sensing of the state of continuous fusion among the elements of self with all life, including the creator" (Dana, 1992, p. 84).

Implicit in this value system is reverence for and acceptance of the gifts from the earth. In their reverence for the earth, a variety of plants, wild and cultivated, were used for both religious and practical purposes as well as for pleasure. Clearly some Indian people, particularly where agriculture was highly developed, used alcohol prior to contact with Europeans, but for the most part, drinking alcohol was a post-contact reality (Waldman, 2000). Native American people believe that to be human is a part of the Sacred, thus there is an acknowledgment that human beings make mistakes (Trujillo, 2000). Nature, in its natural, undisturbed state, is respected, and coexisting (not interfering) with nature is paramount because all things have spiritual energy. The universe, or Mother Earth, belongs to all people. For the Indian, the concept of land ownership was foreign and made

TABLE 4.1   Common Cultural Values among Native Americans and Alaskan Native People

Spirituality (Great Spirit)

Nature (Mother Earth)

The Sacred

Ritual

Tradition

Balance

Harmony

Explanation of natural phenomena according to the spiritual realm

Noninterference

Cooperation

Sharing

Extended and present time orientation

Hozhq (An expression of happiness, harmonious relationships, the beauty of the land)

Tiospaye (Shared responsibility, extended family, reciprocity)

Oral traditions

The extended family (The Tribe)

Selflessness

Deference to and respect for elders

Storytelling

Speak softly at a slower rate

Not holding direct eye contact to show respect

Time is always with us

as much sense as did carving up the sky (which is what currently exists with defined air-space boundaries).

Honoring traditional ways suggests a respect for the past and the contributions of the ancestral spirits. According to Peregoy (1993), "The traditional Indian/Native's system of life is intertwined with the tribe and extends further into a metaphysical belief system" (p. 172).

Native American and Alaskan Natives see the extended family and the tribe as taking precedence over the self (Garrett & Garrett, 1994; Gunn Allen, 1994; Peregoy, 1993). Among many Native American and Alaskan Native people, the concept of self tends to be fluid and includes the individual as well as the tribe, the extended family, and even plants and animal spirits (Dana, 2000). A belief or knowledge in unseen powers and reference to deities and mystery is core to many tribal values, as is the importance of balance (Trujillo, 2000).

Respect for and coexistence with helpful animal spirits are enduring values found in nearly all Native American and Alaskan Eskimo societies. It was believed that the animals made themselves available to humans only for as long as there was respect from the hunters for the animal spirits. This involved ritual treatment of the animals so that the animals would, upon their death, return to the spirit world with a good report, which would ensure the success of future hunters. If a hunter was unsuccessful, it could be stated that the animal spirits had not been treated properly; therefore, proper rituals were needed to restore harmony and to correct the imbalance (Hoxie, 1996).

According to Garrett and Pichette (2000), there are verbal and nonverbal communication style differences between contemporary mainstream American cultural values and those of traditional Native people. More specifically, immediate responses, frequent interruption, and emphasis placed on verbal skills are characteristic of dominant U.S. cultural styles. Delayed responses, less frequent interjection, and emphasis placed on nonverbal skills characterize Native cultural traditions.

ACCULTURATION

Most Native adults whose ancestry is both Native and non-Native retain their traditional values but also seek to live in the dominant culture (Garrett & Herring, 2001). According to Herring (1992), Indian/Alaskan people are "more unalterably resistant to assimilation and integration into mainstream society than are other minority groups" (p. 135); some, however, are acculturated.

Acculturation and *assimilation* influence value structures and are important to an understanding of cultural adaptation. (See Storytelling: "Wrong Note" on page 67.) Garrett and Pichette (2000) identify five levels of acculturation among Native people:

1. Traditional.
2. Marginal.
3. Bicultural.
4. Assimilated.
5. Pantraditional.

These levels exists on a continuum and are a function of a person's life experiences. The Traditional Native person may or may not speak English and will hold traditionally Native values, including tribal customs. The Marginal person identifies with neither mainstream values nor traditional values. Bicultural describes the person who knows and practices both mainstream and traditional values. Assimilated persons hold the mainstream American values in high esteem to the exclusion of those Native. Finally, Pantraditional describes the assimilated person who consciously seeks to return to the "old ways." These people seek to embrace lost traditional values and beliefs and are often bilingual.

Garrett and Pichette (2000) offered a clear definition of acculturation in their discussion of Native American acculturation. It was stated that acculturation is "the cultural change that occurs when two or more cultures are in persistent contact . . . A particular kind of acculturation is assimilation, in which one culture changes significantly more than the other culture and as a result comes to resemble it. This process is often established deliberately through force to maintain control over conquered people, but it can occur voluntarily as well" (p. 6).

Acculturation may take place at the expense of one's original cultural values as one internalizes values and traditions. This process is not always conscious (Sue, 1989), and there is the likelihood of cultural alienation from one's traditional culture because the dominant culture is esteemed over one's own.

One dimension of acculturation is assimilation. Assimilation is different in that it describes those persons who consciously do not desire to maintain their cultural identities and thus seek sustained interaction with other cultures outside their own. The original cultures have been lost or relinquished, and persons have given up most cultural traits of their cultures of origin and assumed the traits, behaviors, and attitude of the dominant culture (Berry & Kim, 1988).

Christianization was one way assimilation was accomplished among many Native Americans. Some Native Americans do not regard the two to be incompatible. In the Native American Church (NAC), Christian and Native beliefs coexist (U.S. DHHS, 2001). In addition to Spanish and French, European colonizers brought English to America. Language is a medium of culture, and English functioned as a way to deny the existence and relevance of Native languages. Such a policy existed in the U.S. government-sponsored Indian boarding schools designed to mainstream American Indian youth. The first school was established in 1879 in Carlisle, Pennsylvania, under the influence of General Henry Pratt. His motto was "kill the Indian and save the man" (Hoxie, 1996; Lesiak & Jones, 1991). In these colonizing contexts, children's hair was cut, traditional clothing was taken away, American Christian names replaced Native names, and only English was allowed. The virtues of White American Christian traditions were espoused and the Native ways were regarded as uncivilized (Cameron & Turtle-song, 2003).

Native Americans and Alaskan Natives who possess a strong sense of heritage and honor tradition may be more likely to feel at peace on the reservation where cooperation with others and respect for tribal values based on ritual are commonplace (Gunn Allen, 1994).

CASE STUDY
A Wounded Mind

Alana is a 46-year-old single woman who cares for her 71-year-old mother who has advanced Alzheimer's. The doctors have explained to Alana that her mother's condition is progressing and eventually she will need to enter into a care facility for people with Alzheimer's. Alana has vowed never to put her mother into such a facility, which she says is typical of White people who throw the old away after they have been used up and are of no use to anybody. During therapy with Connie, a

27-year-old Lumbee Indian counselor, Connie confronts Alana and discloses, "I'm like you, Lumbee, and my grandfather is in a professionally run nursing facility. He has Alzheimer's." Alana asks Connie how she could do such a thing, to which Connie replied, "I needed to put my grandfather's needs above my own and his needs were greater than my ability to adequately care for them." Connie then told Alana that it is clear she is exhausted. Alana begins to cry and says she has not been sleeping well since her mother has started to either leave the house at night or roam about making noise and turning on the oven with empty pots on the stove. Alana locks the doors; however, her mother has been undoing the locks and leaving. The doctors have told Alana that her mother will get to the point where she does not remember how to return home. Alana is also fearful her mother may start a fire. Alana told Connie that her mother forgets that she has eaten and does not remember how to eat—Alana has observed her mom shuffling the food around her plate without actually eating it. Alana also said that her mother hates having to bathe and is often unwilling to allow Alana to bathe her, despite having become incontinent. Alana admits to her fear that the people at the facility will mistreat and abuse her mother, that they will promise to do one thing but will not honor that promise. Alana asks, "How can I say that I love my mother and put her away?"

Connie asks Alana if it is possible to show love for our loved ones by putting them in the hands of people who will make sure she eats, keep her from leaving the house in the middle of the day and night, and attend to her personal hygiene needs.

QUESTIONS

1. What are Alana's value orientations?
2. What are Connie's value orientations?
3. How do counselors and psychologists know when it is appropriate to confront clients and/or disclose personal information?

DISCUSSION AND INTEGRATION
The Client, Alana

Alana's relationship to her situation has to be considered. Collectivistic cultures tend to have a very different way of seeing themselves in relationship to self and others. The person from a collectivistic culture is likely to define "himself or herself in an interdependent fashion . . . Rather than emphasizing personal distinctivenss, this person is likely to stress his or her similarity to a group, view roles and obligations to a group as central aspects of self-definition, and value restraint and harmony" (Enns, 1994, p. 206).

IMPLICATIONS FOR COUNSELORS AND PSYCHOLOGISTS

Being from the same tribe or family does not mean people will endorse similar values—differences in cultural outlook can be seen between Connie and Alana. Much of the emphasis in cross-cultural and, more recently, multicultural counseling and psychology has been on helping counselors work effectively with clients who are different with respect to race, gender, class, disability, sexuality, and other sources of differences. What does it mean when clients and counselors are similar with respect to these differences and yet have different value orientations? Clearly, effective counseling depends on a sound therapeutic alliance (Vontress, 1986). It also depends on clients having a holding environment (Kegan, 1982) that is empathic and allows them to tell their stories while feeling validated (Rayle, Chee, & Sand, 2006; Murphy & Dillon, 2006).

Alana appreciates that Connie, like many Native Americans, views wellness not only in terms of the body but also the spirit and the mind. Alana fears that although her mother's cognitive capacities are leaving, her spirit will feel fear in a foreign place. Connie's ability to use humor appropriately is in line with Alana's culture of not taking herself too seriously (Garrett & Herring, 2001). Humor is also a way for Connie and Alana to maintain Native Culture and create unity, and, for Alana, it is a way for her to learn how to cope with a difficult situation (Garrett, Garrett, Torres-Rivera, Wilbur, & Roberts-Wilbur, 2005).

Connie chose to self-disclose or share some of her personal or demographic information with Alana (Murphy & Dillon, 2008). Connie felt that appropriate self-disclosure could be helpful and even therapeutic. Murphy and Dillon agree with this perspective and said, "We believe that judicious self-disclosure can help develop trust, especially for clients who are not comfortable with what may seem like artificial distance and anonymity" (p. 341). In addition, self-disclosure can be helpful when working with people from marginalized groups. Within the context of counseling Native Americans, Murphy and Dillon state that greater levels of trust may be present within the therapeutic relationship if clinicians use some self-disclosure and demonstrate cultural sensitivity prior to asking Native American clients personal questions. Clinicians should ask the following prior to disclosure:

1. Why am I choosing to self-disclose?
2. What is the impact of the disclosure on my clients?
3. Whose needs are being served by this disclosure, mine or that of the client?

As part of her assessment and treatment of Alana, Connie considers Alana's level of acculturation, her life off the reservation, and the fact that Alana honors more of the tribal (the presence of the medicine man and traditional ceremonies) than some of the mainstream customs (the Native American Church, which has been influenced by Christianity and psychotherapy where the client is sharing personal information with a professional and a stranger).

What helps Connie is her awareness that she is an insider. Alana told Connie that she would not counsel with a European. Still, Connie understands the importance of developing trust with Alana and working in conjunction with local and tribal resources (Dana, 2000). Finally, Connie, although younger than Alana, feels prepared to deal with the extent of Alana's pain and anger around generations of loss, transgression, and trauma (Olson, 2003) that have resulted in treaty violations, loss of land, and broken promises between American and Native people.

SUMMARY

This chapter provided a history of Native American and Alaskan Native people. Representation in the United States, demographic information, history, and common cultural values among American Indian/Alaskan Natives were provided. A summary of these values can be found in Table 4.1. A case study was provided for purposes of application of material and relevance to counseling.

Chapter 5

Latinos

Pray to God and hammer away.

Puerto Rican proverb, *Eyes That See Do Not Grow Old: The Proverbs of Mexico, Central and South America*

This chapter profiles Latinos, an extremely diverse ethnic group. A brief look at history, cultural values, and demographic trends is included. A case study is provided for the integration of material in a therapeutic context.

THE SPANISH, PORTUGUESE, INDIANS, ASIANS, AND AFRICANS

The racial diversity among Latinos is very old and connected to political movements, slavery, family, conquest, defeat, geographic movement, love, and war. The term *Hispanic* comes from España, Spain, the country from which the conquistadors hail. The Spanish encountered various Native people throughout millenia and across the various lands: the Arawak, Mayas, Aztecs, and Incas. African people who were brought involuntarily to the Caribbean and to North and South America as slaves intermarried and intermixed with the Spanish and the Native Indians. In the Phillipines, the Spanish encountered Asian people and made their claim to the land in 1522; thus, Filipinos are categorized as Asian but have Spanish ancestry. Also in 1522, the Spanish infiltrated Central America, including Nicaragua, Honduras, El Salvador, and Guatemala. These countries were conquered two decades later. During the colonial period when Spain ruled these countries, a Spanish elite ruled. Others were considered of a lower class. Class divisions were connected to skin color. Unions between the Spanish and the indigenous Indian people resulted in *mestizos*. Mestizos were not regarded as equals to the Spaniards but emerged as a higher class than pure Indians. Once African slaves arrived, new class and color configurations emerged.

During the 1700s slave trade, Europeans brought Black Africans to the Americas. The Garifina people, a group of Africans believed to have come from Ghana, were taken to Central America. African slaves on the island of St. Vincent revolted and, led by Marcos Sanchez Diaz, fled to the island of Rotan in Honduras. From there the Garifina people spread out along the Caribbean to Belize, Guatemala, and Honduras (www.worldtrek.org/odyssey/ latinamerica).

Today, non-White Latinos still experience discrimination that is politically, socially, and racially motivated (Hernandez, 1996). In addition to European, Indian, and African ancestries, some Latinos claim an Asian heritage (Santiago-Rivera, Arredondo, & Gallardo-Cooper, 2002). Latinos can be of any race and represent a range of phenotypical characteristics, including white, brown, red, and black skin-color hues.

GEOGRAPHY

Central America includes Belize, Costa Rica, El Salvador, Guatemala, Honduras, Nicaragua, and Panama. The countries of **South America** include Argentina, Bolivia, Brazil, Chile, Paraguay, Peru, and Uruguay. Columbia and Venezuela represent the northern part of South America. Brazil is another country in South America; however,

Brazilians speak Portuguese and are of Portuguese, not Spanish, descent. Millions of Latinos from countries such as Argentina and Costa Rica are not of Spanish or Indian descent, but rather descend from European or Antillean nations (Beals & Beals, 1993). Some British left England during the 18th century and other Europeans went to Latin America to escape Nazi oppression (Santiago-Rivera et al., 2002).

Latinos in the United States are united by the Spanish mother tongue, yet there are language differences. Beals and Beals (1993) stated that the majority of Spain's citizens speak Castellano, whereas the majority of Chicanos (Mexicans) speak Pocho. According to Carballo-Dieguez (1989), many Latinos are fluent in both Spanish and English, others know very little English, others have limited knowledge of Spanish, and others speak "Spanglish," a mixture of both languages.

One of the discourses about Latinos is that they are foreigners. Actually, the majority of Latinos were born in the United States, with most speaking only English at home or speaking English very well. In 2004, nearly 75% of Latinos were U.S. citizens (61%) or became naturalized citizens (11%). The 20th century witnessed the mass migration of Latinos to the United States, with most foreign-born Latinos entering in 1990 or later (U.S. Census Bureau, 2007). Their points and periods of entry have differed from legal to illegal, from post-Castro for Cubans to citizenship status issues for Puerto Ricans, to the illegal and extralegal status of Mexicans and other Latinos who die daily en route to America. America has been enhanced, enriched, and truly transformed as a function of the presence of Latino people (Sanchez, 2002).

Mexican Americans represent 64% of Latinos. Mexico has been and continues to represent a country with one of the highest immigration rates to the United States. Central Americans are 7.2% of the population, with El Salvador and Guatemala representing the largest numbers of people from this area at 1.2 million and nearly 700,000, respectively. South Americans are 5.5% of Latinos, with people from Columbia and Ecuador representing nearly 700,000 and half million people, at 686,000 and 453,000, respectively. Puerto Ricans are 9.6%; Cubans, 3.6%; and other countries, 6.7% (U.S. Census Bureau, 2007).

About one in two Latinos lives in two states: California and Texas (30% and 19% of the Latino population, respectively). Florida and New York have 8% and 7% of the Latino population, respectively. Nearly two thirds of Latinos reside in these four states. In addition to these states, Illinois (4.3%), Arizona (3.9%), New Jersey (3.2%), Colorado (2.1%), and New Mexico (2.0%) are home to four out of every five Latinos. Mexicans are more likely to live in the West (57%) and in the South (33%). Puerto Ricans are highly concentrated in the Northeast (64%), and Cubans are most likely to live in the South (80%). Central and South Americans are concentrated in the Northeast (32%), the South, (35%), and the West (28%) (U.S. Census Bureau, 2001a).

MIGRATORY PATTERNS FROM MEXICO

Mexico is currently one of the largest sources of new immigrants to the United States. Mexicans in America represent the largest group of Latinos and number nearly 21 million. Nearly 90% of Mexicans live in Texas, California, New Mexico, Arizona, and

Colorado. North Carolina had the largest percentage of growth of Latinos between the 1990 census and the 2000 census. A number of push and pull factors influenced the migratory patterns of Mexico's people to the United States. During the early 1900s, there was a great need for cheap labor to work in U.S. agriculture. The harsh economic conditions in Mexico and high unemployment, along with Mexico's proximity to the United States, set the stage for large-scale migration (U.S. Department of Health and Human Services [DHHS], 2001).

There was a time when the land that the majority of Americans now occupy was once Mexico. In 1821, Mexico won its independence from Spain, but this freedom was truncated. In 1848, the Treaty of Guadalupe Hidalgo was the result of Mexico's defeat in a series of wars a decade earlier. Through this formal agreement between Mexico and the United States, Mexico lost 50% of its territory. The cultural and geographic decimation was enormous. Mexicans who had lived on their own land, where their *almas* (souls) resided, now became migrant farm workers. Mexicans who had been landowners found themselves working for White men. Once Texas, New Mexico, California, Arizona, Nevada, and half of Colorado officially became United States territory, the Spanish language was ousted, with English becoming the primary and official mode of school instruction.

DEMOGRAPHY

The Western world's Latinos are *la raza,* which means, "the race" or "the people." Places of origin among Latinos are diverse and varied: Puerto Ricans *(Puertorriquenos),* Cubans *(Cubanos),* Central Americans and South Americans, Latin Americans (which include Dominicans *[Dominicanos]*), and Mexican Americans *(Mejicanos).*

The federal government defines *Hispanic* or *Latino* as a person of Mexican, Puerto Rican, Cuban, South or Central American, or other Spanish culture or origin regardless of race (U.S. Census Bureau, 2007). Novas (1994) clarified that for many Latinos, "'Hispanic' is merely a bureaucratic government census term." The term *Latino* or *Latina,* depending on gender, is widely used and refers to persons with Spanish ancestry. Many Latinos prefer to be called by their country of orgin.

Representing 14.2% of the U.S. population, or 40.5 million people as of 2004 (U.S. Census Bureau, 2007), Latinos exceed the number of African Americans and continue to be the largest group of color. High rates of immigration, low median age, and high fertility rates account for this increase. For instance, among the 31.1 million people from the 2000 census reporting to be foreign born, 51.7% are from Latin America (U.S. Census Bureau, 2000).

Latino women have a higher fertility rate than non-Hispanic White women. About 75 out of every 1,000 Hispanic women aged 15 to 50 gave birth in the 12 months prior to being surveyed in 2004, compared with 50 of every 1,000 non-Hispanic White women aged 15 to 50. In 2000, one in five births in the United States was to Latinas, and the fertility rate for Latinas then was 47% higher than the overall average. In comparison to native-born Latinas, foreign-born Latinas have a higher fertility rate (U.S. Census Bureau, 2001b), with Guatemalan and Mexican women having the highest fertility rates of the specific Hispanic-origin groups and Cuban women having the lowest. For example, there were 92.1 births out of 1,000 to Guatemalan women and 41.7 births out of 1,000 to Cuban women (U.S. Census Bureau, 2007).

In 2004, 50.8% of Latinos were married while 35% were not married. Nearly 19% of households among Latinos were females with no husband present, whereas 9% of households were males with no wife present. Among Latinos compared with the general population, there are higher rates of female and male households and lower rates of nonfamily households, which is 23%. Among Dominican and Puerto Rican women, their situations are different from other Latino groups. Nearly one third of Dominican and 26.5% of Puerto Rican women are in female-headed households only with no husband present. The lack of a male present has enormous implication for economic stability (Santiago-Rivera, 2003).

Divorce and widowed rates were lower at 7.5% and 3.3%, respectively, compared with 10.2% and 6.1%, respectively, in the general population. Rates of separation were slightly higher, at 3.5% compared with 2.1%. It should be noted that there are considerable within-Latino group differences with respect to marriage stability. Cubans have the highest rate of divorce, compared with Guatemalans who have the lowest: 12.4% and 4.1%, respectively. Cubans were also the least likely to have never married at 25%, whereas Hondurans and Salvadorans were the most likely to never have married at 40.4% and 40.3%, respectively. Struggling with transition from one cultural context to the next, working long hours to support themselves and to send money to family remaining at home, and dealing with survival issues can eclipse dating and looking for a mate. Regardless of specific group, Latinos tend to have larger household sizes at 3.4 compared with 2.6 for the general population. Guatemalans had the most people in their households (3.90).

Whereas the median age of non-Latinos in the United States is 40.1, the median age among Latinos is 26.9 years (U.S. Census Bureau, 2007). Mexicans have the lowest median age, 25.3 years, and Cubans had the highest, at 40.6 years. In fact, one third of Mexicans, Puerto Ricans, Dominicans, and Hondurans are children. In 2000, the largest 5-year age group among Latinos was children under the age of 5. Among non-Latinos, the largest 5-year age group is 40- to 44-year-olds. Latinos have had the lowest proportion of elderly in each census, although Cubans have had a larger proportion of people aged 65 and older. For the remaining specific Hispanic groups, the proportion of the population that was 65 and older was 7% or less.

SOCIAL, PSYCHOLOGICAL, AND PHYSICAL HEALTH ISSUES

Sounds like U.S.

The diversity among Latinos is tremendous. Despite this diversity, Latinos are descendents of the oppressed and the oppressor with a history marked by social oppression, conquest, liberation, and struggle (Garcia-Preto, 1996). Among the diverse group of Latinos, differences exist across geography, country of origin, race, class, traditions, acculturation, and the time and sociopolitical circumstances in which persons entered the United States (Beals & Beals, 1993; Nicolau & Santiestevan, 1990). Stavans (1995) said, "We Latinos have an abundance of histories, linked to a common root but with decisively different traditions. At each and every moment, these ancestral histories determine who we are and what we think" (p. 20).

Variations are striking among ethnic groups across the educational pipeline with respect to educational attainment. More than one quarter, or 27%, of Latinos have less than a ninth-grade education compared with 4% of non-Hispanic Whites. The high school graduation rate for all Latinos is 60% compared with 88.6% for non-Hispanic Whites. South Americans (Peruvians, Columbians, and Ecuadorians) have much higher graduation rates (84.5%) than Central Americans (Guatemalan, Honduran, Salvadoran) with an average of 53%. Puerto Ricans have the next highest graduation rate at 71%. Mexicans have a graduation rate similar to Central Americans, at 52%. The college attainment rate among Latinos is 10.6% compared with 28% of non-Hispanic Whites. Cubans have the highest college attainment rate at 23% compared with 7% for Mexicans (U.S. Census Bureau, 2001a).

In addition to geographic diversity, income varies as well. Latinos are more likely to be unemployed at 6.8%, compared with 3.4% of non-Hispanic Whites. Puerto Ricans have the highest unemployment rate at 8.1%, with 5.1% among Central and South Americans. When employed, Latinos are more likely to work in service occupations, at a rate of 19.4%, or in operator or labor positions, at 22%. Compared with non-Hispanic Whites, their rates in these positions are 11.8% and 11.6%, respectively. Non-Hispanic Whites are more than twice as likely to work in managerial positions at a rate of 33.2%. In 2000, only 14% of Latinos worked in managerial or professional positions, with Mexicans being the least likely of all Latinos to work in such positions, at a rate of 11.9% (U.S. Census Bureau, 2001a).

Unlike in 1995, many of the Latino workers who had newly arrived in the United States in 2005 were less likely to work in agriculture and more likely to work in construction. These workers were also older and thus less likely to be low-wage earners. Nonetheless, many Latinos who are foreign-born are in poverty (Kochhar, 2007).

Twenty-one percent of Latinos live in poverty compared with 12.3% for the general population (U.S. Census Bureau, 2007). Among Latino children under the age of 18, 29% live in poverty. Among the various groups of Latinos, Dominicans, Puerto Ricans, and Mexicans have the highest poverty rates at 28%, 24%, and 24%, respectively. Columbians have the lowest poverty rate at 11%. The poverty rate among Central Americans is 18%, which is higher than for South Americans (13%).

The poverty rate among Latinos is more than twice that of the non-Hispanic White population, which is 8.8%. High poverty rates contribute to Latinos having the highest (35%) probability of being medically uninsured (Institute of Medicine, 2003). Despite the high poverty rates among Latinos, substantial income gains have been made. In 2004, the median household income for Latinos was $35,929, or nearly $10,000 less than the median income for the general population. Dominicans have the lowest median income at $29,624, and South Americans, particularly Ecuadorians, had the highest at $43,788.

Income is related to status of housing. The majority of Latinos are more likely to own their homes than to rent them, but there is tremendous variation across ethnic groups. More than half, or 52%, of Latinos owned their homes in 2004 compared with 48% who rented. Only 25% of Dominicans own their own homes, whereas 61% of Cubans are homeowners. The median value of owner-occupied homes was $152,000, which was similar (a few dollars higher) to the general population. The median value of homes among Mexicans was $136,468 compared with nearly $300,000 among Ecuadorians. Latinos are more likely than the general population to carpool via a car or truck, at 18% compared to 10%, but less likely to drive alone, 67% compared with 78%. Latinos are also more likely than the general population to use public transportation, 8% compared with 5%.

Latinos also have extremely high rates of not having health insurance, 34% compared with 16% in the general population (DeNavas-Walt, Proctor, & Smith, 2007). Yet Latinos along with African Americans and Native Americans have a 50% to 100% burden of illness and mortality due to diabetes compared with White Americans (Institute of Medicine, 2003). In addition, high blood pressure and obesity rates are also higher among this group (U.S. DHHS, 2001).

The Epidemiologic Catchment Area (ECA) Study investigated rates of psychiatric disorders in five communities. Los Angeles was one of the sites studied and Mexicans were oversampled. Mexican Americans born in Mexico were found to have lower rates of depression and phobias compared with those born in the United States. Another study examined rates of psychiatric disorders in a large sample of Mexican Americans residing in Fresno County, California. Lifetime rates of mental disorders among Mexican American immigrants born in Mexico were remarkably lower than the rates of mental disorders among Mexican Americans born in the United States. The length of time that Latinos had spent in the United States was a factor in the development of mental disorders. Immigrants who had lived in the United States for at least 13 years had higher prevalence rates of disorders than those who had lived in the United States fewer than 13 years (U.S. DHHS, 2001).

Vulnerabilities among youth have been reported as well. A large-scale survey of primarily Mexican American teens in both Texas and Mexico found higher rates of depression, drug use, and suicide among Texas-based youth (U.S. DHHS, 2001). Living in the United States was related to a higher risk of mental health difficulties than not living here. Texan youth were more likely to report high rates of depressive symptoms than Mexican youth, 48% compared with 39%. Youth residing in Texas who reported illicit drug use in the last 30 days was also higher among Texas-based youth as was suicidal ideation compared with youth who lived in Mexico. Among Latino college students, the numbers are growing, and yet there are few studies that have examined acculturative stress and psychological distress (Crockett, Iturbide, Stone, McGinley, Raffaelli, & Carlo, 2007).

The HIV/AIDS epidemic is a major threat to the Latino community. In 2001, HIV/AIDS was the third leading cause of death among Hispanic men aged 35 to 44 and the fourth leading cause of death among Hispanic women in the same age group. In 2002, Hispanics accounted for more than 8,000, or 20%, of the more than 42,000 new AIDS diagnoses in the United States. Of the rates of AIDS diagnoses for all racial and ethnic groups, the second highest was the rate for Hispanics (U.S. Centers for Disease Control and Prevention, 2004).

Of inmates under state or federal jurisdiction in 2004, 19.2% were Latino males, whose numbers were 260,600 with a sentence of more than 1 year. There were 75 Latino women per 100,000 inmates compared with a total of 64 per 100,000 for non-Hispanic Whites. (Harrison & Beck, 2006).

MIGRATION AND ACCULTURATION

Given the disproportionately higher levels of poverty, stress, and trauma of immigration and adapting to a foreign culture, and cultural isolation upon arrival, Latinos are in need of mental health services. On average, Latinos have relatively low educational and economic status. Despite the fact that the United States is referred to as the second largest Latin American country in the world (Arredondo & Rodriguez, 2005), migration experiences and the psychological impact of these on mental health and well-being is an area of research that needs further exploration (Santiago-Rivera, 2003).

Feelings of personal loss and grief are part of the experience even if, in the process, a person's and/or family's economic outlook improves. Political turmoil may prevent some families from returning to their homeland. For some, there are tears of deportation if they return home. These circumstances can heighten a person's longing for home and the family and friends left behind (de las Fuentes, 2007).

Since September 11, 2001, xenophobic attitudes have increased, and Latinos are vulnerable to such personal attitudes as institutional structures impinge upon their lives. Acculturation stress is the emotional, physical disharmony and spiritual imbalance that is part of the acculturation process following immigration. Lack of a solid social network, not having facility with the English language, intergenerational conflicts, and overcrowded and unsafe living conditions and neighborhoods have been documented as part of the acculturation process (Arredondo & Rodriguez, 2005).

In working with Latinos, it is important to consider the client within the broader context of the family. In this chapter's case study, Ami (the counselor) inquires about Tania's role in the family and how this role is manifested in her life, particularly in the chronic caregiving to Jaime. Tania is a wife and mother to Jaime. A multidimensional ecological comparative model can help mental health professionals devise a relevant and respectful treatment approach. There are four domains to the model:

1. The impact of migration and cultural change.
2. Family organization.
3. The current ecological environment and the family.
4. The family life cycle or transitions.

How the couple has traditionally dealt with stress was a question that Ami asked (Santiago-Rivera et al., 2002). (See Case Study: "War.")

Colorism refers to differential and often inequitable treatment because of skin color hue (Robinson & Ward, 1995). As with African American communities, colorism affects Latino communities. Sue and Sue (1990) indicated that "the more a person resembles an Indian, the more prejudice and discrimination he or she will encounter" (p. 298). A variety of hues—white, tan, black, brown, and red—compose the Latino population. This attests to roots from Africa, Asia, the Carribean, Spain, and other parts of Europe, and a Native American heritage. Research is needed to investigate the role of brown and black skin color hues among many Dominicans and Puerto Ricans and higher rates of poverty and family instability.

CULTURAL ORIENTATION AND VALUES

Cultural heritage commonalities are strong. Among most Latinos, cooperation rather than competition is stressed. The extended family and friendship networks are held in high esteem and are the basis of Latino culture (Gloria & Peregoy, 1995). (See Table 5.1.) Family members feel a sense of obligation to provide for, and receive support from, one another both emotionally and materially (Vasquez, 1994). *Familismo* (familialism) is considered to be one of the most important cultural values that Latino people have (Santiago-Rivera, 2003) and "involves the strong identification and attachment to nuclear and extended family. Loyalty, reciprocity, and solidarity among members of the family are associated with this attachment" (p. 50).

Latino cultures tend to be collectivistic, which means individual goals are subordinated to the larger group. Relationships in collectivistic cultures also tend to be more

TABLE 5.1   Common Cultural Values among Latinos

Personalismo (intimacy)

Dignidad (personal honor)

Familismo (faith in friends and family)

Respeto (respect)

Confianza (the development of trust)

Simpatia (being a nice, gentle person)

Carino (a demonstration of endearment in verbal and nonverbal communication)

Orgullo (pride)

Loyalty to family

Collectivism

Service to others

Education as a means of development

Religion (for most, the Catholic Church—but not for all)

stable and even involuntary "because they arise from the fewer, yet closer knit, in-groups that permeate this orientation" (McCarthy, 2005, p. 110).

In many Mexican American families, the extended family is strong and includes *compradazgo,* or godparents, and among Puerto Ricans, *compadres,* or special friends, who often act as co-parents and receive a high place of honor, affection, and respect in the family (Santiago-Rivera et al., 2002). Gloria and Peregoy (1995) stated that more status is given to a person who honors family than to someone with material possessions.

Family structure and personal honor are highly valued. *Dignidad* is linked to both *personalismo* and *respeto. Personalismo* is an orientation in which the person is more important than the task. Warm and interpersonal relationships are valued (Santiago-Rivera, 2003). *Respeto* refers to "sensitivity to a person's position and creates a boundary within which conversations should be contained to avoid conflict" (Santiago-Rivera et al., 2002, p. 113). *Dignidad* encourages actions that cultivate pride for people independent of their position and refers to a strong sense of self-worth and personal dignity. A focus is also placed on being in the moment, with emphasis on the present.

Family structures are often formal and hierarchical, in that deference to elders and males is practiced. Although often misunderstood as related to men's sexual prowess and women's objectification and subjugation, *machismo* is a part of Latino culture that describes stoicism, the need for *dignidad,* or dignity, *respeto*, or respect, and in some instances, dominance within the family (Vasquez, 1994). Adherence to family roles, such as males outside the home and females inside, represents another value orientation practiced by some Latino families (Arredondo, 1992). Preserving the Spanish language within the family is a common practice in many Hispanic homes.

In Latino culture, a premium is placed on personal relationships. *Personalismo*, or a desire to be close, to know one another intimately, and to communicate personally rather than impersonally, represents a value orientation common to many Latinos (Arredondo, 1992; Gloria & Peregoy, 1995). *Simpatia* refers to the value of smooth and harmonious interpersonal interactions (Gloria & Peregoy, 1995). It also speaks to the importance of harmonious and polite interactions (de las Fuentes, 2007).

STORYTELLING: El Caballo

During my first job out of graduate school, I traveled for work to Puerto Rico. At the end of the work day, a few of us decided to go horseback riding. It was my first time on a horse, so I was excited as well as apprehensive. I had been instructed how to pull back the reins on the horse when I wanted to slow down. I came to a spot where I wanted to do just that, slow down. I pulled on the reins and told the horse to stop. I found that it was not working. The horse ignored me. I pulled harder—again the horse went on his merry way did not pay me any mind as he trotted along. Sensing my frustration and anxiety, the guide calmly said, "the horse does not understand English." Once I used the right language, the horse complied and we got along famously!

Latino families are more likely to live within family units and, similar to Asian Americans and Pacific Islanders, are least likely to live alone. Children also tend to remain with the family (especially girls) until they marry (U.S. DHHS, 2001).

Demonstrated through loyalty for one's family, cultural pride is significant (Rendon & Robinson, 1994). According to Comas-Diaz (1993), the concept of *respeto* "governs all positive reciprocal interpersonal relationships, dictating the appropriate deferential behavior toward others on the basis of age, socioeconomic position, sex, and authority status" (p. 250). (See Storytelling: "El Caballo.") Within the concept of *respeto,* parents desire to raise children who are polite and well mannered *(bien educados)* as opposed to children who are not well behaved *(malcriados)* and is an indication of poor parenting (Arredondo & Rodriguez, 2005).

For most Latinos, the bond to Catholicism is strong. In fact, the concept of *Marianismo* "is based on the Catholic cult of the Virgin Mary, which dictates that when women become mothers they attain the status of Madonnas and, accordingly, are expected to deny themselves in favor of their children and husbands" (Vasquez, 1994, p. 202). Clearly, conflicts can emerge within this cultural value system, particularly for Latinas who may be more acculturated. Overall, the church and faith play a crucial role and shape core beliefs, such as the importance of sacrifice; charitability and service to others; and long suffering, even in the face of adversity (Sue & Sue, 1990). As is consistent with other groups who are more oriented toward collectivism than individualism, there is a holistic connection between the mind and body. *Curanderos,* or spiritual and herbal "folk" healers, who are primarily women, practice an ancient Native American art (Novas, 1994). They hold special status in many Mexican and Mexican American communities and often work in consultation on psychiatric cases with priests and other religious authorities (Arredondo, 1992). *Espiritistas* are spiritual guides, and *Santeros* (a reference to worshipers of Catholic saints and African gods) are consulted to diagnose conditions, both physical and psychological. Oils, prayers, holy water, candles, and special herbs are items used to perform rituals (Santiago-Rivera, 2003). Aztecs have a rich history as herbalists, healers, botanists, and medical doctors (Padilla, 1984). That some of their descendants would have the gift of healing is understandable.

Communication styles represent a significant part of the way meanings are expressed and interpreted. Many Latinos tend to speak softly, avoid eye contact when listening to or speaking with persons perceived as having high status, and interject less. Often, the manner of expression is low-key and indirect (Sue & Sue, 1990). For many Latino youths and adults, being a linguistic minority represents a real barrier to education and employment. Families gather to celebrate holidays, birthdays, baptisms, first communions, graduations, and weddings. Latino families teach their children the importance of honor, good manners, and respect for authority and the elderly. Importance is given to physical appearance as a sense of honor, dignity, and pride. Formal attire is commonly worn to church, parties, social gatherings, and work (Clutter & Nieto, n.d.)

Culture-bound syndromes are defined as "recurrent, locally specific patterns of a typical behavior and troubling experiences that may or may not be linked to a particular *DSM–IV* diagnostic category" (Shiarev & Levy, 2004, p. 244). Folk illness such as *empacho*, which is a bad upset stomach, *nervios* (nerves), and *mal de ojo* (evil eye) are often related to supernatural causes, particularly among Puerto Ricans, Cubans, and Dominicans. *Susto* refers to fright, and it originated from and is a combination of medieval Spanish, African, and indigenous beliefs (Santiago-Rivera, 2003). An expression of distress commonly linked to Latinos and Mediterranean groups is *ataques de nervios* or attack of nerves. Symptoms of an *ataque de nervios* include screaming uncontrollably, crying, trembling, heat in the chest rising to the head, and verbal or physical aggression. Death of a loved one, divorce, or interpersonal conflict can bring this syndrome about (Shiarev & Levy, 2004). Dissociative experiences, seizures, or fainting as well as suicidal gestures are known to occur in *ataques* (U.S. DHHS, 2001).

CASE STUDY
War

Monteo Loraso is a 49-year-old father of three sons. Monteo was born in Guatemala and is married to Tania, his wife of 31 years who is also Guatemalan. They have lived in the States for 11 years. Monteo and Tania are present at a support group through the local diocese for parents with children stationed in Iraq. Monteo and Tania have already lost their oldest son to HIV just 2 years ago. Monteo Jr. had a heroin addiction for years; intravenous drug use was the means by which he contracted the disease. Although Monteo and Tania each pleaded with their second eldest not to join the military, 19-year-old Esteban was very eager to serve his country and felt committed to protect the freedoms that allowed his parents to come to America. Esteban was also having run-ins with the law and was not working a steady job. He is father to a little girl. Esteban felt that the military would help him get his life on track.

Monteo and Tania are worried that something bad will happen to their son. The loss of Monteo Jr. and their fears about Esteban have not rattled their faith, but their mental health seems affected. Their youngest child, 12 years of age, is autistic and will need care and supervision for the rest of his life due to his developmental delays. Their group facilitator is 32-year-old Ami. She is a European American counseling psychologist and a member of another parish. She is fluent in Spanish.

Although the couple have lived in the States for 11 years, Tania is not fluent in English whereas Monteo is. Monteo owns a landscaping business. Tania is a homemaker. Neither one of them graduated from high school. Upon first meeting the couple, Ami referred to them as Mr. and Mrs. Loraso. Ami listens to all of the family's stories and encourages them to schedule an appointment for individual/family counseling if desired. Monteo and Tania do so. Tania reports that for 3 months, she has been having neck, chest, and head pain. After making several phone calls, Ami is able to identify a daily program for their youngest son, Jaime, to participate in during the day. She also encourages Monteo and Tania to continue with both individual and group counseling for support.

Ami also helps Monteo and Tania grieve the lost of Monteo Jr. Their multiple concerns about finances, caring for Jaime, and helping Esteban avoid similar trouble as his older brother did not allow them to process their tremendous loss. Ami told them, "Other families are suffering with this war, but your suffering is unique to you." Ami also asks them about their spirituality and how their faiths have managed not to have been affected by their losses. Monteo said God will provide. Tania is silent. Ami asks Tania where she is spiritually, and Tania begins to cry and say that she knows God is with her son but she worries about him all the time. Ami explores with Tania the meaning of God being with her in life and death. Ami also asks Tania want she wants for her life. Tania tells her that she would like to be able to read her son's letters as soon as she gets them in the mail. Ami encourages her to take the English as a Second Language courses available through the diocese. Prior to the end of one of their sessions, Tania says in Spanish to Ami, "I feel like more light is coming in."

QUESTIONS

1. What are cultural dimensions that may affect orientation to their situation?
2. How did Ami help "more light to come in" for Tania and Monteo?

DISCUSSION AND INTEGRATION
The Clients, Tania and Monteo

First it is important to regard Monteo and Tania as immigrants within a context that understands their place of birth and circumstances that contributed to their migration to the States. According to Falbo and De Baessa (2006), Guatemala is divided between Indian (40%) and non-Indian groups. The Indian groups are considered to be descendents of the ancient Mayans, who dominated the area during first millennium AD. Beginning in 1523 and typical of the colonizers' mindset, who were determined to extinguish the indigenous peoples' language and ethnic identity, the Indians were compelled to assimilate into the Spanish colonial system. Ladinos, a term used to describe non-Indians, refers to a mix of the descendents of the ancient Mayans and Spanish colonists—who are part of the dominant national culture. *Ladinization* is the process of shifting from Indian to Ladino. Although a diversity of experiences exist, Ladinos on average have higher social status than Indians (Falbo & De Baessa, 2006).

Monteo and Tania's psychosocial identities and orientations to their situation have been shaped by a constellation of factors, including ethnicity, gender, culture, family, geographic region, education, religion, and personality, as well as other dimensions, such as acculturation level. To see Tania and Monteo holistically, it is imperative that Ami not define the couple by one visible identity construct, such as

being Latino. There are other dimensions in Monteo and Tania's life that shape presenting issues, such as grieving the death of a child and fears about a child fighting a war where thousands have been killed and thousands more have been physically and psychologically maimed and/or permanently afflicted by a traumatic brain injury or post-traumatic stress disorder. The affective dimensions of the couple's life need to be addressed. Prior to getting help through family and group counseling, they were experiencing tremendous repressed emotions, high levels of stress, and anxiety/depression. Jaime, their youngest son with autism, relies on them for his basic needs. Ami, through advocating with social services, located a program that has tremendous benefits for Jaime and Tania—who is now able to relax and attend to her needs and errands. Tania is also more traditional than her husband. In addition, her limited use of English restricts her movements. She also does not drive.

Acculturation is a psychosocial stressor. For first-generation immigrants who are attempting to adjust to a new environment, acquire a new language, and deal with a host of internal and external demands, the stress may be much greater than previously thought, with chronic acculturation stress having enormous psychological implications (Santiago-Rivera et al., 2002). According to the U.S. Department of Health and Human Services (2001), "Recent immigrants of all backgrounds, who are adapting to the United States, are likely to experience a different set of stressors than long-term Hispanic residents" (p. 133). Acculturation, according to some epidemiological studies, may even lead to an increase in mental disorders. Thus, the length of time that Tania has resided in the United States need not preclude the presence of culture-bound syndromes that could be associated with the stress of acculturation (Gonzalez et al., 1997).

Tania's headaches and chest pains could be a function of somatization, in which she is expressing her emotional and psychological discomfort through physical sensations within her body. One of Ami's effective skills was her skillful questioning and listening. She asked Tania to tell her what she thought her physical symptoms meant and how they may be related to her concerns about her children (U.S. DHHS, 2001).

As a woman and a Latina, Tania has been socialized to see herself within the context of her relationships with others. Her multiple identities as an immigrant with little formal education and limited facility with the English language enhance her vulnerabilities, which Ami identified as connected to her level of anxiety and fear. She could not bring Monteo Jr. back from the dead; she has no control over whether Esteban is going to return home alive. Jaime's condition is per-manent. Ami's goal was to provide Tania and Monteo with greater coping skills. Balancing multiple roles and conflicting demands produces stress for women (Comas-Diaz & Greene, 1994) and men.

As parents, Monteo and Tania worry about their children. Latino youth are at higher risk for poor mental health outcomes, and they are more likely to drop out of school and to report feelings of depression and anxiety. This was the case with both Monteo Jr. and Esteban. Latino youth also represent 18% of juvenile offenders in residential placement (U.S. DHHS, 2001).

IMPLICATIONS FOR COUNSELORS AND PSYCHOLOGISTS

Ami is an effective therapist. Her bilingual, listening, questioning, counseling, and diagnostic skills aided symptom relief and allowed the clients to have more hope and see possibilities. There is such informality in Western culture—everyone is on a first-name basis—but some clients of color as well as some White people are put off by a casual air that feels disrespectful. Ami referred to Tania and Monteo as Mr. and Mrs. Loraso. This is a basic concept when working with clients who are older. The concept of *falta de respeto* (lack of respect) is considered to be a major cause for breakdowns in communication across a number of relationship dyads (Santiago-Rivera et al., 2002). The Western view of the nuclear family is limiting for many Latinos and is connected to the cultural tendency to bifurcate and separate the self into discrete categories.

Like other Latinos, Guatemalans have a variety of phenotypes. Given Tania's dark skin, Ami, upon first looking at her, assumed Tania was Dominican and not Guatemalan. There were African slaves in Guatemala, and many, due to their African roots, have dark skin and other Negroid features. Guatemala is home to more than 6,000 Black Guatemalans. A key ingredient to effective counseling is to wait and listen for valuable information that the client and the counseling process can and will reveal. In time, ask appropriate questions. Ami knew her geography and was aware that Guatemala was a Central American country. She also knew that Spanish was spoken, the dominant language of the conquistadores. However, Indian languages are spoken as well, namely Kiché and Q'eqchi' (Falbo & De Baessa, 2006). Ami also knew that poverty rates were very high among this particular group of Latinos. Tania and Monteo speak Spanish, but they also speak Q'eqchi. In Guatemala, Q'eqchi people tend to have less formal education and lower earnings than other Indian groups (Falbo & De Baessa, 2006).

Ami relied on an understanding of collectivistic frameworks and their influence on people's problem orientation and resolve. Ami knew that many Latino families value close and intimate communication styles in which there is greater emphasis on the group and less on the individual acting as a lone agent. Ami did not view this closeness as enmeshment or dysfunctionality. In many Latino families, the husband is the primary and only breadwinner, with gender roles well prescribed. This was also apparent in Monteo and Tania's home. At the same time, this family structure was not a source of oppression for either party. The crisis in their lives allowed Tania to realize that there were other experiences, such as education, that she wanted to have.

Monteo and Tania came to the United States with the same dreams as other immigrants—to have access to economic opportunity and to give their children a good life. Political instability, unemployment, wars, and devastation of a country's infrastructure compel people in search of a better life to leave their homes. Although their homelands are rich in beauty, culture, and natural resources, economic and social development opportunities are often lacking (Suarez-Orozco & Paez, 2002).

Diagnosing Tania's health condition might be challenging. Oftentimes, the symptoms associated with a particular disorder or level of distress may fall short of meeting all of the diagnostic criteria. This could result in a failure to adequately diagnose a condition, particularly when cultural patterns may affect the manifestation of a disorder (U.S. DHHS, 2001).

Ami helped Monteo and Tania to deal with their stress through a variety of stress reduction activities, such as prayer and deep-breathing exercises. People across a variety of ethnic groups use alternative forms and sources of health care. Tania's family traditions, proverbs or *dichos*, and reliance on prayers or religion were extremely helpful to Ami in integrating spirituality within therapy. Ami knew that if Tania did not use stress-reduction techniques, she was going to be immobilized by the stress (Comas-Diaz & Greene, 1994).

Ami helped Tania, within a culturally respectful framework, to identify her priorities and helped her receive help. Among many collectivistic cultures, mental health services are not sought because in-group members' reliance for help (usually received from family or church) from persons who are members of the out-group might be viewed with mistrust and suspicion (McCarthy, 2005). Ami's affiliation with Tania and Monteo's church was an asset.

SUMMARY

This chapter focused on Latinos. A demographical snapshot was provided and included information about representation in the population by ethnic group, the most populated states where Latinos reside, and educational attainment. Immigration was discussed, as were push and pull factors contributing to immigration. A detailed case study was included, and cultural elements were discussed. Death of a child through HIV and the stress of war along with acculturation and gender expectations were addressed through a case study.

Chapter 6

People of African Descent

And for all the faithful ones, courageous enough to believe that hard times can make way for good outcomes and even happy endings, may God bless you.

Bebe Moore Campbell, 72 *Hour Hold*

This chapter is about people of African descent. The majority of Black people in this country are descendents of African slaves. The term *people of African descent* is used to recognize this majority as well as refer to people who have origins in any of the Black racial groups of Africa.

HISTORY, 500–1500 A.D.

According to social historian Bennett (1982),

> Civilization started in the great river valleys of Africa and Asia, in the
> Fertile Crescent in the Near East and along the narrow ribbon of
> the Nile in Africa . . . Blacks, or people who would be considered
> Blacks today, were among the first people to use tools, paint pictures,
> plant seeds, and worship gods. (p. 5)

The skeletal remains of the earth's earliest human come from East Africa, representing all of our ancestors—we are family in the truest sense of the word!

Between 500 and 1600 A.D., Africa had empires, governments, and systems of trade in regions throughout the continent. The West African empires of Ghana, Mali, and Songhai emerged in the western Sudan and were in existence during that time (Christian, 1995). Each of these three states had a powerful king and was very wealthy, with an abundance of gold, thriving agriculture, manufacturing, and successful international trading efforts. Ghana dominated the Sudan for three centuries and reached its peak in the early part of the 11th century. Mali rose in the 13th century, and Songhai was a formidable power in the 15th and 16th centuries. During this time, Timbuktu represented one of the world's greatest cities, with a reputation as the intellectual center of the Songhai empire.

THE SLAVE TRADE

The majority of Blacks in America trace their ancestry to the slave trade. The slave trade operated for four centuries. In 1501, for instance, the Spanish government authorized the use of African slaves in the Americas. Portugal was actually the first country to land a cargo of slaves in the Western Hemisphere (Christian, 1995) and remained the dominant slave trader well until the end of the 16th century (Stewart, 1996). In addition to the Portuguese, the Spanish, Dutch, British, and the colonies provided fierce competition for this lucrative industry in which human beings were traded for gold, salt, sugar, wine, and tobacco. Nations that controlled most of the American waters controlled most of the trade. Slaves were shipped to Cuba, Spain, the West Indies, and to the colonies. The first American slave ship bound for Africa was called the Rainbow and sailed from Boston.

During the slave trade throughout Europe, the Americas, and the Carribbean, nearly 12 million people were taken out of Africa, mainly from West and Central Africa. Slave ships brought kidnapped Africans to the Western Hemisphere, which included the colonies, Brazil, and the Caribbean. Most slaves came from an area bordering a 3,000-mile stretch on the West Coast of Africa. They hailed from different tribes, including the Hausas, the Mandingos, the Yorubas, the Efiks, the Krus, the Ashantis, the Dahomeans, the Senegalese, and the Fantins (Bennett, 1982).

It is estimated that as many as 2 million people perished at port, at sea, or upon arrival during the slave trade. The **middle passage** typically refers to the journey from Africa to the Americas, Europe, or the Caribbean. From roughly 1450 to 1600, about 367,000 Africans were removed from Africa, with this number increasing dramatically to more than 6 million during the 18th century.

Africans played a role in capturing other Africans for sale to White slave traders. Prior to European enslavement of Africans, slavery existed in the African states. This historical reality was used to justify the use of African slaves among Europeans. Although enslavement of any human being is morally reprehensible, there were two important differences between the slavery of Africans by other Africans and the slavery of Africans by Europeans. African slavery was not plantation or mining slavery. It did not strip African people of family linkage, nor was it based on racial hatred that reduced people's humanity. African slaves owned by other Africans would sometimes marry, own property, and become a member of the family (Zinn, 2003). The extent of Africans' participation in the selling of other Africans to Europeans depends on which version of history we read. According to Bennett (1982), there has been an attempt to overemphasize the degree of African involvement. Bennett said, "It is true that some Africans, corrupted by Europe's insatiable desire for human flesh, sold their countrymen. But many Africans, like King Almammy and Captain Tobba, loathed the whole business and forbade their subjects to take part in it" (p. 47). According to Stewart (1996), "Most of the Africans who became slaves were sold into slavery by other Africans . . . A lucrative trade for European goods, especially weapons, facilitated the selling of slaves to the Europeans" (p. 10). Africans captured by other Africans and sold to White slave traders who sold them to the highest bidder in Virginia became part of the social structure of the colony (Christian, 1995).

The year 1619 is designated as the date when the first African settlers reached North America on a Dutch man-of-war ship in Jamestown, Virginia. This group of African indentured servants were not regarded as slaves. In exchange for their passage over, people sold their labor for a period of time. Thousands of Whites used this method as a means of coming to the colonies, and life for them was often similar to that of Black indentured servants. They worked alongside each other farming, clearing forests, and cutting tobacco. For these first 40 years, Black settlers moved about with relative ease and had voting rights, and even—after surviving indentured servitude—purchased other Blacks. This system began to erode with the arrival of greater numbers of Africans, which made the profits from the slave trade escalate for both the slave trader and slave owner.

These servants were not, however, the first Africans to arrive in North America. Estevanico was the most important African explorer of America and the first foreigner to discover New Mexico. He was born in Morocco around 1500 and left Spain in 1527 as the slave of Andres Dorantes. These two were members of the expedition of Pánfilo de Narváez, the Spanish governor of Florida. Estevanico became the first foreign explorer of the southwestern United States and explored the area that became Arizona and New Mexico (Christian, 1995; Stewart, 1996). In 1539, Estevanico was murdered by Zuni Indians who were protecting their land.

During the latter part of the 1700s, southeast Native American tribes, such as the Choctaws, Seminoles, and Creeks, were slave owners, with the Cherokees having the largest number of slaves. Prior to Native people's removal to Indian Territory, Native Americans used Black slaves on their plantations in both Georgia and Tennessee.

The slave trade was outlawed in the United States in 1808. At that time, there were approximately 1 million slaves. By 1860, there were close to 4 million, with Virginia leading all other states followed by Georgia, Alabama, and Mississippi. These states, along with Texas, Louisiana, Tennessee, and Arkansas, were the cotton kingdoms, and half of the Black population worked in these states.

RESISTANCE TO SLAVERY

A history of resistance and revolt characterize the African slaves. In 1526, in the San Miguel settlement, now known as present-day South Carolina, slaves set fire to the settlement and fled to live among the Native Americans. Those slaves who managed to make it safely to the Gracia Real de Santa Teresa de Mose settlement, founded by escaped slaves, were granted their freedom by the King of Spain.

The resistance to slavery was multifaceted: it was political and literary, and it appeared on the podium as preachers spoke against this abomination to humankind. Many slaves ran away, often seeking to be reunited with loved ones and risking life and limb to escape their enslavement. Frances E. W. Harper, a Black poet, was born to free Blacks in Maryland. Some thought her to be a man or a White person with a black painted face given how intelligent and articulate she was (talk about discourses!); however, she protested the unequal treatment of people on the basis of gender and race. Her poem "The Slave Auction" appeared in her 1854 *Poems of Miscellaneous Subjects*:

> And mothers stood with streaming eyes,
> And saw their dearest children sold;
> Unheeded rose their bitter cries,
> While tyrants bartered them for gold.

Slavery was a barbaric institution supported by the government and often sanctioned by the Christian church. The impact on and implications for Black people's mental health, self-image, psyches, and earning potential can never be truly assessed.

The ways in which Black people coped or resisted took on a number of different forms, with religion and spirituality being critical. "In the slave quarters, African Americans organized their own 'invisible institution.' Through signals, passwords, and messages not discernible to Whites, they called believers to 'hush harbors' where they freely mixed African rhythms, singing, and beliefs with evangelical Christianity" (Maffly-Kipp, 2000, p. 2). Negro spirituals had double meanings of salvation and liberation. It was in this context that spirituals were created and remain to this day.

Although the slave trade had been outlawed, slavery itself continued in the South until Lincoln, out of military necessity, signed the Emancipation Proclamation in 1863. The purpose of this document was to deplete the South of its slave labor power. Lincoln had no authority to free slaves in the loyal states, only in the states of rebellion. In 1865, on June 19th, a day better known as "Juneteenth," slavery was outlawed in Texas. Later that year, on December 18, slavery became illegal with the passage of the 13th Amendment to the U.S. Constitution.

The only way for many Blacks to gain access to opportunity was to leave the South. Baltimore was considered a border city and represented a popular place for newly freed slaves to start a new life, after looking from town to town for displaced loved ones. In the same year the 13th Amendment was ratified, the Ku Klux Klan was organized in Pulaski, Tennessee. Its purpose was to undermine racial equality through acts of terrorism, which often went unpunished and, in some municipalities, were sanctioned by political officers who were themselves Klan members.

The 14th Amendment in 1868 extended citizenship to African Americans, whereas the 15th Amendment was put in place to ensure the right to vote. Poll taxes, grandfather clauses, and literacy tests prevented Blacks from voting. *De jure* (by law) **segregation** replaced slavery—also known as Jim Crow. This inferior status of Blacks was sanctioned by law and required that Blacks ride at the back of the bus, sit in different sections of movie theaters and sports stadiums, drink at separate water faucets, live in separate neighborhoods, and eat at separate restaurants.

After passage of the 13th Amendment, many Blacks sharecropped. Sharecroppers worked the landowner's land for a share of the profit once the crop went to market. Landowners kept the accounts. Keeping landowners honest was very difficult for sharecroppers who had little power or literacy.

The majority of Blacks in the United States continue to reside in the South. This percentage declined during the 20th century. World War I created a huge demand for unskilled labor in the urban North; recruiters went to the South to bring Black workers to northern cities such as Pittsburgh, Chicago, Detroit, and Indianapolis. Between 1916 and 1919, 500,000 African Americans migrated north (Stewart, 1996). After World War II, nearly 5 million Blacks went north between 1940 and 1960.

DEMOGRAPHIC TRENDS

As the second largest group of color in the United States, the 36.6 million people of African descent come from diverse cultures, including Africa, Haiti, Dominican Republic, Jamaica, central Europe, North and South America. African Americans are 12.8% of the population (U.S. Census Bureau, 2007). Of all African Americans, 8% are foreign born. About 66% of foreign-born Blacks come from Latin America and 30% come from Africa. Since 1983, more than 100,000 refugees have come to the United States from African nations (U.S. Department of Health and Human Services [DHHS], 2001). Actually 33% of foreign-born Blacks came after 1990 and 18% in 2000 and after. Roughly 1 in 4 Blacks in New York, Massachusetts, and Minnesota were foreign born.

The majority of Blacks in America reside in 10 states: New York, Florida, Georgia, Texas, California, Illinois, North Carolina, Maryland, Virginia, and Louisiana. In 2000, 55% of Blacks lived in the South, with 19% residing in the Midwest, 17.6% living in the Northeast, and only 9% living in the West (U.S. Census Bureau, 2000b).

States in the West have low proportions of Blacks in the population. Blacks were less than 5% of the population in the West, and Blacks were less than 1% in Idaho, Utah, Wyoming, and Montana. A similar situation exists in New England states, where Blacks are less than 1% of the population in Vermont, New Hampshire, and Maine. In Washington, DC, 57% of the residents are Blacks and in Mississippi, Alabama, Louisiana, Maryland, Georgia, and South Carolina, more than 25% of the state's residents are African Americans.

SOCIAL, PSYCHOLOGICAL, AND PHYSIOLOGICAL HEALTH ISSUES

The median age of African Americans is 31.2 years, which is about 9 years younger than the median age of non-Hispanic Whites, or 40.1. Persons between the ages of 18 to 44 are 39.1% of the population, followed by children under the age of 18 at 31.2%. Persons 45 to 64 are 21.4% of the population, with people 65 and older at 8.2% (U.S. Census Bureau, 2007).

In 2004, Black women had higher rates of fertility than White women, and 62.4% of the Black women who gave birth in 2004 were unmarried, compared with 20.5% of White women. The greatest percentage of Black people were in nonfamily households at 35%. A nonfamily household is defined as people who live alone or people living with unrelated individuals. Thirty percent of Black households had women only with no male present, 29% percent were married couples, and nearly 6% were male only. Blacks are also more likely than Whites to live with and care for grandchildren. About 7% of Blacks aged 30 and older were grandparents living in the same household with their co-resident grandchildren under the age of 18.

To understand demographic data and the experience of Blacks living in America, sociopolitical factors need to be considered. Compared with the population at large, Blacks have higher rates of marital divorce, separation, and never-married status. Between the race and Hispanic-origin groups, Blacks have the lowest sex ratio, with Black females outnumbering Black males throughout every decade. In 2004, 42.5% of the Black population over the age of 15 had never been married, compared with 23.8% among Whites. Rates of separation are double those in the general population: 5.1% among Blacks compared with 2.1% for the total (U.S. Census Bureau, 2007). In 2006 the poverty rate for African Americans was 24.3% (DeNavas-Walt, Proctor, & Smith, 2007), compared with 12.3% for the nation at large. Black children are more likely to live in female-headed households, which are disproportionately high among the poor. More than two thirds, or 66%, of Black children live in poverty. Black people are more likely to live in severe poverty in comparison to Whites. Blacks tend to have less money saved, have lower rates of home ownership (54% of Blacks live in renter-occupied homes), and have few investments (U.S. DHHS, 2001; DeNavas-Walt et al., 2007).

Among Black people who own homes, the median value of their homes is $104,000, which is $50,000 less than the median value of White owner-occupied homes. There is another side to Black economic conditions. More than 30% of Blacks in America have incomes between $35,000 and $75,000. Nearly 32% live in the suburbs (U.S. DHHS, 2001). Although there is a discernible middle class among African Americans, regardless of income, Black people in America tend to have fewer resources (e.g., public services, access to health care) and tend to be segregated in neighborhoods and have higher levels of health risks (Institute of Medicine [IOM], 2003). Compared with Whites, Black people are more likely to use public transportation to commute to work (12% of Blacks compared with 3% of Whites).

There have been increases in the high school graduation level, now at 80% among Blacks 25 years of age and older. This compares with 83.9% for the general population (U.S. Census Bureau, 2007). Just over 17% (17.3) had completed a bachelor's degree (U.S. Census Bureau, 2007). Nearly half, or 27%, of Blacks are employed in management or professional occupations compared with 38% among non-Hispanic Whites. Nearly 24% of this group work in sales and office occupations, which is similar to non-Hispanic Whites, 27%. Nearly one quarter of Blacks work in service occupations, with 6% in construction jobs. Among non-Hispanic Whites, 14% are in service and 10% work in construction jobs. Higher percentages of Blacks are in production and transportation in comparison with Whites, 13.1% and 11.7%, respectively.

Compared with the general population, Black people are more likely to be exposed to violence, which has implications for mental illness symptoms such as depression and post-traumatic stress disorder (PTSD). More than 20% of Blacks do not have health insurance despite the fact that more than 8 in 10 African Americans are in working families (IOM, 2003). Access to mental health care is limited. Among Blacks who have health insurance, treatment-seeking behavior for mental health services does not automatically increase. Reluctance to seek mental health services is related to the stigmatizing attitudes that exist regarding mental health care. One study found that the number of Blacks who feared mental health treatment was 2.5 times greater than the proportion of Whites (U.S. DHHS, 2001). Other research found that Blacks were less likely than Whites to be properly diagnosed when suffering from affective disorders, such as depression. The tendency of clinicians, both Black and White, was to diagnose Blacks with schizophrenia (Good, James, Good, & Becker, 2003).

African Americans are less than 13% of the U.S. population, yet in jails and state and federal prisons, they represent 41% of the incarcerated population (Harrison & Beck, 2005). Among Black males ages 25 to 29, 8.4% were in prison compared with 2.5% of Hispanic males and about 1.2% of White males in the same age group. Black women are 2 and 4 times more likely to be incarcerated compared to Hispanic and White women, respectively.

The higher rates of nonmarriage and female-headed households descriptive of Black people needs to be considered in light of the socioeconomic data. According to the Washington-based research and advocacy group Justice Policy Institute (JPI), African American men are more likely to go to jail than to college. Between 1980 and 2000, the number of African American men in jail or prison grew three times as fast as the number in colleges and universities. The JPI report compared two decades of data from the Bureau of Justice Statistics and the National Center for Education Statistics and found that although states had plenty to spend on prisons, they had much less to devote to education (Schulte, 2002). It should be noted that in 2000, 32% of Black men were not in the civilian labor force compared with 25.8% of men in the general population (U.S. Census Bureau, 2000b).

Health outcomes are related to lifestyle choices, such as smoking and nutrition. Blacks have myriad health challenges that must be examined in conjunction with the experiences of poverty, substandard housing, underemployment, unemployment, unequal access to quality health care, and chronic racial discrimination. Blacks have diabetes at a rate more than three times that of Whites; heart disease is 40% higher than that of Whites; prostate cancer is more than double that of Whites; HIV/AIDS is more than seven times that of Whites; and infant mortality is twice that of Whites (U.S. DHHS, 2001). Relative to Whites, African Americans (along with Latinos) are less likely to receive appropriate cardiac medication (e.g., thrombolytic therapy, aspirin, and beta blockers) or to undergo coronary artery bypass surgery even when insurance status, income, co-morbid conditions, age, and symptom expression are taken into account (IOM, 2003).

PHYSICAL APPEARANCE

Skin color has social power and status within the African American community (Okazawa-Rey et al., 1987). Mullins and Sites (1984) found that the inheritance of light skin color, which generally came from the mother, who tended to be lighter than the father, along with the mother's education, occupational attainment, and income, served to bolster a family's social position over time. Within a society preoccupied with skin color and where white skin is valued, the desirability of lighter skinned women stems from their closer proximity to European beauty standards. Research has found that skin-color hue affects income, educational attainment, and perceptions of success (Rockquemore, 2002).

Intraracial conflict around **colorism,** or stereotyped attributions and prejudgments based on skin color, has been documented in the literature (Okazawa-Rey et al., 1987; Robinson & Ward, 1995; Rockquemore, 2002). As children, many African American women remember being cautioned by their mothers that unless their newly washed hair was done (which meant being pressed and curled or braided), they could not go outside. The implicit and sometimes explicit message in this statement was that a female's natural state was synonymous with being unpresentable and unkept. Among Black Americans, appearance is not solely linked to skin color but to a variety of phenotypical traits, such as body shape, facial features, and hair texture (Rockquemore, 2002).

Colorism is often manifested as a preference for lighter skin tones over darker ones because color-consciousness is rooted in the social, political, and economic conditions that existed during and after slavery (Hall, 1992; Hall, 2005). Discrimination against persons with lighter skin tones occurs as well. Colorism in the Black community may be a double-edged sword, affecting those who are seen perhaps as "too black" and those who may be seen as "not black enough." Robinson and Ward (1995) found that African American adolescents reported high levels self-esteem, yet students who were at the extremes of skin color, lighter or darker than most African Americans, were less satisfied with skin color than students who were somewhere in the middle. Skin color attitudes are connected to several variables, including the particular ethnic group; group cohesiveness; the group's status in society; family, school, peers, and majority vs. minority status (Phinney, 1992). For instance, Harvey, LaBeach, Pridgen, & Gocial (2005) found that at a predominantly Black university, students placed more emphasis on skin tone than students at a predominantly White university. According to Ward (2000), unhealthy strategies of surviving racism include adopting hairstyles for the sole purpose of looking White and discriminating on the basis of skin color. She maintains that Black children and arguably adults must be taught to value their bodies for their strength and to appreciate the diversity of beauty found in Black people.

CULTURAL ORIENTATION AND VALUES

There is great diversity among people of African descent in country of origin, language, ethnicity, class, education, acculturation level, point of entry into America, and religious orientation. Despite struggle and hardship, values that transcend within group diversity are spirituality, persistence, forgiveness, resistance, humor, wisdom, and resilience (Exum & Moore, 1993). (See Storytelling: "Protective Parents and Picnics.") Spirituality is typically cited as a primary value in helping men and women survive prostate and breast cancer diagnoses and endure the strains of caregiver burden (Dilworth-Anderson, Boswell, & Cohen, 2007; Hamilton, Powe, Pollard, Lee, & Felton, 2007; Halbert et al., 2007). Black people are united by strong and rich spiritual traditions that infuse educational systems, cultural values, kinship networks, and political revolutions. Cultivating the spirit and maintaining a strong connection with the church represent a foundation for the experience of most Blacks in America. Black people may not go to church or even have a church home, but they may still "pray to the Lord" (Boyd-Franklin, 2003, p. 270) when confronted with difficult times, such as illness, death, loss, and bereavement.

STORYTELLING: Protective Parents and Picnics

A colleague of mine from the Deep South told a story of his parents' wisdom and ingenuity while he and his siblings were growing up in the segregated south during the 1950s. During this time, most Blacks were not allowed to eat in restaurants or at least enter through the front door. During family vacations and road trips, my colleague's parents would pack a picnic feast complete with silverware, a lovely tablecloth, a beverage, and his mother's dessert. The children thought it was fun to look for a park or open space and have a family picnic. It was much later in life that this man realized his parents were protecting their children from the brutality of racism. The parents knew their innocent children would be discriminated against at public eating establishments. His parents were not going to allow that to happen and protected their children from discrimination and, in doing so, showed them a grand time.

This story speaks to the sociopolitical awareness that many Black parents have about racial inequity and the wisdom needed to protect young children from information before they are able to receive it.

Historically, the Black church has been a focal point in the African American community and a place where advocacy and social and political change have taken hold. The Black church played a prominent role in the civil rights movement, voter registration, fund-raising for college students, health promotion, and personal and spiritual development. Many musicians and other celebrities had their talents recognized and nurtured by participating in the choir, youth programs, and leadership forums. Growing numbers of Blacks are counted among Islamists, Buddhists, Jews, and agnostics; the majority of Blacks in American regard themselves as Christians.

Values common among many Blacks in America include the extended family and others who are not blood relatives. Collateral relations are valued over highly individualistic styles (Sue & Sue, 1990). Education as a means of self-help and a strong work ethic are often taught to children from a very early age. Communication patterns are not limited to verbal dialogue or to standard English—the Black dialect has survived rather well as has a sense of humor when dealing with injustice and all things ludicrous. (See Storytelling: "Protective Parents and Picnics.") Most Black people depend on nonverbal modes of communication patterns—*how* something is said rather than *what* is actually verbally spoken. Body movement, postures, gestures, and facial expressions represent dominant patterns of communication within the African American community. These tend not to be strictly linear as in Western society (Exum & Moore, 1993). Another value often manifested in the Black community is giving people status as a function of age and position. A present-time orientation is seen at church, parties, and other events. The event may formally begin at one time, but the majority of people may arrive at a later time. This fluid relationship with time varies by individual differences and acculturation levels. Value is also placed on the use of proverbs (e.g., "Every goodbye ain't gone") and spiritual wisdom ("If a door closes another one opens") to not only cope but to resist and to thrive. (See Table 6.1.)

TABLE 6.1 Common Cultural Values among People of African Descent

Oral traditions

Reliance on proverbial wisdom

Spirituality and faith

Firm child-rearing practices

Education as a means of self-help

Collateral interpersonal relations

Formal communication styles with elders and authority figures

Respect for elders and authority figures

Nonverbal modes of communication

Extended family based on blood and strong ties

Unity and cooperation

Resistance

Purpose

Creativity

Fluid time orientation

According to Nobles (1972), African Americans' cultural traditions have been derived from several cultural and philosophical premises shared with West African tribes. Myers (1991) states:

> Afrocentricity refers to a worldview that believes reality is both spiritual and material at once . . . with highest value on positive interpersonal relation-ships between men/women; self knowledge is assumed to be the basis of all knowledge, and one knows through symbolic imagery and rhythm. (p. 19)

Within Africentric thought, the self is extended in unity with others and emphasis is on the collective. An African proverb, "I am because we are and since we are, there-fore I am," summarizes the saliency of the collective. Among some African Americans, **consubstantiation,** or the sense that everything within the universe is connected as a part of a whole, is a way of seeing the world (Parham, 1992). Myers (1991) stated that, in the Africentric paradigm, spirit and matter are one and are a representation of one spirit manifesting good.

The *Nguzo Saba,* or classical African values, also provide insight into African American values (Karenga, 1980). The first and third principles are *Umoja* and *Ujima* and refer to unity and collective work and responsibility, respectively. These principles endorse solidarity, harmony, cooperation, and connection with others toward a com-mon destiny. The second principle, *Kujichagalia,* means self-determination and naming for the self who the self will be, despite others' definitions. *Ujaama,* the fourth principle, refers to cooperative economics, in which resources are shared for the good of all. Within an Africentric framework, the *I* is not separate from the *We. Nia,* the fifth principle, is purpose that benefits not only the self but also the collective, for which everyone has responsibility. The sixth principle is *Kuumba,* or creativity. Creativity is inextricably linked to imagination, ingenuity, and leaving the world a better place than it was when you first arrived. *Imani,* or faith, is the last principle and encompasses the past, present, and future.

Worldview refers to the way people make meaning. Adapted from Hilliard's work, Exum and Moore (1993) summarized elements of African American worldview. These include emphasis on the whole as opposed to the parts, preference for approximations over accuracy, focus on people rather than things, and acceptance and integration with the environment. In addition to these values is a respect for nature and emphasis on groupness.

Several publications reflect a theory of resistance based on the Nguzo Saba principles (Brookins & Robinson, 1995; Robinson & Ward, 1991; Robinson & Kennington, 2002). The goal of resistance theory is to empower marginalized groups with optimal tools to name, confront, repudiate, and replace dominant and demeaning messages with knowledge of self and community. (See Storytelling: "My Aunt Mary.")

Resistance theory is an important response to the chronic stress of racism, particularly given the limited research related to the use of specific modes of coping with perceived racism (Clark, Anderson, Clark, & Williams, 2002). African tradition includes a strong tie between the living and the world of the dead in defining the scope of community. J. A. Opoku (personal communication, April 3, 1994) said about Ghanaian culture, "The dead are still with us."

STORYTELLING: My Aunt Mary

My Aunt Mary was married to my grandfather's brother. My Uncle Clarence died in the 1970s. They were from Alabama and had traveled North like so many other Black people during the 1940s in search of better employment opportunities and an opportunity to get away from the oppressive cloak of institutional racism. During one of my visits to her in her secluded West Virginia rural home, Aunt Mary offered me a hot dog. I told her, "No, thank you, Aunt Mary, I don't eat meat." I then asked her if she was eating a turkey dog. She bent her head and said, "What?" We both laughed at that one. I later read the ingredients on the hot dog package—it was not an all beef dog. Aunt Mary drank a can of Pepsi every day and I suspect she had tasted wheat bread in her life but I never saw a loaf at her house; she ate white bread. The last time I saw her in 2004, arthritis in her right leg was her only complaint. She was spry, healthy, and full of life. She drove herself to church and lived contentedly alone until a male relative on her side of the family from Alabama came to reside with her. My 95-year-old Great Aunt did not die 9 months after I last saw her because of heart disease or from a low fiber/high fat, sugary diet, Alzheimer's, diabetes, or natural causes. My Aunt Mary, with the twinkle in her eye and a laugh that arose from deep within her soul, who practiced an abiding faith in God's protection, was a victim of domestic violence—she died from savage injuries received at the hands of the nephew she had welcomed into her home.

IMPLICATIONS FOR COUNSELORS AND PSYCHOLOGISTS

Sometimes our client's stories make us sad—we may even react to the hearing of a tragic story with tears. The profession does not require us to be robotic. If our tears incapacitate us and render us ineffective, then this is a problem. It may indicate we have some unfinished work in our own personal lives that we need to address on our own time. Showing compassion and sharing our humanity are not consistent with losing professional objectivity.

Part of our competence as mental health professionals is to realize our limitations. It is important not to get overwhelmed by the magnitude and sadness of clients' difficult situations. Listening, advocacy, attending, and empathy are crucial skills. We must not underestimate how hugely valuable these gifts are, particularly in a time of crisis.

These skills allow clients to feel cared for and held within a stable and nonjudgmental therapeutic environment. Such environments are not dictated by racial similarity between the client and counselor but by a connective capacity. For most African Americans, contending with racism is part of living in America. Professional status and being middle class may mediate or attenuate the effects of racism, but they do not negate it. Multicultural competence requires knowledge of this sociopolitical reality and awareness of how racism and oppression against the poor heighten people's vulnerabilities to negative mental health outcomes.

CASE STUDY
Anxiety Attacks

Vera is a 64-year-old African American grandmother who has cared for her two grandsons since they were 4 and 6. They are teenagers now. Her daughter died of a drug overdose, and the children's father is incarcerated for beating a man to death—which his sons both witnessed. Vera continues to work as a public health department administrative assistant. She resides in the same home she has lived in for 33 years. Because of the need to get a second mortgage on her home in order to care financially for her grandchildren, her home is not yet paid for, making it necessary for her to work. Vera had breast cancer and had a bilateral mastectomy 8 years ago. At her last doctor's visit, routine blood work was done. The tests showed that Vera's cancer had returned and was in her bones. For several months, Vera had felt pain in her shoulder but assumed it was all of the housework she was doing. Ever since her diagnosis of the cancer's return, Vera has been experiencing heart palpitations and intense nausea. She also has tremendous headaches and at times feels like she can't catch her breath. Her doctor suggested she get counseling. Vera resisted at first and instead prayed about it, asking God to steady her nerves. She also called her "prayer warriors" from her Bible Study class. The panic attacks have worsened and are now interfering with her work performance. Vera reluctantly presents for counseling.

QUESTIONS

1. What might be helpful to Vera to encourage relaxation?
2. How might therapy help Vera's grandchildren?
3. How might a counselor help Vera to live and to prepare for her death?

DISCUSSION AND INTEGRATION
The Client, Vera

Vera is distressed and is dealing with existential issues, facing death, and the stress of raising the grandchildren who depend on her. She sounds anxious. The *DSM–IV* defines Generalized Anxiety Disorder as (1) excessive anxiety and worry (apprehensive expectation) occurring more days than not for at least 6 months, (2) the person finds it difficult to control the worry, (3) the anxiety and worry are associated with three or more of the following six symptoms: (a) restlessness or feeling keyed up or on edge, (b) being easily fatigued, (c) difficulty concentrating, (d) irritability, (e) muscle tension, (f) sleep disturbance.

Vera is in need of help. She has stepped up to the responsibility of caring for her grandchildren and now the disease that cost her her breasts has returned and lives in her bones. As a praying woman, Vera has a important coping tool. According to research by Hamilton, Powe, Pollard, Lee, and Felton (2007), many breast and prostate cancer survivors believe that God is with them, healing and protecting them, and is ultimately in control of their lives. In another study by Dilworth-Anderson, Boswell, and Cohen (2007), 303 African American caregivers stated that their spiritual beliefs greatly helped them with giving care to others. Spiritual beliefs helped caregivers endure, experiencing a sense of reciprocity in giving back to those who had helped them, faith, and gratification to foster positive feelings about giving care.

After her grandchildren came to live with her, they had some of the classic symptoms of PTSD, namely, avoidance of the stimuli associated with the trauma, nightmares, difficulty concentrating, and physiological reactivity on exposure to internal or external cues. There is tremendous stress associated with growing up in violence, and Black children are more likely to be exposed to it. As Boyd-Franklin (2003) stated, "many are acquainted from an early age with violence in their homes in the form of child abuse, sexual abuse, drug overdose, and AIDS" (p. 266). Vera's grandsons were diagnosed as hyperactive— they ran incessantly and stayed busy at all times. Vera did not accept the diagnosis and concluded that her boys just "needed to run all the chaos out of their

systems." Vera was right. Children can evidence difficulty with emotional and behavioral regulation when exposed to trauma (Rampage, Eovaldi, Ma, & Weigel-Foy, 2003). In time, her boys adjusted well at home and at school.

Vera is the only parent her grandchildren have— Black people are more likely than Whites to reside with their co-resident grandchildren, with more than half having responsibility for the care of these children. On one hand, the responsibility of being the sole provider of her grandchildren gives Vera the strength to go on. On the other hand, it fills her with fear.

A counselor is needed who can comfortably integrate Vera's need to pray prior to the therapy session. Vera may also want to discuss dreams or other messages that God might be giving her. Prayer could even be used as visualization to rid her body of the cancer that is now in her bones. Vera continues to be very active, despite her diagnosis, with work and caring for the children. Parham (1992) noted that among some African Americans, depression manifests not as psychomotor retardation but as increased activity in order to "keep on keeping on." Much of the Black experience in America is coping, surviving, and putting up with injustice and stressful aspects of racism. People have to function—go to work and school, feed the kids, and pay the bills. In a doing-oriented culture, a counselor needs to avoid mistaking Vera's behavior for adaptive functioning when it is more descriptive of a disordered mood.

As teenagers, Vera's grandsons have the task of growing up and dealing with their only parent's illness. They, too, could benefit from having a place to process their feelings and learn the truth of their grandmother's cancer.

The Counselor

Vera's therapist may consult Vera's minister about the spiritual aspects of healing. Doing so may provide the therapist with a sense of how to complement this core value of Vera's during psychotherapy. Vera's spirituality may also offer some clinical insight. For instance, her counselor says to Vera, "Think of a hymn that gives you the most comfort. What are the words that help you to feel peaceful?" Vera could be encouraged to become mindful of the worry thoughts and interrupt these thoughts with a song or a scripture.

Part of Vera's anxiety is not just for her own life but for those of two young men as well. She knows they "walk alone." It may be important for the therapist to challenge Vera's idea of what it means to walk alone. Perhaps her therapist could help Vera find a Big Brother program and inquire as to whether the church has a support group for teens. If not, they might start one. If there are no other extended family members to help support Vera through this difficult time, perhaps a family through the church or another civic/community group could be identified. Although increasingly common in our society, the idea of a single adult having the sole care of children and working a full-time job is not logical and does not allow the village to raise the children. The therapist must acknowledge that this is a difficult and terrible time for Vera and assure her that she will not have to walk this path alone.

SUMMARY

This chapter provided history, demographic trends, and cultural values for people of African descent. A case study was presented for students to gain practice with integrating multiple issues: a grandparent raising her grandchildren and dealing with the reoccurrence of cancer, existential issues, and integrating spirituality into the therapeutic event. Counseling with people of African descent is discussed in the case study.

Chapter 7

People of Asian Descent, Native Hawaiians, and Pacific Islanders

MIGRATORY PATTERNS

DEMOGRAPHY

SOCIAL, PSYCHOLOGICAL, AND PHYSICAL HEALTH ISSUES

ACCULTURATION AND EXPERIENCES IN AMERICA

CULTURAL ORIENTATION AND VALUES

IMPLICATIONS FOR COUNSELORS AND PSYCHOLOGISTS

CASE STUDY

SUMMARY

**Those who cannot feel the littleness
of great things in themselves are apt
to overlook the greatness of little things
in others.**

Okakura Kakuzo, *The Book of Tea*

This chapter is a focus on people of Asian descent. The diverse ethnic groups among Asians are highlighted. Demographic information, history, and cultural values are also presented.

Tremendous diversity is found within the Asian community. As Uba (1994) pointed out, "The term 'Asian culture' is technically a misnomer. The tenets of these belief systems are shared by many cultures—there are also significant differences among Asian cultures" (p. 12). More than 100 languages and dialects are spoken, and in some communities such as the Hmong and Cambodians, high rates of linguistic isolation exist, which describes the phenomenon of persons over the age of 14 not speaking English "very well" (U.S. Department of Health and Human Services [DHHS], 2001).

Ethnicity, nationality, migration or generational status, assimilation, acculturation, facility with the English language, political climate in country of origin, religion, socioeconomic status, occupation, transferability of skills, foreign credentials to the United States, and educational level depict some of the many sources of differences within the group (Sue & Sue, 1990; Tsai & Uemura, 1988).

MIGRATORY PATTERNS

The Chinese are the Asian ethnic group with the longest history in the United States and were the first Asian ethnic group to be recruited to the West Coast during the 1840s. At that time, there was a need for cheap labor to work on the transcontinental railroads (Tsai & Uemura, 1988). U.S. policymaker Aaron H. Palmer predicted that with a connection to the East Coast, San Francisco would become the "great emporium of our commerce on the Pacific" (Takaki, 1993, p. 192). Chinese were perceived to be more suited for "cleaning wild lands and raising every species of agricultural product" (p. 192).

In 1863, Congress authorized construction of the U.S. transcontinental railroad. The eastward track was laid from Sacramento, California, through the Sierra Nevada, and eventually into Utah. During the winter months, working conditions were often brutal, and snowdrifts would bury entire work crews. Come spring, their frozen bodies would be discovered. The westward track was built mainly by Irish immigrants and started in Omaha, Nebraska. Both the Irish and Chinese received a monthly wage of $31. Unlike the Irish, the Chinese worked longer days and slept in tents near the side of the road. The Irish worked 8-hour days and resided in boarding rooms.

Despite the harsh realities of work on the railroad, many Chinese were motivated to come to America. In China, floods were making it difficult to harvest their crops. Political instability, such as taxation and ethnic conflict, were also factors. Between 1865 and 1869, the total number of Chinese railroad workers increased from 50 to almost 12,000 (Avakian, 2002). Finding gold in California was also a dream of many Chinese (Cao & Novas, 1996).

Life was not only difficult for Chinese men, Chinese women were suffering as well. In 1860, more than 80% of Chinese women were prostitutes, and many were teenage girls of 15 and 16 years of age. As a result of slavery, kidnapping, and deception, Chinese girls found themselves on the auction block, where they worked as concubines or prostitutes, sexually serving both White and Chinese men (Avakian, 2002).

Shortly after the arrival of the Chinese in 1840, 141 Japanese men, women, and children arrived in Hawaii in 1868. The Japanese, along with Koreans, Filipinos, and Puerto Ricans who came later near the turn of the 20th century, were recruited to work on the Hawaiian sugarcane plantations.

Known as the Meiji Restoration (after Emperor Meiji), the Japanese migrated to the United States during Japan's period of rapid modernization. Because of tax increases levied to pay for sweeping reforms, Japan's peasant farmers suffered greatly from economic hardships and lost their land. Persons from the districts of Yamaguchi, Hiroshima, and Kumamoto were hit hardest by poverty and comprised the majority of immigrants hailing from Japan (Avakian, 2002).

Between 1885 and 1925, 200,000 Japanese left for Hawaii, and another 180,000 went to mainland United States. By the turn of the 20th century, 70% of Hawaii's sugar plantation labor was from Japan. In 1900, with the passing of the Organic Act, the U.S. Congress voted for the creation of the Territory of Hawaii. Despite the fact that Chinese and Japanese Hawaiians represented more than half of the population, they were not allowed to vote. Whites, the minority, represented the elite and ruling class. Fortunately, the Organic Act allowed laborers to have greater power in organizing themselves more effectively. Such resistance, led by the Japanese, encouraged planters to look for new labor sources, primarily from Korea and the Philippines.

Prior to the arrival of other Asians into the United States, Congress passed the Chinese Exclusion Act of 1882, which barred the "immigration of all Chinese laborers, lunatics, and idiots into the United States for a 10-year period" (Avakian, 2002, p. 51). This act was the first and only law in U.S. immigration that ordered an entire group of people of a specific nationality to be banned from the United States (Avakian).

On December 7, 1941, a major base of the U.S. Navy, the Oahu port at Pearl Harbor, was attacked by the Japanese. Bases in the Philippines, Guam, the Midway Islands, and other ports in the Pacific were also attacked. Nearly 3,000 soldiers, sailors, and civilians were killed. This surprise attack fueled existing anti-Japanese sentiments. With the passing of Executive Order 9066, wartime curfew and internment measures were enacted primarily against the Japanese—most of whom were the *Nisei,* or second-generation, American-born Japanese. In addition, small numbers of Germans, Italians, and Eastern Europeans were also relocated to camps to safeguard the security of the United States. Although the order was a constitutional violation as well as a legal violation of due process, more than 110,000 Japanese Americans were forced to leave their homes and move to cramped internment camps. The construction plans used were for unmarried army recruits, thus up to six families resided in long army barracks with very little privacy. The traditional diet of many Japanese people, such as fresh vegetables and fruits, was not available, and waiting in lines for meals and bathroom facilities was commonplace (Avakian, 2002).

Compared with the Chinese, Japanese, Koreans, Filipinos, and Asian Indians, the Vietnamese are the most recent immigrant group to arrive in the United States.

Between April and December 1975, 100,000 refugees from Vietnam and Cambodia were admitted to the United States as parolees, as announced by the U.S. attorney general (Avakian, 2002).

Southeast Asia represents the Asian subcontinent south of China and east of India. Persons from Vietnam, Laos, and Cambodia are neighbors. Indonesia, Malaysia, Thailand, Burma, Bhutan, and Bangladesh are also included. According to Sandhu (1997), more than 40 cultural groups comprise Asian and Pacific Islander Americans. Many of these groups are less researched and perhaps less well known than other groups who have lived in the United States for several genera-tions. Asian newcomers speak hundreds of languages and dialects and practice a broad array of religions. Many ethnic Asian newcomers are more likely to identify with specific national or regional ties (e.g., Vietnamese, Korean, Hmong, Punjabi Sikh, Cantonese, Taiwanese). Many Pacific Islanders reside across more than 22 islands, including Micronesia (Guam; Belau; and the Carolines, Marianas, Marshalls, and Gilberts) and Melanesia (Fiji).

The 20th century witnessed the migration of diverse groups of Asians to the United States. About one third of foreign-born Asians entered during the 1990s, and about 17% arrived in 2000 or later (U.S. Census Bureau, 2007a). Their points and periods of entry have differed and have been largely influenced by work (railroads, cotton, sugarcane, technology, medicine, and war (World War II, Korean, and Vietnam).

DEMOGRAPHY

There are 12.1 million Asians living in the United States (U.S. Census Bureau, 2007a). Although Asians comprise 4.2% of the U.S. population, they represent one of the fastest growing groups in the nation. Between 2000 and 2004, the Asian population in the United States grew by more than 2 million people. In the 2004 American Community Survey, a quarter of a million people reported themselves as other Asian, which includes Bhutanese, Burmese, Indochinese, Iwo Jiman, Madagascan, Maldivian, Nepalese, Okinawan, and Singaporean (U.S. Census Bureau, 2007a).

In 2004, almost 743,000 people reported being Native Hawaiian or other Pacific Islander, which includes Guamanians or Chamorros, Samoan, Tongan, or those of another Pacific Island (U.S. Census Bureau, 2007b). Pacific Islanders also encompass dispersed areas, including Australia, New Zealand (the Maori), Tasmania, Polynesia, Fiji Islands, the islets of Micronesia and Melanesia, and extending through New Guinea (U.S. Census Bureau, 2000b). Polynesians are 63.5% of Native Hawaiians and other Pacific Islanders. Polynesians include Native Hawaiians, Samoans, Tongans, and other Polynesians. *Micronesians* are 25% and include Guamanians and other Micronesians such as Marianas Islanders, Marshall Islanders, and Palauans. *Melanesians,* at 6% of this group, includes Fijians and other Melanesians such as Papua New Guineans and Solomon Islanders (U.S. Census Bureau, 2007b).

In 2004, another 1.4 million people identified themselves as both Asian and one or more other races (U.S. Census Bureau, 2007a). Sixty-four percent of the population reporting as Asian with another race were Asian and White, or 881,813 people. High rates of intermarriage between Asians and Whites, particularly among Asian women and White men, explain respondents' report of their biracial heritage. According to Wu (2002), "Among Asian Americans under the age of thirty-five who are married, half have found a spouse of a non-Asian background" (p. 263). In 2000, 138,802 biracial respondents reported they were Asian, Native Hawaiian, and other Pacific Islander; 106,782 were Asian, Black, or African American.

The Chinese are the largest group of Asians, representing 2.8 million, or 23% of the Asian population. In 2000, Filipinos were the second largest group of Asians. As of 2004, Asian Indians represent the second largest group of Asians, at 2.2 million, representing 19% of Asians. Filipinos are the third largest group at nearly 18% with 2.1 million. Sixty percent of Asians are Chinese, Asian Indian, or Filipino. The fourth largest ethnic group among Asians are Vietnamese, who are 10.5% of Asians and whose numbers are 1.3 million. Koreans are the fifth largest Asian group at slightly under the numbers of Vietnamese, 1.2 million and 10.3% of Asians. Although the Japanese were the second group of Asians to enter America, more recent newcomers have exceeded this group in numbers.

Highly concentrated in the West, California alone had 35% of the Asian population. Half of all Asians lived in three states: California, New York, and Texas. The seven other states with the largest Asian populations are New Jersey, 5%; Hawaii, 4.3%; Illinois, 4.2%; Washington, 3.2%; Florida, 2.9%; Virginia, 2.7%; and Massachusetts, 2.3%. Hawaii had the largest Asian proportion in its population in that Asians accounted for more than 40% of the total household population in Hawaii. In 2000, 9 of the 10 cities in the United States with more than 100,000 Asian residents were in California. The Northeast has nearly 18% of the Asian population. Less than 6% (5.7%, 5.6%, and 5.6%, respectively) of the Asian population reside in New Jersey, New York State, and the South.

The median age among Asians of 34.8 years is about 5 years younger than the median age of non-Hispanic Whites, at 40.1 At the turn of the 20th century, the median age was approaching 40 years and was a function of the predominantly adult male migration to the United States from mainland China. Persons between the ages of 18 and 44 are 45.2% of the population, followed by people 45 to 64 at 23.5%. Children under the age of 18 are 23% of the population, with people 65 and older at 8.3% (U.S. Census Bureau, 2007a).

One of the discourses about Asians is that they are foreign-born. Although the majority of Asians are U.S. citizens, the majority of Asian Americans were foreign-born. In 2004, 33% of Asians were native to the United States; 37% were foreign-born, naturalized citizens; and 30.5% were foreign-born, not a citizen. About 63% of Asian aged 5 and older spoke only English at home or spoke English very well. More than 75% of Asians speak a language other than English at home, with most speaking only English at home or speaking English very well. Nearly 75% of Asians were U.S. citizens (61%) or became naturalized citizens (11%). Among Pacific Islanders, 78% were native to America (U.S. Census Bureau, 2007b).

SOCIAL, PSYCHOLOGICAL, AND PHYSICAL HEALTH ISSUES

Compared with the population at large, Asians have higher rates of marriage. In 2004, 62% of the Asian population over the age of 15 had married, compared with 57.3% among Whites. There is also much less divorce among Asians compared with the general population. Rates of divorce are less than half of those in the general population: 4.7% among Asians compared with 10.21% for the total population (U.S. Census Bureau, 2007a). Approximately 10% of Asians are separated, widowed, or divorced compared with about 19% among non-Hispanic Whites. There are interethnic group differences. Asian Indians were most likely to be married, about 69%. People who were biracial (Asian and White) had the highest never-married rates, at 50.5%, as well as higher divorce rates, nearly 7% compared with less than 5% among Asian-only groups.

A different picture exists for Native Hawaiians and Pacific Islanders compared with other Asians. One third of Pacific Islanders had never married in 2004. In addition, about one of every eight Pacific Islanders was separated, widowed, or divorced compared with about one in five of non-Hispanic Whites (U.S. Census Bureau, 2007b). (See Table 7.1.)

In 2004, Asian and Pacific Islander women had higher rates of fertility than White women, with 59 and 78, respectively, births per 1,000 in the past 12 months preceding the survey. About 36% of Pacific Islander women who had given birth were unmarried compared with 8% of Asian women. Again there are group differences. Vietnamese and Asian Indian women have the highest rates of fertility, 74.5 and 72 births per 1,000, respectively. Chinese and Korean women have the lowest rates of fertility, 48.5 and 46 births per 1,000, respectively.

TABLE 7.1   Characteristics of Asians and Pacific Islanders

Characteristic	Asians	Pacific Islanders
Median age	34.8	29.2
Native-born	33%	78%
Total poverty rates	12%	18%
Poverty rates of children	13%	24.5%
Bachelor's degree	48.2%	15.4%
Never married	28%	33.3%
Marriage	62%	53%
Divorce	4.7%	7.3%
Median income	$56,161	$47,442
Median values of homes	$306,000	$230,000
Owner-occupied homes	57.6%	46.4%

The greatest percentage of Asians were in family households at nearly 75%. A nonfamily household is defined as people who live alone or people living with unrelated individuals. Sixty percent of households were married couples, 26% were nonfamily, 9% were female households only with no male present, and nearly 5% were male only with no female present. Unlike with Blacks and Latinos, Asians were not more likely than Whites to live with grandchildren; however, Pacific Islanders were. About 10% of Pacific Islanders were living in the same house with co-resident grandchildren.

In 2006 the poverty rate for Asians was 10.3% (DeNavas-Walt, Proctor, & Smith, 2007), compared with 12.3% for the nation at large. Asian children are more likely to live in married-couple households, although 13.2% of Asian children live in poverty—this is above the national poverty rate. Overall, Asians tend to have higher rates of home ownership at 58% in owner-occupied homes. Koreans were less likely than other Asian groups to own their homes (U.S. Census Bureau, 2007b). Among Asians who own homes, the median value of their homes is $306,000, which is nearly twice the median value of White owner-occupied homes ($154,000).

Not surprisingly, the poverty rate for Pacific Islanders was much higher at 18.1% (U.S. Census Bureau, 2007b). One quarter of Pacific Island children live in poverty. Among White children, the rate is 11% in married-couple households. Pacific Islanders have lower rates of home ownership compared with other Asians, or 46.4%. Among Pacific Islanders who own homes, the median value of their homes is $230,000, which is higher than the median value of White owner-occupied homes ($154,000).

Along with Arabs, Asians are among the most highly educated groups of color in the nation. Among Asians age 25 and older, 85% have graduated from high school. This compares with 83.9% for the general population. Nearly half of all Asians (48.2%) have completed a bachelor's degree. Educational attainment among Pacific Islanders is a very different situation. Among Pacific Islanders age 25 and older, 84% have graduated from high school. Fifteen percent of Pacific Islanders (15.4%) have completed a bachelor's degree (U.S. Census Bureau, 2007a).

One in five Asian adults has an advanced degree compared with 11% of Whites (U.S. Census Bureau, 2000b). Asian Indians, more than any other Asian group, occupy higher percentages of managerial and professional positions. In 1980, 47% of Asian Indians held professional managerial jobs in the United States, compared with 30% of Chinese, 28% of Japanese, and 22% of Koreans. Based on 1997 data, 58% of Americans who descended from the Indian subcontinent (Bangladesh, India, Pakistan, and Sri Lanka) had undergraduate, graduate, or professional degrees (U.S. DHHS, 2001).

Nearly half, or 46%, of Asians are employed in management or professional occupations compared with 38% among non-Hispanic Whites. Nearly 24% of this group work in sales and office occupations, which is similar to non-Hispanic Whites (27%). Comparable to the total in the general population, 15.5% of Asians work in service occupations, and very low numbers of Asians are in construction jobs (4%). Among non-Hispanic Whites, 14% are in service and 10% work in construction jobs.

Sue and Sue (1990) cautioned against acceptance of well-known myths and stereotypes concerning Asians in America as "model minorities" who do not face difficulties

STORYTELLING: Activism and Peace

I met a Black woman recently who was a native of the Solomon Islands, which is east of Papua New Guinea and northeast of Australia in the South Pacific. Soloman Islanders are Melanesians, one of the broad groups of Asian peoples. In 1999, a militia group called the Isatabu Freedom Movement, made up of indigenous Isatabus from Guadalcanal, expelled more than 20,000 Malaitans or people from Malaita. The Malaitans had migrated in search of employment. Many had jobs in the capital, which led to resentment from the indigenous people, the Istabus. The Mailitans formed their own group in response to the ethnic tensions. They were called the Malaita Eagle Force. Over the years, there was unrest, corruption, and instability. This woman became a peace maker. Although it was dangerous to speak to the men, many of whom saw women as subordinate and inferior, she was courageous in her actions, taking her brother with her not only for protection but to have the status of a man with her. This resistance and activism is part and parcel of the experience of the diversity among Asian people worldwide, who are often given hope and ideas by the struggles of people in America. Many young Asians, including the Maori people in New Zealand, were inspired to develop a sense of ethnic pride and self-esteem when leaders in the Black Power movement encouraged African Americans to find empowerment (Avakian, 2002).

that other groups of color experience. (See Storytelling: "Activism and Peace.") The model minority myth also denies the tremendous diversity that exists among individual Asian Americans. According to Takaki (1994),

> Asian-American "success" has emerged as the new stereotype for this ethnic minority. While this image has led many teachers and employers to view Asians as intelligent and hardworking and has opened some opportunities, it has also been harmful. (p. 57)

The model minority cannot be broadly applied. Wong and Halgin (2006) observed that the label cannot acceptably capture "the lives of all Asian Americans subsumed in this panethnic category" (p. 41). The model minority myth interferes with economically disadvantaged Asian American communities receiving the necessary emotional and financial resources and creates division among groups of color as one group is pitted against another (Wong & Halgin, 2006). Some suffer because of unemployment, and some newly immigrated groups, such as Southeast Vietnamese, have very high poverty rates and difficulties with social adjustment due to the trauma they experienced prior to immigration. In fact, Vietnamese Americans have an average family income that is about half that of Asian American Pacific Islander (AAPI) populations as a whole (Byrd & Clayton, 2003).

Pacific Islanders tend to have higher rates of poverty than other Asian groups, with Tongans and Samoans having some of the highest rates (U.S. DHHS, 2001). (See Table 7.1.) Because of autonomous governments with a variety of political relationships with the United States, varying levels of health and health care exist for Pacific Islanders. For instance, Guam has a relatively high level of health care, with the Republic of Belau and the Federated States of Micronesia having older hospitals that provide a "generally poorer level of care" (Byrd & Clayton, 2003, p. 480).

Much of the literature that is available would suggest that Asian Americans, in comparison with the general population, consume less alcohol and drugs (Mercado, 2000). The myth of the model minority fuels this dearth of information. The truth of the matter is that Asians, like other groups, contend with substance addictions as well. There is research to suggest that substance abuse among Asians is on the rise (Zane & Huh-Kim, 1998). To best treat substance abuse issues, Mercado (2000) suggests a family counseling/therapy intervention. Respecting cultural values and understanding the extent of acculturation are critical to treating the client, even if the client is being seen alone (Chang, 2000).

Among refugees, such as Cambodians, Laotians, and the Vietnamese, post-traumatic stress disorder and depression are common given war and poverty. Prime Minister Pol Pot is known for Cambodia's "killing fields," which references an inhumane period of genocide led by the Khmer Rouge, a communist guerilla organization. Between 1975 and 1979, one third of Cambodia's population, or between 1.5 and 2 million Cambodians, were slaughtered. Anti-communists, students, intellectuals, the wealthy, and doctors were considered to be enemies of the state and tragically lost their lives (Avakian, 2002). One study found that Cambodian high school students had symptoms of PTSD as well as depressive symptoms. Among Cambodian adults who had been resettled in Massachusetts, 43% reported the deaths of between one and six children (U.S. DHHS, 2001). This distress was captured as intense sadness that is invisible to other people.

Asians also suffer discrimination on the job, and career choices are skewed because of racial inequities. Educationally, some Asians have problems with the English language on standardized tests, and conflicts exist between American and Asian values. The stereotype of the model minority permeates the culture. Asian students who internalize this myth may find it extremely hard to ask for needed assistance or feel increasingly isolated in their attempts to achieve academic success (Gloria & Ho, 2003).

For some youths, the pressure to succeed academically can cause enormous stress. Chang's (1996) research on coping styles of Asian students is a welcome contribution to the literature, given the stress experienced by many Asian youths. He found in his study of 111 Asian college students and 111 White college students that Asian students used more problem avoidance and social withdrawal than the White students. Also, the Asian students, although more pessimistic in their orientations than the White students, were not less optimistic. Amid the expectation of negative events, the Asian students employed active coping styles.

The concept of talk therapy is foreign to many Asian American clients (Hong & Domokos-Cheng Ham, 2001). Asian Americans may be hesitant to discuss their feelings and problems openly and question the effectiveness of counseling. Some of the same attitudes that discourage Asian Americans from seeking mental health services discourage them, once in therapy, from discussing their problems. In spite of a lack of familiarity with psychotherapy, many Asian Americans might expect quick relief from their symptoms. Deferring to nonprofessionals, elders, and older relatives within the community (Yeh & Wang, 2000) is a way that Asian American communities deal with mental health challenges.

In addition to concerns about traditional coping strategies, there are other reasons that explain the reluctance among Asian Americans to discuss their problems. According to Uba (1994), it is not uncommon for Asian Americans to perceive talking about themselves or disclosing private personal information to a stranger as reflective of low maturity and lack of discipline.

Facility with the English language is one of the factors, from a study of Chinese Americans in the Bay Area of California, found to be associated with a more positive attitude toward help seeking for a nervous or emotional problem (Ying & Miller, 1992). In a study by Lin (1994) of 145 adult Chinese Americans, when qualified ethnic and language-matched therapists were provided, the Chinese Americans were found to stay in therapy as long as the general American public.

According to Dana (2002), "Somatization constitutes an attempt to communicate an experience of bodily symptoms and distress in response to psychosocial stressors often associated with depression and anxiety disorders, or worry and preoccupation with well-being" (p. 37). Research suggests that some groups of Asians may have higher rates of somatoform issues compared with the general population. Headaches are one way in which somatization is manifested.

ACCULTURATION AND EXPERIENCES IN AMERICA

There are differences in the values expressed in Asian cultures and in the United States. Much of this difference, in addition to personality, is related to acculturation. Length of time in the United States, access to resources, facility with the English language, educational level, and employment status are factors that affect adjustment. Other moderator variables include generational status, age, ethnic density of neighborhood, country of birth, kinship structures, and purposes of immigration. According to Berry and Sam (1997), cultural maintenance and contact and participation are important issues that groups and individuals consider in their interpersonal interactions. Two different immigrant streams are associated with huge diversity within the Asian and Pacific Island populations. The first stream represents people from countries that have large populations in the United States and tend to have better health. Included are Chinese, Filipinos, Koreans, and Asian Indians. The second stream consists of lower socioeconomic groups. Many refugees are included in this number (Frisbie, Cho, & Hummer, 2002).

Cultural maintenance refers to cultural identity characteristics that are considered important and for which people strive. **Contact and participation** refers to the extent to which groups deem it important to become involved with other cultural groups or remain primarily among themselves. **Assimilation** is defined as what takes place when persons do not wish to maintain their cultural identity and seek interactions with other cultures. **Separation** refers to what happens when the nondominant group places a value on holding onto their original culture and wishes to avoid interactions with persons from other cultures. **Segregation** is the term used to describe the dominant group's stance with respect to the nondominant group. **Integration** refers to the maintenance of cultural integrity while seeking to participate in the larger social network of a multicultural society. **Marginalization** is defined as little possibility or interest in cultural maintenance and little interest in having relations with others.

Research conducted by Sodowski, Wai, and Plake (1991) with 524 Latino and Asian American students, faculty, and staff at a large midwestern university revealed that Vietnamese were less acculturated into the majority society than were Japanese and Korean Americans. No significant acculturation differences were found among Chinese and Japanese Americans and Asians from the Indian sub-continent.

Prior to arrival in the United States, most Asian immigrants and refugees have primary exposure to their own culture. Upon arrival, cultural adaptation is required, and a relinquishing of native aspects of their culture to function in school and work contexts is part of this process. In addition to the factors cited earlier that affect adaptation, age of migration (before or after the age of 12), reason for migration (economic development or political refuge), and mode of migration (with or without parents or family members) are critical issues (Tsai & Chensova-Dutton, 2002).

Among many Asians, arranged marriages are still practiced. Another practice is that of Asian-born children being adopted by primarily White American parents. During the Korean War, there were growing numbers of children in Korean orphanages. After the passage of legislation that made the adoption process easier, the practice became increasingly common in the 1970s. In addition to Korea, India, Vietnam, the Philippines, and Cambodia experienced upheaval that exacerbated poor living conditions. Vulnerable families relinquished their children for adoption. Between 1989 and 2003, according to the U. S. Department of State, China sent 7,044 children to the United States. Russia was second with 5,865. Third was South Korea at 1,716 (Le, 2008). (See Storytelling: "Mother and Child.")

The successes and creativity of many newly migrated groups from Asia have been attributed largely to the informal network system of valuing the group, being a member of the group, and attending to the needs of others through sharing financial and

STORYTELLING: Mother and Child

A White woman and her husband had adopted a baby from an Asian country. The proud mother was out one day with her child when she was approached by another White woman. Upon seeing the baby, the woman expressed sympathy and said she was "sorry for her child." The mother was confused and said, "I beg your pardon." The stranger said she was sorry that she had a "mongoloid child." The stranger thought the woman's baby was mentally retarded. It had not occurred to her that she was looking at an Asian baby boy and his White mother.

human resources, from employment information to housing, for the betterment of all (Chang, 1996; Sue & Sue, 1990). Among some Asian groups, even among newly arrived immigrants, a substantial number have higher education and extensive career experience. Much of the success in business noted among many Korean Americans can be explained by a system called *kae,* which is similar to the Chinese concept of *woi* and the Japanese system known as *tanomoshi*. These systems enable success-ful people to help newcomers through a lending and borrowing system. In addition, many of the Korean banks in America are under the authority of banks in Korea. In this way, newcomers face less discrimination than would be seen at an American bank (Avakian, 2002).

CULTURAL ORIENTATION AND VALUES

Confucianism, Taoism, and Buddhism underlie many Asian cultural values. Founded in the 5th and 6th centuries B.C. by followers of Siddharta Gautama, later known as Buddha (Avakian, 2002), the basic teachings of Buddhism maintain that there is suffering, the first Noble Truth. Understanding the roots of suffering, the cessation of suffering, and being on the path to refrain from that which causes suffering are also emphasized (Nhat Hanh, 1998). Older than Buddhism is Hinduism, which dates back to 1500 B.C. Hindu beliefs are presented in two sacred books, the *Vedas* and the *Upanishads*. People are ranked into caste systems from the Brahmans or priests to the sundras or peasants and laborers. Confucius, born in about 551 B.C., was China's most influential philosopher. Family loyalty, hard work, and respect for parents and elders were emphasized. In addition to being a philosophy, Taoism was also a religion. It emphasized harmony in nature and contemplation (Avakian, 2002). Such a philos-ophy is seen in the eighth chapter of the *Tao Te Ching:* "In dwelling, be close to the land. In meditation, go deep in the heart. In dealing with others, be gentle and kind. In speech, be true. In ruling, be just. In business, be competent. In action, watch the timing. No fight: No blame" (Lao Tsu, trans. 1972). *We wei,* which literally means "doing nothing" or inaction, was emphasized, but it could also refer to modesty, sim-plicity, and absence of ambition for power (Hong & Domokos-Cheng Ham, 2001).

Values common to Asian ethnic groups include emphasis on harmony in relation-ships, emotional restraint (emotional expression may be interpreted as a sign of immaturity), precedence of group interests over individual interests, extended family, deference to authority, obedience to and respect for parents, emphasis on hard work, fulfilling obligations, and high value associated with education (Sandhu, 1997; Uba, 1994). (See Table 7.2.) According to Ying (2002), "The primary objective of socialization is *tsuo jen* (which literally means to make/become human), that is, to teach a child proper social rules of conduct and submission of personal desires to that of others in order to avoid interpersonal conflict and social disapproval" (pp. 174–175).

Among the Chinese, selflessness, obedience to authority, or deference to the collective unit is a primary value and is manifested in relations with elders or those in

TABLE 7.2   Common Cultural Values among People of Asian Descent

Enryo (reserve, constraint)

Jen (benevolence, personhood, humanity)

Yuan (the influence of past relationships on present social relationships)

Face (concern for maintaining face)

Thrift

Interpersonal harmony in relationships

Ren qing (social favors exchanged in the form of money, goods, information—according to an implicit set of social rules)

Precedence of group interests over individual interests

Educational attainment and achievement

Obediance to authority

Marriage

Emotional self-control

Honor given to elders

Modesty and humility

Patriarchy

authority. Body parts are used to describe intimate relationships. For instance, biological children are referred to as bone and flesh and siblings are referred to as hand and foot (Ying, 2002). The concept of *jen*, or personhood, is emphasized. Jen is a Confucian virtue and is written with two strokes. Each represents one person and refers to responsibility for kin as expressed through respect, loyalty, and love (Dana, 1993).

Among collectivistic people, the self is conceptualized in a social way (Ying, 2002). In the West, the self is primary and exerts influence on expectations concerning psychological well-being. For instance, personal happiness is considered an inalienable right and an essential goal, almost an entitlement. In many Asian cultures, including Chinese but also Southeast Asians, achievement of personal happiness may be a less salient goal and constructed within a collectivistic framework because appraisal of the self is based on external social standards (Tsai & Chensova-Dutton, 2002).

Despite diversity among Asians, certain ethnic groups share some similarities, such as the Chinese and the Japanese. According to Sue and Sue (1995), in both cultures, the families are patriarchal and communication styles tend to be formal, well defined, and flow from the top downward. Relationships among family members are highly interdependent, with one person's actions reflecting on the entire family unit. Control of the children is maintained by fostering feelings of shame and guilt. Although parenting children in this manner may characterize many Asian families, it also applies to other cultures as well. Hsu (1953) observed that the most important issue to Americans is what parents should do for the children; to Chinese, what children should do for their parents is of greatest importance.

Family is given respect and honor. Among the Vietnamese, it is not uncommon for multiple generations to reside collectively in one home. Elders are honored, respected, and cared for because of the importance of family. Compared with other groups, Asian Americans are more likely to live in households comprised of family members only. They are less likely to live on their own and are characterized by low percentages of female-headed households. Pacific Islanders are also more likely to have larger families than most Asian Americans and Americans (Byrd & Clayton, 2003; U.S. DHHS, 2001). According to McFadden (1993), Asians tend to believe that marriage is the most important event that can occur in a person's life and is perceived to be long-lasting, until the end of the person's life, with divorce being considered the greatest possible tragedy that could occur. "Most Asian cultures are historically patrilineal and patrilocal and favor male offspring over female. Consequently, women often grow up feeling devalued and suffer emotional and psychological consequences from these sexist customs throughout their lives" (Chang, 2000, p. 201).

Restraint of emotions represents a value for many Asian Americans. This is not to be confused with the absence of a sense of humor; however, *enryo*, or reserve and constraint, is important and represents a primary mode of communication. Uba (1994) said, "This syndrome may be manifested in a number of ways, as in a hesitancy to speak up in class or to openly contradict a person in a position of authority . . . Another part of the *enryo* syndrome is a modest devaluation of oneself and one's possessions" (p. 18).

Humility is a cultural value, as is the notion of loss of face. Self-effacement and modesty are highly valued and reflect wisdom and function to increase social harmony (Ying, 2002). Leong, Wagner, and Kim (1995) stated that communication styles among Asians allow participants to maintain face. Therefore, direct communication styles, reflective of a Western style and involving confrontation and challenges, tend to be less desirable.

IMPLICATIONS FOR COUNSELORS AND PSYCHOLOGISTS

There is tremendous diversity among Asians with respect to nationality, language, immigration status, educational and occupational levels, and income. Despite this heterogeneity, the myth of the model minority for the entire group of Asians prevails. The disadvantages of ignoring this level of diversity among Asians is problematic. Monolithicizing a group reflects racism in its failure to honor important intragroup differences. In addition, the unique challenges and concerns that do not reflect success and achievement are obscured. Poverty, mental illness, gang affiliation, school failure, and racism are realities for many Asians. The stereotypes of Asians—China doll, Tokyo Rose, savage, mysterious, Charlie Chan, dragon lady, exotic, insolent, diminutive, mail order bride, and little brown brother (Zia, 2000)—are still with us today.

Although the median value of homes among Asians homeowners exceeds that of Whites, there was a time in this country when Asians could not own land. Known as the Alien Land Law, this law prohibited anyone of Asian ancestry from owning land.

Internalized racism was also part of the experience of many Chinese after Pearl Harbor was bombed. Signs were seen posted in stores that announced, "This is a Chinese shop." Some people wore buttons that said, "I am Chinese" or "I hate Japs worse than you do" (Zia, 2000). Despite discourses that Asians are passive or politically safe, Asians have a history of resistance to oppression. The Japanese American Citizens League and the Chinese Consolidated Benevolent Association were centers of organization for equal rights and social justice. In a study investigating the benefits of Asian cultural values to Asian clients in counseling, Kim, Li, and Liang (2002) found that Asian American clients who had high adherence to Asian cultural values, as measured by the Asian Values Scale, perceived greater client–counselor working alliance and counselor empathic understanding than did clients who had low adherence to Asian cultural values. Such values representing related aspects of Asian cultural values included collectivism, conformity to norms, emotional self-control, family recognition through achievement, filial piety, and humility. The authors concluded, "Asian Americans who adhere to Asian cultural values try to be understanding, accommodating, conciliatory, and not directly confrontational, and they expect the same from others" (pp. 351–352). In providing mental health services to Asians, it is imperative to consider acculturation, facility with English, religious and cultural values, generational status, and social supports as part of diagnoses and treatment.

CASE STUDY
Dual Diagnosis

Khanh is a single, 34-year-old graduate student in counseling. She was born in Vietnam and is attending graduate school in the South. She and her family have lived in the United States for 18 years. As part of her counseling practicum, she is assigned Brie, a 23-year-old White female client struggling with body image, an eating disorder, and a recently failed relationship with a woman. Brie is bisexual. Khanh can gather from Brie's body language that she is uncomfortable with having an Asian counselor. Within a 30-minute period, Brie apologized three times for the use of slang and certain English expressions that she assumed Khanh did not understand, given her accent. Khanh assured Brie that she both understands and also uses slang and expressions specific to American culture. The following is an excerpt from one of their sessions.

BRIE: I don't think you understand me.

KHANH: What makes you think I don't understand you?

BRIE: I'm not sure. It's just a sense that I have.

KHANH: Does my accent bother you?

BRIE: I wouldn't say your accent bothers me. Sometimes I have a hard time understanding what you're saying.

KHANH: It's important to me that you understand me. I'm happy to repeat myself when you don't understand me if you would just let me know.

BRIE: Ok. I can do that.

KHANH: Does my accent make it difficult for you to accept me as your counselor?

BRIE: I would like an American counselor.

KHANH: (pause) I will share your concerns with my supervisor. I'm most concerned about you and your needs and how your concerns about our ability to work together may interfere with my meeting your needs. Would you be willing to come for one more session?

BRIE: I agree to come back for one more session.

KHANH: Although we were born in different countries, I had bulimia when I was in my 20s. I share that with you so that you know there are some challenges that you have now that I have also experienced and might understand.

BRIE: That surprises me—that you had an eating disorder. What helped you?

KHANH: I had a really understanding counselor—a White woman who I did not think would understand my situation and would judge me for not being like other Asian women.

QUESTIONS

1. Why might Brie want an "American" counselor?
2. What are Khanh's cultural values that may help her counsel clients who are culturally, racially, and linguistically different from herself?
3. How critical is it for supervisors to have personal and professional awareness of race, racism, and racial identity?
4. Why might Brie have been surprised to hear about Khanh's eating disorder?

DISCUSSION AND INTEGRATION

During the next session, Khanh questioned Brie about her ideal of an "American counselor." Over time, mutual feelings of openness and reciprocity were part of the sessions between Khahn and Brie. Khanh sought help from her supervisor, who helped her realize that for many people, American means White and not foreign-born. Her supervisor also pointed out that it was possible Brie perceived Khanh to be culturally conservative, which would mean her inability to appreciate some of Brie's choices to live on her own, have sexual relationships with women and men, and not communicate with her father. Khanh was initially confused by her supervisor's meaning of conservative. She pointed to Chow (1994), who identified four cultural dilemmas facing Asian American women: (1) obedience versus independence, (2) collective (or familial) versus individual interest, (3) fatalism versus change, and (4) self-control versus self-expression or spontaneity (p. 186). Although it was hard to acknowledge, some of these very forces were operating in Khanh's life, particularly obedience versus independence and the construction

of the self from a collectivistic orientation. She continued to live at home with her parents despite her desire to have a place of her own.

The supervisor helped Khanh appreciate that her client, Brie, may not have thought a foreign-born woman would know much about or be able to relate to bulimia. In addition to the supervision, Khanh relied on her Buddhist beliefs, which helped her operate more from a place of compassion and less from her own ego. At the same time, Khanh was willing to look at her shadow side, which felt angered and dismissed by what she perceived was Brie's racism. Bradshaw (1994) discussed the cultural inconsistency of anger among Asian women in light of the values of deference and meekness.

Khanh began to be more open and accommodating of Brie's needs as well as more open to accepting whatever the outcome was: that Brie may decide she ultimately wanted a different therapist after all, which had more to do with Brie and less about who Khanh was as a capable and multiculturally competent counselor. By not being closed to future consequences in her work with Brie, Khanh found she was more relaxed about therapy with Brie and all of her clients. Brie continued on with Khanh and was able to gain insight into her disordered eating and her role in her relationship conflict.

To address family dynamics with Brie's mother and father, Khanh suggests a genogram going back to three generations within the family. Khanh also recognizes America's obsession with external standards of beauty amid a growing obesity epidemic. Brie is not alone in feeling the burden of this inordinate emphasis on being thin, which translates into being pretty.

Phan and Tylka (2006) conducted research on 200 Asian American women to examine whether several variables and paths included within one empirically supported model of eating disorder symptomatology were supported. More specifically, researchers examined ethnic identity, self-esteem, pressure for thinness, eating attitudes, and body shape. They found that Asian American womens' perceived pressure for thinness slightly predicted their self-esteem and moderately predicted their body preoccupation both directly and indirectly. It was also found that Asian American women's body preoccupation strongly predicted their eating disorder symptomatology. What was most interesting and contradictory to previous research was that ethnic identity actually intensified the pressure for thinness—body preoccupation relation. More specifically, "pressure for thinness and body preoccupation were strongly related for women with high ethnic identity but moderately related for women with low ethnic identity" (Phan & Tylka, 2006, p. 45). It was hypothesized that within collectivism, a value endorsed often by women who have high ethnic identity, Asian American women are more likely to be concerned about how their weight may have an adverse impact on significant others, which can then lead to body preoccupation.

Khanh endorsed collectivism and had a strong ethnic identity, yet to her own surprise, she struggled with disordered eating. Lee (2003) concluded from his research studies on two types of perceived discrimination (minority group discrimination and personal ethnic discrimination) that ethnic identity did not moderate or mediate the negative psychological effects of personal ethnic discrimination or minority group discrimination. He surmised, "it is possible that ethnic identity functions primarily as a psychological asset that contributes to well-being but it does not—in and of itself—protect against the effects of discrimination" (p. 139).

Given Khanh's history with bulimia and that one of her clients has bulimia, her supervisor was concerned about countertransference. Vontress (1986) defined *countertransference* as the reverse of transference. He defined *transference* as psychological transposing. Although positive transference, which refers to fondness, tenderness, and respect, can contribute to a healthy therapeutic relationship, counselors need their own therapy in order to avoid countetransference, which stems from unresolved negative feelings that the clients' transference can stir within themselves. Unresolved issues in counselors can be a source of countertransference. It is important that Khanh had personal therapy where she examined the multiple forces in her life—cultural, familial, and institutional—that contributed to her eating disorder.

SUMMARY

This chapter focused on people of Asian descent. A case study provided insight for counseling, where an Asian counselor was working with a White bisexual female client with an eating disorder who exhibited discomfort with her therapist who was foreign-born, not-White, and had an accent. The therapist's negotiation of the therapeutic relationship required her to examine her own history with bulimia and the meaning of her clients' discomfort with her race and accent. The counselor and clients' multiple identities—gender, ethnic, and cultural—were discussed and considered as dimensions of problem presentation and resolution.

Chapter 8

People of the Middle East and Arab Americans

THE AFRICANS, ASIANS, EUROPEANS, AND ARABS

MUSLIMS AND ARABS: DIFFERENCES AND SIMILARITIES

MIGRATORY PATTERNS FROM THE MIDDLE EAST

DEMOGRAPHY

SOCIAL, PSYCHOLOGICAL, AND PHYSICAL HEALTH ISSUES

CULTURAL ORIENTATION AND VALUES

IMPLICATIONS FOR COUNSELORS AND PSYCHOLOGISTS

CASE STUDY

SUMMARY

The Sun Never Says
The sun never says to the earth,
"You owe
Me"

Hafiz, The Great Sufi Master, from *The Gift*

This chapter profiles Arabs and people of the Middle East. A brief look at history, cultural values, and demographic trends is included. A case study is provided for the integration of material in a therapeutic context.

THE AFRICANS, ASIANS, EUROPEANS, AND ARABS

The Middle East represents a region that encompasses southwestern Asia and northeastern Africa. It spans from Morocco to Pakistan and includes the Caucasus Mountains, which is a mountain system between Europe and Asia (or Eurasia) and between the Black and Caspian seas. Spanning two continents, Africa and Asia, the Middle East is home to the beginning of civilization and all three monotheistic religions. The region's history has been influenced by Persians, Greeks, Roman Empires, Crusaders, Mongols, Mamluks, Ottomans, Europeans, and many others. The majority of the countries that comprise the region have only gained independence in the last century. The Middle East has been transformed by the discovery of oil, the creation of the state of Israel, the revival of Islam, the Iranian Revolution, the Iran-Iraq War, the Arab-Israeli conflict, the Persian Gulf War, and America's wars in Afghanistan and Iraq. The future of the Middle East is uncertain as it struggles to balance the importance of religion, development, and stability in an ever-democratizing global world (Middle East Institute, 2004; Dwairy, 2005).

The term *Arabs* originally applied to the Semitic peoples of the Arabian peninsula. It is now used for populations of countries whose primary language is Arabic. Arabic was named as the sixth official language of the United Nations and is currently ranked as the fourth most widely spoken language in the world. Extremely difficult and grammatically complex, a good command of the Arabic language is highly valued (Dwairy, 2005).

The Arab League of Nation includes 22 countries: Algeria, Bahrain, Comoros Islands, Djibouti, Egypt, Iraq, Jordan, Kuwait, Lebanon, Libya, Mauritania, Morocco, Oman, Palestine, Qatar, Saudi Arabia, Somalia, Sudan, Syria, Tunisia, United Arab Emirates (UAE), and Yemen. According to de la Cruz and Brittingham (2003), "a person is included in the Arab ancestry category if he or she reported being Arab, Eyptian, Iraqi, Jordania, Lebanese, Middle Eastern, Morocaan, North African, Palestinian, Syrian and so on." Some people from these countries may not self-define as Arab, whereas people who identifiy as Arab may not have their country listed. Although Maritania, Somalia, Djiboti, Sudan, and Comoros Island are part of the Arab League of Nations, the 2000 census did not consider people from these countries to be Arab. Groups such as Kurds and Berbers, who are usually not considered Arab, were, included in the U.S. Census definiton of Arab for consistency. Iran, although located in the Middle East, is not one of the countries in the Arab League of Nations. The languages of Iran are Farsi and

Persian. Bedouins are Arabs who reside in Israel and who, until a few decades ago, had lived in the desert in a tribal social system. Now, they reside in small villages (Dwairy, 2004).

The term *Palestinian* refers to people whose ancestors orginated in Palestine prior to the establishment of the State of Israel in 1948. The majority of Palestinians who are Muslims are of the Sunni sect, whereas the majority of Christian Palestinians are Orthodox (Abudabbeh, 1996). Palestinians identify as Arabs and speak a dialect of Arabic that is shared with Syria and Lebanon. Subsequent waves of Palestinian migration prior to the first World War were highly educated and or politically motivated—migrating because of loss of their homeland.

The Arab homeland covers 5.25 million square miles (the United States is 3.6 million square miles). Nearly three quarters, or 72%, of the Arab homeland is in Africa, with 28% in Asia. Long coastlines give it access to vital waterways and include the Atlantic Ocean, the Mediterranean Sea, the Arabian Gulf, the Arabian Sea, the Gulf of Aden, the Red Sea, and the Indian Ocean (Dwairy, 2005). Another way to think about it is that 15% of Muslims live in the Arab world and another 25% in Africa.

MUSLIMS AND ARABS: DIFFERENCES AND SIMILARITIES

Islam is a younger religion than Christianity. It is the second largest in the world following Christianity with more than a billion followers and had its beginnings in the early 7th century (610 A.D.) in Mecca, a town in the western Arabian Peninsula. According to Islamic tradition, God *(Allah)* conveyed to Muhammad, a tradesman, a series of revelations that form the basis of Islam. *Islam* means submission to the will of God and comes from the Arabic word meaning "peace" and "submission" (Dwairy, 2005). A Muslim believes in the Islamic tradition and has submitted himself to Allah and acknowledges Muhammad as His prophet. The Prophet Mohammed called upon people of the Arabian Peninsula to submit to God's will expressed in the Qur'an. The Qur'an represents the "direct instruction from Allah and articulates the message that family members are expected to fulfull rules of behavior and family roles, such as husband, wife, child, etc without dissonance or disobedience" (Hall & Livingston, 2006, p.144). For Muslims around the world it is a way of life requiring absolute submission to the will of God. The Qur'an provides guidance just as the Bible provides guidance to Christians. A large percentage of the Arab world practices Islam, yet there is considerable overlap between Arabic and Muslim cultures (Nassar-McMillan & Hakim-Larson, 2003).

The three main Islamic sects are the Sunni, who comprise about 90 percent of all Muslims, the Shiites, and the Sufis. The Sunni are the largest branch in Islam and are sometimes referred to as the "orthodox Islam." The full name is

Ahlus Sunnah wal-Jamaa'h, which translates to "the people of Summa and consensus." Although a fundamental creed is shared with the second largest division of Islam, the Shi'ite, after the death of Muhammed, there was a split regarding leadership. The Shi'a of Ali, which literally means "the party of Ali," insisted that it was the Prophet's intention for his son-in-law, Ali, to succeed him. The Sunni accept the legitimacy of the first four caliphs or successors to the Prophet. They maintained that the caliph should be elected and did not have to belong to the Prophet's family. Shi'ite legal tradition is generally regarded as the most conservative. Ali's followers insisted that a *caliph*, or imam, be a lineal descendant of 'Ali and his wife, Fatimah' (www.answers.com). There are also numerous small sects and subsects, such as Ahmaddis, Alawites, and Wahhabis, that differ in degrees of orthodoxy and practice. Sawy (2005) discusses the beauty of Islam and refers to it as a peaceful religion, saying there is an "element of poetry in a Muslim's everyday life. One says, 'Allah' or 'ma sha'a Allah' (as God wills) upon seeing something beautiful, like a sunset or a newborn baby" (p. 571).

Five Basic Obligations of Muslims refers to the Pillars of Islam. The first is oral testimony that there is only one God and that Mohammed is his prophet. The second pillar is that ritual prayer must be practiced five times a day with certain words and certain postures of the body. The giving of alms is the third pillar. Keeping a strict fast including no liquid or food from sunrise to sundown during October, the month of Ramadan, is fourth. And the fifth pillar is the holy pilgrimage to Mecca once in a lifetime at a specific time of the year (Dwairy, 2005).

Many of the world's people who consider themselves to be Arabs are also Muslims, but being Arab does not mean the person is Muslim and being Muslim does not mean the person is Arab. Substantial parts of Asia are predominantly Muslim. For example, the largest population of Muslims in the world is in Indonesia, which is the fourth most populous nation in the world. Indonesia is located in Southeast Asia and is not part of the Arabian Peninsula known as the Middle East. In addition, Indonesian, a standardized dialect of the Malay language, is the official language, not Arabic. Yet, Arabic script is used today in Indonesia, Afghanistan, Malaysia, sections of China, and in the Muslim areas of the Philippines and the former Soviet Union. Millions of people throughout Africa and Asia write their languages in the Arabic alphabet. Farsi, the language of Iran, and Urdu, the language of Pakistan and some parts of India, are written in the Arabic script. There are also significant Muslim populations in Europe and the Americas.

One of the dominant discourses in this country is that to be Arab means to be Muslim. However, the term *Arab* is based on a person's language and culture; it is not an ethnic origin (Abudabbeh & Nydell, 1993). The majority of Arab Americans are Christians, not Muslims. Approximately 14 million Arabs follow the Christian faith. Forty percent of Arab Americans are Catholic (Roman Catholic, Maronite, and Melkite), 23% are Orthodox, 23% are Muslim, and 12% are Protestant (American Arab Institute, 2006). The largest Christian denomination in the Middle East is the Coptic Orthodox Church. Orthodox also includes Antiochian, Syrian, and Greek. Lebanon contains the largest Christian population, and nearly half of the population are Christians (Abudabbeh, 2006).

MIGRATORY PATTERNS FROM THE MIDDLE EAST

The first wave of people from the Arab homeland came to the United States between 1890 and 1940. Merchants and farmers emigrated for economic reasons from regions that were part of the Ottoman Empire. Ninety percent of this first wave were Christians from Syria and Lebanon. Lebanese families, like many other Arab families, are "traditionally patrilineal, endogamous, and extended, with wide and complex kin relationships that help to sustain traditional functions of the culture" (Simon, 1996, p. 365). Simon also pointed out, "Identity for the Lebanese does not exist apart from the family. In fact, the proper introduction of a Middle Easterner does not end with the announcement of his name—his family group must also be established" (p. 365).

The second wave came after the World War II, after the creation of the State of Israel in 1948. Unlike the first wave, those coming later were mainly people with college degrees or those seeking to earn them. People came with an Arab identity and were from regions of post-European colonization as well as from sovereign Arab nations. The third wave to the United States came after the 1967 Arab-Israeli war and included people from various Arab countries. Like many immigrants from around the world, people were seeking refuge to escape political unrest from their home countries. Lebanese immigrants and Iraqis following the Gulf War were also included. Nassar-McMillan and Hakim-Larson (2003) maintain that Arab Muslims have a more difficult time assimilating into mainstream society than Arab Christians.

DEMOGRAPHY

Arab Americans number almost 4 million and are one of the fastest growing immigrant groups, mainly due to the war and political unrest in the Middle East. They live in all 50 states; 66% reside in 10 states (Hill, Weglicki, Thomas, & Hammad, 2006). Arab Americans are very diverse geographically, religiously, and linguistically. Arab Americans speak many languages in addition to Arabic, such as Farsi or Persian, Urdu, French, and Kurdish.

In 2000, 1.2 million people reported an Arab ancestry in the United States. This represents an increase of 38% since 1990. Arabs represented 0.42% of the U.S. population in 2000 compared with 0.27% in 1980. More than one third of those reporting an Arab ancestry in 2000 were Lebanese, or 37%. The next largest group was Syrian and Egyptian, at 12% each; however, the number of people with Egyptian ancestry grew by 64,000, the most of any specific Arab ancestry group, increasing from 79,000 to 143,000 between 1990 and 2000. Nearly half a million people (473,863) reported other specific Arab ancestries, with the largest group being Palestinian at 6.1% of the total Arab population. Jordanian, Moroccan, and Iraqi population were at 3.3%, 3.3%, and 3.2%, respectively (U.S. Census Bureau, 2003).

In 2000, people of Arab ancestry were evenly distributed among the four regions of the United States, with 27% in the Northeast, 26% in the South, 24% in the Midwest, and 22% in the West. The five largest concentrations of Arab Americans with populations of 100,000 or more are in New York, Dearborn (Michigan), Los Angeles, Chicago, and Houston. According to the U.S. Census Bureau, 30% of Dearborn, Michigan, is Arab.

SOCIAL, PSYCHOLOGICAL, AND PHYSICAL HEALTH ISSUES

There are variations among Arabs and people of the Middle East as a function of gender, education, level of acculturation, income, phenotype, and geography. For example, life expectancy is lower in poor Arab (e.g., Somalia) and Muslim countries (e.g., Afghanistan) compared with rich Arab (e.g., Kuwait and UAE) and Muslim countries (e.g., Malaysia).

Arab countries have the highest level of extreme poverty in the world, with one out of five people living on less than $2 per day with, Saudi Arabia, Qatar, United Arab Emirates, and Bahrain being wealthy countries. The oil that was discovered in the middle of the 20th century is the main source of wealth.

Although Arabs in America are more likely than the general population to have a college education, two thirds of illiterate Arabs are women. Adult literacy in the Arab world is about 60% compared with 79% in the world at large. Approximately 85% of Arab Americans have a high school diploma, and more than 4 out of 10 Arab Americans have a bachelor's or higher degree—this is compared with 24% of the American average. Twice as many Arab Americans as Americans have postgraduate degrees (Abudabbeh, 2005a).

Nearly two thirds, or 64%, of Arab Americans are in the labor force. Among workers, 42% are in management and professional positions; 31% in sales, office, and administrative support; 12% in service industries; 10% in production, transportation, and material moving; and 5% in construction, extraction, and maintenance (Arab American Institute, 2006). The median income for Arab Americans in 1999 was $47,000 compared with the American median of $42,000. Close to 30% of Americans have an income of $75,000 in contrast to 22% of Arab Americans.

Arab Americans have a tendency to display emotional distress in terms of physical complaints. This somatization may be partially explained by the mind-body connection descriptive of many people from collectivistic cultures. Many Arab Americans come from Middle Eastern countries where tobacco use is high. On average, 45% of the men and 5% of the women in the Middle East smoke cigarettes. Tobacco use by women in the Middle East was traditionally very low, but it is now on the rise. The Middle Eastern nations with the highest adult cigarette-smoking rates include Iraq (40%), Yemen (45%), Lebanon (58%), and Tunisia (60%) (World Health Organization Tobacco Free Initiative, 2005b).

In terms of mental health problems presented clinically by the Arab immigrant population, Abudabbeh and Nydell (1993) describe them as physical abuse, identity confusion, loss of extended family support system, adjusting to a lower social and economic status, intergenerational value conflicts, changes in the role of family members, and parenting problems.

Given that sexuality discussions are regarded as taboo for many people of the Middle East, where does the Arab homeland stand in the fight against HIV/AIDS, where sexual transmission remains one of the primary ways to contract the virus? Estimates by the World Health Organization (WHO) and the joint United Nations program on HIV/AIDS show that HIV prevalence is low in the Middle East and North Africa region (0.2%). The most recent estimate of the number of people living with HIV/AIDS in the Middle East and North Africa is a half million. It has been suggested that the low prevalence of HIV in these regions is linked to Islam and its influence on the behaviors that affect the transmission of HIV (Obermeyer, 2006). Traditional Muslim approaches tend to be conservative; some even regard HIV as divine punishment for deviance, whereas religion is regarded as a protection.

Certain risk factors increase the spread of the epidemic such as unprotected extramarital sex, war, migration, and the population of intravenous drug users who may constitute a "bridge" to the general population. Compared with sub-Saharan Africa, HIV rates in the Middle East and North Africa are relatively low. Low alcohol intake as well as male circumcision may also account for this low prevalence rate. Governments in several countries are breaking the silence and allowing information about prevention and treatment to be disseminated.

A cultural context exists where marriage is universally expected. A high value is placed on virginity, which means unmarried young women are subject to judgment and stigma from health workers if they try to obtain contraception (DeJong & El-Khoury, 2006). Moreover, women are pressured to have children as soon as they marry. Tunisia is cited as the only country that legalizes abortion; however, unsafe induced abortion occurs throughout the Arab homeland.

Following the events of September 11, 2001, many Arabs were personally subjected to discrimination or knew someone who had experienced discrimination because of anti-Arab attitudes. In research with 108 Arab Americans, the constructs of discrimination, self-esteem, and personal control were examined. A direct link was found between perceived discrimination events and psychological distress (Moradi & Hasan, 2004). This study also found that "perceived discrimination events were related to lower levels of perceived control over one's life and lower perceived control in turn was related to lower self esteem and greater psychological distress for Arab American individuals" (p. 425). (See Storytelling: "Racial Profiling.") Arab is often coded for potential Muslim extremist, terror suspect, foreign-born and foreign-looking,

STORYTELLING: Racial Profiling

Her son is now 16. Prior to his arrival into the world in 1991, his mother, a very pregnant African American Christian woman in her last trimester, was dressed in a head scarf and a long coat. As she walked alone down the street, a White man in a business suit quickly approached her. Upon passing her, he stared directly into her face and angrily uttered the words, "Sand Nigger Bitch". He then spat on her. Terrified, she stumbled away as quickly as her swollen body would allow. This impeccably dressed stranger had verbally and physically abused her. Due to her light skin and head wrap, the man assumed she was Muslim and an Arab, which meant something to be hated during America's involvement in the Persian Gulf War. There are countless stories like this that happen to Latinos, African Americans, Asians, Indians, and Arab Americans since 9/11, illuminating the terror and threat surrounding groups who are marked and at times targeted.

oppressive toward women due to patriarchy and sexism, and non-Christian. Research suggests that such discourses are damaging and affect the psychological well-being of Arab Americans, who represent an understudied group. As multicultural competence is developed through workshops, classes, supervision, and continuing education, clinicians will hopefully become mindful of their proximity to these and other discourses.

CULTURAL ORIENTATION AND VALUES

According to Abudabbeh (2005a), the Arab family can be described as "patriarchal, pyramidcally hierarchal with regard to age, sex, and extended" (p. 427). (See Table 8.1.) Communication styles are restrained and formal, making it difficult for an Arab client in therapy to disclose personal feelings and problems to someone outside of the family. Persons who are subservient to authority by virtue of age or gender communicate accordingly. In terms of communication between parents and children, Abudabbeh also says that children respond to parental authority by censoring themselves, crying, or withholding information. An Arabic saying goes, "to satisfy God is to satisfy parents" (Hall & Livingston, p. 144). For the majority of Arab people, the family is the primary means of support. Men have specific duties toward their wives and children. Similarly, wives are given instructions regarding the proper treatment of their husbands and children. A collectivistic orientation prevails in that the good of the family is elevated above the fulfillment of personal and individual needs and wishes. Talking negatively about the family is unacceptable. Sexuality is a taboo subject (Abudabbeh, 2005a).

TABLE 8.1   Common Cultural Values among Arab Americans

Hospitality and generosity in giving and spending

Respect for elders and parents

Wealth and preeminence of male children

Subordination of women to men

Modesty and privacy

Intensive religiosity

Marriage

Group values over individual interests and career

Equality of all human beings

Health and strength

Communication patterns dictated by authority, age, and gender

Family cohesion

Loyalty

Cultural values recognized by the Qur'an include hospitality and generosity in giving and spending, respect for elders and parents, wealth and preeminence of male children, subordination of women to men, modesty, intensive religiosity, equality of all human beings, and health and strength (Hall & Livingston, 2006). In addition, final authority rests with the father. Individualistic pursuits in the West, such as when and where to go to graduate school and who to marry, are seen as selfish. Privacy is primary and is connected to honor and the good name of the family. Family structures are often formal and hierarchical, in that deference to elders and males is practiced. Because of the central place of family, going outside the family to seek help for personal problems may be seen as disloyal or a threat to group honor. There is a concern of being seen as *manjun* or crazy (Shiraev & Levy, 2004).

According to Dwairy (2004), women's treatment is inferior in the Arabic world. More specifically, their freedom is limited as is their mobility, social behavior, and decision making. Currently, women are not allowed to drive in Saudi Arabia. Domestic violence at the hands of brothers, husbands, and fathers is a reality for many. In countries struggling to keep their integrity because of war, famine, upheaval, and corruption, mental health needs are not a priority for women or men (Souter & Murthy, 2006).

Traditional Islamic law allows men four wives; however, polygyny is rare in modern Arab societies. Men are also instructed by the Qur'an to not marry more than one woman unless he is able to treat the wives equally. Tunisia forbids the practice of polygyny, whereas some Arab countries require the man to secure a court's permission to take on a second wife, which is the case in Iraq. In some countries, such as Lebanon and Morocco, a woman can insist on a premarital contract that allows her to divorce her husband if he decides to marry a second wife (Abudabbeh, 2005a).

IMPLICATIONS FOR COUNSELORS AND PSYCHOLOGISTS

The Western view of the nuclear family is limiting for many Arabs and other groups of color in that there is a cultural tendency to separate the self into discrete categories. Interventions with Arab clients need to be considered within the context of the family, the extended family, community, and even tribal background (Al-Krenawi & Graham, 2000). Clients may even expect the therapist to provide them with solutions to their problems and see the mental health provider as an authority figure. Treatment can be enhanced if the therapist is willing to relinquish traditional approaches (Abudabbeh, 2005a). Therapists are encouraged to use didactic and structured therapies, calling other family members personally if they refuse to present for therapy, and be willing to accept gifts and invitations to their home. Refusal may be perceived as rude. Therapists should also remember that some topics are taboo, such as sexual problems or homosexuality. Flexibility to accommodate the client and the family's needs is an important therapeutic skill. Among Arab Americans, distrust of outsiders is not uncommon. Many Middle Eastern clients turn to fortune tellers, priests, imams, physicians, and Koranic healers for assistance with mental health issues (Nassar-McMillan & Hakim-Larson, 2003).

Informality is an aspect of Western culture. For example, children and adults are on a first-name basis. Some Arab clients as well as members from White European groups may be put off by a casual air that can feel disrespectful. Al-Krenawi and Graham (2000) maintain that "an assessment of the client's personal background and level of acculturation will alert the sensitive practitioner to potential cultural conflicts with regard to treatment" (p. 12). Among first-generation immigrants who are attempting to adjust to a new environment, acquire a new language, and deal with a host of internal and external demands, the stress may be much greater than previously thought, with chronic acculturation stress having enormous psychological implications. Finally, an Islamic concept of predetermination or fate can make primary prevention a challenge (Nassar-McMillan & Hakim-Larson, 2003).

CASE STUDY
A Nonreturning Client

Adia Fahid is a 36-year-old Egyptian Muslim woman living in Detroit. She is a registered nurse and the only child of her parents who immigrated to the United States when Adia was a teenager. Her parents were originally from Palestine and left there for Egypt shortly after Israel became a state in 1948. Adia has been divorced for nearly a year from her husband.

Although her marriage was arranged by her parents, there were irreconcilable differences, such has her ex-husband's excessive drinking, that drove Adia out of the marriage. She has been living with her parents since the divorce. Actually, she has the same bedroom she had when growing up under her parents' roof. Adia enjoys her career as a health professional in a large hospital; however, she struggles with being single. Adia desires children and her parents also desire grandchildren from her. Upon the suggestion of a colleague at work over a 2-year period to see this "amazing therapist," Adia reluctantly presents for therapy at a private practice to discuss her shame about her troubled, and eventually failed marriage and her ex-husband's alcohol addiction. Her future feels uncertain, and as a result, she has growing concerns about being single and never having children. These are issues she wants to discuss. She has been having heart palpitations and has felt dizzy and has noticed shaking in her hands. She has also been plagued by headaches and has difficulty relaxing.

Adia's therapist is Sara, a 35-year-old biracial (Chinese and White American) counseling psychologist who was born in the states but whose maternal grandparents immigrated from China. Her father's family is from the Northeast. Sara's specialty is the empowerment of women. During the initial intake, Sara queries Adia about her living situation. Adia indicates that she resides at home with her parents. Sara asks, "Do you struggle with not having privacy?" Adia looks at Sara curiously upon hearing the questions and indicates that privacy has not been a problem. Sara then listens to Adia discuss her 5-year marriage and the difficulties with her ex-husband's drinking problem. Sara asks if Adia went to AA—Adia is unfamiliar with this expression and asks Sara to explain AA. Eventually Adia shares with Sara her desire to remarry and have children. She also mentions that she lives at home. As Sara listens patiently to Adia discussing her intense desires for a family, her concerns about getting older and not being able to conceive, and her parents' aging as well as wanting grandchildren, Sara warmly but firmly confronts Adia and asks, "Can you help me understand how you expect to date men while living with your parents? A growing number of women in America are single parents and some even conceive on their own. Have you ever considered artificial insemination with donor sperm?" Adia is rather taken aback by the question and explains to Sara that living at home with her parents is not a problem for her and is an expectation of her parents given that she is now single. Adia had never considered parenting on her own, particularly with reproductive technology, and the thought is upsetting to her. After an awkward silence, Sara asks, "Don't single women from your culture live alone?" Adia replies, "Not if they come from good families." Adia decides not to return for therapy with Sara and instead plans to look for a Middle Eastern therapist. Adia is struck by Sara's directness and begins to feel that she has been disloyal to her family for talking about her personal problems outside of her family and with a perfect stranger.

QUESTIONS

1. What are Adia's cultural dimensions that influenced her problem presentation?
2. What are Sara's cultural assumptions that influenced her conceptualization of Adia's issues?

DISCUSSION AND INTEGRATION
The Client, Adia

Adia's identity and orientation to her problems have been shaped by multiple influences. These include her nationality, gender, immigration status, religion, education, personality, and acculturation level. To see Adia holistically, it is imperative that Sara not define Adia by their commonalities: they are both young, educated, heterosexual, and able-bodied women. Being a Muslim woman from a collectivistic and pyramidic culture that often expects young women to stay at home until they marry, and even after they marry and divorce, is not consistent with a Western and individualistic framework where young women are encouraged to do what they choose and assert their independence from parents. A person from a collectivist culture is likely to define him- or herself "in an interdependent fashion; the self may vary across situations or contexts. Rather than emphasizing personal distinctiveness, this person is likely to stress his or her similarity to a group, view roles and obligations to a group as central aspects of self definition, and value restraint and harmony" (Enns, 1994, p. 206). Adia's actions honor not only the expectations of her parents but of her entire cultural context, even if she is no longer living in Egypt with her family and has never lived in Palestine where her parents' values about family and womanhood were largely formed. At the same time, divorce rates have risen in Arab countries and certainly among Arabs in America. Adia's therapist could help her appreciate that although not ideal, divorce is preferable to being in a marriage that is lonely and unhealthy, which can be expected when the other partner is addicted to substances. There are choices available to Adia in the 21st century and in America that would not be available to women who existed under similar circumstances in the Middle East and other parts of the world.

Adia's insomnia, irritability, and loss of appetite could be an indication of a mood disorder. Her uncertainty about the future is a source of stress. She needs the skills of a good therapist to help her reframe her situation. For example, Adia questions her decision to leave her marriage given that she is now single and without children. Yet, would Adia be better off in an unhealthy marriage with a partner who, due to his own addictions, was not fully present as a husband and would be impaired as a father to any offspring they might have had? At the same time, her choice to marry her husband was in keeping with the traditions of her culture and family. Muslim law allows a woman to be contracted for marriage by her guardian. In most cases, this is the woman's father (Abudabbeh, 2005a). Adia married at age 25; the more education a woman has, the older she is likely to be when she marries.

Adia may need help in sorting out her emotions associated with her decision to marry this particular man. Were their signs that would have informed her that he was addicted prior to the marriage? What did she not see, and how can she use this lesson in the future as a means of wisdom? As a woman—and an Arab woman—Adia has been socialized to see herself within the context of her familial relationships and to respect and honor the wishes of her parents and culture at large.

It is not surprising that Adia had such reservations about going to seek help. Al-Krenawi and Graham (2000) identified that clients of Arab origin tend to have a negative view of mental health service delivery and may even mistrust it. Unlike an individualistic frame of reference that privileges mastery over nature and control, many Arab clients tend not to see the origins of illness from a biomedical point of view but rather as stemming from an external locus of control. The intervention of supernatural elements such as spirits and angels is a belief held by some within the culture as well as a belief in fate.

The Counselor, Sara

There are several mistakes that Sara made during the first session. Primarily, she did not see Adia as a person from a collectivistic culture where group needs are held above those of the individual. Consequently, the therapeutic event was hampered by Sara's challenges with multicultural competence.

Viewing Adia from a place of disadvantage because she appears, from a Western woman's perspective, compliant and obedient, does not benefit Adia. There is strength in her commitment to tradition, family, and honor.

Although both Adia and Sara are women of color with an immigrant history, there are important differences, largely as a function of acculturation. It would help Sara to know where Egypt is and to understand aspects of Arab American culture regarding family roles and adult children's responsibilities to their parents.

Immigrants come to the United States with the same dreams as people born in the United States—to have access to economic opportunity and to raise their families in peace. Devastation of a homeland compels people, in search of a different and better life, to leave their homes. For Adia's family and other Palestinians, their homeland was taken from them. Seeing Adia whole means attending to visible and invisible aspects of her identity: a Muslim woman from a traditional and collectivistic culture that for Adia is not synonymous with oppression.

SUMMARY

This chapter focused on Arab Americans and people of the Middle East. A demographical snapshot was provided and included information about the Arab homeland, distinctions between Muslims and Arabs, religion, and the most populated areas where Arab Americans are from and now reside. The three dominant waves of immigration were discussed as were the factors contributing to immigration. A detailed case study was included that featured a clinician's cultural frame that did not make room for the client's. Emphasis was on clinical skills in working with people from the Middle East and/or Arabs.

Part Three
Converging Identities

Chapter 9

Converging Race

People, I just want to say, you know, can we all get along?

Rodney King

Race intersects with other dimensions of identity and across situations and contexts. For most clients, and for some people of color, race does not exist as a source of clinical exploration. Throughout this chapter, racial identity theory is discussed. The discussion expands race beyond the limiting and essentializing domains of phenotype and skin color.

THE SOCIAL CONSTRUCTION OF RACE

Historically, the multicultural counseling and psychology literature has emphasized race. This is understandable considering both the legacy and current reality of racism in America and the power that people give to racial differences to privilege, stratify, and stigmatize. Omni and Winant (2006) argued that although particular meanings, myths, and stereotypes about race can and indeed change, "the presence of a system of racial meanings and stereotypes, of racial ideology, seems to be a permanent feature of U.S. culture" (p. 23).

Written predominantly by heterosexually identified and racially diverse men, the initial writings on cross-cultural counseling and psychology emphasized race, ethnic, and cultural identities. As U.S.-born women and people of color, racially and ethnically diverse immigrants, transgendered people, gay people, and people with disabilities began writing from their personal and clinical experiences, gender, sexual, and disability identities were added to the literature. Increasingly, a much needed emphasis on spirituality is found. This expanded focus on disability, spirituality, sexuality, and socioeconomic class is crucial to a more integrated cultural paradigm.

To what extent are recently added identities perceived to trespass on the rightful terrain and turf of race and ethnicity? It is important to ask if and what the legitimate and perceived illegitimate dimensions of diversity are. Convergence asks that we honor race and ethnic identities in our clients while simultaneously incorporating other identities that are just as legitimate in the never-ending process of meaning-making (Robinson-Wood, in press).

Within the discourse of diversity, who is included? The current discourse suggests that it is not White people. Although whiteness is unremarkable and unexamined (Newman, 2007), it is against whiteness that discussions about diversity occur. Lipsitz (2005) said "whiteness is everywhere in American culture, but it is very hard to see . . . As the unmarked category against which difference is constructed, whiteness never has to speak its name, never has to acknowledge its role as an organizing principle in social and cultural relations" (p. 402).

When White people choose to get up close to their skin color privilege, they are perceived by other Whites as well as some people of color as noble and exalted in ways that people of color are not when they tackle similar issues. The discourse is that Whites are special when they challenge racism, particularly because they do not have membership in the group, which is usually the target of racism—people of color. It is presumed that people of color would naturally focus on race, women would logically be interested in gender, and gay and lesbian people would devote their time and attention to sexuality. Regardless of the constellation of our identities and membership in privileged groups, a concern about social justice is a reflection of commitment to diversity.

How do discourses about whiteness and other race discourses show up and affect the profession, our students, clients, and clinicians? Where do White people who are not gay, female, or disabled go to explore their whiteness? More importantly what is the motivation for doing so? Without being named in the dialogue, White people who do not have a marginalized identity are given a message that it is not necessary for them to be engaged in and embraced by the work of diversity. We know this to be untrue.

Despite the tremendous heterogeneity among racially similar groups and homogeneity across different racial groups, race functions as a master status in society. As a social construction, race has the power to eclipse other identities that are just as potent to identity construction. Race, then, is not only a master status, it is a grand-master status.

The social construction of race is sociopolitical and looms large. Racial categories contribute to race labeling. **Race labeling** is a function of phenotype and skin color characteristics to assign people to categories that are castelike in nature. **Race** typically refers to appearances, such as skin color, hair type (straight, curly, kinky), skin hue, eye color, stature, body size, nose, eyes, and head shape. Clearly, these characteristics alone do not accurately assign a particular racial classification or negate the larger biological similarities that homo sapiens are destined to share.

Representations of race are used by police, mortgage lenders, judges, teachers, employers, potential suitors, health care professionals, and the public at large to categorize people into racial groups. Socially constructed discourses about race and individual and institutional proximity to discourses contributes to differential treatment. Compared with Whites within a similar income bracket, Blacks and Latinos are given loans with higher interest rates and are not provided the same quality of health care treatment. In sum, race and ethnicity discourses affect the nature of people's daily experiences. (See Table 9.1.)

At the time in U.S. society when the U.S. Census Bureau listed five races, to be *colored* (Black or mulatto) was not just a source of difference. Race functioned as a status variable. More specifically, the experience of being "colored" meant no voting rights, no educational access to predominantly White institutions, inexistent or woefully inadequate health care, extreme vulnerability to being lynched, and no legal protection under the law. (See Storytelling: "Race and Dangerousness.") Yet, the mere classification of race was not solely responsible for differential treatment. Attitudes about race were pivotal to the creation of a social structure in which institutional policy bestowed privilege and conferred disadvantage on persons because of race (Cornell & Hartmann, 1997; McIntosh, 1988; Pinderhughes, 1989). The 2000 census, for the first time, enabled people to select more than one race as a way of describing themselves. Of the 282 million Americans who responded to the 2000 census, 2.4% indicated that they belonged to more than one race—that is nearly 7 million people.

TABLE 9.1 Dominant Race and Ethnicity Discourses

Whites	Blacks and Maori	Arabs	Latinos	Asians
Upper middle-class	Low-income/poor	Wealthy	Low-income/poor	Successful
Qualified	Special affirmative action admit	Dangerous	Lots of children	Model minority
Oblivious about Whiteness; unsure allies in ending racism	Emotionally unrestrained (angry, loud)	Conservative, suspicious	Brown (monolith, e.g., Mexicans)	Emotionally restrained (quiet, not angry like Black people and Latinos)
Smart, capable, successful	Not intelligent as Whites, Asians; Blacks "sound or act White" if articulate	Intelligent; studious	Non-English-dominant and in need of remediation	Brilliant in math and science; smarter than White people
Benficiaries of God's grace	Spirituality among women; dangerous-ness among men	Muslim extremists	Catholics	Buddhists
Hardworking	Gang bangers among youth	Terror suspect	Gang member	Studious, hardworking
Normal Americans	Diverse; urban	Foreign-born	Foreign-born	Foreign-born
Necessary	Lazy; oppressed	Women as oppressed	Illegal/immigrant	Scientists
In-charge, powerful	Great athlete; good dancer; fine entertainer	Sexism among men	Sexism among men	Exoticism among women

STORYTELLING: Race and Dangerousness

My husband and I had just arrived in South Africa. As we drove to our lodging in Hout Bay, I noticed a lot of rolled wire on buildings. I naively said to myself, "Boy, there are a lot of jails here." After seeing the barbed wire everywhere, I soon understood that these fortified buildings were not jails, they were people's very large and protected homes. Upon arriving at our lodging, the owner—a White man—warmly greeted us as we were buzzed though a secure gate. He took us inside the apartment, which had a deadbolted door in addition to a steel-grated gate, and explained to us how to arm the alarm system. Finally, he informed us that a guard would be outside of the apartment every night. I asked why there was so much focus on security. He indicated that there were some "baddies," mainly from the townships nearby. The townships are in full view as soon as you leave the Cape Town airport. The residents of these crudely erected townships are primarily Black South Africans, many from the Eastern Cape looking for work and a better life, as well as African immigrants from Zimbabwe, a northern neighboring country. Since 1994, South Africa has been led by the Black-run

African National Congress, which seeks to address the historical discrimination against Black Africans. While advancements have been made and are in the making, the color caste system is firmly in place and manifested in educational attainment, housing quality, income, and occupational stratification.

In an effort to address racial and gender inequity, affirmative action was created through the provision of opportunity for groups that had been targets of historical discrimination. Takaki (1994), a scholar on race and ethnicity, stated that:

> Affirmative action is actually designed to address the legacy of past racial discrimination and existing inequality by training and identifying qualified individuals of excluded racial minorities and allowing them greater access to equality and opportunity in education and employment. (p. 7)

That affirmative action seeks to impose quotas, which results in unqualified people (meaning people of color and women) taking jobs away from those who are qualified, meaning White males, is a myth. The goal of affirmative action was to encourage college admissions and employers to create opportunity for people of color, given their exclusion throughout history and in current-day America. Eventually, this provision extended beyond racial classification to include gender, sexual orientation, physical disability, and religion.

RACE AND SCIENCE

A substantial portion of the dialogue about race includes conceptual frameworks that attribute inferior yet inherent biological deficiencies to African and Semitic people. In October 2007, Dr. James Watson, a 1962 Nobel Prize recipient for his role in discovering the structure of DNA, found himself in trouble for making statements that were interpreted as racist. He stated that he was "inherently gloomy about the prospect of Africa because all our social policies are based on the fact that their intelligence is the same as ours, whereas all the testing says not really" (Nugent, 2007). Watson later apologized for his remarks.

Charles Darwin's (1859) work *The Origin of Species by Means of Natural Selection* was used to support the genetic intellectual superiority of Whites and the genetic inferiority of non-Whites, who were referred to as the "lower races." There are claims regarding racial purity and racial superiority, but these are bogus and represent a false hope (Cooper, 2002). Everyone comes from the same source (Zuckerman, 1990). Still, outdated racial categories such as Negroid (Black), Mongoloid (Asian), and Caucasoid (White) remain. Human beings are products of migratory patterns and world conquests throughout the centuries; thus, the argument of a pure race does not exist (Dobbins & Skillings, 1991).

The recently completed Human Genome Sequencing Project has confirmed what scientists have known for a very long time— humans do not fit into the biological criteria that define race. The widely held belief in the biological differences between racial groups is simply incorrect (LaVeist, 2002). "Any way you measure, the amount of divergence between people is essentially zero," according to Joseph L. Graves, an evolutionary biologist. He went on to say that "the scientific case for the nonexistence of human race is overwhelming" (Genetic research confirms, 2003).

As early as 1870, the U.S. Bureau of the Census divided the U.S. population into five races: White, Colored (Black), Colored (mulatto), Chinese, and Indian (Root, 1992). Since this time and in even the present day, controversy among biologists, anthropologists, and other scholars has surrounded the topic of number of races.

For instance, Gossett (1963) recognized the diversity of opinion and observed the following:

> Linnaeus had found four human races; Blumenbach had five; Curvier had three; John Hunter had seven; Burke had sixty-three; Pickering had eleven; Virey had two "species," each containing three races; Haeckel had thirty-six; Hurley had four; Topinard had nineteen under three headings; Desmoulins had sixteen "species"; Deniker had seventeen races and thirty types. (p. 82)

Zuckerman (1990) sought to clarify misconceptions surrounding racial similarity and difference. He reported that, in his analysis of 18 genetic systems (blood groups, proteins, and enzymes) in 40 populations within 16 subgroups around the world, "the major component of genetic diversity is between individuals in the same tribe or nation; it accounts for 84% of the variance. Of the remaining variance, 10% is accounted for by racial groupings and 6% by geographic regions" (p. 1300). The existence of definable groups or races is not self-evident although human variation is (Cooper, 2002).

Alan Goodman, dean of natural science at Hampshire College, said that depending on which trait is used to distinguish races, "you won't get anything that remotely tracks conventional race categories" (cited in Begley, 1995, p. 67). Spickard (1992), a scholar on biracial identity, argued, "The so-called races are not biological categories at all. Rather, they are primarily social divisions that rely only partly on physical markers as skin color to identify group membership" (p. 17). (See Storytelling: "Across the Pond Discourses.") Scientists studying the human genome announced recently that "the DNA of human beings is 99.9 percent alike, meaning that no matter what the color of our skin, when you look at humans on the genetic level, we are indistinguishable from one another" (*Race and the human genome*, 2004).

STORYTELLING: Across the Pond Discourses

I was in New Zealand recently presenting my research on White mothers of non-White children. Half my sample is from New Zealand. It dawned on me while preparing my presentation that many, if not all, of the discourses associated with being Black applied to the Maori, the indigenous people of New Zealand. I shared my observation with the audience and a hush fell over the room followed by head nods and conversation. The audience agreed that discourses associated with Black people in American were "spot on" to the Maori. Discourses are an outgrowth of the social construction of race and are not specific to the United States. The question we have to think about is why there are so many similarities between these two groups of color with so much water between them.

ORIGINS OF RACIAL GROUPS

Considerable uncertainty surrounds racial origins. Rogers (1967), a historian, wrote that "for us of the present day, the earliest history of all peoples and nations is lost in a fog" (p. 21). Agreement among reputable historians and archaeologists is that the color of primitive humans was Black. Zuckerman (1990) concurred and wrote, "Although there is considerable speculation on the origin of races, little can be proved other than that a species, *Homo sapiens,* gradually evolved from its predecessor *Homo erectus* about 200,000 years ago in East Africa and spread through Africa and Eurasia" (p. 1297). It had been thought until recently that Homo habilus was a direct ancestor of Homo erectus, but evidence shows they were sister species, living side by side. For about 500,000 years, Homo habilus and Homo erectus co-existed side by side. A 1.5-million-year-old skull and jaw bone found in Kenya have given rise to a rewriting of early man/woman.

Early humans are thought to have been of "small stature, probably from four and a half to five feet tall. Their nearest living descendants are believed to be the Bushmen of South Africa; the Mincopies of the Andaman Islands off the coast of India; the hill-folk of Southern India; the Tapiro of New Guinea; and the Negritos of the Philippines" (Rogers, 1967, pp. 28–29).

Given that the origins of the human race are Black, the White race is a function of lack of pigmentation, lost over time because it was not needed in cold environments. Sergi, of the University of Rome, stated that European man was African man, *Eur-African,* transformed by European environmental effects. There are three categories of *Eur-African:* "(a) the African with red, brown, and black pigmentation, (b) the Mediterranean or brunette complexion, inhabiting the great basin, including part of Northern Africa . . . and finally, (c) a Nordic variety of blond skin and hair, blue or gray eyes, most universally represented as Scandinavia, North Germany, and England" (Rogers, 1967, pp. 29–30).

RACIAL AND ETHNIC IDENTITY DEVELOPMENT

The importance of and a search for racial and cultural understanding is a tenet of racial identity development. Nonetheless, the need to develop a racial identity is coupled with the oppression of racism (Gillem, Cohn, & Throne, 2001), wherein stigma is attached to people of color and privilege is embodied in whiteness.

Racial identity theory assumes that individuals at early levels of development have the potential to change over time as they encounter dissonance to existing cognitive schema (Robinson, 1999). The models reflect movement and change over time. By integrating racial identity with a discussion of race, a focus is placed on development, an achieved characteristic, and not solely on skin color, an immutable one.

Until recently, within the past 15 years, the racial identity development literature has focused primarily on White, Black, and other monoracial groups. Helms's (1995) work on a model of racial identity for people of color and the earlier racial/cultural identity development model (originally called the minority identity development model) by Atkinson et al. (1983) are exceptions. A problem with traditional racial identity models is their failure to include people who are biracial and/or multiracial. Chapter 10 is devoted to an in-depth discussion of biracial and multiracial issues with a goal of becoming familiar with models of racial identity for people with more than one racial identity. In addition, a focus on identity moves the discussion of race beyond the narrowness of phenotype traditionally associated with race.

Experiences with racism differ among groups of color and within groups of color. A number of factors may moderate the experience of racism for people of color such as physical appearance or skin color hue and class markers (e.g., income, occupation, country of origin, and facility with the English language).

Pieterse and Carter (2007) conducted research wirth 220 Black American men, recruited primarily from barbershops in New York and Washington, DC. The purpose of the study was to examine the influence of perceived racism-related stress on psychological health and to explore the predictive quality of racism-related stress on psychological health when controlling for general life stress. All of the men reported experiencing some type of racist incident in the prior month and year. Although racist events were stressful, racism-related stress did not seem to influence the well-being of working-class men. The researchers concluded that for Black men in particular, "social mobility encompasses hidden costs, one of which could be a greater sensitivity to experiences of racism and discrimination" (p. 106).

Ancis, Sedlacek, and Mohr (2000) studied 578 African American, Asian American, Latino, and White college student responses to a questionnaire assessing perceptions and experiences of the Campus Cultural Climate Questionnaire (CACQ). This scale has 100 statements regarding campus climate. The 11 factors include racial tension, fair treatment, cross-cultural comfort, racial pressures, comfort with own culture, and lack of support. The researchers found racial differences among respondents. African American students reported more negative experiences in comparison with Asian American, Latino, and White students. More specifically, Black students experienced "greater racial-ethnic hostility, greater pressure to conform to stereotypes, less equitable treatment by faculty, staff, and teaching assistants, and more faculty racism than did the other groups" (p. 183). The Asian American and Latino students reported experiences of stereotyping and prejudice. They indicated limited respect and unfair treatment by faculty, teaching assistants, and students and pressure to conform to stereotypes. Compared with other racial groups, Latinos experienced the least racism and a campus climate relatively free of racial conflict. White students reported less racial tension, few expectations to conform to stereotypic behavior, an experience of being treated fairly, a respectful and diverse campus climate, and the most overall satisfaction.

ETHNIC IDENTITY

Because there are conceptual differences between ethnicity and race, it makes sense for there to be a difference between racial identity and ethnic identity. *Representations of race* typically refer to phenotype or genetic heritage, whereas *ethnicity* is defined as sociocultural heritage. There has not traditionally been a difference in the psychological literature between racial and ethnic identity. Recently, Cokley (2005) argued that confusion exists among racial identity, ethnic identity, and Africentric beliefs. Ethnic identity refers to the extent to which a person identifies with his or her ethnic group—"it is the meaning, strength, and salience of one's ethnic identity" (Cokley, 2005, p. 517).

In the early days of ethnic identity, Phinney (1990) acknowledged that there was no widely agreed upon definition of ethnic identity. At the same time, the components of ethnic identity include self-identification as a group member, a sense of belonging to the group, attitudes about group membership, and ethnic involvement (social participation, cultural practices, and attitudes) (Phinney, 1990).

Ethnicity is often presented as a subset or is subsumed under race, although people can be of the same ethnicity while representing different races. An example is Dominicans, an ethnic group. There are dark-skinned Dominicans whose ancestors came from Africa, whereas some Dominicans' ancestors were African and also Spanish and/or Indian. People can be from the same race and have different ethnicities. There are people of African descent who are Nigerian; some are Cape Verdean, some are Jamaican, whereas others are U.S. born.

At adolescence, ethnic identity has particular relevance given the pressure of peer groups and the upheaval associated with identity search across multiple levels of identity, including sexuality, gender, and race. In her study of 669 American-born African American, Latino, and White high-school students, Phinney (1997) found that ethnic identity was clearly an important contribution to an adolescent's sense of self and that this finding was consistent across ethnic groups. Among Black and Latino teens, being an American was not closely tied to the sense of self. American identity had no contribution to their self-esteem. For White students, however, ethnic identity and American identity were strong predictors of global self-esteem. Many African American and Latino teens may feel ambivalent about being American given their uncertainty along the meaning of American and the discourses about American actually referring to White people. (See Table 9.1.)

A challenge with the concept of ethnic identity is its confusion with acculturation. *Acculturation* "deals broadly with changes in cultural attitudes, values, and behaviors that result from contact between two distinct cultures" (Phinney, 1990, p. 501). In other words, acculturation speaks to changes that occur over time when two cultures not only come into contact but stay in continuous contact (Phinney & Flores, 2002). Acculturation is mentioned with ethnic identity due to the importance of considering the ethnic group member's relationship with the dominant group. Ethnic identity can be approached as a state in terms of the self-defining labels that a person may use to label himself or herself at a given point in time. Stages of ethnic identity chart changes over time in a person's way of identifying as an ethnic group member.

In pathmaking research, Phinney (1989) was instrumental in providing a framework of ethnic identity development. Ninety-one American-born Asian American, Black, Hispanic, and White 10th-grade students, all from integrated urban high schools, were interviewed. The subjects were also given questionnaire measures of ego identity and psychological adjustment. On the basis of the interviews, the minority subjects were coded as being in one of three identity stages: diffusion/foreclosure, moratorium, and identity achieved. Among children of color, nearly one half of the subjects had not examined their ethnic identity, which was conceptualized as diffusion and foreclosure. *Diffusion* referred to a lack of interest in or concern with ethnicity. *Foreclosure* reflected the views and opinions held by others (Phinney, 1990). In Phinney's (1989) work sample, about one quarter were considered to be in *exploration* or *moratorium*, understood as seeking to understand the personal meaning of ethnicity for oneself. One quarter were identified as *ethnic identity achieved* in that they had explored and were committed to an ethnic identity and had a clear and confident sense of their own ethnicity. This last group had the highest scores on a measure of ego identity and psychological adjustment. Although identity development was similar across the three groups of color, the issues specific to each group differed.

Several racial identity development models are discussed in the following sections. Core differences exist within groups rather than between them. As such, differences in racial identity and value orientation are to be expected among racially similar individuals. Racial identity development theory underscores the reality of psychological differences within monoracial and ethnic groups.

BIRACIAL IDENTITY DEVELOPMENT

The majority of the research conducted on biracial populations has focused on children and teens. Until recently, this literature has been scarce. Concerns about identity diffusion, low self-esteem, academic difficulties, and heightened risk of problem behaviors among multiracial children have been feared, found, and/or predicted (Choi, Harachi, Gillmore, & Catalano, 2006; Kerwin, Ponterotto, Jackson, & Harris, 1993; Gibbs & Hines, 1992).

Although the focus was on adults, Miville, Constantine, Baysden, and So-Lloyd (2005) conducted a qualitative investigation with 10 self-identified biracial and multiracial individuals. People were asked to describe their experiences with growing up, a time when the person first became aware of racial group membership, general observations about monoracial and multiracial people, and joys and hardships related to being multiracial. Four essential themes related to identity development were found:

1. Encounters with racism.
2. Racial identity label and/or reference group orientation.
3. The "chameleon" experience.
4. Identity development in context.

ENCOUNTERS WITH RACISM This research found that all participants had encounters with or experiences of racism that facilitated their understanding of racial group membership. Being asked the question "What are you?" was common fare for these participants as were encounters with "monocultural" racism through work or other contexts.

REFERENCE GROUP ORIENTATION Participants discussed their racial or ethnic label, such as Puerto Rican or Asian, but also saw themselves as multiracial. Identification as a person of color facilitated community building, racial intimacy and pride, and social support networking. Some participants also talked of feeling alienated by groups with whom they were unable to fit.

THE CHAMELON EXPERIENCE The importance of strategies to negotiate their multiple racial identity was a finding from this research. The ability to be flexible across and cross rigid social boundaries was seen as an advantage, although a sense of not belonging to any group was echoed by some.

IDENTITY DEVELOPMENT IN CONTEXT: CRITICAL PEOPLE, CRITICAL PLACES, CRITICAL PERIOD Parents were cited as the most influential people in participants' lives regarding the expression of their racial identity. The authors said, "In general, it seemed that participants adopted the racial-ethnic label of the parent to whom they felt emotionally closest or whom they viewed as most dominant in the household" (Miville et al., 2005, pp. 512–513). Social settings were identified as possibly playing a major role in the development of a positive racial identity with respect to acceptance or tension. Critical periods were connected to school: elementary, high school, and college.

NATIVE AMERICAN IDENTITY

Bryant and LaFromboise (2005) conducted research with 103 Lumbee Indian high school students using the People of Color Racial Identity Attitude Scale (PCRIAS) by Helms (1995). This instrument was developed to provide a measure of racial identity attitudes among Asians, African Americans, Latinos, and Native Americans. There are four stages. *Conformity* represents conformance to the dominant ideology and a devaluing of a person's own racial group. *Dissonance* reflects confusion about a person's racial group. *Immersion* describes identification and even idolization of a persons's racial group. Lastly, *internalization* refers to commitment to a person's group and an ability to integrate a person's racial identity into his or her life. Internalization attitudes were dominant among this group, followed by immersion, dissonance, and conformity.

Bryant and La Fromboise concluded that the internalization findings "suggests they posses a positive American Indian racial identity and also have the ability to acknowledge the positive aspects of White society" (p. 86). In addition, immersion attitudes may suggest some level of psychological as well as physical retreat into the Lumbee American community. Given the students' level of awareness about the impact of race on a daily basis, the conformity and dissonance attitudes may reflect some confusion, albeit minimally, about the sociopolitical constructions of race. Scholl (2006) had similar findings in his research with 121 Native American college students. Internalization attitudes were dominant and conformity (or preencounter) attitudes were least likely to be represented.

Ethics, or the principles or moral values that guide people's actions, provide Horse (2001) with a clear conceptualization of Indian identity. Part of this ethic is within the context of a collective consciousness. Consciousness requires memory, which Gunn Allen (1994) remarked is not encouraged in the West. "The American idea that the best and the brightest should willingly reject and repudiate their origins leads to an allied idea—that history, like everything in the past, is of little value and should be forgotten as quickly as possible" (p. 192). According to Horse, consciousness is influenced by multiple issues: the degree to which someone is grounded in the native language, tribe, family, and culture; the worldview that is embraced; recognition as a member of an Indian tribe by the government of the tribe; and the validity of a person's genealogical heritage as an Indian. Concerns over human-made laws, such as blood quantum amounts (Wilson, 1992), is not as relevant as is someone's consciousness and identity as an Indian.

ASIAN AMERICAN IDENTITY DEVELOPMENT

Myriad challenges face Asian people, as a heterogeneous group, in America. One of the most pervasive is related to the psychological conflict around racial identity. This conflict is connected to the experience of institutional racism, which is often subtle but damaging nonetheless to people who are targeted as inferior due to being different from a standard of White acceptability (Kim, 2001). According to Kim, "At some point in their lives, many Asian Americans have either consciously or unconsciously expressed the desire to become White, and tried to reject their identity as Asians" (p. 70.).

Very few studies exist on Asians and racial identity development (Chen, Le Phuoc, Guzman, Rude, & Dudd, 2006). Research was conducted on 344 self-identified Asian American adults recruited through Asian American electronic mailing lists, professional organizations, and snowballing. The study authors investigated racial identity profiles, racial attitudes, and racism-related stress among Asian Americans using the PCRIAS, the CoBRAS (which is used to measure Color-Blind Racial Attitudes), and the ASRRSI (or the Asian American Racism-Related Stress Inventory). (See Table 9.2.)

Within the context of other groups of color, the social construction of race is such that Asians occupy an intermediary position in the racial hierarchy, with Whites on the highest rung and Blacks on the lowest (Chen et. al, 2006). The Clusters found in their research are illustrated in Table 9.2.

TABLE 9.2   Cluster Definitions

Cluster One: Internalization	Cluster Two: Conformity	Cluster Three: Dissonance	Cluster Four: Immersion
High internalization	High conformity	High dissonance	High immersion-emersion
Low other PCRIAS	Low immersion-emersion	Moderately high conformity and immersion-emersion	Lower dissonance and internalization
	Low internalization	Low internalization	Low conformity
Elevated color-blind attitudes	High color-blind attitudes	Lower color-blind attitudes	Lower color-blind attitudes
Low racial-related stress	Low racism-related stress	Higher racism-related stress	High racism-related stress
Stage might be more consistent with pseudo independence	Denial or minimization of racial issues on personal and societal levels	High conformity of White values	Greater awareness of racial inequality
Role of race may be unclear for some		Immersion-emersion—idealization of own group norms	Ethnic identity precedes race—becoming aware of race can be dissonant provoking

Source: Chen, G. A., LePhuoc, P., Guzman, M. R., Rude, S. S., & Dodd, B. G. (2006). Exploring Asian American racial identity. *Cultural Diversity and Ethnic Minority Psychology*, 12, 461–476.

Kim (2001) has identified grounding principles of an Asian American identity development model.

1. The predominance of White racism and its impact on Asian American identity development must be acknowledged.
2. Internalized racism has to be unlearned unconsciously.
3. A healthy identity requires the transformation of a negative racial identity into a positive and healthy one.

The proposed stage model is sequential but not linear. This model is influenced by other racial identity development theories, yet takes into consideration the unique experiences of Asian Americans.

STAGE ONE: ETHNIC AWARENESS   This first stage represents the period prior to children's entry into the school system. The social environment and reference group consists largely of family. The extent of participation in Asian-oriented activities can bolster a sense of positive ethnic awareness.

STAGE TWO: WHITE IDENTIFICATION   This stage is marked by children's painful awareness that they are different from White people and that this difference is not regarded as a good thing. Feeling a sense of shame for being Asian can result in desperate attempts by Asian children to fit into White society. To compensate for feelings of inferiority, many Asian children will seek leadership in organizations and excel academically. Active White identification refers to the Asian student not consciously perceiving herself as different from Whites, thus there is a desire to alienate herself from and not be regarded as Asian. Passive White identification Asians enter this stage during their later years and are buffered by early exposure to predominantly Asian communities that nurtured self-esteem. The distancing from Asians and seeking to pass for White is not evident here, but fantasizing, (e.g., "I wish") about being White does occur.

STAGE THREE: AWAKENING TO SOCIAL POLITICAL CONSCIOUSNESS.   A shift from personal to social responsibility for racism allows Asian Americans to understand racism and transform their negative sense of self into a positive one. At this stage, White people are no longer the reference group and Asians do not regard themselves as inferior. The person essentially asks the question, "Why should I be ashamed of who I am?" There is a connection to other people of color.

STAGE FOUR: REDIRECTION TO AN ASIAN AMERICAN CONSCIOUSNESS   In this stage, the sense of self as a minority is crystallized into a sense of being Asian. There is often an immersion into the Asian experience, and the ego is centered on things/people Asian. Racial pride is experienced as is a positive self-concept. In addition to pride, people feel angry at the way in which the dominant White culture perpetuates racism and cultural violence.

STAGE FIVE: INCORPORATION   A person's racial identity is blended into other social identities. The self is seen as whole, with race representing only one aspect of social identity. The immersion of the previous stage is relaxed. A clear Asian American identity has been achieved, yet people in general are the person's reference group.

AFRICAN AMERICAN RACIAL IDENTITY

Cross's (1991) theory of racial identity development, called the **Negro-to-Black conversion experience,** or **Nigresence,** is the most widely used racial theory about African Americans. It presumes a sociopolitical perspective and refers to the process of developing healthy racial collective identities as a function of discrepancies in sociopolitical power across racial groups. In Cross's work, a distinction is made between *personal identity (PI)* and *reference group orientation (RGO)*. The former refers to self-esteem and interpersonal competence; the latter refers to racial identity and racial self-esteem. Cross's work on Black racial identity has been extremely influential in the development of models related to other aspects of identity, including racial and cultural identity models for other groups of color and the womanist identity model (see Ossana, Helms, & Leonard, 1992).

Within Cross's (1991) theory, identity development is a maturation process whereby external negative images of the self are replaced with positive internal conceptions. Cross's five-stage Nigresence model—preencounter, encounter, immersion and emersion, internalization, and internalization and commitment—refers to "a resocializing experience" that "seeks to transform a preexisting identity (a non-Africentric identity) into one that is Africentric" (p. 190). Robinson and Howard-Hamilton (1994) discussed **Africentricity** as a conscious ideology with a strong connection to spirituality and kinship via African culture, culminating in the shared belief, "I am because we are and since we are, therefore I am." An optimal Africentric worldview can be measured by an instrument called the Belief Systems Analysis Scale (BSAS), developed by Fine and James-Myers (1990). Africentrism involves an awareness of Black identity, knowledge of cultural customs and traditions, liberating psychological resistance strategies, and an understanding of oppression and strategies to resist it (Dana, 1993; Robinson & Howard-Hamilton, 1994).

Cross developed the Cross Racial Identity Scale (Vandiver, 2001) to measure the revised dimensions of his 1997 Nigresence model. Vandiver reviewed the Cross Racial Identity Scale (CRIS), a 40-item, 7-point Likert-type inventory, to measure Cross's revised theory of Nigresence. Reference group orientation and race salience are also assessed. There are six scales: Preencounter Assimilated (PA), Preencounter Miseducation (PM), Preencounter Self-Hatred (PSH), Immersion/Emersion Anti-White (IEAW), Internalization Afrocentriocity Black Nationalist (IA), and Internalization Multiculturalist Inclusive (IMCI). The psychometric properties of the CRIS report acceptable Cronbach alphas: PA = .85, PM = .89, PSH = .85, IEAW = .85, IBN = .79, IMCI = .76.

At *preencounter,* the acculturated African American views the world through the lens of the White dominant culture. Essentially, race has low salience. When people are asked to describe themselves, identifiers other than race, such as work, church, profession, and club affiliation, surface as key descriptors. Cross (1991) maintained that many preencounter African Americans are psychologically healthy and that anti-Black attitudes among African Americans in this stage are rare, although they do exist. Despite indices of psychological health among African Americans at this initial stage of racial identity, Cross stated, "Preencounter Blacks cannot help but experience varying degrees of miseducation about the significance of the Black experience" (p. 192). African Americans in this first stage are more likely to operate from a Eurocentric cultural perspective in evaluating beauty and art forms.

According to Jones, Cross, and DeFour (2007), the assimilation subscales measure pro-American and assimilationist attitudes (e.g., "I think of myself as an American, and seldom as a member of a racial group"). The miseducation subscale taps into the extent to which the respondent adheres to negative stereotypes about Black people as group (e.g., "Blacks place too much importance on racial protest and not enough on hard work and education"). Racial self-hatred assesses racial self-hatred attitudes (e.g. "When I look into the mirror at my Black image, sometimes I do not feel good about what I see").

At the *encounter* stage, a person's new view of the world, as a result of a shocking personal experience, is inconsistent with the old. According to Cross (1991), the two aspects of this stage are experiencing an encounter and personalizing it. In every year of a person's life, myriad encounter experiences could encourage movement from preencounter to encounter. If the experiences are not internalized and personalized, however, movement up to this next stage cannot occur. Other identity constructs, such as religion, class, and education, can delay racial identity formation, particularly when similarity with the referent group (e.g., being Christian, middle class, academically gifted) is encouraged and differences (e.g., race) that may be perceived as threatening or divisive are ignored (Robinson, 1999).

In the *immersion and emersion* stage, the focus is on being Black to the exclusion of others, particularly Whites. Cross (1991) indicated that this is a transitional stage with respect to identity transformation: "The person's main focus in life becomes a feeling of 'togetherness and oneness with people' " (p. 207). The anti-White subscale assesses dislike for White people and culture (e.g., "I have a strong hatred and disdain for all White people").

The fourth stage of Cross's model, *internalization,* is characterized by more peace and calm. At this juncture, dissonance regarding an emerging identity has been resolved, evidenced by high salience attached to Blackness.

Internalization and commitment persons seek to eradicate racism for all oppressed people. According to Cross, this stage is similar to the internalization stage but is reflective of sustained long-term interest and commitment, as opposed to a brief period in that person's life. Here, the African American is more able to reconceptualize the self outside across multiple identities. At initial stages, the African American has little awareness of racial oppression because race has minimal importance. The Afrocentric and Multicultural subscales assess this internalization stage. The Afrocentric subscales measure Black Nationalist attitudes characterized by empowerment (e.g., "I see and think about things from an Afrocentric perspective"). The Multicultural subscale measures Blacks' acceptance and connection with others from diverse cultural contexts (e.g., "As a multiculturalist, I am connected to many groups").

Jones, Cross, and DaFour (2007) administered the CRIS, the Rosenberg Self-Esteem Scale (RSE), the Schedule of Racist Events (SRE), and the Center for Epidemiologic Studies Depression Scale (CES-D) to 118 African American and 144 self-identified Caribbean women. They discovered that racist stress events and racist stress appraisal play a role in negative mental health, particularly depression. In their sample, multicultural identity attitudes lessened the negative mental health impact of racist stress events and racist stress appraisals, particularly as they related to depression. There was an increase in depression scores as racist stress appraisals increased, but "not to the same degree as those with multicultural identity attitude scores 1 standard deviation below the mean" (p. 222).

LATINO IDENTITY DEVELOPMENT

That Latinos can be and are of any race is often confusing and difficult for counseling students to grasp. When students are told that Latinos are not a racial group but an ethnic group with different ethnic and racial subgroups, the confusion magnifies. When I make the point to students that sharing race does not mean sharing ethnicity and sharing ethnicity does not mean sharing race, I often draw a Venn diagram or say something like: "A White-skinned woman with blond hair and blue eyes might identify herself ethnically as Cubana but racially she considers herself to be White. Is she Latina?" Yes. At the same time, a sister Cubana may have African roots, dark skin, and very curly hair. Ethnically, she is also Cubana but considers herself Black. Cubans hail from Africa,

Europe (Spanish), or Asia (Chinese) and/or are indigenous (Indian). The difficulty with understanding Latinos both racially and ethnically is related to the dichotomization of racial categories. A bifurcation of people—"you are either this or that"—has had implications for a racial/ethnic identity development model for Latinos. The dialectic embraces a "both/and" way of being in the world and is needed to appreciate multiple identities within and across groups of people. In addition, the existing models of racial identity cannot be applied to Latinos. Latinos are not a racial group.

According to Ferdman and Gallegos (2001), there are key dimensions involved in defining a nonlinear Latino identity: how a person prefers to identify herself, how Latinos as a group are seen, how Whites are seen, and how race fits into the equation.

LATINO INTEGRATED   Persons who are Latino integrated are able to embrace the fullness of their Latino identity and integrate this into other identities, such as class, profession, and gender. A dialectic, as mentioned earlier, is characteristic of the Latino integrated. This person is comfortable with all types of Latinos as there is a broad lens used to see themselves, White people, and others.

LATINO IDENTIFIED   This group has more of a pan-Latino identity, with a view of race, *la raza*, as uniquely Latin. There is a deep and abiding understanding of a history of political struggle and a desire to be united with other Latinos in racial unity. Despite the awareness of and vigilant stand against institutional racism, Latino-identified persons may see Whites, Blacks, and other groups in rigid ways.

SUBGROUP IDENTIFIED   Persons of this group see themselves as distinct from White people but do not necessarily identify with other Latinos or with people of color. The broad pan-Latino orientation discussed in the previous orientations is not reflected here. Other Latino subgroups may be viewed in an inferior way. People's allegiance to a particular subgroup is nearly exclusive. Race is not a central or clear organizing concept, but nationality, ethnicity, and culture are primary.

LATINO AS "OTHER"   Persons with this orientation see themselves as people of color. This may be a function of biracial or multiracial status, ambiguous phenotype, or dominant constructions of race. In certain contexts, persons see themselves as minorities and not White. There is no identification with Latino cultural norms or with White culture, and an understanding of Latino history and culture is missing.

UNDIFFERENTIATED   Persons with this orientation regard themselves as simply "people" with a color-blind eye. The emphasis on racial classification is not a part of their framework. The desire to associate with other Latinos is not prominent because contact with others is distinct from a person's race or ethnic identity. Life is lived apart from attention to and thoughts of difference.

WHITE IDENTIFIED   White-identified persons perceive themselves as White and thus superior to people of color (*non-White-skinned people*—emphasis mine). Assimilation into White culture is a possibility as is connection primarily to only one other group (e.g., light-skinned Cubans) while denying connection to other subgroups.

There is an acceptance of the status quo and a valuing of Whiteness to the extent that marrying White is preferred over marrying dark. Latinos with this orientation are *mejorar la raza* (i.e., improve the race).

The strength of this model is that it helps counselors and clients ascertain identity development for Latinos who differ greatly across acculturation level, skin color, national origin, and political ideology. This is also not a linear model; nonetheless, it is clear that there are orientations more conducive to unity with others across race and skin color wherein people are valued because they are human and not because of what they look like.

Umaña-Taylor (2004) studied ethnic identity and self-esteem among 1,062 Mexican-origin adolescents who attended one of three schools: predominantly Latino, predominantly non-Latino, and balanced Latino/non-Latino. Phinney's Multigroup Ethic Identity Measure was used to assess ethnic identity. Rosenberg's Self-Esteem Scale measured self-esteem. A significant relationship emerged between ethnic identity and self-esteem for adolescents attending the predominately non-Latino school, the balanced school, and the predominantly Latino school. This finding suggests that the relationship between self-esteem and ethnic identity may not be context specific. Maternal education was higher among students at the pre-dominantly non-Latino school. Students attending the predominantly non-Latino school were more likely to have been born in the United States than students at the balanced school. Finally, students at the predominantly non-Latino school reported higher levels of ethnic identity than teens at the predominantly Latino and balanced schools. These data suggest that "ethnic identity appears to be more salient for Mexican-origin adolescents when they are in a minority context than in a majority context" (p. 144). However, the relationship between self-esteem and ethnic identity did not differ across schools. Predominantly Latino school students are a minority in the larger society, irrespective of their majority presence at school, which may account for this finding.

WHITE RACIAL IDENTITY DEVELOPMENT

Traditional conceptions of race refer to people of color, but European Americans are also racial beings and experience racial identity development. As racial beings, White people are shaped by the construct of race in their and other people's lives, affected by both skin color privilege and the adverse consequences of racism (Robinson, 1999).

It is an infrequent experience or encounter that would encourage a White person to assess her attitudes about being a racial being (Pope-Davis & Ottavi, 1994). In a society where unearned skin color advantages are conferred, European American counselors need to develop a positive racial identity that does not emanate from oppression and domination. This transformation may be difficult for two reasons:

1. It is possible for White people to live in U.S. society without having to acknowl-edge or give much consideration to the meaning of being White.
2. Denial about one's own race impedes self-awareness, a crucial factor in racial identity development.

Helms (1995; Helms & Parham, 1984) has been the predominant voice in the development of White racial identity theory. Hardiman (1982, 2001) developed the White identity development (WID) model, which was the first model on White racial identity development. Helms's (1984, 1995) White racial identity development model (WRID) has six statuses. The term *status* is preferred over *stage* in that the latter is more reflective of a fixed state. Helms believed that people could be characterized by more than one status at a given time. These statuses are contact, disintegration, reintegration, pseudoindependence, immersion-emersion, and autonomy. Helms's revised model includes information-processing strategies for each of the six statuses.

A person enters the *contact* status from encountering the idea or actuality of Black people. Family background and environment affect whether the attitude toward Black people is one of trepidation or naive curiosity. In contact, the European American automatically benefits from institutional and cultural racism without the conscious awareness of doing so. The identity ego status and information-processing strategy for contact is obliviousness. White people are satisfied with the status quo and are fairly oblivious to the role of racism and their involvement in it.

White people in the contact status tend to have positive self-esteem. They are idealistic about the equal treatment of African Americans; however, in actually interacting with Blacks, they may experience some anxiety or arousal. Through interaction with African Americans, the European American realizes that, independent of economic conditions, clear distinctions exist in the treatment of people across race.

Continuing to have socialization experiences will move the person into Helms's second status, *disintegration*. Entry into disintegration is characterized by conscious conflict that has its origins in dissonance. Here, the White person realizes that people are treated differently as a function of race. The identity ego status and information-processing strategy for disintegration are suppression and ambivalence. White people in this status are truly confused by anxiety-provoking racial moral dilemmas that require them to choose between own-group loyalty and humane behavior.

The third status is *reintegration,* which is entered as the White person realizes that, within the dominant culture, the covert and overt belief of White superiority and Black inferiority exists. The desire to be accepted by the White racial group is very strong. It is important in reintegration that a racial identity be acknowledged. Here, White privilege is protected even though it is unearned. People of color are not entitled to privilege because they are morally, socially, and intellectually inferior. Because honest dialogue about race between racially different people does not often take place, it is fairly easy for a person to fixate here. A jarring event can trigger movement into the fourth status, *pseudoindependence*. The identity ego status and information-processing strategy for reintegration are selective perception and negative out-group distortion. White people are idealized and others are not tolerated well at all.

According to Helms (1990), "Pseudoindependence is the first stage of redefining a positive White identity" (p. 61). This status is primarily one of intellectualization, wherein the person acknowledges responsibility for White racism. The negativity of the earlier stages does not exist; nonetheless, White norms continue to be used to interpret cultural or racial differences. Socially, the person is met with suspicion by both Whites and

Blacks. Discomfort with their ambiguous racial identity may move the person into the fifth status. The identity ego status and information-processing strategy for psuedoindependence are reshaping reality and selective perception. The commitment to racism is largely intellectual. The goal is to reach out and assist other racial groups.

This fifth status, *immersion-emersion,* is characterized by the replacement of old myths and stereotypes with accurate information. It is a period of unlearning. Here, the person may participate heavily in White-consciousness groups in which the goal is to help the person abandon a racist identity. The focus is not on changing Black people but rather on seeking to change White people. The successful resolution of this status requires that the individual recycle or reexperience earlier emotion that was distorted or repressed. The identity ego status and information-processing strategies for immersion-emersion are hypervigilance and reshaping. There is a diligent search for the personal meaning of racism and the ways in which people can benefit from racism.

Autonomy, the sixth and last status of Helms's model, is an ongoing process. In this status, a primary goal is internalizing and experiencing new ways of being racial that were learned from previous stages. Race, your own and other people's, is not a threat. The identity ego status and information-processing strategy for autonomy are flexibility and complexity. Internal standards are used for defining the self, and there is a capacity to relinquish the privileges of racism. Helms (1990) stated that the second phase, development of a nonracist White identity, begins with the pseudoindependent status and ends with the autonomy status.

Watt, Robinson, and Lupton-Smith (2002) conducted a study of ego identity and Black and White racial identity among 38 graduate students (30 White, 6 Black, and 2 Middle Eastern) at the beginning, middle, and end of their counseling training in a program that included student counseling, community agency, and school counseling tracks. The researchers used the Washington Sentence Completion Test to measure ego identity and used Black and White versions of the Racial Identity Attitude Scale. It was hypothesized that the ego developments of students enrolled in Prepracticum (a second-year class) would be higher than the ego development of students enrolled in Theories and Cross-Cultural (both first-year classes). It was found that students in Theories had lower ego development than students in Cross-Cultural and Prepracticum; however, there were no differences in ego development between students in Cross-Cultural and students in Prepracticum. It was also found that students enrolled in Theories had a lower mean score at the pseudoindependence status than did the Prepracticum students. In addition, the racial identity status of students enrolled in Cross-Cultural was higher than the racial identity status of students enrolled in Theories. These data are important in understanding ego and racial identity development for students at different developmental stages in their programs. The study needs to be replicated with a much larger and racially and culturally diverse sample.

Leach, Behrens, and LaFleur (2002) make a distinction between white racial identity and white racial consciousness. They define White racial consciousness as the ways that White people think about people who are not White or the racial out-group. The model "attempts to identify commonly held constellations of attitudes and attempts to determine, which, if any best characterize the racial attitudes held by White individuals" (p. 69).

Seven types of attitudes have been grouped into two categories: achieved, which is the result of personal consideration and commitment to some set of attitudes about racial material (four types), and unachieved, or lack of exploration or commitment or both with respect to racial attitudes (three types). Unachieved attitudes include

1. Dependent, or attitudes determined by a significant other.
2. Dissonant, or uncertainty about attitudes.
3. Avoidant, which is attitudes that ignore and/or minimize racial issue.

Achieved attitudes include

1. Conflictive, which describes fairness but where rugged individualism is strong.
2. Dominative, which describes ethnocentric or pro-White attitudes.
3. Integrative, which reflects positive and pragmatic attitudes.
4. Reactive, which are strong pro-groups of color attitudes.

OPTIMAL THEORY APPLIED TO IDENTITY DEVELOPMENT

Myers et al. (1991) developed a theory of optimal identity that is neither linear nor categorical. In criticizing some psychosocial identity models, they observed that the models have limited the role of the individual in the identity process, did not consider people with multiple identities, and were based on a Eurocentric worldview. Myers et al. maintained that the dichotomy of the spirit world and matter within American society make it difficult to attain a positive self-identity in the United States, regardless of race, because self-worth is based primarily on external validation. Persons who turn outside themselves for meaning, peace, and value have adopted a suboptimal worldview. According to Myers et al., within an optimal perspective, self-worth is intrinsic in being. Thus, the purpose of life is becoming clearer about how the self is connected with all of life. Spiritual development is an integral part of identity development.

In Phase 0, known as *absence of conscious awareness,* the person lacks awareness of being. This is regarded as an infancy stage. Phase 1 is *individuation.* Here, the world is the way it is in that people simply lack awareness of any view of self other than the one to which they were initially introduced. They rarely assign meaning or value to the various aspects of their identity. Phase 2 is *dissonance;* persons begin the exploration of their true self and effectively explore dimensions of the self that may be demeaned by others. In Phase 3, *immersion,* persons' energy is focused on those who are regarded as similar. Phase 4, *internalization,* occurs as people feel good about who they are and have successfully incorporated feelings of self-worth. Phase 5, *integration,* happens as people's deeper understanding of themselves allows them to change their assumptions about the world. The self is more secure internally, and peaceful relationships are a manifestation of this. The final stage, Phase 6, is *transformation.* The self is redefined toward a sense of personhood that includes ancestors, the unborn, nature, and community. The universe is understood as benevolent, orderly, and personal.

IMPLICATIONS FOR COUNSELORS AND PSYCHOLOGISTS

In a survey conducted by the Kaiser Family Foundation (U.S. Department of Health and Human Services, 2001), it was found that 12% of African Americans and 15% of Latinos, compared with 1% of Whites, felt that a doctor or health care provider would judge them unfairly or treat them with disrespect because of their race or ethnic background. There is a climate of mistrust around race. Poor Black families are often stigmatized as disorganized, lazy, and deprived (Boyd-Franklin, 2003).

Part of multicultural competence is knowledge of these sociopolitical dynamics and resources for counteracting them. Day-Vines et al. (2007) introduced the concept of **broaching**, which refers to the initiation on the part of the clinician to bring issues of race and diversity, often regarded as fugitive topics, into the therapy room. The purpose of doing this is to encourage the client's exploration of these difficult topics. Due to fear of being perceived as ignorant, insensitive, or racist, counselors will asking particular questions. This fear can paralyze the therapeutic event and interfere with the client's growth. Leadership requires therapists to introduce conversation about difficult and sensitive topics. A source of resistance may be an internal reluctance to talk about race, even after taking the required graduate-level cross-cultural diversity course.

The therapeutic relationship is influenced by a client's racial identity development in that it can directly affect the client's preference for a counselor. Clients of color in preencounter (Black), White identified (Latino), or White identification (Asian) are more likely to prefer a White counselor over a counselor of color. The belief exists that "Whites are more competent and capable than members of one's own race" (Sue & Sue, 1990, p. 108). In this scenario, if the counselor is White, the client will typically be overeager to identify with the counselor. If the counselor is non-White, then the counselor will experience feelings of hostility from the client even if the client and the counselor are of the same race. Independent of the counselor's race, the counselor has a responsibility to help reeducate the client as they work together through the client's conflicts. Regardless of race, counselors who choose not to face their biases with courageous introspection are not appropriate candidates for the mental health profession.

During the encounter and dissonance stages, clients are preoccupied with questions concerning the self and identity. They may still prefer a White counselor; however, counselors can take advantage of clients' focus on self-exploration toward resolution of identity conflicts. During the immersion/emersion and resistance and immersion stages of racial/ethnic identity, clients of color tend to view their psychological problems as an outgrowth of oppression and racism. In this stage, clients of color are prone to prefer counselors of their own race. In fact, people of color may tend to perceive White counselors as enemies. Thus, it is important for White counselors to not personalize attacks from clients of color. Statements regarding the unjust sociopolitical nature within the United States have legitimacy. It is also wise for counselors to anticipate that resistance/immersion clients will test their clinicians, as this stage is one of great volatility. Finally, counselors are apt to be more effective with a client when they use action-oriented methods aimed at external change.

Clients of color at more integrated phases of racial identity often experience an inner sense of security regarding their identities. They are able to choose therapists, not necessarily on the basis of race but on the basis of the professional's ability to be empathic and understanding of the issues clients bring to counseling. Sue and Sue (1990) stated that "attitudinal similarity between counselor and client is a more important dimension than membership-group similarity" (p. 112). Nonetheless, clients at higher stages of racial identity may accept a counselor of a different race while preferring one of their own racial, ethnic, or gender group. This preference need not be an indication of discriminatory attitudes but may instead reflect a desire or need for a cultural connection that may or may not occur.

All mental health professionals need to acknowledge their biases and assess their personal readiness prior to engaging in counseling across sources of diversity. (See Storytelling: "Requests for Same-Race Therapist.") Not to do so is to place the client in jeopardy. If need be, licensed professionals may want to contact a supervisor at parallel or more integrated levels of racial identity to facilitate their racial identity progression (Ladany, Brittan-Powell, & Pannu, 1997).

Richardson and Molinaro (1996) found that the reintegration therapist may be impatient toward clients of different races and less likely to establish rapport with these clients. Cook (1994) suggested that White counselors may also engage in ethnocentric behavior if they operate at Helms's reintegration stage and recognize their own race as standard for "normal" behavior of the client. Not until the immersion/emersion stage do White clinicians acknowledge clients' race, respect cultural influences, and examine the sociopolitical implications. At the pseudoindependence stage, the White counselor will discuss racial issues but only when interacting with persons of color (Cook, 1994). Ethnocentric assumptions still frame people's thinking.

Ultimately, our beliefs and attitudes will inform the quality of our listening and our talking. Delpit (1997) eloquently said, "We do not really see through our eyes . . . but through our beliefs. To put our beliefs on hold is to cease to exist as ourselves for a moment—and that is not easy . . . but it is the only way to learn what it might feel like to be someone else and the only way to start the dialogue" (p. 101).

STORYTELLING: Request for Same-Race Therapists

I recently received two requests from colleagues looking for Black clinicians to work with Black women, one a graduate student and the other a working adult. These women specifically asked for professionals of color. Fortunately, there were licensed professionals available to whom I could refer these women. It does not surprise me that some Black clients prefer other Black professionals, particularly when issues of racism and/or White privilege are at the core of the presenting issue. Preference for a counselor on the basis of race can and does occur. An agency or practice or group may not have an appropriate match but may have gender compatibility. The literature is inconclusive regarding the link between racial identification and counselor preference (Pope-Davis, Liu, Toporek, & Brittan-Powell, 2001). Being a therapist of color or a woman or both does not ensure that one is able to work effectively with women clients of color. Wilkinson (1997) pointed out that Black educators and mental health professionals internalize racism and the negative scripts around race just as White people do.

This in turn can contribute to Black professionals' ignorance about class discrimination and its influence on people's lives (p. 271) and make Black people unable to relate to other Blacks who are of a lower income bracket or who were born on the African continent. Despite this reality, a same-race counselor has often had "similar emotional and physical experiences with racism, and more of a willingness to confront this external barrier" (Washington, 1987, p. 198). It is important for multiculturally competent White therapists to broach the topic of race and explain to their clients that discussions of race and racism are welcomed—that the focus of therapy is on the clients' healing, not on protecting the therapist from topics of White racism. Part of the everyday experience of Black people is comporting themselves so as not to offend or censuring themselves in order to get along. Therapy should not reproduce these experiences. Multicultural competence is an awareness of sociopolitical issues such as structural inequalities that affect people's attempts to be agentic and have control over their economic lives. Knowledge and assessment of proximity to race and ethnic discourses, skills about broaching difficult topics, referral, and advocacy, as well as an understanding of racial identity development and multicultural terminology are all skills of multiculturally competent counselors (Holcomb-McCoy, 2000).

CASE STUDY
Teaching Privilege to the Privileged

There are a host of emotions that accompany undergraduate and graduate students' awareness of unearned privilege. Guilt, anger, minimization, rationalization, humor, sadness, and confusion are common emotions. The following themes are intended to assist instructors with teaching privilege to the privileged. This discussion is relevant for skin-color privilege as well as gender, ability, class, religious, and sexuality privileges.

QUESTIONS AND DISCUSSION

1. Realize that unearned privilege and entitlement go hand in hand. Entitlement is the belief that one has the right to be acknowledged, protected, respected, and rewarded. When denied any of these, shock and anger emerge.

2. Respect the difficult and redemptive feelings that accompany unpacking the invisible knapsack. Allow yourself and students to feel their feelings, knowing that such feelings are necessary for transformation. Most students have been taught that society is fair and just, and

White people tend to not confront the role of racism in their own lives (Tatum, 1992).

3. Although race, gender, class, and sexuality are identity constructs that have status, race in America is a grandmaster status and often eclipses and overwhelms other markers, such as class. Working-class Whites are often quick to invoke their modest class origins and may attempt to compare their class oppression with racism. Skin color is an immutable characteristic and is not fluid as class often, but not always, is. Universities are filled with White professors whose families of origin were low-wage earning and working class and yet, unless people identify this as part of their experience, how do we distinguish this group from those whose parents and grandparents were academics? Finally, working-class status among whites and working-class status among Blacks and other groups of color is different. Being low-income and Black represents two marginalized identities, not one.

4. Not having White skin-color privilege or other sources of privilege does not render a person powerless. Having White skin-color privilege does not result in people feeling powerful.

5. "Counselors need to enhance themselves personally and professionally by reading and exposing themselves to various artistic art forms" (Lee, 2001). Reading newspaper articles and attending films and other culture-specific activities can inform a professional's sense of another person's culture.

6. Engage in an inventory of your life. Who are the people you invite into your home? What level of comfort do you feel with certain groups of color compared with others? Culture-free service delivery does not exist; therefore, it is impossible to help clients examine cultural identity and self-esteem issues if counselors and psychologists have not done this important work for themselves (Pinderhughes, 1989).

7. Encourage narrative with students as well as their exposure to others. Psychosocial narrative questions that I ask students include:

   a. What does it mean to be the race(s) you are?

   b. What impact has spirituality had on your development as a counseling professional?

   c. What did your parents teach you about race and skin color?

   d. What are the privileges and oppression in your life?

   e. How do you feel about the presence and/or absence of privilege and oppression in your life?

   f. Tim Wise (2005) suggests this question for White students, "What does it mean to be White, especially in a nation created by people like you, for people like you?" (p. 2)

8. Healing yourself from racism is an evolving but important process. Ellis (2004) wrote that healing promotes self-discovery, people discovery. Healing also provides a person with the rest needed when involved with race-based information from a personal and historical onslaught of racial inequity.

9. Multicultural competencies and guidelines encourage counselors and psychologists to understand how gender, race, class, sexuality, ethnicity, and nationality intersect in the lives of their clients (Salazar, 2006).

SUMMARY

This chapter examined race as a social construction and a status variable. Other constructs were considered in relationship to race in an effort to provide an understanding of the saliency of race as an identity construct that intersects with other multiple identities. Also discussed in this chapter were theoretical advances in ethnic and racial identity models for biracial and monoracial groups. Both qualitative and quantitative methodologies were highlighted. Race and ethnic discourses were identified as were strategies for instructors of diversity courses.

Chapter 10

Converging Biracial and Multiracial Identities

I believe that we have a righteous wind at our backs and that as we stand on the crossroads of history, we can make the right choices and meet the challenges that face us.

Barack Obama, *Dreams from My Father: A Story of Race and Inheritance*

This chapter on converging biracial and multiracial identities explores race as a shifting construct in American society. In doing so, demographic data reflecting increases in biracial and multiracial populations are reviewed. A case study is provided, recent research is discussed, and stories are presented that emphasize the narrative tradition.

DEFINITIONS

STORYTELLING: Hair Care

One of the mothers in my research with White mothers of non-White children had adopted a female child of African descent from South America. One day when the child was about 7 years old, the mother, a White woman, and her dark-skinned child were in a large super discount store. A Black woman—a stranger to both the mother and the child—walked up to them, took the mother by the hand, and led her over to the hair care aisle. She then proceeded to point out to the mother the products that the mother needed to purchase for her child's hair. I asked the mother how she felt about this experience and she said, "Well, I felt two things. On one hand, I was grateful. My daughter's hair did look bad and I didn't know what to do with it. On the other had, I was indignant. How dare this woman tell me how to take care of my child?" The Black woman looked at this White mother with a Black child whose hair was unkempt and concluded that an intervention was necessary. Help offered with greater humility would most likely have felt less intrusive and invasive.

Racial purity is myth; however, for the purpose of clarity, definitions are provided. The child described in Storytelling: "Hair Care" is *monoracial*—she is of African heritage and both of her biological parents are of African heritage, which can mean having European, Indian, and Spanish ancestry, particularly in Latin America. Thus, there is considerable *intraracial* diversity among people from the same racial group. Her adopted mother is White, and therefore, the child and her mother are part of an *interracial* family. Their neighbors are an interracial family as well, and they have biological children who would be considered *biracial*. As a group, biracial people are also referred to in the literature as biracials. The mother is monoracial, Asian, and the father is monoracial, White. This couple is also *bicultural* in that the mother was born in China and moved to the United States when she was 19. The father was born and raised in America. They celebrate Chinese New Year, cook traditional Chinese dishes, and celebrate the Fourth of July with hot dogs and hamburgers (vegetarian). If their son marries the daughter next door and they have biological children, their children would be considered to be *multiracial*, with White European, Black African, and Asian ancestry.

People may choose an identity that may be inconsistent with others' perceptions. In addition, identities are fluid and can change over time. Hopefully, the world in which these children live will be *multicultural* in spirit and in truth.

DEMOGRAPHY

The U.S. Census Bureau documents the reality of increasing numbers of persons who are biracial and multiracial. In the 2000 census, people were asked to report one or more of the following races: White, Black or African American, American Indian or Alaskan Native (AIAN), Asian, Native Hawaiian or other Pacific Islander (NHPI), and some other race (SOR).

There are 7.3 million, or 2.6%, of the U.S. population reporting more than one race. Twelve of the 57 race combinations made up about 93% of the two or more races population and were the only combinations with more than 100,000 people (Jones, 2005). The combinations are listed in Table 10.1. Children under the age of 18 represent nearly 42% of the two or more race population (Jones & Symens Smith, 2001). Of the total two or more race populations, 93% reported two races. The largest race combination was White and some other race (SOR), which represents 32% of the total two or more races population. The next four largest combinations were White and American Indian/Alaskan Native, White and Asian, White and Black, and Black and SOR at 17.3%, 11.9%, 10.9%, and 6.4%, respectively. Thirty-one percent of the total two or more races population was Hispanic compared with about 13% of the U.S. population. The American Indian and Alaskan Native population and

TABLE 10.1 Two or More Races Population by Combination: 2000

White and some other race	7,270,926
White and American Indian and Alaskan Native	2,322,356
White and Asian	1,254,289
White and Black	791,801
Black and some other race	462,703
Asian and some other race	280,600
Black and American Indian and Alaskan Native	206,941
Asian and Native Hawaiian and other Pacific Islander	138,556
White and Black and American Indian and Alaskan Native	116,897
White and Native Hawaiian and other Pacific Islander	111,993
American Indian and Alaskan Native and some other race	108,576
Black and Asian	106,842
All other combinations	507,340

the Native Hawaiian and other Pacific Islander population had the highest percent-ages reporting more than one race.

People who reported more than one race were considerably younger than the total U.S. population. The median age for two or more races was 23.4 compared with 35.4 for the total U.S. population. Among two or more races, a quarter, or 25.2%, were under the age of 10 compared with 14.1% in the total population who were under 10 years of age. White and Black races were particularly young with 71% of the population under the age of 18 compared with 25% in the general population. More than 2 million Hispanics, or nearly one third, of two or more races in the pop-ulation reported more than one race; 43% were under 18. Among non-Hispanics, the comparable rate was 24% (Jones & Symens Smith, 2001). The median age for White and Black races was 9.7 years. The next youngest was White and Asian, with a median age of 18.1 years.

Only 5% of two or more races were 65 and older compared with 12.4% in the total population. There are differences between groups. Among the White and American Indian/Alaskan Native population, 7.5% were 65 and older. This group has the highest median age among the two or more races, at 32.9. Among two or more races, there were similar numbers of males per 100 females while the U.S. population had more females than males (Jones, 2005).

About 27% of the total population 15 years of age and older had never been married. Among two or more races, it was 37.3% who had never been married. The group with the lowest rates of never married were White and American Indian/Alaskan Native, at 28.3%. Among two or more races, 45.6% were married compared with 54.4% in the total population. Asian and Native Hawaiian/Pacific Islanders and Whites and SOR had higher than average rates of marriage among this group, 50.6% and 50.4%, respectively.

More than one half of all households in the United States were maintained by a married couple, 52.5% compared with slightly less than one half of households, 46.6%, with two or more races householder (Jones, 2005). Two or more races had slightly lower than average separated, widowed, and divorced rates than the total population, 17.1% compared with 18.5%. There was, however, a greater likelihood of female householder families among two or more races compared with the total population. The average is 11.8% compared with 16.3% among two or more races. White and Asian races have lower female householder rates, at 10%. The highest is among Black and American Indian/Alaskan Native, Black and SOR, and White and Black races, 29.8%, 26.5%, and 25.6%, respectively.

People who reported two or more races were more likely to be foreign-born, at 24% compared with 11% of the U.S. population that is foreign-born. About 46% of foreign-born people who reported more than one race entered the United States between 1990 and 2000. Nearly 40% of people aged 5 and older who reported more than one race in the 2000 census spoke a language other than English at home, compared with less than 20% of the U.S. population. Three of the combina-tions involving Asian (Black and Asian, White and Asian, and Asian and Pacific Islander) had about 25% to 35% of individuals who spoke a language other than English at home.

Nearly 20% of people who reported two or more races had attained a bachelor's degree or higher compared with 24.4% of the total population. White and Asian races had the highest percent, 34.8% with a bachelor's degree or higher. Asian and SOR were the only group with 25% or more of people in the same group with less than a high school diploma and 29.5 with a bachelor's degree or higher. American Indian and SOR had the highest rates of less than a high school diploma, at 43.8% compared with 19.6% in the total population.

Compared with the U.S. population 16 and older, the two or more races population had a larger proportion employed in service occupations but a smaller proportion employed in management, professional, and related occupations. White and Asian and White and Black and American Indian/Alaskan Native individuals were the most likely to hold management, professional, and related occupations at 36.8%, and 35.7%, respectively. The group with the highest proportion working in service occupations was Black and SOR at 27%.

A range of median earnings exists between the two or more races population and across gender. Although the average earnings for all working males was $37,057, it was $31,035 among men of two or more races, $37,055 among White and Asian men, and $24,665 among American Indian/Alaskan Native/SOR men. The average earnings for all working females was about $10,000 less than for men at $27,194. It was $25,399 among women of two or more races, $29,973 among White and Asian women, and $29,988 among American Indian/Alaskan Native/SOR women (Jones, 2005). White and Asian households had a median family income of $52,413, which was higher than the average for the total population. The next highest was Asian and Native Hawaiian/Pacific Islander at $51,664 and White and Native Hawaiian/Pacific Islander at $45,758.

The poverty rate for children under the age of 18 in the two or more races population was 19.9% compared with 16.6% for all children. (See Table 10.2.) For people

TABLE 10.2   Characteristics of Two or More Races and Total Population

Characteristic	Two or More Races	Total Population
Median age	23.4	35.4
Native-born	76.5%	88.9%
Poverty rates of elderly	16.9%	9.9%
Poverty rates of children	19.9%	16.6%
Bachelor's degree	19.6%	24.4%
Never married	37.3%	27.1%
Marriage	45.6%	54.4%
Divorce	17.1%	18.5%
Median-income women	$25,399	$27,194
Median-income men	$31,035	$37,057
Owner-occupied homes	46.6%	66.2%

aged 65 and over, the poverty rate was 16.9% for the two or more races population compared with 9.9% for the U.S. population (Jones, 2005). Among children, Black and American Indian/Alaskan Native and Black and SOR combinations had higher poverty rates than children in other race combinations. White and Asian was the only population in which a larger proportion of the elderly than children lived in poverty, 16.6% compared with 7.5% among White/Asian children.

In the United States, about two thirds of occupied housing units were owner occupied compared with less than one half of those maintained by individuals who reported more than one race, or 46.6%. Four of the race combinations had home ownership rates of 50% or higher, which is greater than that of the total two or more races population: White and American Indian, 59.6%; Asian and Pacific Islander, 51.9%; White and Pacific Islander, 51.4%; and White and Asian, 50.5%. Black and SOR and White and Black householders were the most likely to be renters, at 69.3% and 65.1%, respectively.

Because race is a social construction, it is possible that the 2000 census might have yielded a different estimate of the size of the biracial and multiracial population had a alternative measure been selected than the one given, which was to report one or more of the following races: White, Black or African American, American Indian or Alaskan Native, Asian, or Native Hawaiian or other Pacific Islander (Harris & Sims, 2002). In other words, who in the household completed the census? Who identifies as multiracial on a daily basis? Whose ancestors come from more than one racial group?

Nearly two thirds of all people who reported more than one race lived in just 10 states (Jones & Symens Smith, 2001). The 10 states with the largest two or more race populations are California, New York, Texas, Florida, Hawaii, Illinois, New Jersey, Washington, Michigan, and Ohio. More specifically, the cities of Los Angeles and New York had the largest two or more races populations. Chicago, Houston, San Diego, and Honolulu also had two or more races populations greater than 50,000.

People with two or more races were more likely to reside in the West, at 40%. Twenty-seven percent resided in the south, 18% in the Northeast, and 15% in the Midwest. Counties forming the metropolitan corridor from Washington, DC, to Boston, Massachusetts, had higher percentages of people reporting two or more races. In the South, several metropolitan areas were cited and anchored by Huntsville, Alabama; Chattanooga, Tennessee; and Atlanta, Georgia. Counties with percentages of more than one race reporting lower than the percentage for the country were in nonmetropolitan counties in the Midwest and the South (Jones & Symens Smith, 2001).

THE ONE-DROP RULE

The **one-drop rule** emerged in the South during slavery and is traditionally understood as disavowing a White identity to anyone who had one sixteenth Black ancestry, regardless of physical appearance. People were considered Black or Negro if either of their parents was Black and if their only Black ancestor was a great-grandparent.

People who were not considered to be White were classified as Negroes and other races. During this time, race was not a social construction but one steeped in biology. Spickard (1992), a scholar on biracial identity, argued, "The so-called races are not biological categories at all. Rather, they are primarily social divisions that rely only partly on physical markers as skin color to identify group membership" (p. 17).

A castelike naming system existed. Whites had the most social power, followed by light-skinned and often mixed-race Blacks: mulattos, quadroons, and octoroons. Darker-skin Blacks were on the bottom rung of this ladder (Brunsma & Rockquemore, 2001). Mulattos had one Black parent and one White parent, usually a Black mother and a White father. Quadroons had one-quarter Black blood with one Black grandparent. Social privileges such as indoor housework instead of field work in the hot sun and educational opportunities were provided to offspring of White fathers, which served to create division in the Black community and gave rise to colorism. Octoroons had one-eighth Black blood or a Black great-grandparent. They were classified as non-White regardless of their phenotypical presentation. Passing was an option, that is, presenting as White, as long as the person did not maintain contact with family members who were counted as and/or identified as Black.

Sharfstein (2007) argues that the one-drop rule did not automatically make all mixed-race people Black. Communities co-existed with contradiction and allowed people to "cross-over" the color line—not because they were liberals or abolitionists but because the individual doing the crossing may have held segregationist and anti-Black attitudes as well and not because they were passing as White. Defining and demarcating race is shifting as is the discourse on race. White college students, in contemporary times, claim a Black identity to get into college. Others do not claim a Black identity despite knowledge of Black people in the family. There are increasing numbers of multiracial people with biracial and multiracial children representing the fastest growing groups of children.

Despite changes, the one-drop rule is still alive; however, it is not as pervasive as it used to be (Rockquemore, 2002). Increases in biracial and multiracial populations and different, hybrid identities of race in a post–civil rights age contribute to the lessening grip of this antiquated way of defining people's racial identities. Nonetheless, society has difficulty with multiracial individuals' alignment with more than one racial identity. Rigid and binary notions of race are being contested, and the cultural dimensions of race in the United States are shifting (Brunsma, 2006). Biracial and multiracial identities do not obfuscate the construct of race, but they do challenge the one-drop rule that denies a claim to a White identity if a person is also Black.

For some, a denial of multiple aspects of their racial and ethnic identities is likely to occur when a monoracial identity is claimed. Within the Black community, biracial and multiracial identities have existed since slavery. The one-drop rule, which is cloaked in a racist ideology that assumes racial purity, disallowed other than a Negro identity for people with both White European and Black African ancestry. Thus, mutlattos were considered Black due to the concept of *hypodesent*, or the process wherein biracial people were assigned to the social group with less social status (e.g., the Black mother during slavery). Due to the violence of slavery, the Black/White offspring conceived during this time were predominantly between Black slave women and White slave-owning men, but such was not always the case.

Biracial and mixed-race identities have existed in the Black community for centuries. What has not always existed, and is still highly contested, is whether Black/White biracial identities occupy a space that is different but not altogether separate from blackness. Claiming a biracial identity is neither a rampant negation of African ancestry nor an unbridled introjection of whiteness, but this is not collectively known or believed. Although rooted in and derived from White racist supremacist notions, in contemporary times, plenty of people of color resist multiracial identity claims among Black/White people.

The elevated social status associated with lighter skin, a characteristic among many monoracial and biracial people, has served to pit Black people in this country, and arguably throughout the world, against one another. Some people of color believe that a single racial definition reflects unity and power, while some political groups oppose a multiracial category. There is concern that allocations for school and social-based programs will be adversely affected by a multiracial designation (Schwartz, 1998), that a biracial identity might lead to further divisions among Black people, result in a loss of political clout, or be interpreted by the dominant society as biracial people's rejection of blackness in a racist world that already does that.

THE FLUIDITY OF RACE

Confusion exists as to who is considered multiracial. How past generations racially identified, phenotype, and self-identification have all been used to define multiracial people. Among Native Americans, blood quantum has been considered. The concept of race as fluid suggests it, like class, social experience, and custom, is not static, is shaped by social circumstances, and extends throughout the developmental life (Hall, 2001).

Shih and Sanchez (2005) maintain that several approaches exist for understanding multiracial people. One approach is the problem approach, which sees non-monoracial groups as marginal, susceptible to poor psychological outcomes such as low self-esteem and an inferiority complex, lability in mood, and hypersensitivity. The equivalent approach argues that after 1970, there were social movement shifts in the form of civil rights and racial politics. Racial pride was invoked and miscegenation was outlawed. Although racial identity models for monoracial groups were in development, their application to biracial people was deemed appropriate; in reality, this was short-sighted. They did not account for being able to identify with more than one racial group simultaneously.

The variant approach is the most recent approach and views "multiracial identity as a unique category, separate from any monoracial category (e.g., Asian, White, or Black)" (Shih & Sanchez, 2005, p. 571). It seems that it is interdisciplinary in focus, drawing on sociology, psychology, anthropology, literature, and feminist studies, and it encourages the perspective that multiracial people have multiple understandings of their racial identities (Brunsma & Rockquemore, 2001).

Race as a fluid construct is fundamentally different from passing. What does the fluidity of race mean, across contexts (home, school, and work), if biracial or multiracial persons were not denying any one identity or were not choosing to pass as something they were not but were identified according to contexts? Harris and Sims (2002) examined data from Wave 1 of the National Longitudinal Study of Adolescent Health (Add Health), a school-based, longitudinal study of health behaviors for youth in grades 7 through 12 collected in 1994 and 1995. More than 83,000 in-school interviews were conducted with students from 80 high schools and 52 middle schools. In addition, in-home interviews were conducted with more than 18,000 youth from the school sample. Finally, in-home interviews were conducted with a primary caregiver of each of the youth interviewed at home. All children who identified as Hispanic were excluded given that Hispanicity is deemed separate from race. The sample was also restricted to youth sampled both at school and at home.

Great variation in patterns of expressed internal race for multiracial populations was found. Among White/Black, 0.6% identify as White and Black at home and at school. White and Asian students did not differ between the school and home interviews in terms of their identities. However, White/American Indian youth were different. More than 2% identified as White and American Indian at school, yet a smaller share (1.5%) claimed a White/Indian identity at home. The researchers concluded that with "respect to racial self-identification, there is not a single multiracial experience" (Harris & Sims, 2002, p. 618). That racial identities are fluid was concluded: only 87.6% of adolescents expressed identical racial identities across contexts. Furthermore, 8.6% of youth reported being multiracial at home and 1.6% identified as multiracial in both contexts, across home and school. Geographical context is important to consider. In the south, White/Black youth were less likely to select White as their best single race. Other people's interpretation of biracial people's appearance places parameters on their own racial self-understandings (Brunsma & Rockquemore, 2001).

BIRACIAL AND MULTIRACIAL IDENTITY DEVELOPMENT

Brunsma and Rockquemore (2001) conducted research with 177 White and Black biracials (people with one Black parent and one White parent) to assess racial identification. Four identities were identified in previous research by Rockquemore (1999):

1. Singular identity.
2. Border identity.
3. Protean identity.
4. Transcendent.

Respondents were asked: Which of the following statements best describes yourself exclusively:

1. Black (or African American).
2. I sometimes consider myself Black, sometimes my other race, and sometimes biracial depending on the circumstances.
3. I consider myself biracial but I experience the world as a Black person.
4. I consider myself exclusively as Biracial (neither Black nor White).
5. I consider myself exclusively as my other race (not Black or biracial).
6. Race is meaningless, I do not believe in racial identity.
7. Other.

Phenotype (skin color), appearance, and interactional experiences (preadult racial composition and negative treatment from Whites and Blacks) were queried.

The majority of respondents (56.2%), despite a variety of skin color hues, defined themselves as "ambiguous though most people assume I am Black," (Brunsma & Rockquemore, 2001, p. 38). Seventeen percent stated they "appear Black, most people assume I am Black" and nearly 17% stated, "ambiguous, most people do not assume I am Black." Ten percent said they "appear White, I could pass as White." The majority of the sample considered themselves to have border identities in that they understood themselves as neither Black and White but as exclusively biracial. Although this is the case, most of the border biracials said they experience the world as a Black person. Their experience as exclusively biracial is not validated by others in interactions. Only 14% of the sample saw themselves as exclusively Black. The same percentage did not apply racial labels to themselves and is considered to be a transcendent identity or with no racial self-understanding. Five percent saw themselves shifting among Black, White, and biracial identities, depending on the circumstances. This is referred to as a protean identity. Nearly 4% saw themselves as singularly White.

Wijeyesinghe (2001) presented a factor model of multiracial identity (FMMI) developed from a qualitative study of African American/European American multiracial adults. This model is nonlinear and represents factors or dimensions of identity. These dimensions include:

- Racial ancestry or family tree.
- Early experiences and socialization, which includes exposure to culture, such as food, music, holiday, dialect, and language.
- Cultural attachment that may influence racial designation.
- Physical appearance, which includes skin hue, body shape, and hair texture.
- Social and historical context, such as the presence of other multiracial people or the 2000 census allowing people to choose more than one box to designate themselves racially/ethnically.
- Political awareness and orientation, which is connected to the awareness of race and racism within a larger sociopolitical context.

- Other social identities, such as sexual orientation and social class.
- Spirituality or being guided by spirit, which fosters connection to others and allows people to transcend the divisions of race and ethnicity.

Kich (1992) developed a three-stage biracial model for Japanese and White Americans from semistructured interviews with 15 biracial adults. The first stage is awareness of differentness and dissonance between self-perceptions and the perceptions from other people. Biracial people are seen as different. Dissonance or discomfort about this difference can occur when the comparison process is regarded as devaluation. The second stage, struggle for acceptance from others, can extend into adulthood and often occurs in the context of school or community settings. In cases where a biracial person is the only one in a particular context, the question "What are you?" may be asked, especially in light of differences in the person's name or phenotype.

The final stage is self acceptance and assertion of an interracial identity. Kich (1992) says, "The biracial person's ability to create congruent self-definitions rather than be determined by others' definitions and stereotypes may be said to be the major achievement of a biracial and bicultural identity" (p. 314).

Kich (1992) also discussed the ways in which biracial Japanese Americans achieved a sense of identity development. Some traveled to Japan and learned the language. Others met and spoke with extended family members who may have been less emotionally available in the past. Others who had endorsed the European American community exclusively may have explored their Japanese heritage anew or for the first time.

It is not uncommon for biracial persons to struggle with converging their various identities. According to Mass (1992), Japanese people in Los Angeles had higher rates of out-marriages compared with other Asian groups. In a study conducted among interracial Japanese Americans, Mass sampled 53 college-age White Japanese respondents and 52 monoracial Japanese American college students. She measured ethnic identity, acculturation, self-concept, and the Japanese American ethnic experience and then administered a personality inventory. No differences in the psychological adjustment and self-esteem of the two groups were found. However, it was discovered that interacial Japanese Americans showed less identification with being Japanese than monoracial Japanese Americans. Japanese Americans who were raised in parts of the country (Hawaii and certain California communities) where there were larger numbers of Japanese Americans tended to have few or no problems with race.

Poston (1990) proposed a model of biracial identity development with five linear stages: (1) personal identity, (2) choice of group categorization, (3) enmeshment/denial, (4) appreciation, and (5) integration. Stage 1 is the initial step in identity process and is seen among young children who have not developed a group self-esteem. Choice of group categorization (stage 2) consists of persons choosing a racial group to identify with. Ethnic background, neighborhood, and social support are factors that can influence this choice. The third stage represents upheaval and confusion about choosing a group with which to identify. Feelings of being betwixt and between can characterize people who may not feel acceptance from either group. Learning to accept their multiple identities describes the fourth stage, and stage 5 is an integrated place where people are able to celebrate all of who they are.

RESEARCH AND BIRACIAL AND MULTIRACIAL POPULATIONS

Although more research is being conducted, there is a dearth of empirical research on multiracial populations (Herman, 2004). Shih and Sanchez (2005) observed that much of the work done was on investigating the psychological impact of having a multiracial identity and the difficulty that multiracial people had in defining a racial identity. There have been difficulties with sample size, methodological issues such as randomization in sampling, and problems with self-report inventories (Herman, 2004). Qualitative research may be best suited for research on biracial and multiethnic populations given that it allows the researcher "to enter the subjective world of other people and groups through interviews and rich descriptions, which is not achieved through quantitative methods" (Jourdan, 2006, p. 330).

Theoretical sampling is a critical concept in qualitative research and refers to the research participants' contribution to the study with less emphasis on numbers. Qualitative methodologies, such as semistructured interviews, are ideal for research with multiracial populations in that they allow for a broader and more in-depth exploration of mixed-race people's life experiences while allowing the researcher to develop hypotheses for future studies from a contextual and cultural perspective (Collins, 2000).

Rockquemore (2002) conducted in-depth, loosely structured, qualitative interviews with 16 Black/White biracial respondents. The primary theme that emerged was negative interactions with monoracial African Americans. (See Storytelling: "Hostile Assumptions.") Women were more likely than men to report negative interactions. The content of these encounters was typically related to physical appearance, such as skin color, body size, and eye color. Competition for Black men was discussed. That Black women have few eligible suitors given that successful Black men are just as likely to marry inside and outside of their race has to be considered within the context

STORYTELLING: Hostile Assumptions

One of the mothers in my research with White mothers of non-White children, along with her husband, had adopted two Black/White biracial children. She was at the grocery store one day with her children and noticed that the check-out clerk, a young Black woman, seemed to be hostile toward her. She chalked it up to a bad day. The same experience occurred when she took her children to buy school clothes. She reflected on these events during our interview and said that it actually happened a lot. I asked her if she thought the women had made an assumption that she was the biological mother of these children, which meant their father was a Black man. She nodded and concluded that this may explain their attitude. This issue of hostility from Black and Maori women toward White mothers, even women who have adopted children or single lesbians, has been discussed in my research.

of this finding. The internalization of negative messages among some of the biracial women in the sample was identified. Black people were broadly characterized as being on drugs, without jobs, and ill-mannered. Many of the respondents were raised by White women, given that White woman/Black man is the most common dyad for Black/White marriages.

Interview respondents raised by White mothers frequently reported dealing with a White parent's explicit racism and dealing with the racialized negativity that the White parent had for their Black father. Rockquemeore (2002) cited that a cognitive dichotomy can emerge when a Black father is abusive or addicted and in contrast a friend's White father is attentive and involved. Blackness can be conceptualized as betrayal and Whiteness as goodness. Rockquemore concluded by saying that for women of African descent, skin color acts as a microlevel manifestation of oppression with respect to the conflicted and contested relationship between Black and biracial women.

CASE STUDY
Color-Blind

Lita Evans, PhD, is a 35-year-old counseling psychologist. For a year she has been working in a private practice with two junior MS-level counselors and another licensed psychologist. Lita is Japanese and was born and raised in Oregon. Her husband, Jake, is a White European American and is also from Oregon. Both sets of his grandparents were from England. Lita and Jake live in Utah with their two school-age daughters. Kati, their oldest daughter, asked Lita why her daddy's and sister's skin and eyes were not dark like theirs. Lita told Kati, "You were kissed by the hot sun and daddy and sister were embraced by the cool moon." Recently Lita and her colleagues were talking about the Korean wife of a mutual acquaintance. One of her White colleagues said, "She may have married white and rich, but she will always look like she was hit in the face with a skillet." Embarrassed, her colleague said, "Don't take offense Lita; I don't see you as Asian." Lita smiled and said, "Hey. We're all human aren't we?"

All of Lita's friends and neighbors and the majority of her clients are White. One of Lita's new clients is Tarisa, an 18-year-old female born in Brazil. Tarisa has caramel-colored skin, green eyes, and curly hair.

She was adopted as a baby by Sheila and Mike, who are White. They were told by the adoption agency that Tarisa's father was White and her mother was very dark. Tarisa's ex-boyfriend, Brad, ended their relationship 3 weeks ago. They had dated 6 months. Since the break up, Tarisa has a hard time getting out of bed in the mornings, has lost weight, cries a lot, is socially withdrawn, and finds it difficult to concentrate at school. She also has headaches and neck pain. Brad told Tarisa that his parents preferred that he date Jewish girls. Tarisa was raised in a racially/culturally diverse community. Her parents exposed Tarisa to her African-Brazilian culture through film, history, art, and travel. Sheila and Mike wanted Tarisa to *fall in love* with Brazil as they had. Sheila takes Tarisa to Lita for therapy. She is perplexed as to why a break-up with a boyfriend has had such a profound impact on her daughter. A transcript from the therapy follows:

LITA: Tarisa, what makes you the saddest?

TARISA: I am a good person. I think Brad wanted to break up with me because I am not White.

LITA: Why do you think that?

TARISA: Brad told me that his parents wanted him to date only Jewish girls.

LITA: Some parents think religion is important.

TARISA: Brad's last girlfriend was Catholic, not Jewish. They dated a whole year.

LITA: Why did they break up?

TARISA: He told me that she broke up with him because he started seeing other people.

LITA: You're going off to college in a few months where you will meet other guys. I met my husband in college and he's American.

TARISA: (pause). I'm American, too.

LITA: My husband is English.

TARISA: Oh, he was born in England. That's cool. I was born in Brazil. I love Brazil!

LITA: No, my husband was born in Oregon; we both were.

TARISA: So, your husband is White? Why not just say that!

LITA: There are many ways to describe people.

TARISA: I'm Brazilian American. My skin is brown. I'm biracial and adopted. My parents are White. How do you describe yourself?

LITA: This session is about you. Let's focus on you.

TARISA: Why do so many people say skin color doesn't matter and the whole time, they act like it's more important than anything?

LITA: Is it possible you place too much emphasis on that?

TARISA: Maybe you don't place enough emphasis on "that."

After the session, Tarisa tells her mother that she does not want to continue counseling with Ms. Evans, who "lives in la la land." Sheila is disappointed that the therapy went as poorly as it had. She said, "I was hoping that a therapist of color could help my child explore issues around race and racism and develop strategies to live with agency in a world preoccupied with skin color!" After speaking with some of her friends, Sheila finds a therapy group for young women of color facilitated by a licensed mental health professional through a local Black church.

Tarisa enjoys going and, in time, feels better and eventually is weaned off of the antidepressants prescribed by their family physician. She announces to her parents she wants to travel to Brazil during the summer prior to going away for college and search for her biological mother.

QUESTIONS

1. What are the implications of the counselor's unexplored racial identity on therapeutic practice and effectiveness?
2. What are the discourses and experiences that contribute to people of color not exploring and developing their racial identities?
3. How did Lita's lack of personal exploration about her racial identity get past her clinical and faculty supervisors?
4. What are the discourses and experiences that contribute to White people exploring and developing their racial identities?

DISCUSSION AND INTEGRATION
The Client, Tarisa

There are multiple issues in Tarisa's life. She feels rejection from Brad and attributes his termination of their relationship to her race and his inability to be honest about it. Tarisa is depressed and, given the loss she has experienced, has reason to be—she lost a significant relationship that she values. At the same time, the break-up triggered very old feelings of rejection as an adoptee that she has not consciously addressed. Such feelings of rejection and betrayal have triggered unresolved feelings of personal inadequacy associated with being given up for adoption by her birth mother. Tarisa's headaches and neck pain may be stress related and a somatization of her inner state.

Fortunately, Tarisa seems to have a good sense of her biracial identity. The stable home that her parents have provided her, the racially diverse neighborhood, as well as the validation and acknowledgement of Tarisa's African-Brazilian heritage have played a role in the development of a cohesive identity (Schwartz, 1998). The term *double* could be applied to Tarisa in that she has created an identity that is more than the sum of its parts regarding her White and African-Brazilian identities. "Double denotes those who have a positive reflection of their identity based on the coexistence of their ethnicities" (Collins, 2000, p. 126).

The antidepressant medication prescribed by the family physician may provide symptomatic relief and help Tarisa to cope with her feelings of sadness. The medication may, in time, allow her to function more effectively at school; however, it does not replace the importance of tackling this unfinished business in her life.

A combination of psychopharmacology and group therapy functions well for Tarisa, yet she will need to be monitored by a medical doctor when decreasing her dosage of antidepressants. Sudden withdrawal can be accompanied by physically distressing symptoms. Activities of the young women's group include keeping a journal and walking to relieve stress and maintain physical health and strength, with deep breathing exercises to relax. Sheila and Tarisa take a trip to Brazil after doing some preliminary research from home about Tarisa's birth mother.

The Therapist, Lita

Lita is similar to other Japanese American women who have the highest rates of marriage to Whites among all other Asian ethnic groups (Le, 2007). More than 38% of Japanese women have White spouses compared with 27% of Filipino women, 23% of Korean women, 14% of Chinese women, and 11% of Vietnamese women. Asian Indian women are the least likely of all groups to have a White spouse at 4.3%. Wu (2002) said, "Among Asian Americans under the age of thirty-five who are married, half have found a spouse of a non-Asian background" (p. 263).

Lita takes a color-blind approach to life. Color-blindness refers to the denial, distortion, and/or minimization of race and racism (Neville, Spanierman, & Doan, 2006). In her research with the Color-Blind Racial Attitudes Scale (CoBRAS), Neville and her colleagues found that although there are different types of color-blindness, this phenomenon has been related to higher levels of fear about people of color, lower levels of White

guilt, and less anger and- or sadness about the existence of racism.

To competently respond to clients' issues associated with race as a personal identity and social construct, it is important that the therapist be aware of his or her own racial identity and be at a similar place or preferably further along than the client with respect to racial identity development. It is clear that Lita has an underdeveloped sense of who she is as a monoracial woman in an interracial marriage with biracial children. Her marriage to a White man in no way is a manifestation of where she is developmentally. There are clear examples in the case study that indicate she does not have a clear sense of who she is as a racial being. She provides a mythical explanation to her daughter's question about skin color and eye shape; she allows a derogatory statement about Asians to go unchecked; and she is incapable of providing appropriate clinical insight to Tarisa, whose clinical presentation is partially influenced by race and perceptions of racial discrimination.

Lita, for the most part, lives in an all-White world in Utah, where her biracial children are not exposed to other biracial children or to other Asian people on a regular basis and so do not have an opportunity to see other people who look like themselves. Collins (2000) found, in her qualitative research with Japanese/White individuals who grew up in predominantly White neighborhoods, that they did not acknowledge their Japanese ethnicity, did not have the opportunity to socialize with other biracial children, and thus, their self-definition was devalued. As children grow and seek to belong to others, exclusion from groups may become an issue. Physical appearance, stereotyping, or being given a message that you are excluded from a desired group can provoke dissonance about where a person belongs and even encourage attempts to belong to the excluded group (Ahnallen, Suyemoto, & Carter, 2006).

Because Lita's children have different phenotypes, their experiences with both European and Japanese American groups may differ considerably. More specifically, Ahnallen, Suyemoto, and Carter (2006) found that physical appearance played a role in relation to belonging to European American groups.

Japanese physical appearance showed trends toward relating to both Japanese American belonging and exclusion. The daughter who looks more European may find acceptance as European in ways that her Japanese-looking sister does not, despite the fact that they come from the same parents. Root (1998) found in her investigation of 20 sibling pairs that hazing, which she called "an injunction to prove one is an insider through a demeaning process of racial and ethnic authenticity testing" (pp. 242–243), was reported as an experience among many of these siblings.

Parents who are unable or unwilling to discuss the stratification of race with their children do them a disservice in preparing for a world that continues to be preoccupied with skin color as a means of racial categorization. There are times when family dysfunction (abuse and addiction) result in racial themes not being salient (Root, 1998). In Lita's case, it appears that she is at a place of racial unawareness.

Lita's children are biracial, but they are not being raised to be bicultural. Biculturally identified people take pride in cultural traditions from both ethnic and racial groups. Although there are differences in their appearance, Suzuki-Crumly and Hyers (2004) state that Asian/White biracials may be less noticeably non-White and more ambiguous in their appearance than Black/White biracials. The model minority stereotype, in addition to having a European-looking appearance, may make it more easy to identify as White and gain acceptance into the White community.

IMPLICATIONS FOR COUNSELORS AND PSYCHOLOGISTS

Some of the early research suggested that biracial children had a high incidence of academic and behavioral problems presumed to be connected to identity conflicts and related challenges (Gibbs, Huang, & Associates 1989). Santiago-Rivera, Arredondo, and Gallardo-Cooper (2002) encourage parents of bicultural children not to impose their culture on the child, particularly adolescents. It is suggested that children will internalize a variety of experiences and beliefs into their own value system that encompasses multiple identities and worldviews.

Shih and Sanchez (2005) cautioned researchers who study clinical samples to apply these findings to nonclinical samples. In their review of multiracial literature, multiracial persons in the general population were not more dissatisfied, unhappy, or uncomfortable with their racial identity. Udry, Li, and Hendrickson-Smith (2003), in their analysis of Add Health data comparing mixed-race adolescents to single-race adolescents, concluded adolescents who identify with more than one race were at a higher health and behavior risk when compared with adolescents identifying with only one race. The risk may be related to the stress associated with identity conflict. Without direct evidence, the researchers cautioned against jumping to conclusions.

Schwartz (1998) observed that the racial identity development of multiracial youth is more complicated than for monoracial youth. Herman (2004) affirmed the ethnic identity research, which suggests there are opportunities associated with identity development. Although there is societal racism (negative feelings about interracial marriages) and families that do not emphasize race, children come to see prejudice and racism in society. In addition, some children may feel enormous conflict about choosing one racial identity over another based on the child's phenotype, neighborhood, or, in the case of divorce, the race of the custodial parent. Socialization of children to embrace a biracial or multiracial identity communicates to a child the value and importance of all of his or her racial and ethnic identities. Although more complicated, the experience of identity formation can be a positive and affirming experience (Herman, 2004). Treating race as a social construction as opposed to a biological one was found by Shih, Bonam, Sanchez, and Pick (2007) to help buffer people from stereotype threat effects.

SUMMARY

This chapter provided several definitions, including *biracial, multiracial, bicultural, interracial*, and *interracial*. Research on biracial and multiracial populations was highlighted, and a discussion of research methodologies was examined. The intensely political nature of the topic of race and biracial identities was a theme throughout the chapter.

Chapter 11

Converging Gender

Violence is often the single most evident marker of manhood.

Michael Kimmel

Gender is a crucial part of our daily lives. It takes deviation from gender conformity to get people to notice the undoing of gender. Gender influences what we believe about ourselves and others. Across race, class, culture, disability, and sexuality, common gender themes seem to exist for men and women. Among people of color, gender is often obscured by race, in that race vies for more attention as the salient identity construct.

In this chapter, gender is emphasized as both a social construct and a status characteristic. It is acknowledged that gender differences exist between men and women and within groups of women and men. This truth is neither refuted nor regarded as problematic. However, the way gender inequity is perpetuated as a primary status characteristic within society is examined. Selected literature is presented that examines relationships with the self and others as a function of gender, gender roles, and sex role typology. The subsequent impact on gender identity is also investigated, as is gender from a biological perspective. Myths about biological differences between males and females are exposed.

GENDER DEFINITIONS

Sex roles and *gender roles* differ. Typically, **sex roles** are behavioral patterns culturally approved as more appropriate for either males or females (Worell & Remer, 1992); however, in this work, *sex roles* refer to roles related to the function of one's biology, such as erection, ejaculation, menstruation, ovulation, pregnancy, and lactation. **Gender roles** are a consequence of society's views regarding appropriate behavior based on one's biological sex, such as diaper changing, garbage takeout, spider killing, dinner making, and primary breadwinning. Gender labels are applied to people, and, once done, people behave toward an individual based on a set of expectations held for persons who have the same label. A role is a cluster of expectations for behavior of persons within a specific category. The meaning of **gender** varies among different cultures and changes throughout time (McCarthy & Holiday, 2004). The most common definition is the culturally determined attitudes, cognitions, and belief systems about females and males. Haider (1995) said, "The focus of gender is on social roles and interactions of women and men rather than their biological characteristics which is sex . . . gender is a matter of cultural definition as to what is considered to be masculine or feminine" (p. 35). The male gender role affirms masculine identity around qualities such as self-reliance and success. For women, it is feminine characteristics traditionally associated with noncompetiveness and care of others. The negative consequences of gender role restriction is termed **gender role conflict** (Lane & Addis, 2005) and "describes the detrimental consequences of gender roles either for the person holding them or for those associated with this person" (Mintz & O'Neil, 1990, p. 381).

Masculinity refers to traditional societal roles, behaviors, and attitudes prescribed for men, whereas **femininity** references traditional societal roles, behaviors, and attitudes prescribed for women (Mintz & O'Neil, 1990). Masculinity is construed with hegemonic power and men's dominance over women; however, men are dependent on women and perceive women as having expressive power over them or the power to express emotion (Pleck, 1984). Another form of power that women are perceived to have over men is *masculinity validating power,* or men's dependence on women to affirm their masculinity and validate their manhood. A system of this nature reinforces homophobia and heterosexism in its dependence on rigid adherence to gender and sex role–appropriate behaviors that operate exclusively in the context of heterosexuality, or the semblance of heterosexuality, and gender conformity.

Androcentrism refers to males at the center of the universe, looking out at reality from behind their own eyes and describing what they see from an egocentric—or androcentric—point of view (Bem, 1993).

GENDER AND BIOLOGY

Confusion arises when the sex category to which one is assigned is ambiguous. With the application of rigorous criteria that are socially derived, people are placed within indigenous categories as male or female, man or woman (West & Zimmerman, 1991). West and Zimmerman said, "Not only do we want to know the sex category of those around us (to see it at a glance, perhaps), but we presume that others are displaying it for us in as decisive a fashion as they can" (p. 21).

In each human body cell, chromosomes are the genetic material carried. Except for the reproductive cells (sperm and ova) and mature red blood cells, each cell has 46 chromosomes arranged into 23 pairs. Twenty-two pairs of chromosomes, called **autosomes,** are matching sets in both males and females. The 23rd pair, called **sex chromosomes,** differs between the two sexes. Among genetically normal males, the sex chromosomes are XY; among genetically normal females, they are XX (Moir & Jessel, 1991).

From conception to about the 6th week in utero, all human embryos are anatomically identical. During the 6th week, sexual differentiation begins. The genetic information in the Y chromosome stimulates the production of a protein called *H-Y antigen.* This protein promotes the change of the undifferentiated gonads into fetal testes. The fetal testes synthesize myriad hormones known as **androgens.** Two important androgens are *Mullerian inhibiting substance (MIS)* and *testosterone.* MIS is involved in the degeneration of the female duct system (Renzetti & Curran, 1992). Testosterone promotes further growth of the male Wolffian duct, the duct system that leaves the testes. Testosterone is often referred to as the aggression, dominance, and sex hormone (Moir & Jessel, 1991).

In the 8th week, the hormone dihydrotestosterone encourages the formation of external genitals. It is suggested that, for the female, the lack of testosterone may prompt the undifferentiated gonads of an XX embryo to transform into ovaries around the 12th week of gestation (Renzetti & Curran, 1992).

THE SOCIAL CONSTRUCTION OF GENDER

Gender is a status characteristic that manifests in dominant and multiple ways. For the most part, males tend to enter into the world as the preferred sex and are accorded power within a patriarchal society. Because gender intersects with sexuality, class, and race, some men in society have more power than others and less power than some women. Clearly, not all men feel powerful and exert power over all women within a system of male supremacy. There are women, who by virtue of their race, nationality, skin color, able-body, and class privileges, exert power over some men and other women. Men operate as both the oppressed and the oppressor (McCarthy & Holliday, 2004). An androcentric culture exists and dictates for both women and men images and standards of acceptability, which influence body image and self-esteem.

The devaluation of women and the esteem given to men is culturally rooted. Saucier (2004) noted that "women are set up to fail in a system that defines success for men in terms of productivity and accomplishment and designates beauty and sexiness as the measure of success for women" (p. 420). The process of preparing boys to be masculine men and girls to be feminine women is largely an unconscious one within the culture. The family influences children in their most important identity formation, the gender role. Socializing influences include parents, grandparents, the extended family, teachers, the media, other children, and textbooks. Evans and Davies (2000) found in their examination of first-, third-, and fifth-grade literature textbooks that despite publisher's guidelines and Title IX, males are still portrayed in stereotypical ways, to be aggressive, argumentative, and competitive. It is not uncommon for couples with girl children to keep trying for a male child. This information needs to be contextualized. There are families with boy children who will keep trying for a girl child as well.

An individual's personality develops through the interplay of both biological inheritance and social experience. At birth, males and females are ascribed certain roles, characteristics, and behaviors associated with explicit values and expectations according to a constructed gender role that is socially generated (Haider, 1995). Society places men's work on a higher level for remuneration and recognition. (See Storytelling: "Maiden Name.") Even in female activities, male involvement gives men expertise.

Once upon a time, before satellite and cable television, high speed Internet, cable, iPhones, BlackBerries, video games, PlayStations, and play-dates, children went outdoors and played with other children. Store-bought toys were available, but often imagination and improvisation were used and children made up their own games or toys. As was the case then and is now, parents ensured that children were exposed to games, activities, and household chores compatible with children's gender. Children were rewarded for acting appropriately and punished when there was deviation from a standard. Rewards may be in the form of toys, accolades, encouragement, playing with other children, or actually offering advice and instructions. Punishments may be in the form of ridicule, denial of privilege, or removal of an offensive object (e.g., a Barbie doll for a little boy). Pressure is put on girls to be obedient, good mothers, selfless,

STORYTELLING: Maiden Name

When you call the credit card company and actually speak to a human being to check on your balance, request a credit line increase, or request a lower interest rate, the password is your mother's maiden name. Every time I get asked this question, I complain—ultimately to the representative who has no power to make or change policy but only to enforce it. Heterosexist, racist, and sexist discourses are loaded in the question. First, it is assumed that people's mothers married—some mothers have a child or children without marrying the father. Nonmarriage is not a negation of a child's birth. A large percentage of women across race, but particularly among Black women and Latinas, are single parents. Second, it assumed that a woman is heterosexual and thus married a man. Third, the credit card company policy assumes that upon marriage, all women renounce their birth names and take their husband's name. This practice is antiquated and needs to stop.

dependent, and trustworthy (McBride, 1990). A relationship exists between these types of gender socialization experiences and girls' tendency to attribute their success to luck as opposed to skill (Sadker, Sadker, & Long, 1993). In a recent study of 392 college women, a lack of problem-solving confidence predicted depressive symptoms, which predicted eating disorder symptoms (VanBoven & Espelage, 2006).

Dealing with novelty or the unexpected can be a challenge for girls because they tend to be protected and sheltered. Boys are taught to be outgoing, independent, and assertive. This is not to say that all boys are assertive and feel powerful and that all females do not feel powerful. Race, class, sexuality, disability, and immigrant status are all factors that mediate the impact of privilege and oppression on people's gendered lives. Fortunately, the study of femininity and masculinity is increasingly more focused on cross-cultural contexts (Wester, Kuo, & Vogel, 2006). For instance, immigrant women in the United States experience oppression from xenophobia, racism, class discrimination, and sexism (Yakushko & Chronister, 2005). Research was done with 60 male participants at a school in Massachusetts and 45 male participants at a large public university in Costa Rica. The research was investigating culture, gender role conflict, and likelihood of help-seeking for two different problems from a variety of potential help providers. The Costa Rican men were more likely to report higher levels of restrictive affectionate behavior between men and lower levels of conflict between work and family than were U.S. men. The researchers surmised that the two groups of men might experience similar levels of success, restrictive emotionality, power, and competition but the meaning and importance of these constructs might vary between the cultures (Lane & Addis, 2005).

Good and Mintz (1990) found that boys' games, although rule-governed, rewarded creativity, improvisation, and initiative and involved teams comprised of a larger number of peers while encouraging both cooperation and competition. Boys are also prepared to engage in the world and explore it and to play by themselves. In doing so, they develop improvisational and problem-solving skills and are given important practice in the art of negotiation. Achievement and success are emphasized for boys, which may explain why boys enter an activity with a premise that they should master, create, and make a difference.

The instrument commonly used to measure masculine role conflict is the Gender Role Conflict Scale (GRCS). It is based on the notion that the traditional gender socialization of boys asks more than what is possible to give. To be regarded as masculine, men are expected to have power, compete with one another, demonstrate control over themselves and their environment, and show power over women. Vulnerability is frowned upon, as is weakness and irrationality. The inability to shoulder all of these expectations ushers in distress. Gender role conflict was associated with psychological distress, such as paranoia, psychoticism, obsessive-compulsivity, depression, and interpersonal sensitivity.

One consequence of the male socialization pattern that emphasizes strength, self-reliance, and independence is restrictive emotionality. **Restrictive emotionality,** the socialized practice of men not expressing their emotions, is one of the subscales on the Gender Role Conflict Scale. According to Good et al. (1996), four behavioral patterns emerge when men experience gender role conflict. The first behavioral pattern is *restrictive emotionality,* which refers to men's reluctance or difficulty in expressing their emotions. *Alexithymia* describes symptoms that include a decreased ability to label and communicate affect, confusion of affective and somatic symptoms, and externally oriented thinking. Alexithymia may be linked to a variety of both psychological and physical disorders, including depression (Carpenter & Addis, 2000).

The second behavioral pattern is *restrictive affectionate behavior between men.* Men may be afraid of sharing a full range of emotions for fear of being seen as gay (Good, Dell, & Mintz, 1989). Gertner (1994) said that men may also be limited in how they express their sexuality and affection to others.

Obsession with achievement and success is the third behavioral pattern, which references a disturbing and persistent preoccupation with work, accomplishment, and eminence as a means of demonstrating value. Seeking help may be experienced as the antithesis of being in control and having power. This may explain why men remain less likely than women to seek therapeutic assistance (Gertner, 1994). It is not that women are more psychologically disturbed than men, it is that men's socialization patterns do not encourage them to seek needed psychological help. Feeling sad or depressed may be seen as unmanly (Good et al., 1989).

There has been greater emphasis in the past few decades on *coaching,* defined as an ongoing professional relationship that helps people produce extraordinary results in their lives, careers, businesses, or organizations (McKelley & Rochlen, 2007). Coaching may appeal to men, particularly those who are adverse to receiving professional help. Its emphasis on a collegial relationship (perhaps less of a power differential) and on the teaching of human relationship skills to successful executives over addressing psychological deficits has been cited as the appeal.

Balancing work and family relations is the fourth behavioral pattern. Because men are socialized to focus on achievement, other areas of life, such as home and leisure, can easily be ignored or sacrificed or both. These four behavioral patterns have been related to depression (Good & Mintz, 1990). Gertner (1994) added homophobia and health care problems to this as well.

A study was done involving 103 master's- and doctoral-level male interns in Association of Psychology Postdoctoral and Internship Center (APPIC). The main finding, which investigated gender role conflict and the supervisor working alliance, was that men high in restrictive emotionality tended to deal with less power by turning against themselves in the form of negative perceptions of their own counseling efficacy. This study revealed that counseling students were not immune to internalizing gendered behavior, even if it had negative consequences (Wester, Vogel, & Archer, 2004).

Another way of understanding restrictive emotionality on men's lives is by comparing an underused muscle to the difficulty many men have in receiving assistance during emotional stress or accepting responsibility when necessary. In a study with 207 college students (17% non-White), men were found to experience shame proneness, guilt, and externalization (Efthim, Kenny, & Mahalik, 2001). **Externalization** was defined as the act of shifting blame outward for negative events and is a defensive maneuver in dealing with shame and guilt (Skovholt, 1993). Men's tendency to avoid expressing affection toward other men is associated with increased likelihood of depression, as is their reluctance to seek psychological help.

The psychological distress experienced by women occurs within the context of unfair treatment due to their biological sex (perceived discrimination) and subsequent and negative personal views of women as a group (private collective self-esteem) and of themselves as individuals (personal self-esteem) (Fischer & Holz, 2007).

UNDOING GENDER

Western philosophy dictates the construction of masculinity and femininity as mutually exclusive or dichotomous. Common language used when referring to the two genders is "the opposite sex," or reference is made to one's partner as "the other half." Masculinity in the Western worldview is associated with an instrumental orientation, a cognitive focus on getting the job done, or problem solving. Femininity, in contrast, is associated with a concern for others and harmony with the group. Until gender roles ascribed by society change and the inherent sexism is transformed, men and women alike will be constricted to and suffer from the consequences of inequities based on biological sex and socially constructed roles (Gertner, 1994). Although there are serious consequences associated with rigid sex-based gender roles that limit the range of affect, behaviors, and cognitions perceived to be available to people, they are adopted and perpetuated. This issue was explored by psychologist Sandra Bem, who developed the concept of androgyny. She also designed the Bem Sex Role Inventory (BSRI), which has been used in hundreds of research studies on *gender role socialization* and androgyny. *Androgyny* is from the Greek *andro,* meaning "male," and *gyne,* meaning "female" (Bem, 1993). Androgyny is consistent with the notion of people as gendered beings fully developing without restricting and confining sex roles.

Androgynous refers to persons who are high in both feminine and masculine psychological and behavioral traits, not to persons' biological, male or female, physical characteristics. According to Bem (1993), an individual can be both masculine and feminine; expressive, instrumental, and communal; and compassionate and assertive, depending on the situation. Limiting oneself to one domain could be costly to human potential in that individuals may be required to mitigate agency with communion and strength with yielding. Bem stated that balance is necessary because extreme femininity untempered by a sufficient concern for one's own needs as an individual may produce dependency and self-denial, just as extreme masculinity untempered by a sufficient ability to ask for help from others may produce arrogance and exploitation. An individual with both masculine and feminine characteristics would arguably be more flexible and function more productively than a sex-typed individual. Androgynous persons demonstrate a lack of statistically significant differences between masculinity and femininity scores, thus showing a blend of both dimensions.

Psychological differences between the sexes are not biological destiny but rather are learned after birth through the sex role socialization process (Cook, 1987). Although this is the case, a *uniformity myth* tends to make sex synonymous with gender roles. Men are connected with masculine characteristics that are instrumental, agentic, and goal oriented in nature. Emphasis is placed on self-development and separation from others. Masculine characteristics are associated with goal directedness, achievement, and recognition by others for one's efforts. Highly valued traits within the culture of the United States are also deemed masculine—competitiveness, assertiveness, high achievement, and individualism (Burnett, Anderson, & Heppner, 1995). Saucier (2004) observed that most positive traits associated with masculinity increase with age (e.g., competence, autonomy, self-control, and power). Not only are males elevated, masculinity has greater "social utility" than does femininity. This, according to Burnett et al. (1995), is known as the masculine supremacy effect. "This position suggests a cultural bias toward masculinity such that individuals who are masculine receive more positive social reinforcement and hence develop higher self-esteem" (p. 323). Masculinity was viewed as more valuable not only for men but also for women. Women who were low in individual masculinity were at greater risk for decreased self-esteem. There is, however, a flip side. Women who demonstrate too much masculinity are regarded as aggressive and bitchy, whereas boys and men who exhibit an excess of feminine qualities are ridiculed and called derogatory names, such as fag and sissy (Haddock, Zimmerman, & Lyness, 2003). Femininity may influence how others respond to a person, but masculinity is strongly related to various indexes of psychological health (Burnett et al., 1995). Masculinity had a more positive impact on how one sees oneself. Conversely, women are associated with the feminine characteristics of expressiveness and communality, with a focus on emotionality, selflessness, sensitivity, and interpersonal relationships.

The challenges with measurement of masculinity and femininity were echoed by Hoffman (2001):

> There are numerous instruments that are widely used today by a range
> of individuals from researchers in counseling, psychology, and education
> to human resource personnel. Unfortunately, what is being assessed is
> often given only cursory consideration by researchers and consumers
> alike. (p. 472)

Despite the murky waters of masculinity and femininity, these terms are popular within the culture. Sex role typology, which references a psychological dimension, is not predicated on biological sex. Masculinity or femininity refers to behaviors, not physical makeup. Men can be psychologically feminine and women can be psychologically masculine. Sex-typed persons (e.g., men ascribing to a strictly masculine role, women to a feminine role) have internalized society's sex-appropriate standards for desirable behavior to the relative exclusion of the other sex's typical characteristics. The traditional masculine role, which has been found to be unhealthy on many indexes of functioning, is related to status, toughness, success, achievement, emotional stoicism, and antifemininity (Lane & Addis, 2005).

Sex role rigidity contributes to narrow and restricted behaviors. An example of this was seen in research conducted by Stevens, Pfost, and Potts (1990). They found that "masculine-typed men and feminine-typed women reported the most avoidance of existential issues, with sex-typed persons indicating the least openness to such concerns . . . the findings also complement evidence of behavioral rigidity among sex-typed individuals" (p. 48).

Spence and Helmreich (1978) developed the Personal Attributes Questionnaire (PAQ). Like the BSRI, the PAQ identified four groups: feminine, masculine, androgynous, and undifferentiated. This model recognized that masculinity and femininity coexist to some degree in every individual, male or female. The androgynous person, less bound to the restrictive, sex-appropriate standards for behavior, is theoretically able to develop psychologically to the fullest and respond receptively to a wide range of situations, perhaps in ways that the less integrated person is unable to do.

Cross-culturally, the concepts of *masculinity* and *femininity* have been represented as complementary domains, traits, and behaviors for thousands of years. The yin-yang theory of the harmony and balance of forces in nature is based in Confucian thought and Chinese cosmology. Uba (1994) said that the yin is representative of feminine, negative, inferior, and weak, whereas the yang is symbolic of masculine, positive, superior, and strong. "If this supposedly natural balance is upset (e.g., if a wife domineers over her husband), the equilibrium within the family would be disrupted" (p. 29).

SEX AND GENDER ROLES

Several models describe women's development (Enns, 1991). These models seek to highlight the relational strengths that women embody and, according to Enns, attempt "to correct the inadequacies of mainstream theories and conceptualize women's experiences in their own terms" (p. 209). Evans, Kincade, Marbley, and Seem (2005) reviewed the historical aspects of feminism and feminist therapy in women and men's lives. Feminist therapy skills, an emphasis on social justice and change, and the relationship between the client and the counselor were all highlighted.

Erikson (1968), one of the early and essential voices in identity development, has been criticized for focusing the majority of his attention on the masculine version of human existence. However, the primacy of men in the human life event reflects the sexism of the time (Horst, 1995). Women's psychosocial development is different from men's. Gilligan (1982) criticized major identity development theorists who depict women as inferior to men because of important gender differences. According to Gilligan, women's development "relies more on connections with others, on related-ness rather than separateness" (p. 271). Recently, other psychologists have written about the unique experience of womanhood on development. Jordan (1997a) and Nelson (1996) commented that relational skills are highly functional and involve a complex array of competencies essential to preserving family and culture.

Compared with men, women may emphasize relationships, and the importance of autonomy for women cannot be underestimated. McBride (1990) argued that **autonomy** refers to being able to define oneself, rather than being defined by others. This definition is not seen as an isolated and extremely individualistic self. Rather, autonomy refers to interdependence, mutual cooperation, and individuation. McBride stated that **instrumental autonomy** refers to the ability to act on the world, carry on activities, cope with problems, and take action to meet one's needs. **Emotional autonomy** is the freedom from pressing needs for approval and reassurance. Women are often unaware of how much energy they invest in doing things for others versus developing healthy interdependence. The capacity to commit to concrete affiliations and partnerships and to develop the ethical strength to abide by such commitments, even though they may call for significant sacrifices and compromises, is a source of strength. It is questionable as to whether such commitments and mutuality can be achieved when there is a considerable power differential (Haddock et al., 2003).

GENDER AND EMOTION

The history of gender relationships in this country is steeped in patriarchy and inequality. Elizabeth Cady Stanton, one of the cofounders of the first Women's Rights Convention held in 1840, observed the burden of caring for everyone other than one-self on the faces of women. She said,

> The general discontent I felt with women's position as wife, mother, house-keeper, physician, and spiritual guide, the chaotic condition into which everything fell without her constant supervision, and the wearied, anxious look of the majority of women, impressed me with the strong feeling that some active measures should be taken to remedy the wrongs of society in general and of women in particular. (cited in Zinn, 2002, p. 123)

This socialization process of being selfless contributes to women equating self-care with being selfish. Women who sacrifice their own development to meet the needs of others often inhibit the development of self-expression, self-knowledge, and self-esteem (McBride, 1990). Yet the culture encourages women to sacrifice their development and needs for the benefit of others' needs, usually men's. Depression is associated with the behavior of women constantly putting others' needs first and discounting their own needs. It is important, then, not to pathologize women for behaving in this manner. Women who are selfless and sacrificial have had cultural, institutional, and relational reinforcement (Lemkau & Landau, 1986). Choosing to care for the self might be perceived as an unacceptable proposition, because it is likened to the denial of others (McBride, 1990). When women feel that they have failed to be in nurturing and sustaining relationships, there is a sense of shame. Gender socialization is riddled with shame for women and men. There is not enough room in this book to address the shame heaped upon transgendered people due to nonconformity with gender socialization processes and practices.

Researchers found that shame proneness among women was the dominant affective response related to living up to female gender role norms (Efthim, et al., 2001). For shame to be experienced, a person appraises the self as having violated group norms or as having failed to live up to the standards of the social group. Five factors of the Female Gender Role Stress (FGRS) Scale examined women's gender role stress:

1. Emotional detachment (e.g., having others believe that you are emotionally cold).
2. Physical unattractiveness (e.g., being perceived by others as overweight).
3. Victimization (e.g., having your car break down on the road).
4. Unassertiveness (e.g., bargaining with a salesperson when buying a car).
5. Failed nurturance (e.g., having someone else raise your children).

In the Efthim et al. study, five factors of the Male Gender Role Stress (MGRS) Scale examined men's gender role stress and reinforced the dimensions of masculinity:

1. Physical inadequacy (e.g., losing in a sports competition).
2. Emotional inexpressiveness (e.g., admitting that you are afraid of something).
3. Subordination to women (e.g., being outperformed by a woman).
4. Intellectual inferiority (e.g., having to ask for directions when lost).
5. Performance failure (e.g., being unable to become sexually aroused when you want to).

Many men leave intimacy to women. Consequently, the requirement for intimacy in adult relationships, to join in mutuality and to surrender to another, is a tremendous source of conflict and anxiety for men (Jordan, 1997b). Men need to be educated on the benefits of emotional expression. As human beings, men have basic needs to love and to be loved, to care and to be cared for, to know and to be known, but socially prescribed gender roles tend to require men to be inexpressive and competitive with one another. Evaluating life success in terms of external achievements rather than interdependence is emphasized.

In the Newman, Fuqua, Gray, and Simpson (2006) study, the relationship between gender, depression, and anger was investigated in a clinical sample. There were 65 men and 74 women in the study, with a median age of 31. People were in the low-to-moderate income range and were predominantly White. Despite previous research that women are more likely to be depressed than men, this study found no difference between men and women on any of the affective scales, including depression. Both men and women had high Beck Depression Inventory scores. A significant finding was that 38% of the variance in depression was related to the five anger scales used in the study: state anger, trait anger, anger-in, anger-out, and anger control. The relationship between anger and depression was substantial for both men and women. The emphasis on quantitative methodologies and homogeneity in race and ethnicity represent severe limitations to this research, and yet the findings help us see the benefit of focusing on clinical samples and not relying on and applying findings from nonclinical samples to clinical ones.

Wester, Vogel, Wei, and McClain (2006) provide one of the first studies to examine race and male gender role conflict. In their sample, 130 Black male college students completed the GRCS, the Cross Racial Identity Scale, and the SCL-90 to measure psychological distress. A Bonferroni correction was done to address the multiple independent t tests performed on gender role conflict subscales. Black men's GRCS scores were predictive of their psychological distress. Black men who internalized a racist understanding of themselves as men of color suffered more from their attempts to navigate the male gender role than did men who internalized a racial identity based on an appreciation of their African American heritage. Internalized racism served as a vehicle through which internalized sexism (gender role conflict) affected quality of life. Racial identity partially mediated the effects of gender role conflict on psychological distress. The negative consequence of internalized racism was associated with racialized gender behavior.

Healthy male development can be accomplished with the expansion of gender roles. Skovholt (1993) said that "this narrow funnel of acceptable masculinity may give males a solid sense of gender identity, but it can, in time, also become a prison that constricts personal growth and development" (p. 13). Men are fearful of being perceived as or labeled feminine, which is part of the narrow funnel through which they must conduct their lives. From a psychosocial perspective, this fear stems from the arduous task men must complete: separate from their mothers toward developing their male identities (Skovholt, 1993). This particular socialization process dictates that men should never engage in opposite-sex behaviors and attitudes.

Men travel through their developmental paths unduly conflicted yet trying to maintain power over women and other men (Pleck, 1984). A key task of the men's movement was to articulate the male experience of power and powerlessness, which assumed that female powerlessness translates into male power (Swanson, 1993). It is clear that the wounds of patriarchal power and control are damaging to men and women (Brown, 1994). The roles for men need to be transformed so that men become "acutely aware of their power to influence self and to break the bonds to patriarchy, emotional handcuffs in the form of assumptions and interpretations that favor patriarchal values above the worth of human beings and the meaning of their experiences" (Brown, 1994, p. 118).

GENDER AND THE BODY

Cultural values of independence, thinness, physical strength, and athleticism pervade U.S. society. Both print and audiovisual advertisements are a primary medium for the transmission of images. Chronic dieting and preoccupation with bulk and speed

STORYTELLING: Barbaric Practice or Cultural Rite?

When traveling in Tanzania, our group had the privilege of staying with the Masai—a nomadic people who eschew modern conveniences like electricity and plumbing. We were told that circumcision for women and men is a prerequisite for marriage, and girls know they will not be marriageable (deemed worthy of a Masai man's hand in marriage) without doing so. We were told that women did not fear circumcision; they anticipated it as part of the marriage preparation. Chung (2005) cites that the Western-coined female genital mutilation (FGM) for circumcision is a standard cultural practice in preparing for marriage and adult status in sub-Saharan Africa, Egypt, United Arab Emirates, Bahrain, Oman, Indonesia, South Yemen, Pakistan, Malaysia, and some parts of Russia. It also occurs in immigrant and refugee communities in the Americas and Europe.

among men and women to the point of damaging the health of one's body with steroids and from anorexia and bulimia are epidemic within the culture. Cultural values must be considered when tracing the etiology of gender-based practices. (See Storytelling: "Barbaric Practice or Cultural Rite?") For instance, health behaviors may manifest masculinity. Men "anticipate their world from the experiences of being males in their respective cultures (e.g., being told to be tough, self-reliant, violent, promiscuous) and take (or not take) certain actions based on their understanding of their world (e.g., ignore pain, refuse help, become violent, engage in risky sexual practices" (Mahalik, Lagan, & Morrison, 2006, p. 192). These behaviors have their genesis in culturally laden images that privilege physical power.

In the United States, more than 90% of persons suffering from **anorexia nervosa,** or self-starvation of the body, are young females (Andersen, 1986; Anorexia Nervosa and Related Eating Disorders [ANRED], 2006). Pursuit of the thin beauty ideal has meant different things for women. One percent of the 10- to 20-year-old American female population has anorexia nervosa. It is estimated that 4 percent of college-age women have bulimia nervosa—this could be higher given the secret nature of binge eating. Ten percent of anorexics and bulimics are men. About 72% of alcoholic women under the age of 30 also have eating disorders (ANRED, 2006). Disordered eating is far too often associated with becoming or remaining thin. Large numbers of young women in high school report that they use maladaptive weight control techniques such as fasting (39.4%), appetite suppressants (8.1%), and skipping meals (33.5%) to lose weight (Tylka & Subich, 2002).

Adolescents are particularly vulnerable to eating disorders because anorexia nervosa has its highest incidence at the beginning of adolescence and bulimia nervosa has its highest incidence at the end (Emmons, 1992). From a psychodynamic perspective, the earlier scripts that are set in motion will have a powerful impact on behavior and cognition unless early information is replaced with new information. Arrival to adulthood does not ensure clarity about the existence or elimination of dysfunctional tapes. Thus, one task of adulthood is to unlearn many of the negative tapes received during childhood and adolescence and to replace them with messages that affirm the self and are more reflective of who the individual has sculpted the self to be. The media, church, educational institutions, other women, family members, and men create an environment wherein men "construct the symbolic order" within which gender inequity and male supremacy are reproduced.

In this system, women and men (due to the price associated with the privilege of defining reality) become at war with their bodies. This is particularly true when a gap exists between body image perception and proximity to the socially constructed standard. Learning to define oneself as acceptable amid the aging process where one no longer fits the ideal of beauty is essential in combating appearance anxiety or fear-based thoughts that one's aging body is betraying them in a youth-obsessed culture (Saucier, 2004). Intense body dissatisfaction and a sense of disembodiment can ensue when one's body does not conform to the standard. Hutchinson (1982) stated, "The body is experienced as alien and lost to awareness . . . The body has broken away or has been severed from the mind and is experienced as a foreign object, an albatross, or a hated antagonist" (pp. 59–60).

Alienation from the body hampers appreciation and acceptance of multiple identities. Perceptions of the body amid parts that cause pain, create difficulty, or are defined by society as unattractive and unacceptable can be transformed through paradigm shifts. New discourses or ways of bringing meaning to bear on the value of the body can emerge and take root interpersonally.

Oppressive stereotypes about women of color are pervasive throughout the media. For instance, Root (1990) identified that

> Women of color are either fat and powerless (African American and Latina women); fat, bossy, and asexual; corrupt and/or evil (Asian/Pacific Island Americans and African Americans); obedient, quiet, and powerless (Latinas and Asian/Pacific Americans); exotic (Asian Americans, mixed race); or hysterical and stupid. (p. 530)

Gunn Allen (1992) observed that American society would be different if various traditions from Native American culture were followed, saying, "if American society judiciously modeled the traditions of the various Native Nations, the ideals of physical beauty would be considerably enlarged to include 'fat' strong-featured women, gray-haired, and wrinkled individuals, and others who in contemporary American cultured are viewed as 'ugly'" (p. 211).

Race and skin color are variables in the beauty business. American standards of beauty are based on White or White-approximating ideals. The physical features of many White women, as well as those of women of color, differ from socially constructed rigid and often unattainable beauty standards. In an effort to conform to accepted standards of beauty, many women of color will seek to fulfill Eurocentric beauty standards equated with status, acceptance, and legitimacy. Some Asian women have undergone plastic surgery to make their eyes appear more round or double-folded, as opposed to single-folded, for a more Western look. This drastic physical change may be fueled by Uba's (1994) statement, "There is evidence that Asian Americans have lower self-concepts than Euro-Americans do when it comes to physical appearance" (p. 83).

Rhinoplasty is a surgical procedure many Jewish women have undergone to obtain a smaller, narrower, and finer nose. Black women spend an inordinate amount of time, psychic energy, and money on the monumental issue of hair. Many, along with their Jewish sisters, have for decades been relaxing their hair by applying chemicals or a hot metal comb to naturally curly and coily hair to make it straight. Alice Walker (1987) refers to this relaxing process as "oppressing" the hair.

Emmons's (1992) research points to an erroneous assumption about eating disorders—that they are rare among people of color. She found that African American teenage girls were more likely than any other race and gender group examined to use laxatives as a dieting ploy. In contrast, European Americans were more likely to vomit to lose weight. Cultural factors, values, and institutional variables such as racism and religious discourses all converge to influence the presence and diagnosis of eating disorders in women. Among Black women, stress associated with the struggle to deal with acculturation, success, racism, and family responsibilities may trigger bingeing and purging behavior in some who did not evidence disordered eating during adolescence.

Mastria (2002) maintains that cultural components of Latina culture predispose girls to defer and sacrifice themselves. She said, "From childhood, females are taught to repress sexual desires, and conditioned to be extremely modest and 'virginal' in terms of their bodies, which may cause conflict and shameful feelings about their bodies" (p. 71). Research conducted by Lester and Petrie (1998) on 139 female Mexican American college students found evidence of bulimia nervosa among 1.4% to 4.3% of the sample. Despite strongly entrenched beliefs about the protective aspects of race, a relationship may exist between increasing opportunities for social mobility for women of color and increasing vulnerability to disordered eating (Root, 1990).

The desire to bring honor and not disgrace to the family, coupled with the model minority myth, may contribute to disordered eating among Asian American girls (Mastria, 2002). The changing roles of women within the family and workforce have to be considered when understanding the etiology of eating disorders and its relationship with power and control. According to Chernin (1985), eating disorders "must be understood as a profound developmental crisis in a generation of women still deeply confused after two decades of struggle for female liberation, about what it means to be a woman in the modern world" (p. 17).

Family of origin plays a pivotal role in the life of the girl who has an eating disorder. Brouwers (1990) reported that negative attitudes toward the body begin in the family and that, after self-body evaluation, the daughter's belief that the mother was critical of the daughter's body was the second biggest predictor of bulimia in female college students.

College campus factors or values may influence a girl's vulnerability to eating disorders. Kashubeck, Walsh, and Crowl (1994) discovered that the literature on one college website emphasized physical appearance, attention to fashion, and participation in the sorority-fraternity system. Another college, a liberal arts institution, emphasized political activism and intellectual talent. The rate of eating disorders did not differ between the two schools, but the study found that at the first school, the factors associated with eating disorders were the perceived pressure to dress a certain way, to be smart, and to have a marginal grade point average. At the second school, being a girl and having low masculine gender role identity were the strongest predictors to disordered eating behaviors.

Research by Rogers and Petrie (2001) found that among 97 college women (27 non-White), dependency and assertion of autonomy were important in explaining the variance on the Eating Attitudes Test. It appears that symptoms of anorexia are characterized by dependency on and need for approval from a significant relationship, as well as the need to deny this reliance. Restricting food intake may be a way to assert one's sense of individualism within the gender role. Women's power comes from their beauty and physical allure as approved and esteemed by others.

In research with 200 Asian American college women, self-esteem, perceived pressure to be thin, ethnic identity, body shape, internalization of society's emphasis on appearance, and eating disorder symptomatology were assessed. The following were found: Asian American women's perceived pressure for thinness slightly predicted self-esteem and moderately predicted body preoccupation; self-esteem predicted body preoccupation; and body preoccupation strongly predicted eating disorder sympotomatology. Although ethnic identity predicted self-esteem, ethnic identity did not predict internalization of the thin ideal, body preoccupation, and disordered eating. Ethnic identity only influenced internalization of the thin ideal and body preoccupation through its association with self-esteem (Phan & Tylka, 2006).

Despite African American youths' positive self-esteem (Gibbs, 1985; Gibbs, Huang, & Associates, 1989; Ward, 1989), feeling enormous pressure to look according to European ideals adversely affects self-concept among this group as well as other women of color. They may feel compelled to change hairstyles, dress, body size, and makeup to be accepted and thus keep the doors of opportunity wide open. Robinson and Ward (1991) indicated that obesity among many African American women may be a quick-fix resistance strategy to negotiate the pressures and frustrations of daily racism and sexism.

African American women have been known to bleach their skin, yet, skin-color issues are connected to broader themes of identity and an awareness of the sociopolitical context of race in America. As people of African descent celebrate various hues, skin color as a status variable may hopefully take on less prominence. (See Storytelling: "I Am Beautiful, No Matter What They Say!")

STORYTELLING: I am Beautiful, No Matter What They Say!

While we were in graduate school, a group of Black women gathered in Longfellow Hall at the Harvard Graduate School of Education to discuss hair and skin color. Women told stories about growing up with family members who communicated that *value* was associated with light skin and long, "good hair." Unlearning these damaging messages of internalized racism and coming to a place where a woman honors her whole self is true beauty.

GENDER AND EXPERIENCES IN THERAPY

Qualitative research was conducted with 16 counselors to address how counselors conceptualize and address privilege and oppression within counseling and understand their perceptions of their training with respect to these constructs. Specifically two research questions were asked: how do practitioners see privilege and oppression influencing and interacting in counseling, and what changes in training and practice related to these constructs do they see as necessary to better serve clients? Two themes emerged from the data: (1) the intersection between counselor process and cultural power and (2) transitions in counselor training practice. More specifically, interactions with clients were facilitative in counselors' awareness of privilege and oppression. In addition, counselors felt they lacked a sense of preparedness to address power issues in counseling (Hays, Dean, & Change, 2007).

Bernardez (1987) found three specific reactions to women in therapy: (1) the discouragement and disapproval of behavior that did not conform with traditional role prescriptions, such as mother; (2) the disparagement and inhibition of expression of anger and other "negative" affects, such as hatred and bitterness; and (3) the absence of confrontation, interpretation, and exploration of passive-submissive and compliant behavior in the client. Despite these reactions from therapists, Bernardez reported that female therapists showed greater empathy and ability to facilitate self-disclosure than males. There are exceptions; male therapists may be more inclined to reproduce the dominant-subordinate position by unconscious encouragement of the female's compliance, submissiveness, and passivity.

Fauth and Hayes (2006) investigated the applicability of a transactional theory of stress to understanding countertransference with male clients. Therapists' positive appraisals were linked with more positive diagnostic evaluation of their client. Negative appraisals were linked with increased distance from and hesitance with the client. "Counselors who felt more efficacious in managing their feelings and value conflicts with the client tended to avoid him less" (p. 436). The authors did not find that counselors' male gender role attitudes and male clients' gender role conformity interacted to predict the counselors' stress appraisals and countertransference.

A problem for both sexes is the strong gender role prohibition against female anger, criticism, rebellion, or domination. Anger is often equated with hatred, destructiveness, or bitterness. Helping clients realize that they have the right to take care of themselves, even if those in their environment tell them they are hurting others, is an important step on the road to self-mastery. Some clients "may exclude information that they assume the counselor will not understand or include details designed to counteract the counselor's presumed prejudices" (Hays, 1996, p. 36). The very exploration of bitterness and resentment can lead to the identification of sources of dissatisfaction.

The female counselor–male client dyad represents the typical caregiving pattern in society. Most men would feel very challenged entering therapy and abdicating power to a woman. If a woman is uncomfortable with her power, given her proximity to discourses that sing the power-of-men-over-women song, she may acquiesce her power and view men as greater authorities than herself.

Female counselor–female client is probably one of the most emotionally intense dyads. This dyad was found to allow for a fuller exploration of childhood experiences. Female clients, because of socialization, may challenge the female counselor and question her competence. Because of gender role socialization, therapists of both genders have difficulties with a whole array of aggressive behaviors in their women clients (Kaplan, 1987). When both the client and counselor are lesbian, the therapeutic relationship is shaped by the intersections of gender and sexuality in that both parties attempt to honor the mutuality inherent in empathic counseling (Slater, 1997). The very process of the counselor "coming out" to her client is an act of mutuality, and yet lesbian therapists should not be the only therapists engaging in this type of self-disclosure. It is also the task of the heterosexual counselor to disclose. Robinson and Watt (2001) summarized this point and stated, "The socially endorsed experience of heterosexuality and the unconscious and unearned privilege afforded heterosexuals often deems them unaware of the importance to transition through sexual identity formation. It is presumed that sexual identity formation pertains to gay people only" (p. 594). People who are heterosexually identified are sociopolitically advantaged and privileged (Mohr, 2002). Hoffman (2004) argued that lack of attention to identity development for majority group members is the inadvertent perpetuation of the need for minority group members to explain their realities.

Regardless of the gender of the counselor and the client, empathy is the key ingredient in therapy (Pinderhughes, 1989). **Empathy** is the ability of the therapist to surrender him- or herself to the affect of another while cognitively structuring that experience so as to comprehend its meaning in terms of other aspects of the client's psyche (p. 13). It requires that the counselor be comfortable and familiar with the world of affect and the nature of connections between people (Kaplan, 1987). Empathy allows for a merger of people's experiences and understanding—not toward enmeshment but attunement. "In true empathic exchange, each is both object and subject, mutually engaged in affecting and being affected, knowing and being known" (Jordan, 1997a, p. 15). There are power differentials within counseling that are part of the professional relationship, yet empathy and mutuality are impeded by unacknowledged hierarchies within the counseling event when they reinforce hegemonic power dynamics (Mencher, 1997).

Therapists may disapprove of women who show power and controlling, competitive, and autonomous behavior while disliking behavior typically regarded as feminine (e.g., self-depreciation, submissiveness). Some male therapists may subconsciously dread women dominating them and fear their own vulnerability to female aggression. Female therapists may also fear the eruption of their own anger toward men, which can have an adverse impact on the therapeutic relationship. It is also possible that some therapists are afraid to experience the powerlessness that comes with examining social injustice, racism, and oppression (Bernardez, 1987).

Independent of race, ethnicity, and sexual orientation, male and female children and adolescents receive similar gender-appropriate messages. Poor White men and upper-class men of color are socialized to function and be in positions of control (whether they actually *are* is a different matter). For this reason, seeking help is incompatible with the masculine role. Middle-class White women and poor women of color are socialized to emphasize the needs and wants of others, usually before their own. Despite the similarities, more research is needed on the specific effects of class and other sources of differences as mediating traditional gender role messages.

Depression among college men and the low likelihood of their seeking out psychological services suggests that college counseling centers are in a prime position to do outreach (residence halls, orientations, classrooms, student development). Helping people reclaim the parts of themselves they have forfeited to conform to society's role expectations, both at home and at work, is a form of healing. In addition, men can be encouraged to reframe their notions of counseling. Good and Wood (1995) said that "changing men's view of counseling might consist of efforts to emphasize that participating in counseling is an activity involving personal courage and strength that is displayed through facing and sharing one's concerns" (p. 73).

A primary theme articulated throughout this work is that more differences are found within groups than between them. The need for mental health professionals to be aware of the salience of physical attractiveness as a status variable in everyday life is crucial to understanding clients as whole beings. Narrow definitions of physical attractiveness have implications for mental health attitudes, body validation, and the development of coping strategies to cope meaningfully with both unanticipated and normal maturational changes in physical appearance and ability. Integrated into this discussion is an examination of the culture's clear preference for the able-bodied and intolerance for persons with disabilities.

GENDER IDENTITY MODELS

THE WOMANIST MODEL

Ossana, Helms, and Leonard's (1992) womanist identity model, adapted from Cross's four-stage Nigrescence model, is helpful in illuminating the process of self-awareness. The first stage in the womanist identity model is *preencounter,* which maintains that women at this stage accept traditional or stereotypical notions of womanhood. Such notions are often steeped in women's reliance on others for approval and legitimation. Naturally, the locus of control for women in this stage would be external. The second stage, *encounter,* occurs when a woman has an experience wherein she begins to question notions of womanhood and becomes aware of the prevalence of sexism in society. A woman's discovery that her male colleague with less education and experience is paid significantly more than she is could be described as an encounter. In the third stage, *immersion/emersion,* the woman surrounds herself with other women and literature about and by women. She is critical of the patriarchal context of society and may experience turbulent emotions, such as guilt and anger, toward herself for having been selfless for so long and at society for its history of promoting gender inequity. During the fourth and last stage, *internalization,* the woman defines womanhood on her own terms and is not bound by external definitions or dictates about what it means to be a woman. Research conducted by Carter and Parks (1996), using the womanist scale on Black and White women, found a relationship between womanist identity attitudes and mental health. No relationships were found among African American women, but they were found among European American women. More specifically, White women ($n = 147$) who were not at the highest or internalization stage of womanist identity were more likely to feel depressed, anxious, and scrutinized or under attack. These findings suggest that White women pay a psychological tax for pushing back against the dictates of hegemony. They also pay for their dependence upon hegemony.

WHITE MALE IDENTITY DEVELOPMENT MODEL

Scott and Robinson (2001) presented a circular White male racial identity model. According to the model, movement occurs in multiple directions; however, one type, a term preferred over stage, is most descriptive. It is a theoretically driven model and influenced by Helms (1995), Myers et al. (1991), and Sue and Sue (1990). This model addresses "the convergence of race and gender attitudes that White men exhibit as a result of socially constructed attitudes regarding appropriate displays of manhood" (p. 418). It could be used when counseling White men to help them gain insight into how race and gender intersect and contribute to problem presentation.

Type I, Noncontact, describes men who represent the status quo, deny racism, and seek power and privilege. Type II, the Claustrophobic, characterizes the man who feels that other races are closing in on him. Men whose lives are characterized by this type are disillusioned by the American dream. There is a feeling that power and privilege are going to other races. Type III, Conscious Identity, describes the man who is in dissonance and feels this dissonance between existing belief systems and realities. The Type IV Empirical man questions his role in racism and oppression. Finally, Type V, Optimal, describes the man who understands how his struggle for power and privilege has contributed to racism and oppression.

IMPLICATIONS FOR COUNSELORS AND PSYCHOLOGISTS

One reverberating point throughout this text is that U.S. society is highly gendered and has rather rigid notions about appropriate modes of being for men and women (Kaplan, 1987). Thus, the power of the therapeutic event is found in the interpersonal relationship between client and therapist. The importance of clinical skills and training is not being minimized; however, the relational bond based on mutuality and trust is primary.

Over time, women and men maintain and modify their sex role–related perceptions, attitudes, and behaviors. Sex role typology is complicated. Individual differences in determining sex roles must be allowed so as not to stereotype people, yet it is important to incorporate gender role socialization in working with clients. For instance, educating women about the relationship between perceived discrimination, collective self-esteem, personal self-esteem, and psychological distress may provide tools for understanding their own experiences (Fisher & Holz, 2007).

Gender dyad makes a difference in the counseling event. Often, the male and client roles are rather discontinuous. For instance, the personal characteristics of the male role often focus on physical strength and accomplishment, whereas the client role emphasizes acknowledgment of weakness. In the male role, men are often punished for seeking help, whereas in the client role, help seeking is reinforced (Skovholt, 1993).

Gender can add another dimension to the therapeutic process. Good and Mintz (1990) found that between two men, a male counselor and a male client, restricted emotionality and homophobia present themselves as issues. As unfortunate as it is, homophobia may prevent male clinicians from showing concern and care for male clients. A male client may feel tremendous angst and fear if he experiences warmth toward a male counselor. It is also likely that a male counselor could be embarrassed at his feelings toward another man's intense emotional expressions. The client could also be ashamed to disclose. When the counselor is male and the client is female, a different dynamic can surface. One form of bias is for male counselors to respond to female clients as sex objects. Moreover, because of socialization, a male counselor may adopt a one-up type of position with the client. The client may also have difficulty expressing to the counselor emotions that she may subconsciously feel are intolerable. Kaplan (1987) found that women with male therapists saw themselves as less self-possessed, less open, and more self-critical than did women with female therapists.

More researchers are conducting rich qualitative research to better understand gender themes. Phillips and Daniluk (2004) tape-recorded interviews with seven women between the ages of 30 and 57 who had been sexually abused as children. Women were asked questions such as:

How would you describe your recovery process?

What aspects of who you are as a person do you feel have remained constant or stable throughout your life?

In what ways do you think your past abuse experiences inform your sense of who you are today?

How has this changed over time?

Several themes emerged:

1. An increasing sense of visibility, congruence, and connection.
2. An emerging sense of self-definition and self-acceptance.
3. A shift in worldview.
4. A sense of regret over what has been lost.
5. A sense of resiliency and growth.

In examining the constructs of race and gender among college students, Cokley (2001) conducted research on academic self-concept, racial centrality, and academic motivation of 257 African American college students. Ninety-two were male and 165 were female. Packets were given to students during summer school at two historically Black colleges. The purpose of the study was to examine gender as an important variable in understanding the psychosocial development of African American students. The researchers found that women scored significantly higher on one of the extrinsic motivation scales (the Extrinsic Motivation Identified Regulation scale). Men had significantly higher scores on the Atrinsic Motivation scale, which represents neither intrinsic nor extrinsic motivation. The researchers concluded that Black female students were more motivated about being in college than were Black male students, who evidenced a lack of motivation. In tandem with the larger society, the college experience for many Black males is perceived as alienating. The number of Black males enrolling in and graduating from college has fallen off sharply over the years (Cokley, 2001). The lack of difference in race centrality scores between males and females may suggest that for both genders, race is a central and dominant construct.

The socialization differences for men and women have been widely documented. Men continue to be socialized toward assertiveness, power, and independence—to restrict emotion. Women are socialized toward nurturance, compliance, and direct achievement through affiliation with others, particularly men (Mintz & O'Neil, 1990). Such socialization patterns in early childhood have implications for relationships and can enhance a client's vulnerability to selflessness or excessive individualism. Because humans have myriad emotions, it is important for therapists to confront clients' beliefs about rigid gendered emotions while having the ability to hold women's intense anger and men's overwhelming sadness and fear (Brown & Gilligan, 1992).

The role of women in multicultural counseling and psychology is being explored in greater depth. Initially, the literature took a monolithic approach to counseling that failed to show how gender interacts with other identities as well as forces such as racism, sexism, class elitism, and homophobia. Gender similarities do not negate racial differences, nor do racial similarities negate gender differences.

CASE STUDY
Building Rapport

Malaya is a 41-year-old Latina counseling psychologist in private practice. One of her clients, Tyler, is a biracial 15-year-old. Tyler's mother is Black and her father is White. Tyler presented for counseling at the insistence of her father because Tyler's grades are declining, she is chronically irritable, she swears, she smokes, she fights with other girls, she is disrespectful of her father and other adults, and she skips school. Tyler has been engaging in this behavior for about 3 months. Her father does not know what to do. Tyler rarely sees her mother and, according to her father, "looks just like her." Her father thinks Tyler is being hit by a boy she's been seeing, based on bruising he has seen on her. Tyler explains it away as being from field hockey injuries. Tyler was also sexually abused as a child when under the supervision of her mother. Because of the abuse from one of the mother's boyfriends, she lost custody of Tyler. Tyler has been raised in predominantly White neighborhoods, attended White-majority schools, and has little interaction with her African American heritage. Malaya, after the brief intake with Tyler's father, suspects that Tyler is angry and having an identity crisis due to normal adolescence, being biracial, and being isolated not only from her mother but from the Black community. Her mother has other children with the man with whom she resides. During their first session, Malaya asked Tyler how she felt about being in counseling. Tyler shrugged her shoulders and said she didn't care. Malaya told Tyler she was glad that she was there and that she (Tyler) could talk about what she wanted. Malaya asked Tyler what kind of music she liked. Tyler said, "Why? You ain't gonna know it." Malaya said, "Try me." Tyler said she liked Rihanna. Malaya replied that she liked her song, "Please Don't Stop the Music." Tyler's eyes lit up and she said that was her favorite song along with "Hate That I Love You." Malaya asked her why and Tyler responded that she loved to dance and it was a way for her to forget about all of her drama. Malaya told Tyler she could bring music in to their meetings, and they could talk about what the words meant to her. As Tyler was leaving, she asked Malaya, "Is it true that you can get a boy so excited and mad then he can't control himself and that if he hits you it's your fault but nobody else had better do it?"

QUESTIONS

1. What appear to be the critical issues facing Tyler?
2. What DSM–IV–TR diagnosis might be missed for Tyler?
3. What are some of the gender dynamics operating in Tyler's life?
4. What might help Tyler's father in parenting his child?

DISCUSSION AND INTEGRATION
The Client, Tyler, and Her Counselor, Malaya

A major gender script that both males and females receive is that men are entitled to their sexuality in ways that women are not. Part of this entitlement absolves men of responsibility, given the enormity and legitimacy of their desire. A huge burden is heaped on the woman to control the man's sexuality (Jordan, 1997a). Prior to Tyler leaving the office, Malaya needs to ascertain the meaning of Tyler's question about boys' arousal and aggression. Was she in a situation where she was with a boy who was sexually aroused and forced Tyler into unwanted sexual activity? If so, what happened? Was Tyler sexually or physically assaulted?

Racism and sexism subject Tyler to discrimination that she may not be mindful of. Many Black mothers raise their daughters with the responsibility of educating them about racism and sexism (Turner, 1997). Wilkinson (1997) said, "In the racially structured and multicultural evolution of this country, sex and gender alone have not been the principal determinants of the experiences or self-definitions of Native Americans or Americans, Mexican Americans, Japanese, and certainly not of African Americans" (p. 267). And while this is true, the question becomes, How would the African American community and other communities of color be transformed if gender were more central to the analysis or if the intersections of race and gender were seen as relevant to the improvement of both men and women's lives (Cole & Guy-Sheftall, 2003)?

Although White women contend with sexism, race and racism are constructs that most do not think about (Robinson, 2001). Among White people, race is often not the most organizing construct in their lives. The majority of White women and men are unaware of or may not have personal histories with race to give their non-White daughters socialization messages about race and racism. This is a challenge for the large numbers of biracial and multiracial children with White parents. For girls and women of color, race, culture, social class, and urbanization interact with gender and create female responses and positions that are diverse and fluctuating (Abrams, 2002). It is highly impossible for Tyler to develop healthily as a young biracial adolescent with no direct exposure to or knowledge of her Black identity. At the same time, her choice in music may be a way to become familiar with Black images.

Tyler is angry. Often adolescents who are depressed exhibit irritable behavior that is mistaken for behavioral misconduct (e.g., oppositional defiant disorder) but is actually deep sadness. In some instances, there is a combination of conduct disturbance and a mood disorder; however, the context and, of course, the length of time that the child has had the symptoms needs to be known. Tyler could be angry and depressed for many valid reasons: she rarely sees her mother and thus feels rejected by her, she is a young woman of color in a discriminatory world, she lacks a circle of women with whom to confide about her multiple identities, she is 15, and she has concerns about being objectified sexually. It is highly possible that Malaya, as a Latina therapist who is old enough to be Tyler's mother, is able to hold Tyler's anger. One of the questions Malaya asked Tyler's father was about her early childhood. As a young child of 7, Tyler was reserved yet tended to be oversocialized with somewhat negative appraisals of herself (intropunitive). Block and Block (2006) indicated in their 30-year longitudinal study that depressive tendencies identified in young adulthood are related to prior observer-based evaluations from parents and teachers.

Tyler's father loves her. There are, however, narratives that Tyler has to share that may be hard for her father to understand or hear. Garcia-Coll (1997) identified that White women, and arguably White men, have a difficult time holding Black women's anger and will go to great lengths to suppress, deny, and repress expressions of this anger. White women's historical role in the oppression of Black women and their enjoyment of present-day privileges earned as a function of that history discourage Black and White women from coming together and bearing witness to one another's anger, shame, and guilt. Good and effective therapy is not possible with all of this unspoken angst. The client should neither have to pay for nor wait on a counselor to work through his or her unresolved issues that leave the counselor feeling uncomfortable and/or ill-prepared.

Women tend to be socialized not to express anger; sadness and fear are more readily tolerated. Tyler needs to learn that anger is acceptable and there are positive and nondestructive ways to release it. Brown (2003) is critical of the culture and its suppression of girls' strong feelings. To mediate their frustrations, fears, marginalization, and anger, girls will fight with other girls. Tyler's feelings of rejection and betrayal from a mother she rarely sees and does not know contribute to her anger. These feelings should not be discounted when seeking to better understand her aggressive behavior with other girls.

Tyler can be taught and encouraged to talk to her therapist, cry, write, shout, run, work, study, pray, curse (but not at her father or teachers), eat well, take care of herself, read, dance, resist, and trust that things will get better in time. Tyler is too isolated, and the interpersonal relationships that describe her life are not uplifting. It is common for women who are being battered to not have adequate social support. In fact in qualitative research with women, six Black and five White, who had survived battering, eight had an earlier experience of abuse (Hage, 2006). Experiences of abuse are a risk factor for further abuse.

Tyler's father, Malaya, and other wise people can offer Tyler a circle of stones, a place to go and to be as healing occurs. Tyler would benefit richly from a mentor, someone who can nurture her development and focus on the communal aspects of being in community with others (Portman & Garrett, 2005). May Tyler experience what Duerk (1989) envisions when she asks: "How might your life have been different if, through the years, there had been a place where you could go? A place of women . . . who understood your tiredness and need for rest? A place of women who could help you to accept your fatigue and trust your limitations and to know in the dark of winter, that your energy would return, as surely as the spring, women who could help you to learn to light a candle and wait" (p. 60)?

SUMMARY

In this chapter, the construct of gender in women's and men's lives was considered. The socialization process, as well as biological dimensions, was explored. Counselors need to be aware of the consequences of gender socialization on their personal lives and on those of their clients. Not to do so is to ignore the powerful role of gender in life. Implications for the development of a healthy relationship with the body were presented. Multiple components of physical attractiveness exist and encompass facial beauty, skin color, body size, strength, visible signs of aging, height, weight, and hair length and texture. A case study examined multiple themes in the life of an adolescent biracial teen. Issues in clinical diagnoses were discussed.

Chapter 12

Converging Socioeconomic Class

Anyone who has ever struggled with
poverty knows how extremely expensive
it is to be poor.

James Baldwin

This chapter is dedicated to an examination of the intersections of socioeconomic class with other aspects of identity such as race, sexuality, gender, and ethnicity. A case study is provided to facilitate the integration of the material discussed throughout the chapter. The implications of a middle-class bias on the training of students in graduate counseling programs are discussed.

THE INVISIBILITY OF CLASS AS A VARIABLE IN COUNSELING

Class is ubiquitous and yet it is largely understudied, particularly as it relates to counseling and therapeutic effectiveness (Liu et al., 2004). Social class position is largely determined by income, education, and occupation. According to Liu et al., "social class may be defined as an individual's position within an economic hierarchy that is determined by his or her income, education level, and occupation; the individual is also aware of his or her place in the economic hierarchy and of others who may share a similar position" (p. 8). A primary component of social class is power which exists across individual, institutional, and societal levels (Appleby, 2001).

Disciplines such as sociology, public health, medicine, feminist psychology, and anthropology have devoted ample attention to class issues, particularly because class affects educational equity, access to health care, and collectivistic vs. individualistic societies (Fine, 1991; Lareau, 1997; Ogbu, 1997; Institute of Medicine [IOM], 2003). In counseling, the investigation of class as a status variable has been largely neglected. Researchers are bridging this gap. Liu et al. (2004) conducted a content analysis of the frequency of use of social class in the empirical and theoretical literature in three counseling journals: *Journal of Counseling Psychology*, *Journal of Multicultural Counseling and Development*, and *Journal of Counseling and Development*. Results of social class were typically reported in the method section. In fact, of the empirical articles that used social class, 31% did so in the method section of the article, and only 4% used social class in the data analysis. Liu et al. stated, "although social class may have been regarded as an important demographic variable to measure in the method section, few studies analyzed the participant data or incorporated social class findings into the discussion section" (p. 15). It was concluded that social class is an infrequently used variable in empirical counseling research.

Myths about class might contribute to this neglect. One myth states that we are a classless society and a second that we are a middle-class nation. The third myth is that we are all getting richer and finally that everyone has an equal change to succeed (Appleby, Colon, & Hamilton, 2001). Beating the odds is part of the cultural fabric regardless of one's indebtedness or income. The APA Socioeconomic Task Force (2007) put it well and said, "the belief that anyone, regardless of his or her socioeconomic history or social position, can make it to the top if he or she works hard is undoubtedly one of the most cherished beliefs in the United States. Evidence to the contrary seems to do little to deter this deeply held cultural belief" (p. 7). Meritocracy, capitalism, equality, and egalitarianism are a number of cultural values evident in both the Appleby et al. and APA statements.

Data on class, income, and poverty challenge prevailing discourses about justice and a level playing field for all Americans. Millions of Americans live below the poverty line. In 2006, the poverty rate for the nation was 12.3%, which reflects a decline from 12.6% in 2005 for the first time in a decade (U.S. Census Bureau News, 2007). DeNavas-Walt, Proctor, and Smith (2007) report that in 2006 the lowest poverty rate for any group was non-Hispanic Whites at 8.2; it was 10.3% for Asians and Pacific Islanders and 24.3% for Blacks, and the poverty rate among Latinos, who can be of any race, was 20.6%. The median household income in 2006 rose from $47,845 to $48,201, or an increase of 0.7%. Women had an adult poverty rate of 12.9% compared with men at 8%.

The working class is about 35% of the population, with mainly blue-collar jobs. Tenure is not a reality in most jobs; thus people contend with job insecurity and heavy production pressures. The middle class are roughly 50% of the nation and the upper class or the wealthiest are 20% of the nation who own nearly 80% of the wealth (Appleby et al., 2001).

THE INTERSECTIONS OF CLASS

Social class is multifaceted and complex. In the social sciences, there has been a tendency to minimize race issues and esteem class, particularly in light of increases in the numbers of middle-class families of color. Class, particularly for people of color, does not operate as a primary status trait because race and gender tend to be more conspicuous than class and can override it. "In the race-class-gender-nexus, race constitutes more than a social construction. It is a permanent and salient identity marker, self-indicator, and status locator that defines one's being, along with gender, sexuality, and class" (Wilkinson, 1997, p. 270).

Within a materialistic and consumeristic society, the structural inequities that can work against a person's best efforts to be successful can be overlooked. It is perhaps easy to blame people for failing to transcend their situations despite structural and institutional forces. For instance, women systematically earn less money than men. Often, men in nontraditional jobs (e.g., nursing) earn more money than their female counterparts (Chusmir, 1990).

Ogbu (1977) argued that "the inequality between Blacks and Whites is one not of class stratification but of racial stratification" (p. 766). **Racial stratification** is "the hierarchical organization of socially defined 'races' or groups on the basis of assumed inborn differences in status, honor, or material worth, symbolized in the United States by skin color" (p. 768). With a bachelor's degree, there are tremendous differences in income with respect to race and class. In 2004, the median annual income for White male full-time workers 25 years of age or older with a bacherlor's degree was $60,710 compared with $42,303 for White women, $48,429 for Latino men and $36,919 for Latinas; $44,722 for Black men and $40,180 for Black women (U.S. Census Bureau News, 2005).

Although the percentage of the foreign-born population in poverty decreased from 16.5% in 2005 to 15.2% in 2006 (DeNavas-Walt, et al., 2007), women of color and immigrant women are overrepresented among women in poverty. According to the U.S. Census Bureau (2001a), the poverty rate among single mothers of color is much higher than it is for White mothers. For White women, the poverty rate was 22.4%, 35.2% for Black women, 14.6% for Asians, and 37% for Latinas. Women of color, as a consequence of poverty, are more likely to suffer from inadequate access to medical and mental health services. In comparison to White women, Black women have lower mean earnings due to their overrepresentation in low-status occupations and a disproportionately low level of education (Napholz, 1994). Unlike the large numbers of White women newly entering the workforce, Black women have a history as workers, slaves, servers, domestics, and field and factory hands (Jones, 1985). This identity is imprinted on the American psyche, thus dictating the perception society at large has of Black women, particularly when they newly occupy class positions not initially meant or reserved for them.

Children's poverty rate is higher than any other age group. Nearly 18% (17.4%) of children under 18 years of age are in poverty, compared with 10.8% of adults age 18 to 64, or elders over 65 who have a poverty rate of 9.4% (DeNavas-Walt et al., 2007). Children suffer because of the economic situation of their single mothers. Higher unemployment, underemployment, and incarceration rates of men of color have an adverse affect on women of color, who are most likely to be in relationships with men from their same ethnic and racial background. It is imperative to examine women's and children's poverty in light of the events and circumstances occurring in the lives of the fathers and partners in their lives. Not to do so is to pathologize groups and blame them for their circumstances.

Membership in groups that are socially constructed as having more value is a mediating variable (Robinson, 1999). Middle-class women share some of the experiences of poor women; however, educational status and occupational position afford benefits across a variety of sectors: living in a neighborhood where there is no gun violence, having access to cancer-fighting fruits and vegetables (the healthier food is more expensive), and having access to a doctor when one is sick. Class does not negate the effects of racism, although class may minimize these effects. People who are poor experience more chronic health problems, live in crowded places, contend with noise and injury on the job, and are more likely to engage in behaviors associated with chronic disease. Over time, these experiences contribute to lower life expectancy (Newman, 1999).

In American society, success is defined and measured by material acquisition. Homes, cars, boats, jewelry, and other "things" are indicators of income and occupation; wealth suggests moral attributes such as being honest, hard-working, smart, and morally good. The socialization practices that most men are exposed to tie manhood to being a provider and having success in one's chosen career (Swanson, 1993). The inability to be successful in this fashion has and continues to have far-reaching implications for men who, for a variety of personal and systemic reasons, are unable to attain success.

CLASS: AN IDENTITY CONSTRUCT

Wealth does not translate to feelings of power, security, and privilege, or lower class to feelings of anxiety, depression, and low self-esteem. Low-wage-earning does not translate to feelings of powerlessness, insecurity, and low self-esteem. Class has psychological effects on people's lives. For instance, McLoyd and Wilson (1992) found that working- and lower-class parents placed less emphasis on happiness during the rearing of their children. In the case of these parents, survival issues took precedence over happiness. Robinson (1990) found in her analysis of Black student persistence that the students who were most likely to graduate from college in 4 years came from two-parent households and had participated in anticipatory socialization experiences such as Future Teachers of America and Future Business Leaders while in high school. These variables, associated with persistence and success, and as measured by graduation, are representations of class but not necessarily income and support the effects of class on career commitment and vocational identity. Race affects gender- and class-linked messages. Renzetti and Curran (1992) cited research that stated Black boys and girls tend to be more independent than White boys and girls. Parents' strong emphasis on hard work and ambition and the less frequent gender stereotyping and exposure to strong mothers that characterizes the lives of many Black children may explain this finding (Cole & Guy-Sheftall, 2003).

Storck (1998) proposed that the definition of social class be expanded to include psychosocial class, which is "defined by a person's education and occupation, and correlated behaviors, thoughts, and feelings" (p. 102). She went on to say that a working-class person tends not to be defined as college educated and is typically employed as a factory worker, with thoughts such as, "life starts after working hours," or "psychotherapy means that they will lock you up." Storck also stated that "both 'lower' and 'higher' ranking individuals and groups may feel disadvantaged or disempowered, in different contexts" (p. 101). Yet, a person from a lower psychosocial class may have higher feelings of marginalization or feel ignored and denied access. These class-determined feelings, according to Storck, are important contributors to depressive symptoms.

People can have similar jobs, incomes, and educational levels and have a different perspective about money as a function of environment and context. (See Storytelling; "The Job.") Counselors are encouraged to take a contextualized approach to clients and consider multiple issues: sociohistorical, or the ways in which people's histories have been silenced and misrepresented; sociostructural, which includes legal, economic, and educational systems; and sociopolitical, or the distribution of power (Liu & Arguello, 2006).

STORYTELLING: The Job

I was recently talking with a friend who explained how she had left a teaching position early in her career as a young assistant professor. She did not have another position to go to; however, she was decidedly unhappy where she was, resigned her position, and headed home to her parents. I marveled at her class privileges and the way it served her mental health. There is a tremendous clarity that comes from being able to be still, think, and regroup before making one's next career move. I reflected on a job I had at the same age as my colleague. I was not at all happy at this job. I stayed because it was my only source of income.

MIDDLE-CLASS BIAS AND COUNSELOR TRAINING

Counseling students receive very little information about socioeconomic class as it relates to influences on identity development and subsequent implications for counseling. Moreover, the training caters to the haves, as opposed to other social classes (e.g., working and lower classes). A client's discussions about economic exploitation and oppression can be extremely difficult for a counselor to hear if the counselor is a member of the very group about which the client is talking/bemoaning (Cardemil & Battle, 2003). The therapist's inability to hear should not be the client's problem, but it becomes the client's problem when the counselor is unavailable emotionally.

Part of middle-class bias is related to the nature of graduate education itself, which is steeped in privilege. Graduate students are college graduates who have distinguished themselves from others in the general population as capable of meeting the rigors of an academic program. Having status as a graduate student is an esteemed position in society that carries middle-class connotations, independent of students' class-linked childhood socialization experiences or their current and temporary state of poverty.

The graduate school environment acculturates its members to a middle-class orientation given the emphasis on success, competition, control, and individualism. In addition, there is an expectation of future employment and class mobility. Graduate students are preparing themselves for positions that will designate their middle-class social standing and prestige. It is hoped that students' future salaries will reflect their elite standing. The pay can be modest and yet the significance of the professional service and high status are evident.

Despite the privileged status of graduate school, some students make considerable financial sacrifices (e.g., working and going to school, borrowing money from family, securing substantial school loans) to attend school. Currently at my institution, each credit is $970.00. It costs master's students $60,000 for their 2-year master's degree. The majority, then, of graduate students in the United States could be described as having embodied traditional values anchored within a middle-class framework: success, motivation, perseverance, self-reliance, Standard English, hard work, and delayed gratification. For some first-generation college and graduate students, the delayed gratification and financial indebtedness may not make sense to working-class family members. The family member who has received an education and physically moved away from the family of origin may be perceived by working-class siblings or parents as not belonging anymore due to different ways of speaking and life experiences. (See Storytelling: "Why Don't You Get a Job?")

What does it mean for a middle-class bias to pervade the training of counselors? Is it possible that the effects of socioeconomic class on psychosocial identity have been neglected in the counseling literature because the middle-class bias is so pervasive and has rendered the profession oblivious to itself? Sue and Sue (1990) identified two

STORYTELLING: Why Don't You Get a Job?

I had just been accepted in my master's program and excitedly called a family member to tell her of the good news. There was silence on the other end of the phone and in all earnestness, she asked, "Why don't you get a job?" I was the first person in my family to graduate from college, let alone begin a graduate program. She had worked all her life and could not understand why I just didn't do the same. She was not seeking to discourage me, but she did not have a frame of reference for appreciating my quest for graduate education.

aspects of middle-class bias within counselor training. The first pertains to the emphasis on Standard English within society at large. The second refers to the 50-minute counseling sessions that typically characterize the counseling event.

Standard English represents a class issue because dialect, accent, and use of English are often used in drawing conclusions about a person's educational, occupational, income, intellectual, legal, and ultimately class status. Standard English operates as a form of power and access within society. Delpit (1997) discussed the power embodied in language and dialect. She argued against obliterating the unique cultural or speaking style of a group, yet she advocated educating people about the sociopolitical context in which standards and rules regarding the status quo exist. She advocates speaking honestly to children about the beauty and value of their language and cultural style while helping them understand the political power games at stake. Delpit demonstrates the dialectic: a "both/and" perspective, in which on the one hand the cultural style is embraced and esteemed, while on the other hand students understand that others perceived as powerful (e.g., teachers, prospective employers) may denigrate it. This means having knowledge of two realities: the appropriate contexts in which one's language can be celebrated and contexts where it will not.

Cultural encapsulation, or defining reality on the basis of a limited unidimensional cultural orientation (Wrenn, 1962), contributes to counselors' bias toward normative standards: being White, able-bodied, and heterosexual and using standard English (Reynolds & Pope, 1991). Schofield's (1964) use of the acronym YAVIS (young, attractive, verbal, intelligent, and successful) may enable counselors to see their tendency to favor this type of client. Perhaps it is related to the counselor's perception that the client is more similar to the counselor's actual or imagined sense of self.

Noticeable differences in communication and behavioral styles (e.g., the use of slang, street talk, or non-Standard English) between the client and counselor can contribute to counselors' discomfort with clients from lower socioeconomic groups. If the counselor is bothered that the client is on a sliding scale, countertransference can present a clinical obstacle.

Some counselors from middle-class backgrounds may not be equipped to deal with the multiple challenges and life problems that characterize some of their poor clients' lives, such as homelessness, pregnancy, appalling living conditions, hunger, mistreatment by the police and schools, crime, transience, and chronic violence or the threat of violence (Boyd-Franklin, 2003).

Another middle-class bias in counseling identified by Sue and Sue (1990) is the 50-minute counseling session. Neither the American Psychological Association (APA) nor the American Counseling Association (ACA) ethics codes dictate 45- or 50-minute therapy sessions. Some clients have work schedules that fluctuate from week to week. This disallows having a fixed day and time for therapy weekly. For example, a client may work the 11:00 p.m. to 7:00 a.m. shift at a gas station one week. The next week, their work schedule might be from 3:00 p.m. to 11:00 p.m. Pulling double shifts is a way for people to make considerable overtime—the cost is seen in disordered sleep, which reeks havoc on wakefulness. For some workers, their schedules may not be posted until a few days prior to the beginning of a new shift.

To accommodate each unique client, particularly in the absence of third-party reimbursement schedules that are strict in their requirement of 50-minute sessions, 90-minute sessions every other week might be preferable and should be offered if it is consistent with the clinician's schedule. A flexible schedule applies to a variety of clients across socioeconomic groups, from highly paid physicians on call to shift workers receiving minimum wage.

Which privileges are we as professionals willing to relinquish to better accommodate a diverse clientele? Wachtel (2002) stated it this way,

> What is required of us, however, in working with a broader range of patients, is more than just explaining why we do things the way we do. At times, what is required is that we do things differently...It is extremely difficult to be successful in therapeutic work with patients outside the White middle class if one maintains traditional notions about "the frame." (p. 205)

Class issues are not discussed in counselor training largely because the context in which class occurs is normative and reflective of an American value. An implicit expectation that clients have jobs and conventional work hours based on standard work fuels this oversight. What about clients who do not own cars, live in cities where reliable public transportation is nonexistent, are unable to leave 15 minutes early from their jobs without being docked, or spend an entire afternoon catching and waiting for buses while having to walk as well? Some clients experience obstacles in their efforts to receive therapy as a direct result of the ways class shapes people's lives, including our own. Do we subtract the time from the client's hour, even if another client is not scheduled immediately, because of the middle-class cultural adage that "time is money"? As mental health professionals, we need to make a living. Recruiting full-paying clients to balance those who are on a sliding scale is a way to make our professional services more accessible to all people. Conversely, if clients drive up for their appointments in expensive cars and wear expensive clothing, how are we affected by these indicators of wealth or debt? Components of class include art, music, tastes, religion, food, and furniture (Bourdieu, 1984). When high-status clients appear, how self-conscious do we become of our work environments and other indicators of our proximity to middle-class status? How might our personal reactions, being intimidated or impressed, affect our ability to extend our best professional practice to wealthy clients?

Counselors need to look beneath the glamour of socioeconomic class and privilege to avoid being blinded by its allure. There are clients with financial means who come to therapy with great woundedness.

THE FLUIDITY OF CLASS

Acquiring middle-class status or suddenly becoming poor in one's life does not erase the effects of early conditioning. Middle-class persons can move into a lower income level because of unemployment, physical and mental illness, violence, divorce or loss of another significant relationship, disability, death of the primary provider, or traumatic event. Class is fluid, and this issue can be overlooked if it is assumed that clients and their counselors have had similar and consistent class socialization experiences from childhood to adulthood. A change in income does not translate into a loss of values to which one has become accustomed.

The U.S. economic recession began in March 2001. Between 2000 and 2001, there was a widespread decline in median income; however, things begin to improve for some but certainly not for all. In 2006, the median household income in the United States was $48,201. It was $47,845 just a year earlier in 2005. In 2006, the median income for non-Hispanic Whites was $52,423; $31,960 for Blacks, $64,238 for Asians, and $37,781 for Latinos. Between 2005 and 2006, each of these racial groups and non-Hispanic Whites showed modest increases in income (DeNavas-Walt et al., 2007). (See Table 12.1.)

MIDDLE-CLASS BIAS AND ETHICAL STANDARDS

The roots of a middle-class cultural bias are reflected in the official documents used to standardize the profession and provide its membership with rules and guidelines for professional practice. For example, the ACA Code of Ethics (Section A.10.d) approaches bartering for services with caution. Yet, it has become flexible in its position from just 10 years ago when it stated that counselors "refrain from accepting goods or services in return for counseling services because such arrangements create inherent

TABLE 12.1   2006 Median Income by Race

Asian	$64,238
Black	$31,960
Latino	$37,781
White	$52,423

potential for conflict, exploitation, and distortion of the professional relationship (1995, Section A.10.c). The 2005 ethical code reads as follows:

> Counselors may barter only if the relationship is not exploitive or harmful and does not place the counselor in an unfair advantage, if the client requests its, and if such arrangements are in accepted practice among professionals in the community. Counselors consider the cultural implications of bartering and discuss relevant concerns with clients and document such agreements in a clear written contract. (Section A.10.c)

In some contexts, such as rural, cultural/ethnic, and/or agricultural communities, money may not be as readily available or even esteemed in the same ways as currency. A woman may not be able to afford $140 an hour for therapy (or even a greatly reduced amount based on a sliding scale), but she may value doing housework, gardening, or providing child care as an expression of gratitude and as a means of paying for the therapy services rendered to her. This sounds like bartering and understandably can be and is problematic. Zur (2006) said, "bartering of goods is more likely to constitute a boundary crossing but not usually a dual relationship; bartering of services always creates dual relationships" (p. 19).

The APA (2002) Code of Ethics does not refute bartering within the context of psychotherapy. Section 6.06 states that "barter is the acceptance of goods, services, or other nonmonetary remuneration from clients/patients in return for psychological services. Psychologists may barter only if (1) it is not clinically contraindicated, and (2) the resulting arrangement is not exploitative." Again, in certain contexts, dual relationships may not be readily avoidable and are the "hallmark of interconnected, rural settings" (Zur, 2006, p. 12). Within the context of a small town, dual relationships can look like the therapist shopping at a store that a client owns or going to the same church or temple, or children attending the same school. It is a middle-class bias that presumes such avoidance is preferred. Collectivistic communities are dependent on overlapping relationships where role diffusion cannot be avoided. Counselors, themselves, may be involved in conflicting roles (Pedersen, 1997). If there are few counselors of color in a community (urban and rural), it is likely that clients of color and the select counselors will frequent the same churches and community and recreational activities and may even have the same employer. Thus, the clear division of roles assumes an abundance of resources that are diverse enough so as not to intersect. The assumption is that clients and their counselors function and live out their lives in different social and political circles. This simply is not the case in some rural communities, communities of color, and ethnic communities—where, for instance, the family rabbi might be the marriage counselor and the child's Hebrew tutor.

Understandably, both ACA and APA are concerned with clients' well being and mental health professionals adhering to ethical codes with professional integrity. At the same time, APA recognizes the nature of multiple relationships and says in Section 3.05,

> a. A multiple relationship occurs when a psychologist is in a professional role with a person and (1) at the same time is in another role with the same person, (2) at the same time is in a relationship with a person closely associated with or related to the person with whom the psychologist has the professional relationship, or (3) promises to enter

into another relationship in the future with the person or a person closely associated with or related to the person.

A psychologist refrains from entering into a multiple relationship if the multiple relationship could reasonably be expected to impair the psychologist's objectivity, competence, or effectiveness in performing his or her functions as a psychologist, or otherwise risks exploitation or harm to the person with whom the professional relationship exists.

Multiple relationships that would not reasonably be expected to cause impairment or risk exploitation or harm are not unethical.

b.   If a psychologist finds that, due to unforeseen factors, a potentially harmful multiple relationship has arisen, the psychologist takes reasonable steps to resolve it with due regard for the best interests of the affected person and maximal compliance with the Ethics Code.

c.   When psychologists are required by law, institutional policy, or extraordinary circumstances to serve in more than one role in judicial or administrative proceedings, at the outset they clarify role expectations and the extent of confidentiality and thereafter as changes occur.

The current ACA Code of Ethics does not discourage dual relationships and has changed the ethical guidelines to respect healthy and therapeutic interactions between client and counselor.

A middle-class bias is seen in the very basic tenets of therapy, such as confidentiality. Students learn early in their programs that mental health professionals can be sued for violating a client's confidentiality. Pedersen (1997) said,

> In an individualistic culture, personal space and personal time are valued as property to be privately owned, and any infringement of those boundaries is considered a form of theft . . . In other more collectivistic cultural contexts . . . personal privacy is less valued and may even be perceived as selfish. (p. 25)[*]

Another middle-class bias exists in the expectation that clients will self-disclose. Actually, this is a hallmark of Rogerian counseling, which assumes that after disclosure, people experience a measurable and identifiable benefit and catharsis. Clearly, the roots of positivism are at work. Some clients may find therapy imbalanced due to the unidirectional nature of the exchange. It could be perceived as inconsistent with community, kinship, and mutuality. Another assumption embedded in disclosure is that an individual will be articulate (in Standard English) and be able to match affective experiences to words. It is a tall order for some clients to disclose personal details about themselves and their families with a professional stranger. Many low-wage earners, because of limited education and/or immigrant status, do not speak Standard English. Inability to speak Standard English is not synonymous with illegal status, limited intelligence, or the ability to learn.

[*]Adapted with permission from "The cultural context of the American Counseling Association code of ethics," by P. B. Pedersen, *Journal of Counseling and Development, 76*, p. 23–28. Copyright 1997 by the American Psychological Association.

STORYTELLING: Coming Down the Mountain

I was with a small group of other Americans and we were climbing Mt. Kilimanjaro in Tanzania. We were outfitted with our sturdy sneakers—some of us had hiking boots. I had my fanny pack with my water and energy bars, along with my layered, moisture-licking, wool clothing that you pay too much for at outdoor shops. We were enjoying the splendor of our hike—the birds, the flowers, the monkeys. At the same time we were tired and challenged by the rigor of this uphill climb. All of sudden, two native Tanzanian youth appeared carrying a long and heavy log balanced on both of their shoulders as they came down the mountain in flipflops. They smiled and warmly greeted us as they scampered past us. We were sobered at how limber they were and without all of the water, food, and footwear that we privileged Americans had.

An examination of core and dominant cultural values allows one to see why a middle-class bias prevails in the training of counselors. Competition, the Protestant work ethic, and self-reliance all stem from an individualistic and Western culture (Sue & Sue, 1990). Yet, some communities are more collective, wherein greater dependence on others is the norm. Perceptions of dependence also seem to be fostered by class status. (See Storytelling: "Coming Down the Mountain.") Perhaps it is easier to live without cultivating a relationship with neighbors if one is not financially interdependent on others. The California community in which I was reared was collective and collaborative in orientation. In my community, neighbors depended on one another for community. We borrowed household flour and sugar from one another, helped raise each other's children, shared resources, and even watched television in one another's homes when someone's "tube" was in the shop for repair. Class may dictate one's ability to provide for personal material needs independent of others. Having middle-class status, particularly within an individualistic context, may make it easier not to be in relationships with persons in close proximity to oneself. This is most likely different from poor or collectivistic communities (independent of class differences), where value is placed on kinship networks. Within collectivistic contexts seen among many Arab, African, Asian, Native American, Latino, and agrarian and religious White families, an extension of the personal self is part of the culture or tribe.

CLASSISM

The media plays a role in depicting poor people as invisible and yet responsible for their predicament. They tend to be presented as unworthy and not deserving of more. Being poor in American society and staying poor is not valued. Such a position does not mirror the American values of competition, success, change, progress, rising above one's situation, and controlling one's life. The inability to significantly alter one's station in life is inconsistent with core American values.

Classism is a form of oppression against the poor. Smith (2005) defines *classism* as "an interlocking system that involves domination and control of social ideology, institutions, and resources, resulting in a condition of privilege for one group relative to the disenfranchisement of another. Members of both dominant and subordinated groups are capable of prejudice, but only dominant groups have the institutional and cultural power to enforce their prejudices via oppression" (p. 688).

APA (2007) defines classism as "the network of attitudes, beliefs, behaviors, and institutional practices that maintain and legitimatize class-based power differences that privilege middle and higher income groups at the expense of the poor and working classes" (p. 7). Starting out poor and becoming rich through marriage, promotion, business, or even winning the lottery, is admired. The values of hard work and/or good fortune, pulling oneself up by one's bootstraps, and a belief in a just society are all at work as is the ability to, despite the odds, transcend one's situation.

Socioeconomic class is fluid, which means the so-called lines between class groups are not solid. Many working-class families are governed by middle-class values, such as education as a means of self-help, hard work, money management, perseverance, and delayed gratification. Ogbu (1997) discussed the transient nature of class membership:

> Because the basis for membership in class groups can be acquired by an individual during a lifetime, social classes are open entities. Although they are more or less permanent, the entities have no clear boundaries; furthermore, their membership is not permanent because people are continually moving in and out of them. (p. 768)

Ogbu's words, as well as the most recent and looming recession, acknowledge that the white-collar worker can quickly become the blue-collar laborer. Newman (1999), an anthropologist and researcher on poverty, said, "The working poor are perpetually at risk for becoming the poor of the other kind; they are one paycheck away from what is left of welfare, one sick child away from getting fired, one missed rent payment short of eviction" (p. xiv).

Within the home there are cultural experiences that assist children in their adjustment to school, such as being read to, seeing people read books, waiting in line, and organizing one's work or play. Bourdieu (1984) referred to such experiences as cultural capital that have middle-class connections. The home environment, along with a host of other agents (e.g., school, church, neighborhood, extracurricular activities), socializes children toward a middle-class perspective. Linguistic structures, styles of interacting, and authority patterns characterize cultural resources that can be turned into highly beneficial and socially lucrative cultural capital.

Kenway (1988) conducted research on privileged girls in private schools in Australia. She was interested in looking at self-esteem within an educational context. In talking with the girls about their experiences, Kenway found they used words such as *proper, right, perfect, education, manners,* and *success* to describe their status as upper class and said, "Self-esteem may be bought via the right 'casual-chic' designer label. In the culture of consumption within which private schools are immersed, success also can be bought alongside approval, acceptance, and social honour" (p. 155). Kenway encouraged her readers to see the costs to these young girls in their efforts to maintain an image based on elite class distinctions as measured by an exclusive school environment.

IMPLICATIONS FOR COUNSELORS AND PSYCHOLOGISTS

Schnitzer (1996) asks "how might clinicians best integrate knowledge about the impact of poverty on mental health into their practice" (p. 577). Unraveling the effects of class on one's life is not easy and can be difficult. Dominant discourses within society and particularly within the nation's training programs connect class and self-worth. More often than not, the poor are seen as lazy, unmotivated, and intellectually inferior.

The middle class represent the referents for society. Counselors need to hear the prevalence of class conditioning when listening to their clients' stories and, where necessary, help their clients make important connections between their identity and the effects of class on their lives. For example, an adult client from a working-class family might be reluctant to take certain occupational risks because of socialization experiences that emphasize security, saving for a rainy day, and being practical about the future. Asking, "What is the effect of growing up poor on your willingness now to change jobs?" or "What kinds of messages did you receive about being poor or taking risks?" could further the client's exploration of the relationship between early family experiences and staying at a job that is unfulfilling.

Anxiety about change and taking risk might be higher among clients who, as children and now as adults, have difficulty meeting basic needs. This is not to say that middle-class clients are prepared to embrace uncertainty or change, but having access to an inheritance, a family home, and other financial safety nets that augment one's existing resources may make it more psychologically comfortable and financially possible to engage in risk-taking behavior. Such resources include, but are not limited to, a trust fund, a family loan, the family home, the beach house, an inheritance, and furniture.

Addressing the structural, social, and economic issues that affect clients' lives is essential. In doing so, we approach our clients from an ecological perspective. A focus on personal relationships and the clients' insights are critical to therapy, however, a broader view is warranted (Schnitzer, 1996). The following questions may encourage introspection about class.

1. Was there an event that you did not attend because you did not have the appropriate attire or accessories?
2. Were there sporting events or clubs that you could not participate in because your family did not have the money?
3. Were there friends you did not invite to your home because you were ashamed of where you lived and how your home looked?
4. What are your experiences with low-wage-earning people?
5. Have you consciously downplayed your wealth by dressing in attire or brands that did not display your wealth?
6. Did you choose friends or shun others because of their income or how they looked or what they drove or wore?
7. Have you ever worked hard to convince people that although you had wealth, you were still a kind person?

8. Did you not date a person you were interested in because you did not think he or she would fit into your life because they had inadequate resources or did not come from the "right" family?

9. Were you told that you just did not fit in and yet the criteria for fitting in was not related to money but perhaps other dimensions of identity, such as race or sexuality or body size?

CASE STUDY
Class Divide

Jane is a 35-year-old, African American, single mother of four children. She is a nursing assistant. Jane faithfully goes to therapy. She and her therapist have decided on a sliding scale. Jane does not have health insurance. Several times, Jane was not able to make it to therapy because the car that her boyfriend had purchased for her had been repossessed. Her boyfriend has an unstable work history due to time spent in jail for drug charges. In therapy, Jane wants to strengthen her relationships and be a more involved parent. Jane receives weekly calls from the school regarding her oldest child who is frequently absent, is disruptive in class, and is known to be inappropriate with the teachers (yelling and disregarding their requests of her). Jane feels that the teachers and counselors do not understand her, and she feels angry after most interactions with them. Jane's mother and sister do not understand why she is going to a perfect stranger to discuss private family matters. Jane appreciates the time in therapy to work on herself and get a break from all of the care she provides for everyone else around the clock. All of Jane's top teeth are missing. Although her challenges are multiple, her therapist notices that she does not seem flappable and does not react in ways that convey extreme levels of distress.

QUESTIONS

1. What do psychologists and counselors need to understand in their work with clients who are low-wage-earning?
2. What are Jane's strengths?
3. How and when do therapists advocate for their clients?

DISCUSSION AND INTEGRATION
The Client, Jane

Despite the multiple challenges that describe Jane's life—poverty, single parenting, a significant other's legal problems and substance addiction, and a child with behavioral and learning difficulties—tenacity, hope, and commitment to her personal development describe Jane's strengths. While it is important for counselors and psychologists to appreciate the strain of oppression in their clients' lives and to advocate as appropriate, many people who start out poor as children and remain poor as adults have learned to "roll with the punches," use humor to "keep from crying," shout out a prayer to God for help in times of trouble. They have also learned to hustle and make do out of a system that often renders them invisible and peripheral.

Socioeconomic status is a major component of biological processes, such as higher blood pressure, greater blockage of coronary arteries, and more rapid progression of HIV infection (Anderson, 2003). Jane, like others who are poor, does not have health insurance. Forty-seven million Americans are in poverty and do not have health insurance. In 2006, 28.3% of female-headed households with no husband present were at the poverty line. In addition, the percentage and the number of people without health insurance increased from 15.3% in 2005 to 15.8% in 2006, or from 44.8 million to 47 million people (DeNavas-Walt et al., 2007). Among Latinos, 34.1% were uninsured compared with 20.5% among Black people. Whites and Asians had the lowest rates of uninsured, at 10.8% and 15.5%, respectively. Among people who were foreign-born, 33.8% were not covered by health insurance. For native-born Americans, the uninsured health care rate was 13.2%.

It is inaccurate to assume that low-wage-earning people do not care about their children. Jane, like many other clients dealing with just "one more thing," may react with muted affect or numbing. "Class and racial differences between therapist and client may mean experiences with emotional and physical assault so profoundly variant that the therapist cannot adequately envision the impact on the human psyche" (Schnitzer, 1996, p. 575).

Jane's boyfriend experiences depression and frustration at his irregular employment situation. Regarding Black men, Washington (1987) said, "Economic stressors such as unemployment, underemployment, job losses, health catastrophes, loss of personal property, and gross indebtedness also exert an unacceptable level of chronic stress" (p. 194). The stress is tied into not being able to achieve society's clear standards about manhood, which are synonymous with career and material success. At the same time, addiction grossly impairs one's ability to seek work and maintain positions once offered.

Like Jane, many unskilled parents leave the training and education of their children to teachers while valuing educational success and achievement. Lareau (1997) conducted research on two very different school populations. At the first school, 60% of parents were professionals, compared with 1% at the other. The majority of the professional parents had college degrees, and many fathers had advanced degrees. Parents in the unskilled jobs had either a high school education or had dropped out of high school. Only 1% of parents at the first school were unskilled workers, compared with 23% at the second one. Lareau found that interactions between professional parents and teachers were more frequent and comfortable. Professional parents were also more involved in the academic preparation of their children. Parents at the school at which the majority of parents were semiskilled or unskilled tended to have uncomfortable and infrequent interactions with teachers. Lareau wrote, "In the middle-class community, parents saw education as a shared enterprise and scrutinized, monitored and supplemented the school experience of their children" (p. 712).

Children from middle-class families had greater cultural capital than children from lower income families. This is not to say that the family–school relationship among the middle class was better for children in comparison with children from the working class. Lareau stated, however, that "the social profitability of middle-class arrangements is tied to the school's definition of the proper family-school relationship" (p. 713).

Jane reported that her interactions with the school counselor are awkward. It may be helpful for the therapist to attend such a meeting with her client. School counselors need to be aware of the ways in which culture can work against parents' perception of schools as accessible, particularly for working-class parents and their children. What may appear to be apathy from Jane may actually be feelings of fear and uncertainty. For Jane and others like her, the quality of interactions with school personnel is linked to the discourses predominant from her educational contexts that were alienating and fraught with shame and difficulty. Brantlinger (1993) interviewed low-income parents. She found that many continue to carry the mental baggage from their early school experiences, which detracted from their ability, in some instances, to discuss their children's school experiences.

The Therapist

Jackson (2005) makes a distinction between *poor women* and *low-wage-earning women,* which, she says, "helps us to always keep an eye trained on the economic conditions that create and/or maintain the challenges that many women and their families to seek our services" (p. 238). Low-wage-earning people are more vulnerable within institutional structures, including the school, courts, and the police (Robinson, 1999). For instance, interest rates on credit cards are often near 30%. When making the minimum monthly payment, getting out of debt is nearly impossible. An important skill for Jane's therapist to have is the ability to engage in introspection and to ask questions of herself toward gaining insight into the effects of class on her identity. No standard for training about social class and classism exists in counselor training. Because of this dearth, "counselors in training must seek experiences where they can explore their own social class worldviews and be challenged in a supportive environment" (Liu & Arguello, 2006, p. 9).

What is it about interactions with low-wage-earning people that may feel awkward or conforming or familiar? What are the indicators of one's own privileged financial position that may be a point of disclosure to Jane, albeit unintentionally? Jane's therapist wants to nurture an egalitarian relationship with all of her clients, yet at the same time, there is an unequal power dynamic. Feelings of guilt can contribute to a counselor's acquiesence of her power. This is defeating to both the therapist and the counseling event. As an identity construct, class has a significant impact on development. Like culture, people are often oblivious to it.

To facilitate the process of counselors' becoming more aware of their own class experiences and worldview, the counselor could recall memories from her childhood that were connected to class and that evoked feelings of pride, embarrassment, guilt, superiority, inferiority, and shame. Remember similar stories from college and as an adult. It is important for Jane's therapist—regardless of race, class, sexuality, ability, or gender—to endorse mutuality, reciprocity, and sensitivity in her work. She recognizes that Jane has limited resources but also understands the importance of Jane meeting her financial obligations for therapy. Respecting Jane's situation, she asks, "What do you think you are able to pay for psychotherapy?" The therapist asks Jane to ponder this question until their next session.

SUMMARY

This chapter on class explored the neglect of class within the literature as a psychosocial variable. The middle-class bias in graduate counseling training programs was discussed at length. Work conducted by sociologists on school inequity was an important link in this discussion. A case was presented of a client from a low-income background with multiple challenges and strengths. Implications for counselors and psychologists were explored and questions presented for beginning the personal process of interrogating the dynamic of class in one's life.

Chapter 13

Converging Sexuality

We cannot live without our lives.

**Barbara Deming, lesbian feminist
writer and activist**

This chapter focuses on sexuality. From the beginning, it should be noted that language is in flux and has changed over time. Terms in this chapter will be used that admittedly are contested, such as *gay, lesbian*, and *bisexual* (Eliason & Schope, 2007). Sexuality exists on a continuum representing variations within and between homosexuality, bisexuality, and heterosexuality. There are people who have lived part of their lives with a particular sexual orientation and have come to question that sexuality. Persons who are transgendered do not fit into the binary of woman or man, gay or straight. This chapter recognizes the fluidity of sexuality over the developmental cycle and recognizes sexuality as part of a developmental system. A person's "sexual landscape might change, thus creating new opportunities for self description while transforming or eliminating existing possibilities" (Rust, 2006, p. 174). A possible outcome of this discussion is that the reader will become more conscious of a heterosexual bias that continues to exist in the societal culture at large and the profession in particular. An assumption of heterosexuality can be silencing and offensive to lesbian, gay, and questioning clients. As clinicians increase their awareness of their biases and their proximity to heterosexist discourses, service delivery will hopefully improve. Far too often, graduate counseling programs do not provide adequate training in this area. Unpacking personal biases and receiving knowledge about gay, lesbian, bisexual, intersexual, and transgendered clients provides therapists with the skills and competencies needed for this and other nondominant populations. At the same time, working outside of areas of expertise is a violation of the ethical standards of the American Counseling Association (ACA) and the American Psychological Association (APA).

Definitions are provided, and a case study concludes the chapter.

DEFINITIONS AND TERMINOLOGY

To enhance understanding, definitions are provided. Hunt (1993) said, "as with any group, language has a strong impact on gay and lesbian culture. As times change and as words develop new connotations some words fall out of favor" (p. 2). The following terms are considered nonbiased and accepted terminology among people who identify as gay men, lesbians, or bisexuals. Intersexuality and transgendered will also be discussed. These terms are used as the standard terminology in this chapter. (See Storytelling: "Language.")

Heterosexism is the belief that everyone is heterosexual and that heterosexual relationships are preferred and necessary for the preservation of the family, particularly the nuclear family. Heterosexism is institutionalized through religion, education, and the media and leads to homophobia (Robinson & Watt, 2001). It describes the institutionalization of antigay, antilesbian, and antibisexual beliefs, attitudes, and behaviors. Heterosexism is the deeply ingrained notion that heterosexuality is the superior sexual orientation (Wall & Evans, 1992). Pharr (1988) stated that heterosexism has been defined as a worldview, a value system that prizes heterosexuality, that assumes it is the only appropriate manifestation of love and sexuality, and that

STORYTELLING: Language

The terms *transexxual, transgender, transvestite,* and *gay* are not well understood. As I lectured in class one night, I mentioned that the majority of men who were transvestites were not gay but heterosexual and that people can be transgendered but not gay. The silence was amazing, and the confused looks on students' faces told me that they did not understand what I had just said. Another way to look at transgender was defined by Towle and Morgan (2002), who said that *transers* "has sometimes replaced third gender to designate gender roles and practices which are not definable in terms of local understandings of gender normativity" (p. 473). The term *third gender* was introduced in 1975 by M. Kay Martin and Barbara Voorhies and drew attention to the ethnographic evidence that gender categories in some cultures (as well as our own here in the West) could not be adequately explained in a two-gender framework. The heterosexual man who loves his body and has a girlfriend refers to himself as transgendered because he refuses to restrict his clothing choices to pants only. He wears skirts. At the same time, there are people who are transgendered who are gay or bisexual or questioning their sexuality. Transgendered does not mean gay. Transsexuals may not define themselves as gay but have had or plan to undergo reconstructive surgery to match hormone treatments or electrolysis for men who are transitioning to becoming women. Counselors and therapists have a responsibility to be informed of the correct language so as not to be insensitive or misinformed.

devalues homosexuality and all that is not heterosexual. Dines and Humez (2002) described heterosexism as the heterosexual predisposition that is encoded into and characteristic of the major social, cultural, and economic institutions of our society.

Although similar to heterosexism, **homophobia** is regarded as a sense of dread of being in close quarters with people who are lesbian, bisexual, or gay (Worthington, Dillon, & Becker-Schutte, 2005). *Homophobia* comes from the Latin *homo,* meaning "same" (in this case, referring to same-gender attraction), and *phobia,* meaning "fear of"; thus, the term's original application to individuals was an extreme and persistent fear and loathing of homosexuals (Pharr, 1988). Fear, hatred, and dislike tied to cultural socialization and religious beliefs are often present with homophobia. **Homonegativity** has been defined as negative feelings and thoughts about lesbian, gay, or bisexual orientations or individuals (Worthington et al., 2005). Pharr (1988) said that homophobia is a weapon of sexism because it works to keep men and women in rigidly defined gender roles. **Homosexual** defines attraction to the same sex for physical and emotional nurturance and is one orientation on the continuum from homosexual to bisexual to heterosexual. This term has become associated with the historical belief that homosexuality is unnatural, a sin, and a sickness. For this reason, females who are homosexual/gay often prefer the term **lesbian** to describe their sexual orientation. The difference in terminology, which arose during the feminist movement, reflects the difference between gay men and lesbians. The term *lesbian* gets its origins from the Greek poet Sappho (c. 600 B.C.), who lived on the Greek island of Lesbos in the Aegean Sea. Sappho's poems are exclusively about women.

Someone who acknowledges his homoerotic orientation and incorporates this knowledge into his identity and carries this identity into interpersonal relationships is defined as **gay**. The term *gay* signifies more self-awareness, self-acceptance, and openness than the term *homosexual*. Often, in developmental literature, the process of coming to terms with one's sexuality involves moving from being homosexual to becoming gay. One consequence of homophobia is **internalized homophobia.** It is produced by the negative messages about homosexuality that lesbians and gay men hear throughout their lives. Because gay men and lesbians are stereotyped, uninformed, or fed inaccurate, distorted information about homosexuality, the messages are internalized and result in low self-esteem. Internalized homophobia can lead to self-hatred and other psychological problems (Dworkin & Gutierrez, 1991).

Rust (2006) aptly pointed out that people sometimes misrepresent their identities to avoid judgment and disapproval. She said, "Lesbians and gay men often misrepresent their sexual locations when in heterosexual contexts, and bisexual women often misrepresent their location when in lesbian contexts" (p. 179). **Bisexuality** represents a shifting and dynamic sexual landscape that can be misunderstood, not only among heterosexually identified people but among gay men and lesbian women.

Transgender refers to persons who may be biologically one sex but may identify within their bodies, souls, and minds as the other sex. People may refer to themselves as transgender and still consider themselves gay, lesbian, bisexual, or heterosexual. A male-to-female transsexual might put it this way, "I see myself being with a man, but I did not see myself as a man with a man. I saw myself as a woman with a man." (See Storytelling: "Living Authentically.")

STORYTELLING: Living Authentically

I once knew someone of color who had a wife and two children. This person, who I'll refer to as Hailey, served many years in the military. Although Hailey had an outward appearance that was masculine, in terms of style of dress, mannerism, and voice, Hailey felt that being male was not accurate, that an error had occurred. Hailey also was attracted to men but as a person who identified as female. Hailey felt paralyzed. On one hand, Hailey loved the woman with whom Hailey had two children and had shared a life together for a long time. On the other hand, Hailey felt that the denial was a death sentence. Denial was no longer an option. Hailey decided to get therapy to explore sexuality and identity as well as how to live authentically. Hailey has always felt different because there had been an attraction to men but not as a gay man but as a woman attracted to a man. Hailey did not want to hurt anyone and said in therapy, "My wife has always been good to me and she is such a kind soul." It took Hailey a while to find a suitable counselor. The first therapist, upon learning Hailey was struggling with sexuality issues, suggested Hailey see another counselor, citing Catholicism and Hailey's issues as conflicting with the counselor's personal and religious values. Feeling deflated and defeated, Hailey waited before seaching again for a suitable professional with whom to work. After nearly a year, Hailey found a skilled and nonjudgmental counselor. After therapy for almost a year, Hailey decided to tell the truth: that a divorce was necessary and that to live authentically meant living life as a woman. Therapy helped Hailey realize that no one was going to emerge from this situation without being hurt. Hailey had spent so much of her life hiding and denying what she knew to be true. Because she started to feel her own hurt and pain, she was able to recognize that her coming out would be hurtful to her wife and children. Hurt was one thing but deception was another. Therapy also helped her think about what it meant to be transsexual as a woman of color. Not only had she been battling heterosexism throughout her life but racism and sexism. At the same time, she was committed to being honest, answering people's questions, and staying connected to family.

For as long as Hailey could remember, she felt different, and yet words failed to fully express the nature and extent of this difference, which contributed to Hailey's sense of isolation and confusion about who she was. Not having people in whom Hailey could confide contributed to her loneliness. It was a significant step for Hailey to disclose her struggles with a therapist. In doing so, words again failed her in that she did not have the language to explain who she was: a genetically normal XY male who felt that her gender assignment was wrong and yet did not identify as gay because she saw herself as a female who was attracted to men. Growing up in a rural part of the Midwest only fueled Hailey's self-perception that she was abnormal. Therapy helped Hailey understand the stigma associated with not aligning with the gender binary. It also helped her see how she had internalized oppression and that racism, sexism, and homophobic attitudes were prevalent throughout her life. Hailey's authenticity was noted in deciding to no longer live a lie.

A tremendous amount of oppression and isolation exists within communities of color around homosexuality. A man's expression of interest in another man is construed as homosexuality. In a heterosexist society, homosexuality is often feared. Kimmel (2006) said homophobia is interwoven with sexism and racism. Hailey, as a young man, exaggerated his masculinity and interest in things male: fighting and hypersexuality. Persons of color who are transsexual differ from White people who have similar experiences. Fortunately, Hailey's therapist was attentive to her multiple identities particularly within the context of multiple sources of discrimination (Greene, 1994).

The first counselor Hailey interacted with did not want to work with Hailey because the presenting problem related to sexuality and its conflict with her values and beliefs. While mental health professionals are not supposed to function outside of their scope of training or competence, counselors are encouraged to "gain knowledge, personal awareness, sensitivity, and skills pertinent to working with a diverse client population" (ACA, 2005, C.2.a). The first counselor clearly exhibited biased, inadequate, and inappropriate practice (Garnets, Hancock, Cochran, Goodchilds, & Peplau, 1991).

Hermann and Herlihy (2006) caution counselors about not treating clients because of sexuality issues. In citing the case of *Bruff vs. North Mississippi Health Services, Inc.,* in 2001, they explained that "the most significant legal aspect of the Bruff case is the court's holding that an employer's legal obligation to make reasonable accommodations for employees' religious beliefs does not include accommodating a counselor's request to refer homosexual clients who ask for assistance with relationship issues" (p. 416). In short, counselors cannot use their religious practices and beliefs to defend discriminating based on sexual orientation.

Intersexual refers to people who are (pseudo) hermaphrodites (Kitzinger, 1999), or persons born with genitalia that is different or ambiguous enough to raise concerns as it deviates from a normative appearance. However, intersexuality is not always evident from an external evaluation. A newborn might have genitalia that resemble a very large clitoris and/or male genitalia that have a more masculine appearance. Intersexuality may be caused by congenital adrenal hyperplasia, mixed gonadal dysgenesis, androgen insensitivity syndrome (complete or partial), 5-alpha reductase deficiency, and many other conditions (Chase, 2003). The narrow construction and birfurcation of gender, which translates into males having a designated sized penis and testicles and females not having a clitoris that is too large and a vagina and uterus, does not apply to all children born in the United States and throughout the world (Sterling, 1992).

Queer theory is a field of gender and sexuality studies that emerged in the early 1990s out of the gay/lesbian and feminist studies. Deconstructionists influenced this field, which is a critique of gender and sexual identities, while gazing at the socially constructed nature of identities and sexual acts, normative and deviant. Queer language evolved as a form of resistance to externally imposed structures from the dominant cultures and created by the "queer community" as a means of communicating (Wikipedia, 2007).

When gay men and lesbians come to accept being gay or lesbian as a salient component of their identities, it is descriptive of the process of **coming out.** Numerous developmental models describe the stages of the coming-out process, such as those of Cass (1979) and Coleman (1982). Gay and lesbian people have struggled throughout history with the notion that their sexual identity was a choice—and the wrong choice. Because of socialization, some gay men and lesbians have behaved heterosexually even though their identity was gay or lesbian. Many remember feeling different at an early age and see this as stemming from their gay and lesbian orientation. For this reason, the term **sexual orientation,** rather than *sexual preference,* is preferred. By owning this orientation, gay men and lesbians make a conscious choice to let their behavior conform to their orientation, just as a heterosexually oriented person makes a choice not to behave in a homosexual manner.

Heterosexism affects everyone, covertly and overtly, in this society. It is not only harmful to the victims but to the perpetrators as well. According to Smith (1982), heterosexism is intimately associated with other discriminatory practices (e.g., classism, sexism, racism, ageism) in our society. She stated that verbal and behavioral expressions of heterosexism are acceptable and go uncontested in contexts where other discriminatory comments or gesticulations (e.g., racist, sexist, or anti-Semitic remarks) would be challenged or prohibited.

Sexual politics ensures the dominance of males over females and the dominance of heterosexuals over persons who are gay and lesbian (Pleck, 1984). Within a system of **hegemony** (a historical situation in which power is won and held) and androcentrism (in which the complementarity of women and men implies women's subordinate social position to men), homosexuality becomes a threat for heterosexual men. Heterosexual men are socialized into believing that to reject anything that remotely resembles homosexuality, they must oppress women. For this reason, "any kind of powerlessness, or refusal to compete among men becomes involved with the imagery of homosexuality" (Pleck, 1984, p. 84). Within heterosexuality, a central dimension of the power that men exercise over women is found. Clearly, sexism and homophobia are interlocking paradigms.

Sexual inequality and heterosexuality cannot be discussed without addressing sociopolitical power dynamics within society, such as the suppression of women's sexuality, forced sexuality through incest and rape, the idealization of heterosexual marriage, and the contradicting and confusing roles of motherhood.

Traditionally, a healthy or ideal personality has included a concept of *sexual identity* with three basic components:

1. A sexual preference for members of the opposite sex.
2. A sex role identity as either masculine or feminine, depending on one's gender.
3. A gender identity that is a secure sense of one's maleness or femaleness.

Bem (1993) set out to refute these components by stating that sexual preference ought to be considered orthogonal to notions of mental health. She also indicated that the terms *heterosexual* and *homosexual* should be used to describe acts rather than persons.

NARRATIVE QUESTIONS

It is often through exposure to other people's personal narratives that students gain insight into the lived experiences of others. Gaining insight into one's own personal stories and histories is essential to self-knowledge. Consider your responses to the following questions (Falco, 1991, p. 174):

1. What was the first reference to gays or lesbians you ever remember hearing?
2. What do you remember about the first person you ever saw or met who you identified as gay or lesbian?
3. What did your parents teach you about people who are gay and lesbian?
4. What type of treatment did gay and lesbian clients receive in your therapy or counseling course?
5. How were gay or lesbian student therapists treated in your training program? Gay or lesbian supervisors or instructors?
6. Do you currently have friends or acquaintances whom you know to be gay or lesbian? If not, why do you think this is so?
7. Who do you think might be gay or lesbian? What are they like? Do you think they are typical of gays or lesbians?
8. What is the most memorable same-sex experience of your life? The most traumatic? The most meaningful and/or eye-opening?

THE IMPORTANCE OF A FOCUS ON GAY, LESBIAN, BISEXUAL, AND TRANSGENDER ISSUES IN COUNSELING

To be effective, therapists need to receive adequate training in counseling persons who are gay, lesbian, bisexual, and transgender. First they must understand the terms briefly discussed earlier. Rudolph (1990) projected that approximately 25% to 65% of the gay, lesbian, and bisexual population seeks psychotherapy, a percentage two to four times higher than in the heterosexual population. Moreover, a significantly larger percentage of gay men and lesbians report dissatisfaction with their treatment, compared with heterosexuals.

Although there is a need to provide psychotherapy in the gay/lesbian community, many mental health professionals have not been provided the appropriate training to assist gay men, lesbians, and bisexuals effectively through their coming out or identity development process. Beals and Peplau (2006) found in their study of 144 gay men and lesbians that they have better relationships with people they have directly told about their sexuality compared with people with whom they have not disclosed. Clearly, disclosure of a stigmatized identity can have profound and lasting implications for relationships; nonetheless, this finding suggests that relationship quality is adversely affected when people have not revealed core information about their identity.

Survey and anecdotal literature reveals that the source of dissatisfaction often is the counselor's ignorance or prejudice toward people who are gay (Bell & Weinberg, 1978). Just as clinicians must be aware of their racial biases regarding cultural and racial groups, they must also assess their biases as they relate to gay, lesbian, and bisexual clients (Pope, 1995). Clinicians have been influenced by living in a society that socializes people toward racist and homophobic attitudes. For example, Caroline Pace (1991) conducted an in-depth study on the attitudes of mental health professionals and graduate students in training programs toward gay men and lesbians. She found that "counselors, like other individuals socialized by heterosexist institutions in the United States, hold negative attitudes toward lesbians and gays" (p. 73). The mental health professionals and counselors-in-training scored in the "low grade homophobic" range of the Index of Attitudes toward Homosexuals Scale.

Bradford, Barrett, and Honnold (2002) report that as of the 2000 census, there were nearly 600,000 same-sex couples, or nearly 1.2 million people. The largest proportional increases in the number of same-sex couples self-reporting in 2000 compared with 1990 were in rural and sparsely populated areas. For instance, Wyoming reported 30,000 same-sex couples in 1990 and 807,000 in 2000. The five cities with largest number of same-sex couples were New York, Los Angeles, San Francisco, Washington, DC, and Chicago.

Gay, lesbian, bisexual, and transgender people experience homophobia not only in the counselor's office, which should be a safe place to explore identity issues, but from the general public as well. In a study of 1,669 students, staff, faculty, and administrators at 14 private and public colleges and universities, 29% of respondents reported that they had been harassed because of their sexual orientation or gender identity. Harrassment was defined as "conduct that has interfered unreasonably with your ability to work or learn on this campus or has created an offensive, hostile, intimidating working or learning environment" (Rankin, 2002, p. 26). The harrassment was most likely, at 57%, to occur in public space on campus or while people were walking or working on campus. The harrassment most frequently occurred through derogatory remarks, at 89%; verbal harassment or threats, 48%; graffiti, 39%; and pressure to be silent about sexual orientation/gender, 38%. This study also found that the majority of respondents, 71%, perceived transgender people to be the most likely to be harassed on campus. The actual percentage of harassment that occurred against transgendered people was 41%. In an environment that should support the universe of expression, ideas, and exploration, colleges and universities have been bastions of heterosexist and homophobic activity.

Other crucial issues that face the gay population are substance abuse, depression, running away, HIV and AIDS, partner abuse, and attempted suicide. Researchers maintain that substance abuse among lesbians and gay men is high. The gay bar may be the most accessible and visible place to persons who are "out" to interact with others who are also "out" (Rothblum, 1994). Gay men and lesbians attempt suicide two to seven times more often than heterosexual comparison groups (Durby, 1994; Hammelman, 1993). Gay youth have a plethora of problems during adolescence, such as intensified feelings of isolation, depression, and lack of healthy role models (Browning, Reynolds, & Dworkin, 1994). School counselors should be aware of, and be prepared to work with, a diversity of youths because an estimated 3 million adolescents across the country are gay, lesbian, or bisexual. Unfortunately, because of the lack of role models and sympathetic support systems, another 20% to 35% of these young individuals attempt suicide (O'Connor, 1992). Gay youth are vulnerable and need caring adults. Racism and other sources of discrimination heighten this vulnerability among gay youth (Greene & Herek, 1994).

Asian American gay people find themselves "caught between two conflicting cultural values, between Asian and Western influences" (Chan, 1992, p. 116). Asian American and Native American Indian gay men and lesbians also contend with strong traditional family roles, subsequent expectations, and community values that are often collectivistic, as opposed to individualistic, in orientation (Greene, 1994).

DEVELOPMENTAL PROCESSES

Everyone has sexuality. Sexuality interacts with other aspects of the self, such as race, age, class, and geography. The need to develop a clear sense of one's sexuality is not limited to GLBTIQQ (gay, lesbian, bisexual, transgender, intersexual, questioning, and queer people) only. Robinson and Watt (2001) argued that "the socially endorsed experience of heterosexuality and the unconscious and unearned privilege afforded heterosexuals often deems them unaware of the importance to transition through sexual identity formation" (p. 594). Not thinking about oneself as a sexual being (similar to not thinking about oneself as having race) has implications for therapists' ability to hear their clients talk about matters related to sexuality. Several themes of identity evolution, which is different from formation as it suggests an endpoint, have been identified by Elaison & Schope (2007): differences, confusion, exploration, disclosure, labeling, cultural immersion, distrust of the oppressor, degree of integration, internalized, oppression, managing, stigma, identity transformation, and, authenticity. (See Storytelling: "Living Authentically" on pages 230–231.)

Several linear models of gay and lesbian identity development exist. There are limitations associated with these models. Not all people progress through the stages as prescribed in that they may skip a stage or recycle back through them in the face of a significant event. There are older adults who experience their sexuality differently from youth. Some of the models do not account for development after adolescence. In addition, the experience of being bisexual and/or transgender is different from being gay or lesbian. Being a lesbian is a very different experience from being a gay male.

Erwin (2006) argues that lesbians are frequently overlooked by researchers, except when they are open about their identity, do not conform to societal gender role expectations, or have concerns about their sexual orientation. Being a feminine lesbian does not describe the experience of a woman who is butch in her appearance or lesbian woman of color (Eliason & Schope, 2007). Despite the limitations of stage models, they do provide some understanding of where people might be in their evolution. The models can also help therapists and student development professionals with understanding the questions and themes that describe certain stages or phases. Cass's model is described below. Troiden's and Sullivan's models are also mentioned.

CASS'S MODEL OF GAY, LESBIAN, AND BISEXUAL SEXUAL IDENTITY FORMATION

Vivian Cass (1979) developed a model to assess the growth, development, and awareness of gay, lesbian, and bisexual individuals. Most counselors will work with a gay, lesbian, or bisexual client at some juncture during their professional careers. The Cass model is provided as a guideline for assessing a client's level of development. It is important to note that the client may foreclose at a given stage, skip certain levels, or regress from a higher stage to a lower stage, depending on the events that occur in his or her life.

Coping strategies vary for gay, lesbian, bisexual, and transgender (GLBT) clients. Often, a therapist can assess the gay client's level of identity development in the coming-out process. According to the Cass model (1984), the gay identity formation process occurs in six stages, beginning with the individual having a sexual self-portrait that is heterosexual. For example, if the client were talking about a female, the female would see herself and her behavior as heterosexual as well as perceive others to view her as heterosexual. For the most part, the person's sexual self-portrait is consistent or congruent with heterosexuality. At some point in life, however, a change occurs. It might happen in childhood, in adolescence, in early adulthood, in middle age, or even very late in life.

STAGE 1: IDENTITY CONFUSION   Identity confusion is characterized by a growing awareness of thoughts, feelings, or behaviors that may be homosexual in nature. These self-perceptions are incongruent with earlier assumptions of personal heterosexuality and constitute the first developmental conflict of this model. Entrance into this stage begins with the conscious awareness that information regarding homosexuality is somehow personally relevant. When the continuing personalization of this information can no longer be ignored, the individual's sexual self-portrait feels inconsistent, or incongruent. The process of gay identity formation has begun.

Examples of questions a person in Stage 1 may be asking are "Who am I?", "Am I homosexual?", and "Am I really a heterosexual?" The individual sometimes feels, thinks, or acts in a homosexual way but would rarely, if ever, tell anyone about this. The individual is fairly sure that homosexuality has something to do with him personally.

With continuing personalization of information regarding homosexuality, the person begins privately to label his own behavior (or thoughts or feelings) as possibly gay. Publicly, the person maintains a self-image as heterosexual and perceives others as maintaining the same image. To deal with this incongruity, the person adopts one or more of the following three strategies (Berzon, 1988). The first is the *inhibition strategy* and describes the person who regards the definition of his behavior (thoughts, feelings) as correctly gay, but who finds this definition undesirable and unacceptable. Several actions are taken: the person restricts information regarding homosexuality (e.g., I don't want to hear, read, or know about it) or inhibits behavior (e.g., It may be true, but I'm not going to do anything about it). Denying the personal relevance of information regarding homosexuality is also an action taken (e.g., It has nothing to do with me). Other possible behaviors include becoming hypersexual (e.g., within the context of heterosexual interactions) or becoming asexual, wherein the person seeks a "cure." Another action is to become an antigay moral or religious crusader. If the inhibition strategies employed are successful in enabling the person to inhibit, redefine, or disown responsibility for gay behavior, a foreclosure of gay/lesbian identity will occur at Stage 1.

Personal innocence strategy is a second strategy. Here, the person rejects either the meaning or the context of the homosexual behavior so as not to have to own it. He then redefines the meaning or context of the behavior. For example, in U.S. society, genital contact between males is acceptable in a variety of situations without the participating individuals being defined as gay. Little boys have "circle jerks." Men confined for long periods of time without access to women, such as in prison or other confined situations, have genital contact with one another, and they are not necessarily defined as gay. The shift occurs in the contextual meaning when males develop emotional attachments to the other males with whom they are having sex or when they have repeated contacts with the same male, increasing the possibility of emotional involvement.

For females in U.S. society, just the opposite is true. Girls can be inseparable, experience deep emotional involvement with one another, and spend more time with each other, even into adulthood, than they do with the men in their lives, and this behavior is not regarded as gay or unusual. For this reason, it may be easier for girls and women to hide their lesbian behavior or identities longer. The shift occurs when they have genital contact in addition to their emotional involvement, which is more likely to be considered lesbianism but may not be. Quite a bit of same-sex sexual experimentation occurs in adulthood among persons who had been or currently are in heterosexual marriages. Qualitative research is needed in this area to understand this phenomenon.

Another personal innocence strategy is categorized as redefining context. The individual disowns responsibility for his homosexual behavior by redefining the context in which it occurred. Examples of these rationalizations are "I was just experimenting," "I was drunk," "I just did it for the money," "I did it as a favor for a friend," "It was an accident," and "I was taken advantage of."

Success in the use of the inhibition and personal innocence strategies depends on the individual's ability to avoid provocative situations and to employ the psychological defense of denial. It is impossible to avoid erotic dreams and physiological responses to persons of the same sex to whom the individual is attracted. In this instance, these strategies will be only partially successful, and the individual may very well experience the beginning of a negative or self-rejecting sexual identity.

The person in the *information-seeking strategy* is likely to adopt this third strategy if the meaning attributed to his homosexual behavior is perceived as correct, or at least partially acceptable. Now the individual seeks more information in books, in therapy, or in talking with anyone who might have expertise or experience related to this topic. The question being addressed is "Am I homosexual?" How individuals perceive these characteristics or behaviors will influence the way they seek to resolve the incongruence, either through repression (identity foreclosure) or by moving into Stage 2. This strategy of seeking more information moves the person along to Stage 2.

STAGE 2: IDENTITY COMPARISON   Individuals begin to investigate those qualities first experienced in Stage 1. As they begin to gather information and seek out contacts with gay others, there is increased congruence between self-perceptions and behaviors but increased conflict with others. Stage 2 statements of *identity comparison* would include "I feel like I probably am gay, although I am not definitely sure." "I feel different. I think I may want to talk with someone, maybe someone gay about feeling different, but I'm not sure if I really want to or not."

As the person accepts the possibility that he may be gay, the individual begins to examine the wider implications of being gay. Whereas in Stage 1 the task was to handle the self-alienation that occurs with the first glimmerings of homosexuality, the main task of Stage 2 is to handle the social alienation that is produced by feeling different from peers, family members, and society at large. A particularly troubling aspect of relinquishing one's heterosexual identity is the giving up of behavioral guidelines and the expectations for one's future that accompany them. If marriage and family are not in one's future, then what is? What will give form, structure, and a sense of normalcy to one's life? With the letting go of a perception of a self that is clearly heterosexual, one can experience a profound feeling of loss. Here the person is able to see a gap between the identity of which they themselves are aware and the identity presented to others.

Certain conditions heighten the feeling of alienation from others, such as living in geographic isolation with no other gay people or resources available and being from a family that is deeply religious and with strong convictions about homosexuality as a sin.

Here are four strategies the individual may employ to reject homosexual self-definition while continuing homosexual behavior:

1. *Special case.* The person characterizes what is happening as the product of the liaison with one person and this one person only.
2. *Ambisexuality.* The person says he can be sexual with anybody; it doesn't matter what gender the other person is.
3. *Temporary identity.* The person regards his homosexuality as only temporary: "I could be heterosexual again any minute."
4. *Personal innocence.* The person blames his homosexuality on anyone or everyone else.

As conflict heightens, individuals may move to Stage 3.

STAGE 3: IDENTITY TOLERANCE   *Identity tolerance* is marked by increased contact with the gay community, leading to greater empowerment. At this point, individuals hold an increasingly strong gay self-image but continue to present themselves (outside the community) as heterosexual. There is dissonance, and the person is characterized as reluctantly adopting a gay self-concept based on the stigma associated with this identity and their own internalized oppression: "I'm gay and I tolerate (put up with) it." "I see myself as homosexual for now, but I'm not sure about the future." These are statements that a person would make at this stage. It occurs when the person has come to accept the probability that he is gay and recognizes the sexual, social, and emotional needs that come with being homosexual.

With more of a commitment to a gay identity, the person is now free to pursue social, emotional, and sexual needs. Doing this accentuates the difference between the person and heterosexuals even more. To deal with the increased social alienation from heterosexuals, the person seeks out gay people and the gay subculture. Involvement in the gay/lesbian community has distinct advantages in terms of movement toward a more positive gay/lesbian identity. According to Berzon (1988), it (1) contributes to a ready-made support group that understands and shares the individual's concerns, (2) provides opportunities to meet a partner, (3) gives access to positive gay and lesbian role models, and (4) provides opportunities to practice feeling more at ease as a lesbian or a gay man. However, if the person has poor social skills, is very shy, has low self-esteem, has strong fear of exposure (of sexual identity), or has a fear of the unknown, positive contacts are made more difficult.

A negative experience may occur if the person encounters gay men and lesbians who are still employing the inhibition and denial strategies of Stages 1 and 2. These lesbians and gay men will be perceived as unhappy, self-rejecting individuals with whom one would not want to be affiliated. However, individuals at this stage will be empowered by people who are accepting of their own gay and lesbian identities. A shift occurs when the individual's significant others are gay rather than heterosexuals.

If the contacts made are experienced as negative, a reduction of involvement with gay subculture is probable, resulting in a foreclosure at Stage 3. If contacts are perceived as positive, it is likely that the strategies employed have broken down and that the individual will want to explore further. This breakdown of strategies will result in movement into Stage 4. In any case, the commitment to gay identity is now sufficient for the person to say, "I am a homosexual."

STAGE 4: IDENTITY ACCEPTANCE   At this point, the conflict between the self and nongay others' perceptions is at an intense level. This conflict may be resolved through passing as "straight," having limited contact with heterosexuals, or selectively disclosing to significant (heterosexual) others. A person at this stage may say, "I am quite sure that I am gay/lesbian." "I accept this fairly happily." "I am prepared to tell a few people about being gay/lesbian (e.g., friends, family members), but I carefully select whom I tell." Identity acceptance occurs when the person accepts, rather than tolerates, a gay self-image and contact with the gay/lesbian subculture continues and increases.

The individual now has a positive identification with other gay people. The questions of earlier stages (What am I? Where do I belong?) have been answered. Attitudes toward sexual orientation of the gay men and lesbians with whom the person becomes associated are crucial at this point. If these individuals regard being gay as partially legitimate (being gay is OK in private, but being public about it is not OK), then the person is likely to adopt this attitude as his own philosophy and to live a compartmentalized, "passing," gay life.

To reduce the stress involved in interfacing with a homophobic society, the person has less and less to do with heterosexuals. Some selective disclosure of gayness to nongay family, friends, and coworkers occurs, but as much control as possible is exercised over the potentially discrediting information. The emphasis is on fitting into society and not making waves. If, on the one hand, this strategy is successful, the person forecloses at this identity acceptance stage. If, on the other hand, the person comes to associate with people who regard being gay as fully legitimate (in private and public), this attitude is likely to be adopted. Greater acceptance of one's gay orientation tends to increase the distance the person now feels from a society that is still homophobic. Homophobic attitudes are now particularly offensive to the person characterized by this stage.

To deal with the anger toward a rejecting society, in combination with the increasing self-acceptance that is occurring, the person moves into Stage 5. Those who find that the strategies described effectively manage the conflict may stay at this level comfortably; otherwise, the continuing conflict pushes them onward.

STAGE 5: IDENTITY PRIDE   Identity pride is marked not only by strong pride in the gay community and in identity, but also by intense anger directed toward, and isolation from, the heterosexual society. The conflict is managed through fostering a dichotomized homosexual (valued) and heterosexual (devalued) worldview. How others, particularly those who are not gay, respond to the expression of these feelings influences whether individuals move to the final stage. Persons who have arrived at this stage may say, "I feel proud to be a gay/lesbian and enjoy living as one." "I am prepared to tell many people about being gay/lesbian and make no attempt to hide this fact." "I prefer to mix socially with other gay men/lesbians because heterosexuals are typically antigay." This stage occurs when, accepting the philosophy of full legitimization, the person becomes immersed in the gay/lesbian subculture and has less and less to do with heterosexual others.

As identification with the gay/lesbian community deepens, pride in accomplishments of the community increases. Daily living still requires continuing encounters with the heterosexual world and its homophobic attitudes. These encounters produce feelings of frustration and alienation. The combination of anger and pride energizes the person into action against the heterosexual establishment and creates "the activist."

Confrontation with the heterosexual establishment brings the person more into public view, and earlier strategies to conceal sexual orientation must be abandoned. Doing so precipitates disclosure crises with significant heterosexuals, such as family and coworkers. It is better to tell the folks yourself than to let them hear that you are gay as you are interviewed on a news program.

What becomes crucial at this point is whether those significant heterosexuals in the gay person's life react negatively to the disclosure as expected or react positively. If the reaction is negative, confirming the person's expectations that it would be so, the view of the world as being divided into gays (who are OK) and nongays (who are not OK) gets reinforced. In this instance, the person forecloses at the identity pride stage. If the reactions of the heterosexuals to whom the person discloses are positive and inconsistent with his negative expectations, the person tends to change those expectations, which moves him into Stage 6.

STAGE 6: IDENTITY SYNTHESIS   Movement to identity synthesis most likely occurs when individuals experience positive reactions from heterosexual others. The need to dichotomize the world into gays who are OK and nongays who are not is gone. The gay/lesbian aspect of one's identity can now be integrated with all other aspects of self.

Sexuality is regarded as one part of the individual's total identity. There is some conflict but it is at the lowest and most manageable point. The person at this stage says, "I am prepared to tell anyone that I am gay/lesbian." "I am happy about the way I am but think that being gay/lesbian is not the most important part of me." "I mix socially with fairly equal numbers of gay men/lesbians and heterosexuals and anyone who is accepting of gay men and lesbians." The individual now acknowledges that some nongay people are as supportive of his gay identity as other gay people are. Because heterosexuals as a class are no longer seen as hostile, it is no longer necessary to sustain the high level of anger seen at Stage 5. Increasing contact with supportive nongays produces more trust.

TROIDEN'S HOMOSEXUAL IDENTITY DEVELOPMENTAL MODEL

Troiden (1989) also developed a nonsequential model of homosexual identity. *Sensitization* is the first stage and occurs before puberty. Here the child is more concerned with gender identification than with sexuality. *Identity confusion* is the next stage. Movement occurs during adolescence, around the age of 18 for females and 17 for males. There is a shift to sexuality and conflict exists between the identity developed during childhood and the identity demanded during adolescence. Often adolescents struggle tremendously in this stage because they are ill-prepared from their heterosexual socialization to deal with these feelings and perceptions. *Identity assumption* is the third stage and occurs around ages 19 to 21 for males and 21 to 23 for females. One of the key tasks here is learning to make sense out of and negotiate social stigma. *Commitment* is the final stage and occurs around ages 21 to 24 for males and 22 to 23 for females. It includes commitment to a same-sex love marked by identifying oneself as gay, lesbian, or bisexual. There is less dependence on passing strategies here.

SULLIVAN'S MODEL OF SEXUAL IDENTITY DEVELOPMENT

Sullivan's (1998) model has five stages that include active and passive phases. It is relevant for both gay and heterosexual people. The first stage is *naivete* and reflects little awareness of sexual orientation. The *acceptance* stage is characterized by a predominance of heterosexist thinking. *Resistance,* the third stage, as is consistent with many identity development models, reflects a state of dissonance. Oppression is now seen. *Redefinition* is the fourth stage. Here the person is reformulating his notions of heterosexuality not dictated by the discourses of heterosexism. The final stage is *internalization* and reflects the person's efforts to integrate newfound values into all aspects of his life.

COUNSELING GAYS, LESBIANS, AND BISEXUALS OF COLOR

Within generally supportive gay and lesbian social communities, people of color who are gay, lesbian, bisexual, and transgender are often oppressed and do not receive the affirmation that White GLBT people receive (Loiacano, 1989). Battle, Cohen, Warren, Fergerson, and Audam (2002) conducted a study in conjunction with the National Gay and Lesbian Task Force with 2,465 Black GLBT people—58% men, 43% women, and 3% transgendered. They found that two thirds indicated that homophobia was a problem within the Black community. Half of the respondents agreed that racism is a problem for Black GLBT people in their relations with White GLBT people. Gender differences were found regarding the most important issues facing Black GLBT people. Approximately 72% of the men stated that HIV/AIDS was the most important issue facing Black GLBT people, while 55% of the women responded the same way. Women were more likely, at 50%, to say that hate crime violence was the most pressing issue; less than 40% of the men responded in this way. In addition to contending with hate crime, there is the pressing issue of domestic violence in same-sex relationships, which the National Coalition Against Domestic Violence estimates at 25% to 33% (Peterman & Dixon, 2003). Gay families struggle with many of the same issues that heterosexual families contend with and need support and appropriate intervention (Laird, 2003).

The racism and oppression faced by gay men and lesbians of color often urge them to turn to their same-race communities for the development of coping techniques, help with maintaining a positive identity, and potential support (Icard, 1986). Because of the level of homophobia, few gay men and lesbians of color actually find needed support psychologically and socially. The African American community often reflects the attitude that homosexuality is inconsistent with being Black (Riggs, 1994).

Black gay males are faced with a problem of complying with male role expectations that include propagating the race and holding allegiance to the African American community, which generally maintains an antihomosexual attitude (Icard, 1986). Similarities are found within the Native American Indian and Asian American cultures. Greene (1994) said that "bearing some similarity to Asian cultures, gender roles are clearly delineated among Indian families, and obedience to parents is expected" (p. 247).

In working with Native American Indian gay clients, the devastation of colonialism and Western influences need to be considered in interpreting sexuality. It is crucial that Spirit, and not the material world, be held as sacred in traditional Native American Indian cultures. Gunn Allen (1992) talked about the gynecentric societies, which value the centrality of women, honor the young, and revere all of life that is part of the whole. In traditional society, there were sacred places for men and women who were embodied by Spirit and did not want to marry persons of the other gender, and there were men who dressed and lived like women. Among Native Americans, the term *berdache* has been misapplied to both gay men and lesbians. It is an Arabic word meaning "sex-slave boy" and has no relevance to American men or women (Gunn Allen, 1992). Concerning contemporary Native American Indians who are gay, Greene (1994) stated that acceptance may be less on reservations than in large urban centers. Gunn Allen pointed to acculturation and fundamental Christianity as major influences on homophobic attitudes among some Native people.

The Policy Institute of the National Gay and Lesbian Task Force interviewed 912 Latino gay men drawn from New York, Miami, and Los Angeles as part of a project called Nuestras Voces (Our Voices). The men reported widespread experiences with oppression (homophobia, racism, and poverty). Sixty-four percent were verbally insulted as children for being gay or effeminate; 31% reported experiences of racism in the form of verbal harrassment as children; 35% reported having been treated rudely as adults on account of their race or ethnicity; and 61% experienced a shortage of money for basic necessities, with 54% borrowing money to get by during the last 12 months before the interview (Diaz & Ayala, 2002). The report found that men who were high risk (less likely to use protection when engaging in anal intercourse with a nonmonogamous partner) had higher rates of oppression when compared with low-risk men. To survive or cope with the pain of societal oppression and accompanying feelings of powerlessness, many men turn to drugs or alcohol as aids and comforters. Diaz and Ayala stated, "Substances are used to cope not only with homophobic messages but also with the anger and frustration caused by poverty, racism and many other forms of social discrimination and abuse" (p. 16). The authors proposed that HIV prevention programs must also help men learn to cope with (*and resist*—emphasis mine) the toxic forces of racism, poverty, sexism, and homophobia because these social forces weigh heavily on Latino gay men's lives. It is important for therapists who work with gay immigrant, ethnic, and other clients of color to ask themselves the following questions:

1. Is the client an immigrant or American born?
2. To what ethnic group does the client belong?
3. What are the specific cultural values of this group? Of the client's family? Of the client?
4. How strongly does the client follow traditional customs?
5. What is the client's socioeconomic status?
6. What is the client's level of bilingualism?

IMPLICATIONS FOR COUNSELORS AND PSYCHOLOGISTS

Exposure to people perceived to be threatening, such as lesbians and gays, can in turn reduce antigay attitudes (Moradi, van den Berg, & Epting, 2006). Personal exposure as well as exposure to information about this diverse population would be helpful.

The American Psychological Association (2006) has issued 16 guidelines for psychotherapy with lesbian, gay, and bisexual clients organized across four areas: attitudes, relationships and families, diversity issues, and education. Guidelines 1 through 4 stipulate that psychologists recognize bisexuality and assessment and treatment of LGBT populations, that homosexuality is stigmatized in society, and that psychologists' prejudicial attitudes can adversely affect the LGTB clients' level of disclosure. The second four guidelines state that psychologists strive to respect the important role that relationships have for LGBT people, that parenting can be particularly challenging, that family ties need not be defined by biology only, and that sexuality can have an impact on relationships and communication within one's family of origin. Guidelines 9 through 13 encourage psychologists to understand the struggles that many LGBT people experience, particularly youth, people with disabilities, and persons of color, and that the population as a whole is very diverse. The last three guidelines pertain to education and state that psychologists support training and knowledge development on LGBT issues and are aware of community resources for this population.

Moradi et al. (2006) conducted research with 175 heterosexual persons. It was found that level of lesbian gay threat (which is defined as the self, and LG [lesbian and gay] as "fundamentally incompatible" [p. 58]) was positively correlated with antilesbian and antigay attitudes.

Several helping strategies that counselors can employ in their work with LGBTIQQ people are as follows:

1. Be aware of personal feelings toward gay men, lesbians, and people who are transgendered.
2. Validate confusion.
3. Provide a safe, supportive environment conducive to the exploration of this struggle and confusion.
4. Explore what it means to be gay.
5. Dispute myths about homosexuality and bisexuality.
6. Suggest readings.
7. Help the client move beyond the grief by acknowledging and expressing the loss of a heterosexual blueprint for life.
8. Become familiar with local resources for gay men, lesbians, bisexuals, and transgendered people, and suggest supportive organizations to assist the client in building a support structure within the gay community.
9. Assist the client in overcoming barriers to positive socialization.
10. Be sensitive to the impact a gay/lesbian, bisexual, or transgendered identity may have on the context surrounding the problems and issues faced by the individual.

11. Encourage the client to create a support system within the gay/lesbian/bisexaul/ transgender community before coming out to heterosexual significant others.
12. Have some type of gay, lesbian, or bisexual literature on the bookshelf.
13. Display something as small as a pin (one pin available for heterosexuals says "Straight but not narrow"), a poster, or a quote that depicts a multicultural and nonbiased view of the world.
14. Attend workshops on counseling gay men, lesbians, bisexuals, and transgendered people.
15. Stay informed of local gay events that can serve as a resource to clients.
16. Personally and honestly assess one's level of sexual identity development.
17. Be aware of sexual identity models for heterosexuals as well as models for GLBT clients.

Chojnacki and Gelberg (1995) connected Cass's model to developmental stages of heterosexual counselors. A counselor who is at Stage 1 (confusion) may not clearly comprehend the oppressive contexts in which gay, lesbian, and bisexual persons live. Therefore, such a counselor may not understand the need for clients to be in a support group. Counselors in the latter stages, such as Stage 5 (identity pride), begin to feel pride about the quality of the services they provide to their clients and recognize the importance of understanding "the history, culture, ethics, jargon, and sense of community that define the gay and lesbian culture" (Pope, 1995, p. 302). Counselors at this stage also begin to experience greater alienation from colleagues perceived to be homophobic. Many gay and lesbian clients are cautious about entering therapy because they are aware of the homoprejudice among society at large and even among members of the helping profession (Rothblum, 1994). Gay, lesbian, or bisexual persons are disadvantaged when the helping professional is ignorant of sexual orientation, developmental processes, identity development, counseling techniques, and overall challenges with which this population contends on a daily basis. Referring a client to a different counselor who can be more effective may be an option, particularly when the first counselor is unable or inadequately trained to provide the necessary support to the client. Yet, counselors need to ascertain whether their unwillingness to work with persons who are gay and lesbian is indicative of an intolerance for other sources of diversity, such as race, class, and, ability.

CASE STUDY
Assigning Gender

Justin and Kaitlin are both 25 years old and have been married for 2 years. They were both excited to learn that Kaitlin was pregnant. After 9 months of eating well, exercising, and regular prenatal visits, Kaitlin goes into labor. Justin is with her throughout the 17-hour process. When their baby is born, there is silence in the delivery room. Upon inquiring about the gender of their baby, the doctor says that tests have to be run. After a harrowing wait, their doctor informs them that their baby was born with ambiguous genitalia, more specifically a micropenis. Because the doctors doubt the functionality of the penis, with respect to urination and having intercourse, they recommend that their child be assigned a gender of female after reconstructive surgery. Their child has a 46 XY karatype. Justin and Kaitlin agree with their doctor's recommendation and consent to the surgery. When friends and family call to inquire about the gender of their baby, they tell everyone they had a baby girl and that her name is Katherine. Three weeks later their daughter has surgery (a bilateral gonadectomy and labial skin biopsy). After a few days of recovery, Kaitlin and Justin are relieved that the last month is now behind them. The doctors informed them that prior to puberty, Katherine will need to begin estrogen replacement and have future surgery to create a functional vagina.

QUESTIONS

1. What are the factors that influence doctors' recommendation to perform gender reconstructive surgery at birth?
2. If Justin and Kaitlin had presented for therapy prior to making their decision, what would have been helpful for them to hear?
3. Should Katherine be told of her parents' decision?
4. What type of concerns might arise for Katherine later in life with respect to her reconstructive surgery?

DISCUSSION AND INTEGRATION
Kaitlin and Justin

It is estimated that approximately 1 in 1,000 to 2,000 newborns are considered ambiguous enough to be considered candidates for genital surgery (Phornphutkul, Fausto-Sterling, & Cruppuso, 2000). There are several principles that guide doctors' decision to perform reconstructive surgery. A few of them were mentioned in the case study. Phornphutkul, Fausto-Sterling, and Cruppuso also report that doctors are seeking to avoid stigmatization of the patient and that gender assignment should be made as quickly as possible and prior to the child's discharge from the hospital. In addition, the future potential for sexual function and fertility are considered. That gender identity is fairly malleable at birth and a

long-standing position that ambiguous genitalia should be avoided have influenced the medical profession's thinking on this topic. Even today, a phallus size of less than 1.5 cm at term is considered inadequate for development of a functional penis. A functional penis is defined as the ability to have intercourse and to urinate standing up. The authors stated, "given that reconstructive surgery aimed at achieving functional female genitalia is considered the more effective alternative, XY intersexual patients with microphallus and testes are often assigned female gender" (p. 135).

Kaitilin and Justin as new and young parents did not anticipate the outcome they encountered and most likely do not have a frame of reference for dealing with this situation. Therapy would have encouraged the new parents to express their fears and anxieties about the life of their child with ambiguous genitalia or in the future, coming to find out what had been done to her at less than a month old. Taking time to do some research or secure a second opinion would also be recommended and having some support while making a decision is extremely helpful. Hormonal therapy has been known to have a positive impact on the length of the phallus during puberty. Phornphutkul et al. (2000) take the position that sexual assignment should be based on the underlying diagnosis "even if sex of rearing my not coincide with size and functionality of the phallus. Whenever possible, reconstructive genital surgery should be delayed until the patient's gender identity can be incorporated into the decision making process" (p. 136).

What would it mean for children to be left alone at birth and live their lives as intersexuals? All persons should have an opportunity to receive the services of a well-trained, qualified, and empathic mental health professional. These services should not be offered by a few sympathetic counselors in the field, but rather be available from therapists who seek to empower their clients. What might it mean for a person's mental health, body image, and sexual satisfaction to have as an adult the body they were born with? The couple in the case study did not have a place to hear or work through these questions, and this is a problem. The dichotimization of gender through society—from bathrooms, to sports teams, to dressing rooms—is not respectful or allowing of intersexuality. Therapists working with intersexuals or parents grappling with this enormous decision for their children need to be prepared to help clients merge with a support system within the intersexual community as a way of lessening feelings of isolation and normalizing one's God-given attributes in the event the parents leave their infants' bodies alone. Ultimately, parents want their children to have a good life, to find meaningful work and love. If they were counseled that such a life was possible without surgical reassignment, they may think differently about the finality of surgery.

SUMMARY

This chapter examined sexual orientation and acknowledged that it exists on a continuum. Definitions were provided, and developmental processes, identity models, and implications for mental health professionals working with gay, lesbian, and bisexual clients were discussed. A case study that dealt with intersexuality exposed readers to an issue that is not often covered in the discussion of gender or even sexuality.

Chapter 14

Converging Disability

I wouldn't be able-bodied if I could . . .

A woman living with polio

STORYTELLING: Not Enough

A woman with a "facial difference" told a story in Zitzelsberger (2005) about walking down the street and being approached by a man who upon looking at her said, "You are so ugly." The woman took the message to mean she did not belong, that she was too ugly to participate. I hear it as his castigation of her for having failed to be appropriate, which is not looking the way she did. Privileges of "normative femininity" are often denied to women with disabilities (Garland-Thomas, 2002). From a very early age, girls and boys are conditioned, in both subtle and overt ways, to believe that fulfillment in life is hugely dependent on a girl's physical beauty. One of the discourses associated with disability is that people with a disability are defined by the all encompassing disability and that who they are in their other identities—a loyal friend, lover of mysteries, collector of tea pots, or jazz music aficionado—does not get considered. Personal beauty is far too often considered the most important virtue a woman can possess. Lakoff and Sherr (1984) said, "beauty is power." Due to their heightened levels of vulnerability, women with disabilities are more likely to experience abuse and violence (Hunt, Matthews, Milsom, & Lammel, 2006).

If we are fortunate to live long and prosper, disability will visit each of us in some way, shape, or form. (See Storytelling: "Not Enough.") This chapter has been influenced by the literature on disability studies and feminist disability theory (Garland-Thomas, 2002; Olkin & Pledger, 2003; Olkin, 2004). The status of the lived body, the politics of appearance, the medicalization of the body, the privilege of normalcy, multiculturalism, sexuality, the social construction of identity, and the commitment to integration are all aspects of a feminist disability theory, which also includes genetics, beauty, health, prosthetics, and reproductive technologies (Garland-Thomas, 2002).

UNDERSTANDING DISABILITY

In 2002, 18% of the population, or over 51 million people, had some level of disability (Steinmetz, 2006). Disability encompasses a variety of different conditions, capabilities, and limitations. It can involve the physical, such as muscular dystrophy, systemic (lupus), cognitive (e.g. traumatic brain injury), visual (blindness), hearing (e.g. deafness), developmental (e.g. autism), psychiatric (e.g. bipolar disorder), or multiple impairment (Olkin, 2004, p. 333). A person has a disability if any of the following conditions apply: used a wheelchair, crutches, or a walker; had difficulty performing one or more functional activities such as seeing, hearing, walking, grasping; had difficulty with or needed assistance with one or more activities of daily living such as bathing, dressing, eating, toileting; had a developmental delay or learning disability; had difficulty walking, playing, or moving arms; had a specific condition, such as mental retardation, cerebral palsy, or Alzheimer's disease; had a mental or emotional condition that seriously interfered with everyday activities; or had a condition that made it difficult to remain employed.

Tremendous heterogeneity exists among the disabled. Given the differences, defining this group as a collective is challenging (Smits, 2004). There are people with nonvisible disabilities who do not self-identify or claim an identity that includes having a disability. There are persons with noncongenital or medically defined disabilities. Due to advances in technology, some people are able to work from home and earn a living, whereas for others, technology costs are prohibitive.

Gender, race, and the nature of the disability also contribute to the diversity among the disabled. Persons of color with disabilities represent those with the highest poverty and unemployment rates (Marini, 2001). Overall, the majority of people with disabilities are female. Among Asians or Pacific Islanders, the rate for the presence of a disability was 11.5%. Asians also had the lowest prevalence, both of a severe disability and of the need for assistance. Blacks had the highest rate for the presence of a disability, 19.8%, and the highest rate of a severe disability and the need for assistance. Among non-Hispanic Whites, the rate for the presence of a disability was higher than Asians, at 19%. More than half of people aged 21 to 64 with any type of disability (55.9%) had some employment in the 12 months prior to data collection. Median earnings for people with no disability were $25,000 compared with $22,000 for people with a nonsevere disability, and $12,800 for persons with a severe disability (Steinmetz, 2006). Poverty rate increases with the severity of the disability. The poverty rate for people 25 to 64 years of age with a severe disability is 25.9% compared with 11.2% among people with a nonsevere disability.

Within the psychology curriculum, graduate students are more likely to receive instruction on race, gender, class, sexuality, and other dimensions of diversity then they are on disability (Olkin & Pledger, 2003; Pledger, 2003). Although disability pervades all aspects of culture 9 years after the passage of the Americans with Disabilities Act (ADA), "the modal number of required courses on disability was still zero, as it was in 1989" (Garland-Thomas, 2002, p. 297). The individualistic frame that represents the majority of mental health professionals in the West tends to focus studies of disability on the individual instead of expanding the scope to include the family, the community, and even a political context. With less of an emphasis on a medical model of disability, mental health professionals are encouraged to collaborate with other disciplines when conducting disability research in order to approach the study from a multidisciplinary perspective (Tate & Pledger, 2003).

DISABILITY STUDIES

Disability studies is an interdisciplinary field that incorporates sociology, history, medical anthropology, politics, law, feminist psychology, and literature (Olkin & Pledger, 2003). Important to the foundation of disability studies is a shift in the paradigm regarding people with disabilities as consumers and as part of the independent living movement. A grounding in the social model of disability that recognizes power, oppression, and economic issues must be included in this discussion, that disability is not just a component of identity but "essential to the exploration of humanness" (p. 297), and that disability studies do not reproduce the oppressive discourses that exist in the larger culture is included.

This new and emerging field is not without its critics. Thomas (2004) argued that disability studies as a distinct area of study might lead to segregation of people with disabilities from the rest of society. It was also argued that the name—*disability studies*—placed emphasis on individuals' disabilities and not on their abilities.

Disability studies have shone a light on the traditional theoretical constructions of disability. The biomedical model of disability has predominated. This model is rooted in the scientific method and defined disability in the language of medicine. A focus is on the disability existing within the individual and not on the person's environment, policy considerations, or structural issues. More recently, a sociopolitical model has emerged that defines people with disability as members of a minority group given the prejudice and discrimination that accompany this identity. Smart and Smart (2006) defined three dimensions of this model: (1) definitions about disability must be from an insider's perspective, from persons with disabilities, (2) people with disabilities must advocate for themselves and not allow "experts" to define disability for them, and (3) people with disabilities resist the labels that align them and their bodies with deviance and pathology. This work is in support of the sociopolitical model.

One of the outcomes of disability studies is a new and holistic paradigm of disability that emphasizes new models of research. The integration of participatory action research methods and person–environment conceptualization of disability encourages researchers and clinicians to move away from the limitations of medically oriented definitions and measures of disability (Tate & Pledger, 2003). This emerging research paradigm means collaboration with members of the disability community and involving them in research that is accessible. It is important to not use research participants for the purpose of one's research effort and not offer anything back to the community.

Olkin (2003) identified several avenues to recruiting research participants from the disability community. She recommended disability magazines and newletters, independent living centers, support groups, disability events, and disability-specific Internet sites. Survey Monkey is also a way for persons with disabilities to participate in research. An alternative format should also be used such as very large and dark print.

THE SOCIAL CONSTRUCTION OF DISABILITY

Many of the barriers that people with disabilities face are reinforced through language (APA 2007), encouraging human service providers to be mindful of their use of language. For instance, it is less appropriate to refer to people with disabilities as disabled people. Stating that a person uses a wheelchair is different from the statement that a person is confined to a wheelchair.

Disability is a broad term. Garland-Thomas (2002) critiqued the definition, which, she said, "clusters ideological categories as varied as sick, deformed, crazy, ugly, old, maimed, afflicted, mad, abnormal, or debilitated—all of which disadvantage people by devaluing bodies that do not conform to cultural standards: its structuring institutions, social identities, cultural practices, political positions, historical communities, and the shared human experience of embodiment" (p. 5). Our individualistic and capital-driven culture equates normalcy with bodily control and perfection. Disability is redefined as non-normative, a loss of control, and a departure from an ideal or what is acceptable. Garland-Thomas (2002) saw similarities across marginalized identities and said, "female, disable, and dark bodies are supposed to be dependent, incomplete, vulnerable, and incompetent bodies . . . women and the disabled are portrayed as helpless, dependent, weak, vulnerable, and incapable bodies" (p. 7). Having an able body and mind are not just valued in society, but are considered blessings. The ability to control, produce, reproduce, and master nature are constructed as biological and, for some, as spiritually superior. Fowler, O'Rourke, Wadsworth, and Harper (1992) said, "When one's physical and/or mental abilities are considered as the primary status for characterizing individuals, the resulting polarity implicitly divides all persons into two groups: the able and the unable" (p. 14). Much like race and gender, physical disability is elevated to and exists as a status-determining characteristic, overriding other dimensions of the self. Even achieved traits are eclipsed by immutable characteristics as a function of birth or acquired through injury or a medical condition. Relationships are often constituted on the basis of similarity, not just with respect to race and class but also with disability.

Dominant discourses associated with disability are that people with disabilities are helpless, childlike, dependent, unattractive, asexual, and low-income wage earners. People with visible disabilities encounter hostility in society due to their physical and mental differences that violate deeply held cultural values about productivity, beauty, control, youth, and mastery over nature. Persons with disabilities are discriminated against, stereotyped, ignored, and in many instances presumed to be biologically inferior, particularly if the disability is congenital as opposed to acquired (Marini, 2001).

Just as physical attractiveness has been linked to assumptions of moral character, intelligence, marital satisfaction, dating frequency, and quality of life (Dion, Berschid, & Walster, 1972; Webster & Driskell, 1983), so has disability. In fact, disability is constructed within the context of physical unattractiveness. The socialization process equates self-worth with mobility, thinness, beauty, and not being disabled. Hahn (1988a) said, "The most salient features of many disabled persons are bodily traits similar to skin color, gender, and other attributes that have been used as a basis for differentiating people for centuries and without which discrimination would not occur" (p. 26). Zola (1991) stated that preference for specific body types over others represents another societal "ism." In this work, this form of discrimination has been termed "ableism." Considerable silence surrounds the experiences of those who have disabilities. (See Storytelling: "Campus Access.") This is particularly relevant among able-bodied persons who assume that lack of membership in the disability community entitles them to ignorance or apathy.

Real-life stories in which people experience dramatic and sudden changes in their bodies are numerous. (See Case Study: "Rethinking Manhood" at the end of this chapter.) Wendell (1989), for example, wrote powerfully about the sudden overnight process of going from being able-bodied to being disabled as a result of a disabling

STORYTELLING: Campus Access?

In my role as a faculty senator, I received a call from a colleague who was disappointed and angered by her inability to get the campus to provide her with temporary public transportation from her office to her classroom during recovery from foot surgery. She stated she was not treated well by the various offices with whom she came into contact. I am pursuing her concerns, but I realize that not having available transportation for situations like these reflects a culture that privileges those who are mobile.

chronic disease. "In 1985, I fell ill overnight with what turned out to be a disabling chronic disease. In the long struggle to come to terms with it, I had to learn to live with a body that felt entirely different to me—weak, tired, painful, nauseated, dizzy, unpredictable" (p. 63). Waiting to return to her original state was indeed dangerous because the likelihood of this occurrence was remote. So, in time, Wendell was required to learn how to identify and coexist with her new disabled body but not without struggle. "I began slowly to identify with my new, disabled body and to learn to work with it" (p. 63). Within a culture where normalcy and disability are regarded as antonyms, she wrote, "Disabled women struggle with both the oppressions of being women in male-dominated societies and the oppressions of being disabled in societies dominated by the abler-bodied" (p. 64).

Both Wendell (1989) and Zola (1991) maintained that a theory on disability and the body is needed. Because of the strong cultural assumptions of able-bodied-ness and physical attractiveness, such a theory is beneficial to all, regardless of current or, better yet, temporary physical status.

Many people with disabilities experience their bodies through pain. Wendell (1989) stated that persons who live with chronic pain can teach the general public what it means to share space with that which hurts. Crucial questions emerge, such as how a person welcomes pain into his or her life, especially if it is feared. In turn, are people with chronic pain feared and loathed by those who are reminded of their own vulnerability? Feeling the pain, as opposed to medicating it away (Wendell, 1989), meditating on the pain, engaging in visual imagery, and making peace with it are examples of being in, listening to, and embracing one's body for what it is. This increased consciousness is a gift of pain. Such a gift can move a person to a place of unconditional acceptance of her body despite the circumstances. Writer Audre Lorde (1994) said, "There is a terrible clarity that comes from living with cancer that can be empowering if we don't turn aside from it" (p. 36). It is in the not turning away, the bold and yet humble confrontation of the source of pain, that strength is found for the journey. All can benefit from this truth. Pain, in its various forms, is a feature of living and is independent of physical ability status.

The wisdom among some people with disabilities may benefit persons without disabilities. The tendency to regard people who are different as "other" impedes benefiting from people who do not look normal. "If disabled people were truly heard, an explosion of knowledge of the human body and psyche would take place" (Wendell, 1989, p. 77). Persons with disabilities have much to teach the able-bodied about acceptance, dignity, and empowerment.

PERFECTION, BEAUTY, AND THE ABLE BODY

Despite the valiant and noble efforts of the women's movement, negative body image continues into the 21st century. According to Hutchinson (1982), "Body image is not the same as the body, but is rather what the mind does to the body in translating the experience of embodiment into its mental representation" (p. 59). Birtchnell, Lacey, and Harte (1985) indicated three aspects of body image: (1) *physiological,* which involves the brain's ability to detect weight, shape, size, and form; (2) *conceptual,* which is the mental picture of one's own body; (3) and *emotional,* which refers to the feelings about one's body weight, shape, and size. A survivor of breast cancer (Elder, 2000) spoke movingly about the impact of the disease, but noted the silence around attractiveness and desirability. She worried about her appearance and how the mastectomy would affect her married life. Her husband was more concerned about her than the loss of her breast.

Physicality in the form of an able body as the most valuable commodity that one has is a damning but active message in society. Discourses about the female body's function as a site for others' approval and scorn set girls and women up to have low levels of self-esteem. Adult women are incapable of helping young women celebrate their bodies when they themselves are unable to honor their own bodily desires. The socialization of young girls to see their primary role in life as pleasing others encourages the development of anxiety, depression, and an unhealthy reliance on others for approval. Brouwers (1990) argued that the emotional aspect of body image is at the crux of bulimia, characterized by recurrent episodes of binge eating and subsequent feelings of lack of control. Intense dissatisfaction with body image and strong hatred of one's body is correlated with bulimia.

Dissatisfaction with one's body is reinforced in the face of unattainable standards of perfected beauty. Restricting and denying one's movement and comfort are handicapping and yet this is what women do regularly to appear beautiful to others. Social desirability is aligned with wearing fashions that are uncomfortable, tight, unflattering (muffin top jeans) and inappropriate (exposure of one's anatomy due to pelvic resting jeans), painful, and even harmful to the body. Stilettos are worn because they add height, slenderize the legs, and elongate the body. They also restrict movement and interfere with normal walking. Bunions, corns, and other serious foot problems suffered by millions of women result from the mantra that pain comes with beauty.

More and more women are opting for expensive and risky plastic surgery to achieve the perfect breasts, nose, and buttocks. Garland-Thomas (2002) noted that "the beautiful woman of the 21st century is sculpted surgically from top to bottom" (p. 10). Aging and obesity are big business. The attitude is that beauty is something to be acquired and at any cost (Okazawa-Rey, Robinson, & Ward, 1987). Liposuction, abdominalplasty, face lifts, breast augmentation, and other forms of plastic surgery are commonplace. A closer relationship exists among beauty, thinness, success, power, acceptance, and self-worth for girls and women than it does for boys and men. In fact, one study found that overall body dissatisfaction was higher among girls than among boys (Paxton et al., 1991). This finding may explain why 87% of persons undergoing plastic surgery are women (Steinem, 1992).

Billions of dollars are spent annually on products and services in Herculean efforts to beautify, freshen, deny, and defy the aging process. Looking good is not denounced. The maniacal emphasis placed on physical attractiveness as synonymous with having an able body is problematic. Hahn (1988a) discussed beauty power and its association with mate selection and sexual intimacy. She said, "As long as physical beauty determines sexual choices, human relations will be guided by fortuitous pleasing compositions of bone, muscle, and skin" (p. 27). Hahn observed that inner beauty and character will take a back seat in the competition for partners. Perceived as a prized commodity, beauty operates to "snare a mate who can give her the opportunity to live out her biological and social destiny" (Hutchinson, 1982, p. 60). Rockquemore (2002) said it well: "for women, appearances are power in the mating market" (p. 492).

Age is the one identity construct that has the greatest bearing on beauty. *Ageism*, or discrimination against middle-aged and elderly people, differs between men and women. According to Nuessel (1982), "Ageism is distinct from other forms of discrimination because it cuts across all of society's traditional classifications: gender, race, religion, and national origin" (p. 273). Ageism affects women in that in the normal and inevitable maturational process, men mature and become refined; women wilt and wither. The devaluation of women's bodies among a male-dominated medical community cannot be divorced from lucrative and costly hysterectomies and other surgeries for women. The medical community has used estrogen against women to support a belief that this hormone is essential for femininity and youth. Now women are discouraged from using hormone replacement therapy unless indicated. Although there are benefits, such as relief from the symptoms of menopause, cancer is a risk.

As women mature and develop a sense of personal power and an internal locus of control, they come to perceive their beauty differently. Powerful women recognize that responsible self-care and respect for others is superior to selflessness and that becoming older is a privilege.

IMPLICATIONS FOR COUNSELORS AND PSYCHOLOGISTS

Mental health professionals have a responsibility to address disability issues in addition to having the psychological skills and expertise to assist the client (Pledger, 2003). Helping professionals are not exempt from attitudes that favor attractive children and adults over those regarded as unattractive (Ponzo, 1985). Guidance counselors need to be particularly mindful of the power of words in shaping children's constructions of themselves. Lerner and Lerner (1977) wrote, "Evidence suggests that when compared to the physically attractive child, the unattractive child experiences rejecting peer relations, the perception of maladjustment by teachers and peers, and the belief by teachers of less educational ability" (p. 586).

Professionals are encouraged to ascertain their own beliefs about body image and physical attractiveness. Some may be more inclined to gravitate toward able-bodied and attractive clients. This is biased behavior and discredits a profession that should be oriented toward empowerment and respect. Due to worldview, gender, culture, and/or individual differences, some clients may not value and thus not strive for independence or mastery over their environments. Refusing to do so is not a form of pathology, but such attitudes have to be examined in the context of culture (Marini, 2001).

Mental health professionals need to assess the impact of the culture's messages about beauty, perfection, and disability on their self-esteem and on their perceptions, favorable and otherwise, of others. Smart and Smart (2006) warn, "If the counselor views disability as a tragic inferiority, then he or she will more likely experience a negative, emotional response to the client with a disability" (p. 37). Knowledge about a client's disability and accompanying functional limitations is part of multicultural competence (Marini, 2001).

To improve compliance with the Americans with Disabilities Act and to serve the needs of individuals with disabilities, it is recommended that counselors:

1. Do not deny services to a client with a disability.
2. Do not provide unequal service to clients with disabilities. Different service to respond effectively to a client's needs is not the same as unequal.
3. Provide auxiliary aids such as large print materials, Braille, notepads, and pencils.
4. Evaluate the structural and architectural environment (ramps, curb cuts, elevator control buttons) to ensure access into the building.
5. Involve the services of a contractor when building a new office so that ADA requirements can be followed. (APA, 2007)

CASE STUDY
Rethinking Manhood

Reese is a 24-year-old Latino male from a low-wage-earning family. At the age of 14, he joined a gang and eventually became a person with a VASCI (violence-acquired spinal cord injury). During a gun fight with a rival gang, Reese was shot two times in the back. One of the bullets nicked his spinal cord. Reese survived the gunshot blasts and is now a quadriplegic. The brush with death was sobering for him and has allowed him to redirect his life. He is now going through peer mentoring training, has a stable relationship with his fiancé, and looks forward to starting college some day in the future. Part of Reese's role as a peer mentor is to discuss sex following a spinal cord injury. Reese realizes he needs help in addressing these issues and receives assistance from his mentor.

QUESTIONS

1. How can a mentor assess where Reese is in his own recovery?
2. How does Reese's status as a quadriplegic affect his masculinity and, more specifically, his sexuality?
3. Could a female mentor help Reese?

DISCUSSION AND INTEGRATION
The Mentor, Reese

Disability intersects with gender. In a society where masculinity is equated with virility, strength, sexuality, and self-reliance, it is understandable that men with physical disabilities are perceived as contradictions to hegemonic masculinity. Gerschick and Miller (1994) stated that "men with physical disabilities are marginalized and stigmatized because they undermine the typical role of the body in United States culture . . . Men's bodies allow them to demonstrate the socially valuable characteristics of toughness, competitiveness, and ability" (p. 35). To arrive at a place of acceptance of one's body, there has to be (1) a confrontation of the societal standard that maintains that masculinity is not only narrowly defined but also in contradiction to the disabled man's body; (2) repudiation of this socially constructed norm; and (3) affirmation of the self through a recognition that the norms and discourses, and not the person, are problematic (Collins, 1989). From this perspective, the man is able to reconstruct, for himself and for others, alternative gender roles and practices (Gerschick & Miller, 1994).

Myers et al. (1991) stated that, in society today, with all of its isms, "the very nature of the conceptual system is itself inherently oppressive and that all who adhere to it will have a difficult time developing and maintaining a positive identity" (p. 55). A suboptimal system operates when self-worth is attached to factors separate from the self. Optimally, self-worth is intrinsic to the self. Accidents and illness suddenly change the ability and control over one's body.

U.S. values—Protestant work ethic, individualism, capitalism, and self-reliance—are inextricably bound to notions of physical attractiveness, power, mobility, strength, and dominance over one's body. Vulnerability and uncertainty simply do not coexist well in a society that values domination and conquest. The belief is that illness and subsequent disability are a result of the individual's doing. Wendell (1989) stated, "The demand for control fuels an incessant search for the deep layered explanations for causes of accidents, illness, and disability" (p. 72).

A client who experiences a traumatic loss needs time and space to mourn. Reese's life after being shot can be meaningful; first, however, he has to redefine some of the dimensions of manhood, such as success, attractiveness, masculinity, sexual activity, and function. Because "a disability carries sufficient conceptual power to stereotype an individual, regardless of whether the disability was present at birth or acquired later in life" (Fowler et al., 1992, p. 102), Reese's conceptualization of self across multiple identities has shifted. Part of this shifting self-conceptualization encompasses what it means to be a man.

A multiculturally competent mentor is not reluctant to explore the violence in Reese's past and how he makes meaning of it in the present. Had Reese fallen asleep at the wheel of a car and hit a tree, a different set of events would be represented than someone perpetrating violence on his life. Where is Reese with feelings of anger and perhaps fantasies of retaliation? In Hernandez's (2005) qualitative study with 16 men with newly acquired spinal cord injury from gunshot trauma, she found three main themes: disability was viewed as a wake-up call or blessing, disability was viewed as a turning point, and disability was viewed as identity transforming.

Reese does not have a disease. His disability is from a violent injury, and he is healthy within the context of his disability. Seeing Reese as sick does not encourage the mentor to view him as active, able, and alive—words that tend not to be associated with the experience of having a disability (APA, 2007). Garland-Thomas (2002) identifies resistance to claiming a disability identity as partly influenced by limited ways to talk about disability that are not oppressive.

At the appropriate time, the mentor can help Reese critique traditional and oppressive notions of masculinity for all men, regardless of ability or disability. Boys are socialized to believe that masculinity is synonymous with being a protector, provider, and worker. Athleticism and body strength create the basis for virility. Men with physical disabilities struggle with internalized notions of masculinity that are inconsistent with the presence of disability. Men with disabilities are not perceived by society as strong because a large part of this strength and manhood equation is having an able body, which is synonymous with the ability to achieve an erection. There are different types of strength, physical as well as character, that are not typically identified by society.

Asking for psychological help is a form of self-reliance and control (Roberts, Kisselica, and Frederickson, 2002). Research has shown that supportive social networks are associated with psychological well-being and adjustment to one's disability (Belgrave, 1991; Swanson, Cronin-Stubbs, & Sheldon, 1989). Prior to the accident, Reese had a very active, albeit dangerous, life involving the full use of his legs. Although Reese's mobility has been improved by his wheelchair, which is controlled by mouth, a measure of Reese's healing is his level of physical, social, and sexual activity. The mentor will want to know what Reese's identity means to him, particularly as he will be helping men who are grappling with a lost of identity.

Recently, Reese has noticed his ability to move two of his fingers on his right hand. This change in functional limitation gives him hope that he will be able to do more in the future. Reese's ability to perform is by no means static and fluctuates across situations and environments—this variation in function is known as the enablement/disablement phenomenon (Pledger, 2003). Through journaling, within small groups, and by providing assistance to others, Reese can continue to unravel the strongholds of socially constructed notions of desirability, attractiveness, and worthiness that have had an enormous impact on his self-concept. Reese's mentor reframes meanings of strength, realizing that Reese can exhibit strength through his lived experiences of dignity, interdependence, competitiveness, and wisdom.

Many of the issues Reese and other men grapple with are related to sexual impotence. A woman could be an appropriate mentor to the extent that she is comfortable with the client's transference and is able to frankly discuss sex. When possible, clients should be asked what their preferences are. They should not have to contend with a counselor who remains uncomfortable with intimate conversation the client needs as part of his recovery. Reese has major concerns about his sexual activity and its expression, given his inability to achieve an erection. How will he experience sexual gratification? How will he provide sexual pleasure? A series of technological devices are available that assist couples with achieving satisfying sex lives in the event of spinal cord injuries, medication-induced impotence, and other barriers to erection. Penile implants made of silicone or polyurethane can be surgically installed. One type consists of two semirigid but bendable rods; the other type consists of a pump, fluid-filled reservoir, and two cylinders into which the fluid is pumped to create an erection. Vacuum devices can also be used to increase blood flow to the penis. Problems have been reported with both vacuum and inflatable devices (Balch, 2006, p. 509).

Reese's body, mind, spirit, and heart are sources of giving and receiving intense pleasure. Notions of what constitutes a normal sex life had to be altered for Reese to find the meaning that is now a part of his life. Genital sex is one way to give and receive pleasure but it is not the only way.

Finally, it is crucial to remember that what is perceived as attractive is a socially constructed cultural dictate mediated and perpetuated by society. Many Native Americans do not regard disability as punishment for having sinned and tend not to judge or stigmatize people (Marini, 2001).

SUMMARY

This chapter examined the culture's fascination and preoccupation with physical attractiveness. A case study examined able-body-ism in a male client who had become disabled as a result of a violent incident. Implications for counselors were discussed with respect to the convergence of physical attractiveness, race, age, ability, disability, and gender. Demographic data were presented on the number of Americans with disabilities.

Part Four
Reimaging Cou

Chapter 15

Diversity in Relationships

We never had a pot to piss in when I was small, but my parents left me great riches in the form of a childhood that's traveled with me down every path I've taken.

Sidney Poitier, *The Measure of a Man*

healing interpersonal relationships with others, as well as one's ... ship, are offered.

CASE STUDY
Two White Mothers, One Black Male Child

The following case is presented for students to discuss in working groups.

Thirteen years ago, a White lesbian couple adopted a Black male child, Rodrick, age 12. The couple has now split up. Together they share custody of the child. The child is your client. Each of his moms has a new partner. Everybody is White and female. Rodrick is required to repeat the sixth grade because of failing grades and truancy. For 6 months, he has been stealing repeatedly from the neighborhood store, and throwing rocks at new cars to dent them. He is defiant and disobedient to his mothers and teachers.

QUESTIONS

1. How do you assess the situation, and what additional information do you need?
2. What would be a provisional DSM–IV–TR diagnosis?
3. What resources do you organize to assist the child?
4. How do you feel about working with this family?
5. What are your concerns, judgments, and biases?
6. How do you work therapeutically with the mothers?

DEMOGRAPHIC OVERVIEW OF LIVING AND FAMILY ARRANGEMENTS

According to the 2000 census, nonfamily households were more common and family households less common in comparison to 1970. The most noticeable trend was the decline in the number of married households with their own children present. In 2000, 24% of homes were married couples with their own children. This percentage was 40.3% in 1970. Other-family households were 16% of the population in 2000 compared with under 11% in 1970. This category includes families whose householder has no spouse present and who is living with other relatives with children present. In 2000, women living alone represented 58% of single-person households. In 1970, this figure was 67%, so the number of men living alone has increased.

Households have become smaller, and households with their ⟨...⟩
prised only one third of all households in 2000 (U.S. Census Bure⟨...⟩
fertility changes, and mortality all contribute to declines in the ⟨...⟩
According to Census data, there are now more single-parent fami⟨...⟩
families increased from 3 million in 1970 to 10 million in 2000,⟨...⟩
households also saw an increase, from 393,000 to 2 million durin⟨...⟩
The reasons for single parenting differ across race and ethnici⟨...⟩ ⟨...⟩ white
women, it is most likely a function of divorce. Most Black women who are single
mothers have never been married. Independent of race, one-parent families maintained by women are more likely than those maintained by men to have family
incomes below the poverty line. The rise in the divorce rate over the last several
decades is no surprise. What is surprising is the influence of gender and race on getting married in the first place. Among African American women in particular, there
have been substantial decreases in marriage rates. The percentage of married Black
women declined from 62% in 1950 to 36.1% in 2000. There are a number of factors
that have already been identified throughout this text that contributed to this
decrease, including high rates of unemployment among Black men (people are less
likely to marry during times of economic instability); high incarceration rates among
Black men; high homicide rates among Black men ages 15 to 44; and increases in
the number of Black men, particularly those with some college or a college degree,
who marry outside of their racial group.

People are also delaying marriage. The median age for marriage among men is
26.8. It was 23.2 in 1970. The median age for marriage among women is now 25.1.
In 1970 it was 20.8. The proportion of women ages 20 to 24 who had never married
doubled between 1970 and 2000, from 36% to 74%.

Another trend in marriage is the increase in the number of interracial married
couples in the United States. As of the 2000 census, there were 1.46 million interracial couples. Black–White couples have increased sevenfold between 1960 and
2000, from 51,000 to 363,000, respectively. The majority of Black–White unions are
between Black men and White women. Despite the large increase in Black–White
marriages, they represent only 24.7% of all interracial marriages, which is lower than
the 34% proportion in 1960. Approximately 70% of Latinos marry outside of their
ethnic group. When Blacks and Latinos marry interracially, their spouses are more
likely to be White. Non-Latino Whites who marry outside of their race are more likely
to marry Native Americans and Asians. The majority of Asian–White unions are
between Asian women and White men. Among Native Americans and Whites, there
are equal numbers of unions between White men and Native women and between
Native men and White women.

Increasingly high numbers of children under the age of 18 reside in stepfamilies. In
1996, 5.2 million children lived with one biological parent and either a stepparent or
adoptive parent. This figure is up from 4.5 million just 5 years earlier in 1991 (U.S.
Census Bureau, 2001a). There were 2.1 million adopted children as estimated from
the 2000 census (Kreider, 2003). Disproportionately, African American children are
represented among those who have been separated from families of origin, placed in
foster care, and in need of adoption (Bradley & Hawkins-Leon, 2002).

THE ECONOMY AND RELATIONSHIPS

The United States and other Western cultures have experienced significant social, cultural, and economic changes. Marked economic growth increased the number of available jobs. Rising inflation rates increased the cost of living. The women's movement, the civil rights movement, and associated legal actions improved the access of women, individuals with disabilities, and people of color to the workplace. Politically and economically based transitions in the past two decades have considerably reshaped the family landscape in this country. Family form and structure have been influenced by a host of factors, including the feminist movement, economic insecurity, the increase in dual-earner households, the recession, more mothers in the workforce, the rising rates of divorce, single-parent households, remarriage, and cohabitation (Fenell & Weinhold, 1996).

During the 1990s, the breadwinner–homemaker model of the two-parent family was replaced by dual-earner families, in which both partners participate in the job market for pay. The predominance of dual-earner families has occurred both by choice and by necessity. Some women wanted to work and others responded to economic necessity because of declining family incomes hit hard by the recession that began in March 2001. In 1975, 47% of all American mothers with children under age 18 worked for pay. By 2000, the rate had risen to 73%. High percentages of women with very young children are going to work. In 1975, 34% of mothers with children age 3 and under were doing paid work, and in 2000, this figure had risen to 61% (Hochschild, 2003). Many of these parents with young children are also caring for their aging parents. For the first time in history, more American children live in families with mothers who are working outside the home than with mothers who are full-time homemakers. These trends in maternal workforce participation are dramatic. Their impact, both real and feared, on family functioning, marital relationships, and child development has received national attention. Despite this trend, the labor participation rates of mothers with infant children actually fell from 59% in 1998 to 55% in 2000 (U.S. Census Bureau, 2001b). It should be noted that these "declines occurred primarily among mothers in the workforce who were 30 years old and over, White women, married women living with their husbands, and women who had completed one or more years of college" (p. 1).

GENDER AND RELATIONSHIPS

Statistics and trends describe the families that counselors interact with on a daily basis, professionally and personally. The very definition of family has a bearing on the way family policy is constructed and on those whom counselors will serve. Current family policy rewards and punishes certain kinds of family forms, as it defines and privileges particular relationships within certain groups. Heterosexual marriage is priviliged and protected; single persons with no children or property pay the federal government mightily in taxes for not having legitimate tax write-offs.

Clearly, the form and structure of the American family is changing. Much discussion and speculation surrounds the loss of the traditional father/breadwinner and mother/homemaker pattern to the dual-earner or single-parent family pattern and its impact on child development and family well-being. It is assumed that the traditional family pattern is best and that nontraditional family patterns, which often include nonfamily-related child care arrangements, are less desirable. But the general trend of research findings does not readily identify one family pattern or child care pattern as clearly superior or inferior to the others in terms of children's adjustment, child-rearing practices, or family functioning.

The traditional family pattern with distinct sex role separations between home-making and wage earning always has been and remains the societal norm. In a compelling historical review of the origins of the traditional family, Lamb (1982) noted that although women universally have had primary responsibility for the care of young children, these responsibilities rarely prevented them from relying, to a substantial extent, on supplemental child care arrangements or from contributing to the economic survival of the family. When U.S. society was more agrarian and local-community-based, both parents typically worked in the fields or in a location close to home. Most women entered the paid workforce and remained employed except for brief childbearing and child-rearing interruptions. With the Industrial Revolution, work locations moved farther away from the family home, but most women continued their employment.

The materialistic culture impresses a value of "more is better," and the debt burdens most people carry are staggering. It is no wonder family members are stressed, confused, and dysfunctional because of frequently conflicting work, school, and personal schedules; regimented and chaotic socialized routines; and little or no intimate space to communicate what has been occurring in each other's lives. These situations often create a struggle for the semblance of a shared life; thus, family discord and confusion occur.

Families have been affected by society's infusion of gender role socialization for centuries. The socialization process requires that heads of the household and siblings conform to rigid gender role expectations created by a patriarchal system (Goldenberg & Goldenberg, 1996; Nelson, 1997). Although the patriarchal structures of intimacy that serve as the hegemonic ideal of family are perhaps the structures among all others that have silenced and exploited women, they are the structures—or something like structures—of many feminists' families (Nelson, 1997). The vast majority of families in this society are affected by the covert and overt models of socialization that ultimately form the framework and functioning in most households (Hanna & Brown, 1995; Lott, 1994).

The literature on gender role socialization discusses the power base of men as providers gaining recognition from sources outside the home, whereas females' power base and recognition come from their work as caregivers and relationship-maintenance providers inside the home (Burck & Speed, 1995; Lott, 1994; Nicholson, 1997). Even when women work, traditional roles such as child care and household chores, as well as sustaining contact and communication with family and friends, continue to be part of their daily routine (Hochschild, 2003). These roles are socially sanctioned and imposed on individuals on the basis of gender. The assumption is that these roles are symmetrical and equivalent in power. However, the inherent inequality of power is based on what is valued most highly in this society—economic stability. "The contribution of women's family work continues to be minimized, perhaps because it does not directly produce income" (Hare-Mustin, 1988, p. 40).

Society imposes certain behavioral expectations on women and men within families. Women in families often experience a responsibility to uphold the traditions and rituals in those families. Men are expected to be the financial providers and to play less of an emotional role in their caring networks. The socially sanctioned roles within families have left behind generations of women and men who have, at different stages in their lives, felt inadequate and isolated from others because of their narrow gender experience.

Women are expected to assume responsibility for maintaining family relationships and connections. If they do not take on this role and no one else fills in the gap, the connections in the family unit start to deteriorate. The breakdown of family ties or inability to provide nurturance in relationships leads to women experiencing an overwhelming sense of shame and inadequacy (Efthim, Kenny, & Mahalik, 2001). The socialization of women to assume this caretaking role is handed down from generation to generation within families by the demands of an androcentric society. These positions of gender role rigidity can serve to restrict the experiences of family members. Men can begin to feel like strangers to the family and are defined primarily within the context of money. Women feel responsible for the survival of the family ties while at the same time their position outside the family is limited.

Families in this new millennium are composed of female-headed households, gay or lesbian couples, interracial partnerships, blended (divorced or widowed) families, and grandparents or extended family members raising the family's children. These new families need to be comfortable with the therapist and the therapist with them. Inquiring about gender and family roles allows the therapist to assess the family dynamics operating between and among members and perhaps across generational lines. Questions that could be asked might include:

1. What family traditions or rituals stress specific roles or activities for boys and for girls?
2. Does your family discuss how gender roles affect girls and boys in our society?
3. In what ways, if any, do you think these ideas and traditions might be related to the presenting problem?

These are a few questions the counselor can ask during the assessment process. Care should be taken to eliminate any question that does not seem to resonate with the client. The therapist should always keep the factors of race, gender, disability, religion, sexual orientation, age, and socioeconomic status in mind when talking with the client because the personal is political.

The family system plays a key part in helping the counselor gather background information on the client and determine whether the client has the ability to process his innermost thoughts and connect them with the impact of gender role socialization or race. This structural approach to family therapy is a theoretical framework that provides a conceptual map to understanding families.

COUNSELING THEORIES FOR FAMILY PRACTICE

The theoretical framework and theorist most commonly used for family issues is the **structural family approach,** developed by Salvador Minuchin (1974, 1984, 1991), who began his work with families in the 1960s. The structural family approach gives the practitioner a concrete, conceptual map of what should be happening in a family if it is to be functional; it also provides maps of what is awry in the family if it is dysfunctional (Becvar & Becvar, 1993). The structural family approach gives students and practitioners definite ideas about the therapeutic processes that should be carried out. These processes inevitably vary in practice; however, they should reflect the personality of the therapist and the particular structure of the family. Structural family therapy is one of the most heavily researched models, and its efficacy has been demonstrated with a variety of what are generally termed "difficult families." Thus, families with juvenile delinquents, families with anorexic members, families with chemically addicted members, families of low socioeconomic status, and alcoholic families (Fenell & Weinhold, 1996) have all been successfully counseled with the structural family approach. The influence of this approach may also be seen in other models of family therapy, particularly the strategic approach.

Structural family therapy sees the family as an integrated whole—as a system. Accordingly, it is also a subsystem in that its members belong to other agencies and organizations in the community of which it is a part and that affect its basic structure and pattern of organization. In the language of the theory, there are three key concepts or constructs: structure, subsystems, and boundaries.

STRUCTURAL FAMILY THERAPY

Structural family therapy focuses on the patterns of interaction within the family that give clues to the basic structure and organization of the system. **Structure** refers to the invisible set of functional demands that organizes the way family members interact, or the consistent, repetitive, organized, and predictable modes of family behavior that allow the counselor to consider that the family has structure in a functional sense. The concepts of *patterns* and *structure* therefore imply a set of covert rules that family members may not be consciously aware of but that consistently characterize and define their interactions.

The structure of a family is governed by two general systems of constraints. The first constraint system is referred to as *generic,* an observation that all families everywhere have some sort of hierarchical structure according to which parents have greater authority than children. An important aspect of this generic structure is the notion of reciprocal and complementary functions, which can be discerned by the labels applied to family members that indicate their roles and the functions they serve. Members of a family evolve roles (without a conscious awareness of their roles) to maintain the family equilibrium and to keep it functioning.

A second constraint system is that which is *idiosyncratic* to the particular family. Rules and patterns may evolve in a family, although the reason for such characteristic processes may be lost in the history of the family. The rules and patterns become a part of the family's structure. Family structure governs a family in that it defines the roles, rules, and patterns allowable within the family.

SUBSYSTEMS

Structural family theory defines three **subsystems:** the spouse subsystem, the parental subsystem, and the sibling subsystem. The rule among these subsystems for the functional family is that of hierarchy. The theory insists on appropriate boundaries between the generations.

The *spouse subsystem* is formed when two people marry and thus create a new family. The notion of a spouse assumes heterosexual marriage. The processes involved in forming the spouse subsystem are known as *accommodation,* which implies adjustment, and *negotiation* of roles between spouses. The early part of the marriage formation of the spouse subsystem necessitates evolving such complementary roles. Although some of these roles may be transitory and others more permanent, the keys to the successful navigation of life as a family are negotiation and accommodation, especially as they concern rules and roles. The adjustment for couples may be difficult and slow because each has certain expectations about the performance of various functions and roles. Negotiation and accommodation are enhanced to the degree that each spouse is his or her own person and is not overly tied to the family of origin or its rules, patterns, and roles. Finally, an important requirement of the spouse subsystem is that each spouse be mutually supportive of the other in the development of unique or latent talents and interests. Accordingly, neither spouse is so totally accommodating of the other as to lose individuality. Both sides give and take, each remains an individual, and as each accommodates the individuality, resources, and uniqueness of the other, they are respectfully bound together.

In the *parental,* or executive, *subsystem,* each spouse has the challenge of mutually supporting and accommodating the other to provide an appropriate balance of firmness and nurturance for the children. The parents are in charge, and an important challenge is knowing how and when to be in charge about specific issues. Parents need to negotiate and accommodate changes in the developmental needs of their children. A family is not a democracy, and the children are not equals or peers of the parents. From this base of authority, the children learn to deal with authority and to interact in situations in which authority is unequal.

By establishing the spouse and parental subsystems, structural family theory also defines the sibling subsystem. The *sibling subsystem* allows children to be children and to experiment with peer relationships. Ideally, the parents respect the ability of the siblings to negotiate, to compete, to work out differences, and to support one another. It is a social laboratory in which children can experiment without the responsibility that accrues to the adult. Children also learn to coalesce to take on the parental subsystem in the process of negotiating necessary developmental changes.

BOUNDARIES

Boundaries are invisible, but they nevertheless delineate individuals and subsystems and define the amount and kind of contact allowable between members of the family. Structural family theory describes interpersonal boundaries among subsystems as falling into one of three categories: clear, rigid, and diffuse.

Clear boundaries are firm and yet flexible. Clear boundaries also imply access across subsystems to negotiate and accommodate situational and developmental challenges that confront the family. Indeed, situations that occur each day are a test in how to live that necessitates negotiation, accommodation, and experimentation with a new structure over and over again until the family gets it "right," only to find its circumstances have changed once more. Clear boundaries in a family increase the frequency of communication between subsystems, and thus negotiation and accommodation can successfully occur to facilitate change, thereby maintaining the stability of the family.

Rigid boundaries refer to the arrangement both among subsystems and with systems outside the family. Rigid boundaries imply disengagement within and between systems. Family members in that instance are isolated from one another and from systems in the community of which the family is a part. Members in such families thus rely on systems outside the family for the support and nurturance they need and desire.

The family defined by *diffuse boundaries* is characterized by enmeshed relationships. In this case, everybody is into everybody else's business, and the hovering and the providing of support even when not needed or requested is extreme. The parents are too accessible, and the necessary distinctions between subsystems are missing. There is too much negotiation and accommodation; the cost to both the developing children and the parents is a loss of independence, autonomy, and experimentation. The spouse subsystem devotes itself almost totally to parenting functions, and the parents spend too much time with the children and do too much for them. Such children may be afraid to experiment, perhaps to succeed, perhaps to fail. They may feel disloyal to a parent if they do not want to accept what the parent offers. They probably have difficulty knowing which feelings are theirs and which belong to others. The clear boundary is preferred and represents an appropriate combination of rigid and diffuse characteristics.

For Minuchin (1974, 1984, 1991), the ideal family builds on a spouse subsystem in which each accommodates, nurtures, and supports the uniqueness of the other. The spouses have attained a measure of autonomy from their families of origin. Ideally, in the family of origin, each spouse felt supported and nurtured and yet experienced a degree of autonomy, independence, and responsibility. Similarly, spouses need to be able to maintain a delicate balance between proximity and distance. The couple negotiates complementary roles that are stable but flexible and, through a process of negotiation and accommodation, evolves different structures and role complements to deal with changing circumstances. The spouse subsystem maintains itself even when children are born and the parental/executive and sibling subsystems come into existence.

The ideal family will face expected and unexpected crises appropriately by recognizing and facilitating necessary changes in structure. Such behavior requires a great deal of patience and wisdom. So, with the challenge of each new crisis, a new culture (structure) must be evolved—in many cases, a structure and transition process for which the participants have no direct experience to guide them. That is, families are organisms in a continuous process of changing while trying to remain the same.

GOALS

Problem solving is not the goal of structural family therapy. Symptomatic behavior is viewed as a function of the structure of the family; that is, it is a logical response in the family, given its structure. Problem solving will naturally occur when appropriate structural adaptations have been made. Thus, problem solving is the business of the family; structural change so that problem solving can occur is the business of the structural therapist. Symptom removal without the appropriate change in structure would not be successful therapy from the structural perspective.

The structural therapist must join the family and respect its members and its way of organizing itself. Thus, the therapist gets into the family and accommodates to its usual style. Such joining is a necessary prerequisite of attempts to restructure. The structural therapist also respects the hierarchy of the family by asking for the parents' observations first. Problems thus get redefined relative to the family structure. Structural family therapy is action oriented and aimed at influencing what happens in the therapy session.

Becvar and Becvar (1993) noted specific techniques and activities the structural therapist might conduct while in therapy:

1. Meet with family members separately to discuss therapeutic boundaries.
2. Assist family members who are not communicating effectively toward increasing their dialogue with one another.
3. Help specific dyads find ways to end conflictual relationships without intrusion from other family members.
4. Help family members find ways to cognitively view themselves differently by embracing a positive frame of reference. (pp. 207–208)

Structural family therapy's primary processes include being clear about family structure and having respect for the family's efforts to achieve higher levels of functioning. Additionally, the therapist should respect the family's traditional modes of operation, yet provide a healthier model of behavior. This can be achieved by "supporting members, challenging them to try new methods in session and praising them generously when they are successful. There must be an intensity sufficient enough to gain the attention of the family members" (Becvar & Becvar, 1993, p. 208).

MULTICULTURAL THEORETICAL PERSPECTIVES IN FAMILY THERAPY

The structural family approach and multicultural theoretical paradigms should be viewed and implemented as complementary approaches to treatment. Gushue and Sciarra (1995) stated that two models currently in the counseling literature provide a framework for the impact of culture on family therapy and family systems: (1) the intercultural dimension and (2) the intracultural dimension, which delineates (a) acculturation, (b) racial and cultural identity, and (c) bilingual theory.

When looking at the *intercultural dimension,* the counselors working with White, middle-class, heterosexual males used this paradigm to guide all work with their clients. But they began to realize that, for families, diversity was normative. Different cultures had differing ways of understanding "appropriate" family organization, values, communication, and behavior. Although the family perspective had revolutionized the individual view of the client by taking family context into account, it now needed to understand its own unit of analysis (the family) in the light of a cultural culture.

In the *intracultural dimension,* the counselor must turn to three crucial questions of within-group difference:

1. To what extent does this particular family conform to or differ from the "typical" patterns of family functioning for its culture?
2. What cultural differences may exist within the family itself (among the various subsystems)?
3. If cultural differences exist within the family, what consequences do these differences have for interactions both among the subsystems and between the various subsystems and the counselor? (See Storytelling: "Family.")

Answering these questions leads the therapist to the issues of acculturation, racial and cultural identity, and bilingual theory.

Acculturation initially referred to the potentially mutual influence that two cultures have on each other when they come into contact (Ivey, Ivey, & Simek-Morgan, 1997; Mindel, Habenstein, & Wright, 1988). Over the years, however, it has more commonly come to refer to the interaction between a dominant and a nondominant culture in which one is affected much more profoundly than the other.

STORYTELLING: Family

I was talking to a man in Ghana. He looked liked he was in his late 20s. He told me that he was the only person in his family working. He had several jobs. From his collectivistic orientation, he was responsible for others and they were responsible for him. A sense of worth or contribution was not based on how much money people in his family contributed, if any. A collectivistic mindset is so significant to many people's way of being in the world, that it fundamentally shapes their sense of the self—the self is not constructed apart from the collective. This concept is foreign within a largely individualistic and capitalistic framework.

Bilingual theory questions whether intracultural differences in a given family can be attained by observing and understanding the function of linguistic difference within the family system. As emigration from non-English-speaking countries continues to rise, bilingual persons in therapy will become an increasing phenomenon. Some issues that need to be addressed for the bilingual client are related to the immigration experience, language barriers within the family, and language barriers between therapist and client. "Family therapists must take great care before using norms that stem from the majority cultural matrix in assessing the attitudes, beliefs, and transactional patterns of those whose cultural patterns differ from theirs" (Goldenberg & Goldenberg, 1996, p. 36). The behaviors described in the next section provide important information that the therapist must be keenly aware of to empathize with the issues affecting people of color in this country.

NATIVE AMERICAN INDIANS

Native American Indian children have extended self-concepts by self-descriptions that indicate an emphasis on family ties, traditional customs and beliefs, and moral worth (John, 1988). The extended family network includes several households (Goldenberg & Goldenberg, 1996; John, 1988). Cousins may be referred to as brother and sister. The primary relationship is with the grandparents, which can include a great aunt or godparents. Relationship, not blood, determines family; thus families are blended, not joined, through marriage (Sutton & Broken Nose, 1996). "A non-kin family member through being a namesake of a child, consequently assumes family obligations and responsibilities for child rearing and role modeling" (Goldenberg & Goldenberg, 1996, p. 37). The presence and impact of these strong family ties once made possible the social controls that existed throughout life and that shaped concepts of the self. In some tribes, during earlier periods, control by the family over social behavior and sexuality during all phases of life was absolute (John, 1988).

In the extended Indian family, responsibility is shared. This shared responsibility includes food, shelter, cars, and all available services, including child care (John, 1988). The Native American Indian community expects decisions by tribal consensus, institutional sharing as a source of social esteem, and a characteristic noninterference when interacting with others. As a result of an extended concept of self, the community is enabled to enforce values and to serve as a source of standards by using a loose structure or flexible nexus of support. An example of extended self-concept is *tiospaye.* In Lakota Sioux, it refers broadly to harmonious and reciprocal family ties.

Examples of an extended self-concept include obligations to other human beings and to the Native community. An extended self-concept serves to provide a continued group identity (John, 1988). This group identity increases the likelihood of prolonged individual survival in an alien and hostile mainstream culture in which the natural and social environments are increasingly less responsive to Native persons.

In addition to tribal beliefs, the composition of the self-concept of any individual Native American Indian is affected by the level of assimilation into the larger culture. Despite education, occupation in nontraditional jobs, and bicultural status, many Native American Indians have shown a significant retention of cultural values (John, 1988). Despite the tremendous diversity across tribes, the homogeneity of beliefs among Native American Indians may be greater than is characteristic of other cultural groups in this country. The cultural loss and devastation that many Native American clients feel deeply should be acknowledged and attended to by the counselor (Sutton & Broken Nose, 1996).

LATINOS

Personal identity for Latino Americans is sociocentric in nature, with the self and self-interest often subordinated to the welfare of *la casa* and *la familia* (Becerra, 1988). The balance of group and individual prerogatives, however, depends on the individual manner of dealing with the culture in traditional, bicultural, nontraditional, or marginal terms. For traditional and bicultural persons, the balance will often be in favor of needs in the extended family. For nontraditional and marginal persons, the balance may favor more egocentric decisions and actions.

Traditional sex roles are clearly defined by *machismo* for men and *marianismo* and *hembrismo* for women (Becerra, 1988). *Machismo* is more than male physical dominance and sexual availability. It includes the role of a provider responsible for the welfare, protection, honor, and dignity of his family. *Marianismo* refers to the spiritual superiority of women and their capacity to endure all suffering, with reference to the Virgin Mary. After marriage, the *Madonna* concept includes sacrifice and femaleness, or *hembrismo,* in the form of strength, perseverance, and flexibility. These *hembrista* behaviors ensure survival and power through the children.

Personal identity is also associated with being strong. *Strong* refers to inner strength, or *fuerza de espiritu,* characterized by toughness, determination, and willpower (Dana, 1993). A strong person can confront a problem directly and be active in resolving it, thereby delaying the admission that help may be needed. *Controlarse,* or controlling oneself, is the key to being a strong person and includes *aguantarse*, or being able to withstand stress during bad times; *resignarse,* or resigning oneself and accepting fate; and *sobreponerse,* or imposing one's will or overcoming circumstance. A weak person will have little or no self-control and be less able to exercise responsibility or to display *orgullo,* or pride, and *verguenzza,* or shame. As a result, he is more easily influenced by people or events and is relatively unable to become strong.

The family name is very important to Latinos, with a man, along with his given name, adopting both his father's and mother's names. It is often expected, as well as encouraged, that family members will sacrifice their own needs for the welfare of the family (Goldenberg & Goldenberg, 1996). Thus, the family constellation is loyal, committed, and responsible to each other and has a strong sense of honor.

BLACKS AND AFRICAN AMERICANS

There is great diversity among Black families, yet there are similarities independent of place within the Diaspora. According to Black (1996), people of African descent are set apart from other ethnic groups by the following:

1. The African legacy rich in custom and culture.
2. The history of slavery and its insidious attempts to destroy people's souls while keeping their physical bodies in servitude.
3. Historical and contemporary racism and sexism.
4. The victim system, in which people are denied access and then blamed for their marginalized positions.

African American families have demonstrated a stability and cohesive functioning that is often culture specific. Competence among intact inner-city African American families includes shared power, strong parental coalitions, closeness without sacrificing individual ego boundaries, and negotiation in problem solving. Many of these competent families are at risk because of economic conditions, appalling neighborhood conditions, violence, and uncertainty in employment status (Ingrassia, 1993).

As a result of economic conditions, families often do not include only blood relations but may have uncles and aunts, cousins, "big mamas," "play sisters," and "home boys and girls." In many Black American families, there is a three-generation system. The extended families encourage an elastic, kinship-based exchange network that may last a lifetime. These families exhibit spiritual strength, role flexibility, and interchangeability in which male–female relationships are often egalitarian because of the presence of working wives, mothers, and grandmothers (Hines & Boyd-Franklin, 1996; Staples, 1988). Members of the extended family may also exhibit "child keeping," using an informal adoption network.

Despite a feminist perspective that characterized large numbers of Black homes prior to women's liberation, African American men have identity as the nominal heads of households, tied in to their ability to provide for their families. Women often socialize their daughters for strength, economic independence, family responsibility, and daily accountability (Boyd-Franklin, 1989).

Women are identified as possessing fortitude, perseverance, and strength during adversity. As such, women are also generally more religious than men and function to tie the family into a complete church-centered support system of persons in particular roles, activities, and social life (Boyd-Franklin, 1989; Hines & Boyd-Franklin, 1996). This is especially notable in Black Christian (e.g., Baptist) churches. Other major religious groups with similar functions include the African Methodist Episcopal, Jehovah's Witnesses, Church of God in Christ, Seventh-Day Adventist, and Pentecostal, as well as the Nation of Islam sects to which more Black people are converting (Black, 1996).

This culture-specific description of the African American family is not intended to suggest that all families are extended and nonconsanguineous in composition. Increasing numbers of Blacks are single, and many marriages have an increasing fragility as reflected in the higher rates of divorce and separation when compared with the general population (Boyd-Franklin, 1989; Ingrassia, 1993). Many African Americans are acculturated, have opted for identification with the dominant European American culture, and are more egocentric in lifestyle and less communal in orientation.

ASIAN AMERICANS

Asian Americans typically have patriarchal families with authority and communication exercised from top to bottom, interdependent roles, strict adherence to traditional norms, and minimization of conflict by suppression of overt emotion (Kitano, 1988; Min, 1988; Tran, 1988; Wong, 1988). Guilt and shame are used to control family members, and obligations to the family take precedence over individual prerogatives (Kitano, 1988; Sue & Sue, 1990; Wong, 1988). Under the aegis of the family, discipline and self-control are sufficient to provide an impetus for outstanding achievement to honor the family. Negative behaviors such as delinquency, school failure, unemployment, or mental illness are considered family failures that disrupt the desired harmony of family life. In addition is the belief in external control, a fatalism that allows an equanimity and acceptance without question of life as it unfolds.

In China and the United States, absolute control by the family as a major ingredient in the formation of a traditional self-concept has not only diminished but is being openly questioned (Wong, 1988). Despite questioning of traditional filial identity, strong evidence suggests, at least among Hong Kong Chinese students, the continued presence of an extended self or collective orientation.

Similarly, in Japan the emphasis on the importance of collectivity has been increasing, particularly in the form of corporate family effectiveness instead of intrafamily lineal authority or filial piety (Goldenberg & Goldenberg, 1996; Kitano, 1988). However, this collectivity may also be expressed in humanistic or socialist terms.

The primary tradition is **filial piety,** which is the dedication and deference of children to their parents (Goldenberg & Goldenberg, 1996). In the United States, problems faced by first- and second-generation Chinese may differ as a result of inability to express this tradition properly (Sue & Sue, 1990; Wong, 1988). Although first-generation men in particular are required to achieve and to be good providers for their families, sufficient achievement to fulfill family expectations has not always been possible for them. Second-generation individuals also may fail to be unquestioningly faithful to the traditional values of their parents. Their self-worth is increasingly defined either by dominant culture values or by pan-Asian values, in which a common response to racism and personal pride may take precedence over filial piety. As a result, individuals in both generations may experience considerable guilt and anxiety. It may be argued that the locus of loyalty within the Chinese community is in the process of shifting from the family, including ancestors, to other collectivities, including the pan-Asian community in the United States. Overall, the traditional Asian American family believes in loyalty and devotion to its values (Goldenberg & Goldenberg, 1996).

ARABS

A premium is placed on the family as a core unit. Gender socialization and roles are often prescribed with the fathers having a level of authority and centrality in the home. Girls are raised to exercise discretion and modesty in their interactions with others and through their styles of dress—a lesson America could borrow given our penchant for showing undergarments and body parts (e.g. low-rise jeans) that strangers really have no business seeing. Boys are socialized to be leaders in the home and to be head of their household by showing strength and Godly direction.

DIVERSE HEALING STRATEGIES

Essential as relationships are to well-being, they can be stressful. There is not one of us who could not benefit from therapy, and yet the majority of people will not seek the services of a counselor and/or psychologist. Church, temple, synagogue, and community groups, in consultation with mental health professionals, can and do offer paraprofessional sensitivity training to leaders. Individuals, couples, or groups who are experiencing transition and need support can benefit greatly from these low-cost, highly effective services. Training can also review when to refer people if and when problems exceed the paraprofessional's scope of training. As people recover from various emotional and psychological wounds, supportive community support is needed.

hooks (1993) said that if places of healing do not exist to help people process their grief, they must be created because "bottled-in-grief can erupt into illness" (p. 104). In healing, balance and harmony are restored (Shore, 1995). "Home psychoanalysis" (hooks, 1993), or informal spaces where people feel free to share their stories and receive nonjudgmental support, is not inconsistent with professional help when necessary. Authentic spaces need to be created so that people may heal and move forward, catch their breath, regain and create new rhythms, and reclaim their voices. Granted, therapists and counselors provide valuable service to people in need, but other havens can and do promote healing.

EFFECTIVE LAY-LED HEALING

Toward strengthening relationships with others and the self, the following incomplete list may be helpful:

- *Book and film circles* describe the gathering of people, not just to talk about the books and films they are reading and seeing, but to think reflectively about the connections between the written texts and the motion pictures on their lives and the lives of others. Feelings of isolation are also minimized, and people can see their life stories mirrored in another's.
- *Storytelling* allows people to think of their own personal stories or those told by another person and reflect on their meaning and importance. Alice Walker talks about her mother's blue bowls. Although it seemed like there was nothing to eat in the house, her mother, with creativity and care, would prepare the most delicious and nutritious food. As a child, I, too, remember marveling at my mother's ability to perform this same feat and vividly recall thinking that this had to be the mark of a real woman—to take what looks like nothing and make it into something special. It is empowering for clients to realize that they can author their own lives and live the stories they choose.
- *Affirmations* written on a daily basis provide ritual and rhythm to life while promoting positive thinking. Shinn (1989) offers wonderful examples: (1) My supply is endless, inexhaustible, and immediate and comes to me under grace in perfect ways. (2) Rhythm, harmony, and balance are now established in my mind, body, and affairs. (3) Infinite Spirit, give me wisdom to make the most of my opportunities. Never let me miss a trick.
- *Poetry*—others and one's own. Iyanla Vanzant's (1998) poem, "Yesterday I Cried," is really a story about a woman who cried over losses and disappointment. She ends the poem on a triumphant note, embracing her wisdom, resistance, and power.
- *Kitchen table talk* is an informal gathering of friends around the kitchen table to eat and to talk about whatever is on people's minds. An adaptation of this activity can take place in therapy. (See Storytelling: "Movement.")
- *Burning bowls.* I used to participate in this on New Year's Eve at my church. The minister would direct each of us to write down on a piece of paper that which we did not want to take into the new year. Finances, relationships, physical health, and spirituality were topic areas to consider. We would then place the pieces of paper in a bowl and burn them. People do not have to wait for the end of the year to participate in this activity of literally incinerating the pieces of paper that reflect what is no longer desired. They could be encouraged to think about what they do not want to take with them into the next day, or the next hour. Vanzant (1998) identified several "lessons" one could burn: (1) making decisions in fear,

STORYTELLING: Movement

I have encouraged my clients in therapy to compile a list of any and all adjectives that, in their view, best describes them. I then ask them to compile another list that speaks to who they would like to become. A woman might, on the first list, indicate that she is accommodating and selfless. On the list of who she would like to be, she may say that she would like to have clear boundaries and be less concerned about others' approval of her. One of the goals of therapy could be to move in the desired direction while unpacking the scripts, socialization experiences, others' commentary, and rewards that influenced and perpetuated a woman's tendency to be overly concerned about pleasing other people while denying herself.

(2) being afraid to say no (or yes), (3) believing that I should not get angry, (4) being afraid to trust myself, (5) not asking for help when I need it, (6) not telling the truth, (7) being afraid to make a mistake, and (8) feeling afraid that I want too much.

- *Letters to oneself.* I have asked my students to write a letter to themselves at an earlier point in their lives. In this letter, they need to offer support, forgiveness, understanding, and wisdom to the younger person they are. A graduate student once wrote to herself as a high school student. She had made a decision to attend a college closer to her home to accommodate her boyfriend who had moved to another state to attend college. He expected her, however, to be able to receive him during holidays and breaks, thus not wanting her to attend the college of her choice several states away. As a graduate student, she came to realize that she forfeited her desires for his and had been encouraged to do so by both women and men alike.
- *Who would you choose to be you?* is an activity that can foster understanding of self through identification with another. A person is asked to identify an actor that he would want to portray him in his biography and why.
- *Massage* is a loving way to affirm oneself, relax, and experience soothing human touch.
- *Latin and swing dancing* are high touch, and the music is soulful and stirring.
- *"Howling at the moon"* sessions (J. Weeber, personal communication, March 1996) occur when men and women gather each month during the time of the full moon to celebrate the faithfulness and continuity of nature and the universe, commune with each other, and restore ritual to life.
- *Metaphor* can be very therapeutic with clients who may have a difficult time naming and articulating intense feelings. A client who has a conflicted relationship with her mother could be asked, "What color is the relationship you have with your mother?" "What shape is it?" "Is it an ocean, river, pond, stream, or gutter?" "How does it sound?" and "Who are its friends?" Such questions enable the client to externalize the pain and conflict.

• *Tell me when to stop* is an activity that I have done with clients who have a difficult time clarifying their feelings around conflicting issues. I have asked them
to tell me to stop when the width of my hands arrives at a point that represents
the depth of their feelings. I had one client who told me that my arms were not
wide enough to describe how angry she was at her husband. It was not until
that moment that she became aware of the extent of her rage at his infidelity
during her pregnancy.

OTHER APPROACHES

Other approaches that are instrumental in healing include physical exercise,
prayer, meditation, yoga, journaling, aromatherapy, and hydrotherapy. There are
times when drug therapy or antidepressants under the careful supervision of a
psychiatrist, medical doctor, or nurse practitioner are warranted and can assist
people along their journeys.

CREATIVE ARTS

Creative arts can be very helpful to the therapeutic event. According to Gladding
(1997), "Creative arts refers to any art form, including visual representations (paintings,
drawings, sculpture), poetry, drama, and music, that helps individuals become more
aware of themselves or others" (p. 354). The National Coalition of Art Therapies
Association (NCATA) is an interdisciplinary organization that supports all art therapies.
Drawings, photography, cartooning, drama, cinema, games, poetry/metaphor, bibliotherapy, working with sand, writing, and music and movement all fall under the
umbrella of creative therapies. It helps for counselors to understand the importance of
the creative process as a part of the healing taking place. Shore (1995) said that "when
clients become artists they have tools for activating their own compost and fertilizing
their inner lives" (p. 93).

WELLNESS

To encourage healing, whether using creative therapies or more traditional ones, a
holistic and multidimensional approach in which mind and body are seen as one is
essential. Myers, Sweeney, and Witmer (2001) proposed a Wheel of Wellness. Five life
tasks for healthy functioning are depicted and include spirituality, self-direction, work
and leisure, friendship, and love. There are additional components for self-direction
such as sense of humor, physical fitness, sense of worth, and cultural identity. This
ecological model interacts dynamically with other life forces including religion,
education, family, and community.

IMPLICATIONS FOR COUNSELORS AND PSYCHOLOGISTS

Therapists attempting to develop a process that will take into account the impact of culture could follow Hanna and Brown's (1995, p. 101) assessment questions of racial and cultural factors. Some of the questions are also used in my psychosocial narrative assignment:

1. How does your racial/cultural/religious heritage make your family different from other families you know?
2. Compared with other families in your cultural group, how is your family similar?
3. What did your parents teach you about gender, race, sexuality, and class?
4. What are the values that your family identified as being important parts of your heritage?
5. At this particular time in your (family's) development, are there issues related to your cultural heritage that are being questioned by anyone?
6. What is the hardest part about being a person of color in this culture? In your family?
7. When you think of living in America versus the country of your heritage, what are the main differences?
8. What lesson did you learn about your people? About other peoples?
9. What did you learn about disloyalty?
10. What are the privileges and/or oppressions in your family? How does your family feel about their presence and/or absence?
11. What were people in your family negative about?
12. Does your spirituality and religion differ from your family's?
13. What might an outsider not understand about your family's racial/cultural/religious background?

SUMMARY

This chapter identified some complex and intricate issues affecting diverse families. The role gender plays in the maintenance of relationships was discussed. The approach presented here emphasized the need to attend to both intergroup and intragroup cultural differences when working within relationships. Gender socialization issues, societal trends, and biases the counselor has internalized need to be identified and challenged. It is important to have a factual perspective of the worldview and specific values of a given family's culture. Therapists must also take into account their own worldviews and family values and assess how their personal perspectives may influence or spill over into the therapeutic process. To be effective in cross-cultural contexts, the therapist must be linguistically cognizant and culturally aware. Ethnocentrism, gender bias, and stereotypical beliefs will confuse the counseling process. Multiple identities must be taken into account. The case study provided an opportunity for students to think about how they would approach a family characterized by separation, same-gender relationships, and cross-racial adoption. Interactions between and among family members and the therapist can be rewarding for those in therapy and to society. Diverse healing strategies were presented outside of therapeutic relationships.

Chapter 16

Advocacy and Social Justice

**Do not withhold good from whom it is
due when it is in the power of thine hand
to do it.**

Biblical Proverb

Harry Stack Sullivan once described the therapeutic relationship as "two people, both with problems in living, who agree to work together to study those problems, with the hope that the therapist has fewer problems than the patient" (Stiver, 1997, p. 306). Counselors and therapists possess knowledge of human development and an understanding of how to facilitate client empowerment, yet the counseling process is by no means a magical one in which the therapist is free of any personal conflicts and the client is solely dependent on the counselor (McWhirter, 1991).

A multicultural focus championed by both the American Psychological Association and Association of Multicultural Counseling and Development of the American Counseling Association has implicated racism, sexism, and other forms of oppression as deleterious to health and well-being. An expansion of mental health professionals' roles includes being active change agents against structural inequalities that foster inequity across race, gender, and class. Not only in clients' lives but in our own do the consequences of social inequalities manifest. Social justice is oriented to an understanding of clients' situations as well as transformation of the very conditions that press down on people's lives and render them voiceless (Vera & Speight, 2003). How this is done and to what extent it is done describes a social justice framework.

SOCIAL JUSTICE AND EMPOWERMENT

At its core, social justice is concerned with a just and equitable distribution of resources, advocacy, and empowerment as well as a scrutiny of the processes that lead to inequality (Vera & Speight, 2003). Social justice is concerned with restructuring, outreach, education, and empowerment (Ivey & Collins, 2003). It also

1. Encourages full participation in society.
2. Facilitates awareness of structural forces that contribute to disease.
3. Advocates for people to grow in their awareness of social responsibility.
4. Unifies people with others who are similarly situated and marginalized. (Warren & Constantine, 2007)

Toporek and Williams (2006) conceptualized differences among advocacy, social action, and social justice. In their view, advocacy is a variety of roles that the counseling professional adopts in the interest of clients. This includes empowerment, advocacy and social action. Social action is described as action taken by the counselor external to the client to "confront or act on behalf of client groups" (p. 19). Empowerment is viewed as one goal of counseling and psychotherapy and is often in the service of a social justice paradigm.

According to Pinderhughes (1995), "empowerment is defined as achieving reasonable control over one's destiny, learning to cope constructively with debilitating forces in society, and acquiring the competence to initiate change at the individual and systems level" (p. 136). For McWhirter (1991), empowerment is a process wherein people or groups of people who lack power become cognizant of the power dynamics that operate in their lives (e.g., prejudice, discrimination) and as a result are able to acquire reasonable control in their lives without encroaching on others' rights.

Empowerment involves educating vulnerable people and communities about resources, information, programs, and behaviors that can improve the overall quality of their lives (Helms, 2003). (See Storytelling, "Unable to Accommodate That Request.") Empowerment is a recognition of power disparities and their creation of imbalance, privileging those with the most resources while inferring disadvantage on those who do not. Clients need to trust that they have a competent counselor who is sociopolitically aware and able to bring empathy and skills such as listening, summarizing, confronting, and interpreting.

An example of social justice is educating a homeless woman with clinical depression about the resources and programs available to help her and her unborn child, who she wants desperately to keep and raise. Although adoption is an option—sometimes a good one—it is not always the best one (at least in this case for the biological mother and possibly the child, who may not be able to fathom why he was given away). Empowerment is critiquing the discourse that says "the best picture of mothering does not resemble this woman: destitute, crazy, and single." Cosgrove (2006) said, due in part to the problematic images of the homeless and poor women in research, the media, and public policies, "the U.S. has become one of the most dangerous democracies in which poor women and their children can live" (p. 201). With a just distribution of resources, fiscal and human, this woman may be able to revamp her life and take care of her child. Social justice is oriented to examining why this woman and others like her are perceived to be entitled to less. Failure to recognize the patriarchy and classism may contribute to missed opportunities to make organizational changes that encourage equal participation (Hoffman et al., 2005). Psychologists and counseling professionals need to identify and be able to discuss privileges that they receive in society due to race, class, gender, and sexuality (Arredondo et al., 1996). This skill supports educating the woman in the previous example about resisting people and systems that exploit her and learning to engage in decision making to keep herself and her child safe and secure; a social justice paradigm is thus activated.

STORYTELLING: Unable to Accommodate That Request

I had a client many years ago who had tremendous work stress. She felt powerless in the presence of not only her supervisors but colleagues, who often asked her to take on their share of the work given her reputation of being nice and efficient. What most people did not know about her was that she felt tremendous resentment when people, in her view, shirked their responsibilities. She did not know how to express this without erupting with inappropriate anger or tears. During a role-play one night, I asked her to represent one of her colleagues for whom she had a great deal of anger. True to this role, she sounded and looked different from herself as she provided a list of demands. I looked at her and said, "I am unable to accommodate that request." I offered no explanation, no capitulation, no apologies. She tried this technique at work and was amazed at how effective it was. A boundary had been established. She used this same statement (which was about getting underneath her desire to please people and gain their approval) with her family of origin.

To Dulany (1990), empowerment "is another term for finding one's own voice. In order to speak, we must know what we want to say; in order to be heard, we must dare to speak" (p. 133). A social justice framework asks, "Whose voices are heard first and/or above the others and why?"

Vera and Speight (2003) argue that although a multiculturally competent counselor is trained to look for discrimination and develop sensitivity to oppression, counseling professionals are not directed to advocate for the elimination of oppression or exploitation. **Mandatory ethics**, or action taken to avoid breaking the rules, differs from advocacy. **Aspirational ethics**, conversely, is taking action at the highest possible level or eliminating oppression, which translates into greater emphasis on prevention, not remediation, and less of a focus on the indiviudal and more on sociohistorical contexts. A communitarian model of justice based on collective decision making and community empowerment is advocated. Helms (2003) contends that the multicultural competencies and its predecessors offer a framework for doing social justice within the existing structure of counseling psychology. Helms acknowledges that the reality of social service delivery is not supportive of a communitarian model of justice that Vera and Speight advocate.

POWER AND POWERLESSNESS

Powerlessness is operationalized as the "inability to direct the course of one's life due to societal conditions and power dynamics, lack of skills, or lack of faith that one can change one's life" (McWhirter, 1991, p. 224). It results in persons feeling unable to have any meaningful impact on their lives. Feelings associated with this disempowered state were identified by Pinderhughes (1989) as less comfort and pleasure, less gratification, more pain, feelings of inferiority and insecurity, and a strong tendency for depression.

A disproportionate share of persons in poverty are people of color. Most jobs are stratified by race, ethnicity, and gender, with women of color at the bottom of the occupational hierarchy and White males at the top. Structural and institutional inequities such as racism, higher rates of unemployment, and incarceration among men of color have profound implications on the economic stability and well-being for the women and children in these mens' lives. Race-based inequalities in access to (and quality of) health care, along with higher rates of poverty and lack of insurance coverage, contribute to marginalization and powerlessness. Despite this, low-wage-earning people, unemployed people, immigrants, people of color, and disabled people have relied on kinship networks, faith in unseen forces, and cultural and ethnic practices to live their lives with dignity and power (Robinson, 1999). Acknowledgement of clients' cultural practices and the ability for the counseling professional to change beliefs and think differently and flexibly are critical to empowerment and advocacy skills (Pinderhughes, 1995). With humility, it is important to recognize the limits of our multicultural competency and expertise. Engaging in professional growth experiences to address these limitations is essential (Arredondo et al., 1996).

Strategies of coping and resistance to oppression do not suggest that people are not vulnerable or that the structural inequalities are not crushing; indeed they are. Empowerment and social justice seek to disrupt the forces that habituate in people's lives as a function of class and race oppression. When people are asked what makes them feel powerful, they will respond with, for example, being listened to, being in a loving relationship, having money in the bank, getting a good education, and having physical health. These are individually focused forces, hallmarks of an individualistic society that places the self at the center of analysis. A steady gaze at systemic and historical issues and their impact on the personal is part of a social justice orientation.

More power is characterized by less tendency to depression, more pleasure, less pain, and feelings of superiority (Pinderhughes, 1989). Ours is still a society in which White people, the able-bodied, heterosexuals, the wealthy, Christians, and males are the referent point for normalcy. Power is attributed to these identities and reflects a system of White privilege. There are implications here for curricula and practica restructuring in order to disrupt this orientation. Counseling students in training and professionals need to assess their belief systems. This work cannot be done in a superficial or cursory manner, but in a way that reflects interrogation of socialization processes from parents, religious leaders, and the educational system regarding difference. This work will faciliate an understanding of the experiences of oneself and others within a particular group (Pope-Davis, Liu, Toporek, & Brittan-Powell, 2001).

Gender and race identities do not ensure psychological empowerment or power-lessness (Robinson, 1999). Power and powerlessness are not mutually exclusive categories in people's lives. Each gender and race has unique feelings of power and powerlessness (Swanson, 1993). People with marginalized identities need not inter-nalize feelings of less power, yet many counseling graduate students confuse mar-ginalization with internalization. Exposure to multicultural topics in the format they are traditionally delivered may not increase competence about these and other dynamics (Pope-Davis et al., 2001).

SOCIAL JUSTICE AND THE THERAPEUTIC PROCESS

With insurance co-pays of $30.00 for each weekly visit, money is a factor that hinders clients' access to therapy. Sliding-scale fees can make therapy more accessible to many clients. A social justice paradigm supports pro-bono services as necessary and allowable given professionals' need and right to be appropriately remunerated.

Structural elements to the therapeutic relationship exists (Mencher, 1997), and even though the therapist exercises authority and the client moves into a place of vul-nerability, empowerment and social justice are central to the process (Jordan, 1997). Structural elements that define the therapeutic relationship include the following:

1. The formal beginning and ending.
2. The client or insurance company pays and the therapist is paid.

3. The client asks for help with some clinical distress, and the therapist provides help based on her training and expertise.
4. The client shares more information about his life than the counselor shares about her life.
5. The therapist agrees to keep the information confidential, whereas the client can share this information with whomever he pleases.
6. The relationship is dedicated to the growth of the client.
7. Counselors operate within these structures and, in an effort to empower clients, need to respect their clients and the values that clients bring to counseling.

Helping professionals who operate from clients' strengths and believe in clients' abilities to positively affect the quality of their own lives are in a better position to facilitate client empowerment (McWhirter, 1991; Pinderhughes, 1989). Mental health professionals who maintain that clients are victims because of the oppressiveness of the social context and that they and their clients have little hope of transforming existing power dynamics directly are not instrumental in creating transforming conditions.

Counselors need to be careful about mystifying the counseling event, particularly if it accentuates the power differential between client and counselor. Balancing the power differential between client and counselor requires empathy, a necessary tool. It represents one of the most important themes in therapy or counseling (Pinderhughes, 1989). Kaplan (1987) described **empathy** as a function of both advanced cognitive and affective dimensions. She said empathy is "the capacity to take in the experience and the affect of the other without being overwhelmed by it on the one hand or defensively blocking it out on the other hand" (p. 13). The therapist must be able to yield (yielding is a traditionally female quality) to the affect of another person while being able to interpret the meaning of this affect within the cognitive domains. The act of yielding denotes enormous power. In short, the therapist needs to be comfortable with a range of emotions—hers and those of another. (See Storytelling: "Crying for Ourselves First.") Therapists are not superior, yet clients experience shame from a therapist's haughty attitude that reinforces a power differential or the feeling that the therapist knows better than the client does.

Power can be abused by fostering client dependence; it can also be used constructively to facilitate growth and insight. **Productive and constructive power** is at the center of a counseling relationship when a counselor creates a holding environment for a client to make passage through a difficult period. **Destructive power** occurs when one has access to resources and dominates another and imposes one's will through threats or the withholding of certain desired rewards despite implicit or explicit opposition from the less powerful.

Accepting the reality of one's powerless position can bring a sense of power (Pinderhughes, 1989). Empowering the client in therapy to reframe or resist a situation while engaged in social action outside of the therapeutic event to advocate for living wages or health care legislation for children and other issues is reflective of social justice.

Empathy allows the therapist to be touched, moved, and affected by stories of change and resistance shared by another. The client is in a position of authority

STORYTELLING: Crying for Ourselves, First

A client shared her story of being sexually brutalized by her father and "family friends" for years. Her single-parent mother battled with her own addictions and was not available to this defenseless girl child. Her therapist said, "It was not your fault. You deserved better than what you received and as a little girl you should have been protected." The client began to cry. As she did, the raw, but healing skin cut with a razor from her own hands whispered that this woman's heart and soul were healing as well. We as therapists and counselors must listen—not distract or silence, but hear the storied lives of our clients. It is imperative that we have told the painful and disappointing stories from our lives to our own therapists and counselors. This would represent a gigantic step in the direction of a social justice agenda—for the healers to get help. Mental health professionsals bring themselves into the counseling room. They bring their pain, disappointment, success, arrogance, insensitivity, and empathy. They bring their attitudes about race, gender, class, sexual orientation, culture, abortion, politics, gender roles, and interracial marriages. Some counselors will find it difficult to bear witness to certain stories or emotions from their clients. The stories themselves are not the problem nor is the difficulty that a therapist encounters in hearing them. It is the inability or unwillingness to make sense out of how clients' lives contribute to and affect our feelings, thoughts, and sensitivities that is problematic. The professionals' unwillingness or inability to hear needs an intervention.

regarding her life. In collaboration with the therapist, the client seeks to remove a situation from her life or to cope more effectively. Policy implications also place an appropriate share of the burden on institutional structures. When future challenges arise, insight is available and can be accessed for better negotiating the situation. As an essential component of social justice, empathy supports respectful interactions between the client and therapist. Where appropriate, the counselor advocates on behalf of the client by, for example, making out-of-office interventions. Empowerment and advocacy differ substantially from rescuing. McWhirter (1991) reminded us that taking responsibility for doing what another person is capable of doing for the self is disempowering. There are some acts that require the presence of another, and although this is not rescuing, it is being with another. This process of "being with" describes mutuality in counseling and represents an intimate space inhabited by two people governed by a professional context.

FEMINIST THERAPY AND SOCIAL JUSTICE

Feminist therapy differs philosophically from traditional psychotherapy in that it seeks to understand the experiences of women within their social contexts while challenging systematic gender inequality. It is reflective of a social justice orientation in its observation and open critique of injustice and structural inequalities. More contemporary forms of psychotherapy have challenged the premises of Freudian psychology, such as Adler and Rogers (see Corey, 1991). These theorists, however, have often been silent about the social-political contexts in which men and women exist—contexts constructed by gender and race relations, which for many people are oppressive and marginalizing. Karen Horney, for example, was a trailblazer in feminine psychology, and her work, to this day, continues to offer the profession a refreshing look at the development of neurosis and its etiology in one's family of origin.

Devoe (1990) stated that "feminist therapy emphasizes the need for social change by improving the lives of women rather than by helping them adjust to traditional roles in society" (p. 33). Feminist therapy critiques how a male-dominated and patriarchal society deems women as other, inferior, and invisible. Because psychotherapy is largely influenced by dominant cultural values, the mental health system has participated in the oppression of women and people of color by assessing women from a male and White model. One strength of feminist therapy is that it acknowledges the patriarchal and unjust society in which women and men live and thus seeks to educate people while honoring women's anger and men's sadness (Devoe). A social justice agenda allows us to see that men have been adversely affected under the system of patriarchy and sexism as well (Robinson, 1999).

Western psychotherapy is influenced by a psychoanalytical framework, European philosophers, and a hierarchical structure based on hegemonic power. More specifically, the therapist, most likely a male, is seen as the expert, and the client, traditionally a woman, is recognized as dependent. In therapy and psychiatry, women have been more likely to receive a diagnosis of mental disorder, are more often prescribed psychotropic medication, and take more prescription and over-the-counter drugs than men (Crose, Nicholas, Gobble, & Frank, 1992).

Ethnic minority clients are also more likely to receive inaccurate diagnoses; be assigned to junior professionals; and receive low-cost, less preferred treatment consisting of minimal contact, medication, or custodial care rather than individual psychotherapy (Ridley, 1989, p. 55). Feminist therapy questions this construction of power and injustice. It proposes instead a more collaborative, egalitarian relationship between client and counselor if therapy is to be therapeutic and ultimately empowering.

Devoe (1990) spoke about an egalitarian relationship and the importance of an emotional link between the client and counselor prior to effective therapeutic work occurring. "The counselor must view the client as an equal both in and out of the counseling relationship . . . [T]he personal power between the client and counselor should be equal whenever possible" (p. 35). It means that when our clients ask us about who we are, it is important not to hide behind a mask of professionalism and see therapy as going in only one direction. Certainly some disclosures are inappropriate, but whether we have kids, where we are from, where we went for vacation, or if we watched the Red Sox the previous night beat the Cleveland Indians for the 2007 American League Championship describes joining with clients, not excessive and inappropriate disclosure. Nonetheless, some therapists may not approve of this level of disclosure. Personal differences apply and need to be respected.

Personal power should be egalitarian, whenever possible, between client and therapist (Devoe, 1990). If the therapist's underlying premise is that the woman intuitively knows what is in her best interest, then the therapist accepts a different power position.

Professional training and years of relevant experience provide insight into mental health issues, but this learned and experiential knowledge does not supplant the woman's subjective and constructed knowledge even if she has yet to tap into it. Finally, a feminist perspective allows the therapeutic process to unfold at the pace that is most comfortable for the client.

A substantial number of women and men may not understand the value of psychotherapy in general and feminist or womanist therapy in particular. Participation in movements for social justice can increase gender consciousness, yet some women of color are concerned that uniting with men of color toward racial equality is a higher priority than increasing gender consciousness with White women (Chow, 1991). From a dialectical perspective, increasing both racial and gender consciousness is crucial because women of color are always, at all times, both female and racial and ethnic beings. Comas-Diaz and Greene (1994) spoke about the intersections of these identities: "due to the pervasive effects of racism and the concomitant need for people of color to bond together, women of color experience conflicting loyalties in which racial solidarity often transcends gender and sexual orientation solidarity" (pp. 4–5).

Race intersects and thus shapes gender as well (Tatum, 1997). Privilege and oppression conjointly intensify and/or counter each other, and, along with structural effects of sexism, colonialism, and capitalism, leave some clients not only vulnerable but physically and mentally exhausted (Kliman, 2005). Becoming aware of gender issues may be difficult for many women of color who contend race, class, as well as gender discrimination. It is common for women to feel overwhelmed at the dynamics of multiple layers of oppression. Layers of oppression should not be confused with race and gender. Racism is different from race (from being Black), and sexism is different from gender (from being a woman).

The experiences of the client in therapy with a multiculturally competent clinician is in need of exploration (Pope-Davis et al., 2001). In an effort to honor the client's cultural, gender, religious, and political backgrounds and the cumulative impact on the therapeutic process, each client must be viewed from her worldview (Arredondo, Psalti, & Cella, 1993). Social justice orientation considers the external and internal factors that affect behavior, prior to and within therapy. Toward this end, Pope-Davis et al. (2001) suggest that more qualitative research needs to be conducted to move away from self-reports, focus on context, and lessen researcher bias. Warren and Constantine (2007) recognize the pressure of getting tenure at some institutions and encourage participatory action research (PAR) as an example of social justice research efforts. Within participatory action research, participants are empowered to voice their concerns about structural inequalities and its personal impact.

PATIENT NAVIGATION: SOCIAL JUSTICE EXAMPLE

In 1989, Patient Navigation began as a result of the work of physician Harold Freeman. As he traveled through America, he listened to the stories of poor people diagnosed with cancer. A year later in 1990, the first American Cancer Society (ACS)

Patient Navigation program was initiated in Harlem at the Harlem Hospital Center in New York City. Harlem is a predominantly Black and Brown community, and many residents live in poverty and have low levels of education. The purpose of this program was to reduce the barriers that poor people encountered while seeking health care. What he found was published in the American Cancer Society's *Report to the Nation on Cancer in the Poor*. Key findings were as follows:

1. Poor people meet significant barriers when they attempt to seek diagnosis and treatment of cancer.
2. Poor people and their families make sacrifices to obtain cancer care and often do not seek care because of the barriers faced.
3. Poor people experience more pain, suffering, and death because of late diagnosis and treatment at an incurable stage of the disease.
4. Fatalism about cancer is prevalent among the poor and prevents them from seeking care.

Patient Navigation is meant to empower people and can be used by counseling professionals when working with overwhelmed and physically ill clients who are negotiating health systems for cancer care and chronic conditions. Counseling professionals with a social justice orientation can work with clients overwhelmed by their interactions with hospitals and imposing health care systems. Patient navigators are trained to help patients move through the health care system by educating patients, ensuring that the patient goes through with the treatment process, and assisting the patient in negotiating obstacles to care. Obstacles to care include financial and insurance difficulties, emotional concerns, and other barriers mentioned earlier such as transportation problems. Assisting patients with getting their X rays, test results, and other records; making referrals to community services such as welfare, housing, home care, and transportation; helping the patient deal with health challenges; securing second opinions; and finding hospice care if necessary are all within the scope of navigators' duties (Thomas, 2006).

IMPLICATIONS FOR COUNSELORS AND PSYCHOLOGISTS

The Guidelines on Multicultural Education, Training, Research, Practice, and Organizational Change for Psychologists (American Psychological Association, 2003) and the comprehensive competencies identified in 1996 by Arredondo et al. articulate social justice within an ecological context. Both encourage mental health professionals to engage in culturally competency practice with people across race, ethnic, and class groups. Knowledge of legal issues that affect clients' lives, biases in assessment and diagnostic instruments, and referral sources that can assist clients is deemed critical. Although greater explication of competencies and guidelines in counseling and psychology are needed, both documents represent a significant social justice intervention (Ivey & Collins, 2003).

Action represents a different level of resistance to oppression and is a core component of social justice. Action includes exercising institutional intervention skills on behalf of a client, recognizing situations in clients' lives and addressing the incident or perpetrator, filing an informal complaint, filing a formal complaint, and so forth, as well as working at an organizational level to address change whereby policies that discriminate and create barriers are eliminated (Arredondo et al., 1996).

Many counseling professionals are inadequately prepared to work with clients who present with concerns, such as worrying about physical and environmental safety levels and confronting sociopolitical barriers to health care and quality housing (Washington, 1987). People of color as well as low-wage-earning White people have been treated poorly by the mental health establishment, which is often insensitive to sociopolitical realities that affect mental and social functioning. In some circumstances, having a one-on-one client–counselor relationship is not possible or even desirable due to lack of access, unavailability of clinicians for a given area, or the client's sense of mistrust about the benefits and aims of therapy. For this reason, alternative healing strategies discussed in the previous chapter are essential.

CASE STUDY
Homeless Mother

The number of homeless families has increased and now represents 40% of persons who are homeless. Denials to requests for beds at shelters has also increased (Cosgrove, 2006). Victim-blaming increases as the problem of homelessness is located intraindividually as opposed to an examination of structural issues such as the high costs of housing, a minimum wage that encourages poverty, the pathologizing of women who stay in violent domestic situations due to limited choices, and the long-term effects of psychological trauma.

As I write and as you read, there are children in each of our respective cities who are sleeping in cars, on a relative's couch, or in some other make-shift arrangement.

QUESTIONS

1. How could a counselor who is multiculturally competent, and ethnically responsible, with a social justice orientation help mothers avoid homelessness when shelters are full?

2. What is our social justice responsibility as counselors and psychologists outside of the office for client care?

3. Do current ethical guidelines regarding dual relationships limit the range and scope of advocacy for those in the most need?

DISCUSSION AND INTEGRATION

Both short- and long-term advocacy and social action are evident in this list:

1. Use the Internet to identify emergency funds available through churches, the Red Cross, the YMCA, and similar community agencies for a hotel stay.

2. Contact shelters in adjoining towns and see if transportation can be made to transport a family to a safe place.

3. Contact the local newspaper to write a story about this issue in order to educate the public.

4. Contact social services. They are often connected to food banks and other resources to provide emergency food and clothing.

5. Contact congressional representatives about the need for policy changes that can lead to more shelters for women and children. Write letters and encourage others to do so.

6. Collaborate with schools to inform them of the child's family situation. Tutoring, counseling, and other services may be available to help children who are contending with such stressful life situations.

7. Contact the woman's family and friends to see if there are opportunities for women to reside temporarily—regardless of where the extended family might be located.

8. Encourage the woman to trust that situations change and things do get better.

9. When basic necessities are met, such as shelter and food, encourage the woman to write her narrative and give voice to her experience. This can be empowering.

10. Do not resist the expression of the woman's confusion, uncertainty, fear, and anger.

11. Encourage and help identify a support group to reduce feelings of isolation.

12. Get support while supporting. This work is rewarding but also fatiguing and frustrating as the slow wheels of bureaucracy turn.

13. Collaborate with the woman in her own transformation. Ask her what she wants.

14. Avoid pathologizing the client and viewing her as aberrant and abnormal. Do not stereotype, project, or distance. (Pinderhughes, 1995)

15. Investigate the availability of a patient navigator to help the woman manage and travel to doctor's appointments.

16. Investigate 12-Step programs, family therapy, and other services and referrals to deal with a multiplicity of challenges that arise when human beings contend with poverty and the trauma of not having a safe place to lay one's head at night.

17. Actively engage in an ongoing process of challenging attitudes and beliefs that do not support respecting and valuing of differences.

18. Receive supervision from other professionals about the best course of action.

19. Communicate to clients an understanding of coping skills and behaviors viewed by dominant society as dysfunctional that they may need to maintain.

20. Give the woman examples of where bias is imbedded in institutions and society.

21. Share how others have coped and survived when confronting a similar situation.

SUMMARY

Social justice was defined. Its relationship to social action, empowerment, and advocacy was also discussed. The relationship between multicultural counseling competencies and the guidelines for psychologists and social justice was made. A case study integrated the elements of competence, advocacy, and social action within a social justice context. The importance of counseling professionals taking the opportunity to share their own problems and narratives with a therapist was encouraged given that unresolved issues can rob professionals of their personal power, thus impeding the therapeutic process.

Chapter 17

Converging Spirituality

It is not differences that immobilize but silence. And there are so many silences to be broken.

Audre Lorde, *Sister Outsider*

A case study is presented first and discussed throughout this chapter. Definitions of spirituality and religion are provided. Spirituality as a component of diversity, as an identity construct and as integral to the therapy process, is discussed.

CASE STUDY
Crises of Faith

Tim is a 36-year-old African American man. He has been married for 6 years to Geri, also 36. They met while they were in college and are both from the Northwest. They reside in Seattle, Washington. They regularly enjoy a variety of outdoor activities throughout the year: cross-country skiing, horseback riding, and marathons. Tim is a youth pastor and feels that his work with teenagers is a calling from God. Geri is Director of Music at the church. Tim had been noticing a mild ache in his lower abdomen and pain in his genital area. He figured it was due to a rigorous weekend of cross-country skiing and getting older. When the pain did not go away, he stopped doing strenuous exercise for a while. Geri noticed that Tim was limping slightly and was more reluctant to have intercourse. Geri pleaded with Tim to go to the doctor, but he was resistant and embarrassed. Once the pain increased, Tim could not ignore it any longer.

Tim had a physical, and during the exam, Dr. Wilson noticed that Tim's left testicle was enlarged. Tests confirmed the doctor's suspicions. Tim was diagnosed with advanced testicular cancer. The doctor recommended the use of radioactive rods and chemotherapy in order to give Tim the highest chances for survival. This technique did not eliminate the cancer, and the removal of both testicles was recommended. After much prayer, and second and third opinions, Tim decided to proceed with the procedure.

Six months later, Tim is cancer free and is back to work as a minister. He does not have the same passion for the ministry as he once did. He feels lost when talking with the teens about dating, marriage, and sexuality. As a result of the surgery, Tim is unable to have an erection and is on testosterone replacement therapy to avoid a feminizing direction to his body: weight gain, loss of muscle tone, and an upward shift in voice pitch. Dr. Wilson encourages

exercise that requires less risk of bodily injury, such as walking, gardening, and cycling. He has also recommended medical techniques that would assist Tim and Geri sexually. Tim is really turned off at doing something that was meant to be natural. In the last year, Tim has struggled with depression, irritability, and overwhelming feelings of inadequacy. Because they desire children, Geri has suggested they pursue adoption. Tim is not interested in thinking about this issue. On a weekly basis since the surgery, Geri has heard Tim ask, "What have I done so terribly that God would punish me like this?" On the advice of his senior minister, Tim reluctantly goes for counseling. His counselor is Michael Grant, a licensed professional, European American counselor who specializes in men's issues. He is Jewish.

QUESTIONS

1. How can the counselor integrate Tim's spirituality into the therapy?
2. What are the implications of Michael's spirituality on his work with Tim?
3. How do counselors address crises of faith within therapy?

DISCUSSION AND INTEGRATION
The Therapist, Michael

Among many people, faith helps them cope with stress while making meaning in life, particularly when seeking to answer questions such as, "What will become of me?" or "What am I going to do?" Spirituality provides hope, particularly in the face of distress and uncertainty, and can give some a sense of meaning and purpose in life (Ganje-Fling & McCarthy, 1996). When this belief system fails to provide hope and purpose, a crisis of faith is said to result. Professionals need to first assess their own cultural and spiritual faith and belief systems to help clients navigate this oftentimes uneven terrain.

It is impossible to help clients explore anxiety producing and down-right scary issues around spirituality, death, and sexuality if we, as mental health professionals, have not begun this narrative personally, intrapsychically (Robinson-Wood & Braithwiate-Hall, 2005). Michael cannot afford to overlook faith as key to Tim's identity and recovery. Dissimilarity in religious and spiritual values between Tim and Michael can explain Michael's hesitance to explore religion or self-disclose his values. If Michael lacks knowledge about Tim's culture or religion or both, it is crucial that he close this knowledge gap.

During their first session, Michael discloses that he is Jewish and does not go to temple regularly, but that his faith is important to him. Wiggins-Frame and Braun (1996) wrote of the importance of mental health professionals clarifying their values and religious beliefs in order to deal with such issues successfully in therapy. Michael also tells Tim that he is comfortable discussing religion and that many of his clients are not Jewish but Christians, Protestants, and even aetheists. Through the process of Michael's skillful questioning, he asks Tim to describe his spirituality. Tim became aware that he had subscribed to a belief that punishment came to those who had strayed from God's will and had shown disobedience. Because he saw himself as faithful to God's call on his life to pursue a divinity degree, commit his life to the ministry, and marry his wife, he felt lost in his ability to make sense out of his tragic situation.

Michael had a clinical hunch that Tim held fast to some religious beliefs that were a source of oppression and did not contribute to his experiencing God's protection in his life (Robinson & Watt, 2001). Rather than interpret Tim's difficulty with cognitive restructuring as pathological, Michael understood that Tim's position was largely influenced by his religious beliefs. Michael's understanding of Christianity, along with his awareness of the overlap between his own religion and Christianity, aided him in disentangling spiritual themes from pathology in Tim's life (Schultz-Ross & Gutheil, 1997).

SPIRITUALITY AND RELIGION DEFINED

Religion and spirituality are interrelated but important differences exist. Religion comes from the Latin root *religio*, which means a "bond between humanity and the gods" (Ingersoll, 1995, p. 11). "Religion is the practice of one's beliefs with respect to a higher being. Involved are behaviors, rituals, and routines related to the worship experience" (Robinson & Watt, 2001). Spirituality is understood as the "outward expression of the inner workings of the human spirit" (Swinton, 2001, p. 20).

In their work with African American survivors of breast cancer, Halbert et al. (2007) saw spirituality "as having a personal relationship with a higher power and faith and may be a process used to find meaning in one's life, while religion is defined as a set of practices and beliefs (e.g., dogma) that are shared by a community or group" (p. 282). Spirituality is associated with a transcendent and sacred dimension (Robinson-Wood & Braithwaite-Hall, 2005) and includes a "capacity for creativity, growth, and development of a value system" (Young, Wiggins-Frame, & Cashwell, 2007, p. 48).

Ingersoll (1995) identified spirituality as having seven dimensions:

1. One's conception of the divine or force greater than oneself.
2. One's sense of meaning or what is beautiful, worthwhile.

3. One's sense of relationship with Divinity and other beings.
4. One's tolerance or negative capability for mystery.
5. Peak and ordinary experiences engaged to enhance spirituality (may include rituals or spiritual disciplines).
6. Spirituality as play or the giving of oneself.
7. Spirituality as a systemic force that acts to integrate all the dimensions of one's life. (p. 11)

It is possible to be spiritual and not religious and to be religious and not spiritual (Burke & Miranti, 2001). Religion is often associated with an institutionalized set of beliefs "by which groups and individuals relate to the ultimate" (Burke, 1999, p. 252). It is defined as the specific organized and codified form through which individuals may express their spirituality (Young et al., 2007, p. 48). Miller and Thoresen (2003) conceptualized religion as associated with the social phenomenon and spirituality understood at the level of the individual; nonetheless, spirituality and religion overlap and are related constructs in that they share some characteristics and do not share others.

Hall and Pargament (2003) caution against the polarization of religion and spirituality, which "ignores the fact that all forms of spiritual expression unfold in a social context and that virtually all organized faith traditions are interested in the ordering of personal affairs" (p. 64). These authors also site other consequences association with a bifurcation of religion and spirituality:

1. There is a risk that spirituality emerges as good and religion as bad. The truth is that there are helpful and harmful aspects related to each.
2. Most people experience spirituality within a religious context and frankly do not see a distinction between the two.
3. The polarization could lead to duplication of concepts and measures used in research.

CLINICAL SKILLS IN INTEGRATING SPIRITUALITY AND PSYCHOTHERAPY

Effective therapy does not deny differences between client and therapist but respects completely the multiple identities that comprise the self. Multiculturally competent therapy emphasizes an ecological framework wherein the person and environment interaction is considered along with culture, ethnicity, family, structural issues, history, and spirituality, which is seen as fundamental to who the client is in therapy (Robinson-Wood & Briathwaite-Hall, 2005). Spirituality is a core dimension of life, along with friendship, love, work, and self-regulation (Witmer & Sweeney, 1992), yet there are barriers to an inclusion of spirituality into therapy.

The lack of training about spirituality within therapeutic contexts is a key issue for many therapists, particularly given that spirituality has emerged as a dimension of multiculturalism (Hall, Dixon, & Mauzey, 2004). Unresolved issues in the therapist's life, lack of clarity about spirituality as a mysterious and deep phenomenon, as well as fear of imposing values may lead a therapist to maintain silence. The misguided belief that spirituality cannot and should not be studied have contributed to its absence in research (Miller & Thoresen, 2003).

The connections between spirituality and therapy are strong. "Both psychological growth and spiritual conversion draw the person out of old ways of being, through the deaths such letting go requires, and into liberation forms of life consistent with one's true self" (Berliner, 1995, p. 113). Both spirituality and therapy are oriented to helping the client do the following:

1. Learn to accept himself in relationship to the environment and with the people in one's environment.
2. Forgive one's self and others. Sometimes not forgiving others makes sense, thus allowing the client to release toxic and debilitating resentment and hurt.
3. Acknowledge personal shortcomings and those of others as part of the human experience.
4. Confront corrective and destructive guilt.
5. Modify patterns of thinking, behaving, and feeling that are self-destructive and contribute to a lesser life. (Burke & Miranti, 2001)

Skills that may help Michael and other clinicians approach spirituality as a topic for clinical insight have been identified:

1. The ability to examine one's own prejudice and biases around spirituality and religion, both positive and negative.
2. Becoming familiar with the various literature regarding spiritual experiences.
3. Exploring religion from a different culture than one's own and assessing the relevance of the spiritual domains in the client's therapeutic issues.
4. Using a client's spiritual beliefs in the pursuit of the client's therapeutic goals. (Cashwell & Young, 2004; West, 2000)

Michael realizes that a crisis of faith can lead to spiritual growth and personal trans-formation. Parker (1985) saw faith and development as integrated: "the idea that active participation and struggle is necessary is common not only to discussions of religious development but to discussion of other forms of cognitive growth and change" (p. 45). He demonstrates many of these skills as shown in his skillful questioning. Some of these questions convey his understanding of some of the basic principles of Christianity. To facilitate a discussion of spirituality given Tim's crises of faith, Michael asks Tim the following:

1. How has spirituality failed you?
2. How has spirituality helped you in the past?
3. Would you still perceive God as punishing you if you did not have to have an orchiectomy?

4. How do you make spiritual sense of your cancer-free diagnosis?
5. Do you experience God's presence during prayer and worship?
6. How does your faith affect the way you look at your suffering?
7. Does Jesus's suffering on the cross help you make sense of your suffering?
8. How does the orchiectomy affect your sense of your manhood as a Black man?

SPIRITUALITY, THERAPY, AND CULTURAL CONSIDERATIONS

Tim and Michael have racial and religious differences between them. Michael's multicultural competence has equipped him with the ability to consider Tim's cultural worldview. One of the significant contributions of multicultural counseling and psychology has been to transition from a narrow focus on the individual to viewing the self in relation to a broader cultural context (Wiggins-Frame & Braun, 1996). Concerning African Americans and other groups of color, the authors said, "this shift has prompted recognition of spiritual and healing systems indigenous to racial-ethnic American cultures . . . standards for multicultural counseling competencies all include a call for practitioners to be knowledgeable about and to use religious and spiritual healers and leaders" (p. 22).

Michael is mindful that Tim presents with spiritual issues related to a surgical procedure to treat his cancer. As a multiculturally competent clinician, Michael considers Tim's race and the impact on him, not only as a man but as a young, African American man who has not fathered children. Michael is mindful of the press of dominant discourses on himself and Tim. One of these discourses is that manhood and virility are synonymous, particularly for Black men within a culture that objectifies them sexually.

Vontress (2004) reminds mental health professionals not to impose race on clients but attend to the significance that the client attaches to race as an important issue in their lives. In time, after rapport and trust have developed and Michael has been instrumental in alleviating Tim's depressive symptoms, he might introduce race through a question such as, "What is the effect of the surgery on your sense of your manhood as a Black man?"

Tim's crisis of faith, although understandable and functional, can have adverse implications for his well-being and quality of life. Although spirituality can play a role in moderating health and well-being (Miller & Thoresen, 2003), the converse seems true. In their review of nine hypotheses about the link between religion or spirituality and mortality, morbidity, disability, or recovery from illness, Powell, Shahabi, and Thoresen (2003) concluded that, "religious people who become upset by the belief that God has abandoned them or who become dependent on their faith, rather than their medical treatment for recovery, may inadvertently subvert the success of their recovery" (p. 50).

Having visited a Black church on several occasions, Michael understands the crucial role that the Black church has played in the lives of African Americans. From civil rights organizing to social activism in the form of feeding programs, prison ministries, and educational centers (Adksion-Bradley, Jouhnson, Sanders, Duncan, & Holcomb-McKoy, 2005), the Black church has been a beacon of hope and light for Black Americans.

A multicultural competency of integrating appropriate interventions into the therapeutic event is evidenced by Michael. He is comfortable with the use of scripture in therapy, the therapeutic benefit of Tim sharing his prayers for a miracle of healing, and Tim's conclusion that his earnest prayers went unanswered. Because one of Tim's goals is to restore his relationship with God, Michael queries Tim about whether his church has prayed for him. Michael is familiar with "prayer as an integral part of the process for relieving the pain and suffering often associated with their everyday life experience" (Adksion-Bradley et al., 2005).

As a leader in his role as Youth Pastor, Tim also feels enormous guilt for not being a man of greater faith. The cathartic process of being listened to and speaking one's truth without censor or judgment help Tim. He eventually appreciates that the pressure he put on himself to accept his cancer and loss of his testicles as God's will exacerbated his feelings of powerlessness and did not allow him to express his anger at the unthinkable, God. Halbert et al. (2007) said, ". . . discussing of religious and spiritual beliefs with heath care providers is important to African Americans diagnosed with prostate cancer" (p. 282).

Michael communicates to Tim that surrendering to a situation is not the same as condoning it. This difference was a critical one for Tim, who saw that many of the ministers in his spiritual community took the stance that his cancer was God's will, that his survival was a manifestation of God's faithfulness, and that Tim needed to approach God with a grateful heart. To join with his client, Michael acknowledges that Tim's disappointment in and doubts about God's provision and care have been expressed through the ages by the Old Testament prophets, Jesus himself, and other people of faith across religions.

Unpacking religious teachings is hard and daunting work. Messages such as "don't question God" or "just pray about it and the problem will take care of itself" do not encourage people to get underneath the emotions that contribute to their crises of faith and extreme disappointment in God. Tim feels deprived of God's grace, which, if present, would have meant healing of his cancer. Michael asks Tim to consider if people can pray for healing, die anyway, and yet still be whole, healed, and benefactors of God's grace. (See Storytelling, "Grace?")

Tim's religious beliefs are gendered in nature as well: part of his depression is feeling that he has failed his wife by not giving her children. Tim is also concerned that his wife looks at him differently, with less desire due to his operation. In time, Michael will encourage Tim and his wife to seek out another therapist with whom to have couples therapy.

One of the helpful interventions for Tim was bibliotherapy—this served to reduce his feelings of aloneness. Another intervention for Tim was to eventually join a support group of men who had survived prostate and testicular cancers. Because Tim is a private man, he resisted this suggestion from Michael. For this reason, Michael did not introduce this suggestion until he felt that Tim might be more supportive of it. Michael was also mindful of a support group that was facilitated by a man of color, given the disproportionate rates of prostate and testicular cancer for men of color.

STORYTELLING: Grace?

Years ago, I was talking with one of my dearest friends about a mother and her young son who were traveling on a stretch of highway when their car stalled at a dangerous place. Other motorists would be unable to see them in time to avoid an accident. Before help arrived, their car was hit by another vehicle approaching at a high rate of speed. The mother died. Her son survived. My friend told me that she and her mother, just a few weeks prior to this fatal accident, had broken down near that same spot but shortly afterward, a police officer pulled up behind them, flashed his blue lights, and radioed for a tow truck. In the meantime, he put flares down to alert oncoming cars to go around the stalled car. "But for the grace of God go I" said my friend as she compared her outcome with that of the mother's. I asked, "Do you think the mother who died benefited from God's grace?" My friend answered, "Yes, I do." I said, "So do I." Survival and rescue are not the only examples of God's grace, provision, and protection.

In one study, cancer survivors described helpful communication as empathic listening, allowing the client to talk and weep without interjecting helpful advice or cheerleading, and offering gentle encouragement. Unhelpful communication included admonishing people to overcome their illness, avoidance, and forced cheerfulness (Curtis & Juhnke, 2003).

IMPLICATIONS FOR COUNSELORS AND PSYCHOLOGISTS

Therapy is a gift in that it can help people move toward wisdom, peace, and sanity following tragedy and crises. Therapists who are able to usher spirituality into the therapy room and critique cultural patterns about religion and gender allow clients to experience the healing benefits of spirituality within therapy. What counselors-in-training are being taught about spirituality represents a signficant gap in the research (Young et al., 2007). Toward the articulation of competencies that mental health professionals need in their work with spirituality, nine competencies identified 13 years ago during an initial Summit on Spirituality are provided for both counselors-in-training and seasoned practitioners:

1. The ability to explain the relationship between religion and spirituality, including similarities and differences.
2. The ability for the counselor to describe religious and spiritual beliefs and practices within a cultural context.
3. Personal exploration of one's religious and spiritual beliefs.
4. An understanding of various models of religious/spiritual development across the lifespan.

5. Sensitivity to and acceptance of a variety of religious and spiritual expressions in the client's communication.
6. An ability to identify the limits of one's understanding of a client's spiritual expression and demonstrate appropriate referral skills.
7. The ability to assess the relevance of the spiritual domains in the client's therapeutic issues.
8. Sensitivity to and respect of the spiritual themes in the therapeutic process.
9. The ability to use the client's spiritual beliefs in the pursuit of the client's therapeutic goals.

SUMMARY

This chapter began with a case study that was discussed throughout. An African American man's crises of faith following testicular cancer diagnosis, treatment, and finally an orchiectomy were presented. His therapist was also a male but racially and religiously different. Multicultural competencies for mental health professionals when integrating spirituality and religion into therapy were highlighted. Definitions were provided as were the challenges associated with bifurcating these terms.

Epilogue

If you are not angry, you are not paying attention.

Bumper sticker, late 1990s

There are two parallel tasks: creating and insisting on a world where all people, regardless of their human characteristics, can speak and be heard. Knowing that people will get mad, sad, and confused does not stop this time-honored process of extending our hearts and our ears to listening and being heard. I dream of a world where people can live in peace—have enough to eat and places of safety to dwell. I envision a world where each of us knows the bounty of community during times of celebration and plenty as well as during times of want and struggle. And I dream of a world where people are not afraid to love people who are perceived to be different or the same as themselves—a world where human differences are not better or worse than other human differences.

I have attempted to present a way for the therapeutic event to embrace the multiple, shifting, and simultaneous identities in people's lives. I trust that people will talk about the cases—about the models, and the research, and the census data, and the stories. I hope people share their feelings and listen to others' reactions. And that when all is said and done, we will know that the never-ending process of transformation is under way.

Tracy Robinson-Wood

REFERENCES

Abernathy, A. D. (1995). Managing racial anger: A critical skill in cultural competence. *Journal of Multicultural Counseling and Development, 23,* 96–102.

Abrams, L. S. (2002). Rethinking girls "at-risk": Gender, race, and class intersections and adolescent development. *Journal of Human Behavior in the Social Environment, 6,* 47–64.

Abudabbeh, N. (1996). Arab families. In M. McGoldrick, J. K. Pearce, & J. Giordano (Eds.), *Ethnicity and family therapy* (pp. 333–346). New York: Guilford Press.

Abudabbeh, N. (2005a). Arab families: An overview. In M. McGoldrick, J. Giordano, & N. Garcia-Preto (Eds.), *Ethnicity and family therapy* (pp. 423–436). New York: Guilford Press.

Abudabbeh, N. (2005b). Palestinian families. In M. McGoldrick, J. Giordano, & N. Garcia-Preto (Eds.), *Ethnicity and family therapy* (pp. 487–498). New York: Guilford Press.

Abudabbeh, N., & Nydell, M. K. (1993). Transcultural counseling and Arab Americans. In J. McFadden (Ed.), *Transcultural counseling: Bilateral and international perspectives* (pp. 261–284). Alexandria, VA: American Counseling Association.

Adherents.com. (2007). Major religions of the world ranked by number of adherents. Retrieved from http://www.adherents.com/

Adksion-Bradley, C., Jouhnson, D., Sanders, J. L., Duncan, L., & Holcomb-McKoy, C. (2005). Forging a collaborative relationship between the Black church and the counseling profession. *Counseling and Values, 49,* 147–154.

Ahnallen, J. M., Suyemoto, K. L., & Carter, A. S. (2006). Relationship between physical appearance, sense of belonging and exclusion, and racial/ethnic self-identification among multiracial Japanese European Americans. *Cultural Diversity and Ethnic Minority Psychology, 12,* 673–686.

Alba, R. D. (1990). *Ethnic identity: The transformation of White America.* New Haven, CT: Yale University Press.

Alinsky, S. D. (1990). *Rules for radicals: A primer for realistic radicals.* New York: Random House.

Al-Krenawi, A., & Graham, J. R. (2000). Culturally sensitive social work practice with Arab clients in mental health settings. *Health Social Work, 25*(1), 9–22.

American Cancer Society. (1989). A summary of the American Cancer Society report to the Nation: Cancer in the poor. *CA Cancer Journal for Clinicians, 39,* 263–265.

American Counseling Association. (1995). *Code of ethics.* Alexandria, VA: American Counseling Association.

American Counseling Association. (ACA). (2005). *Code of ethics.* Alexandria, VA: Author.

American Psychological Association. (2002). *Code of ethics.* Washington, DC: Author.

American Psychological Association. (2003). Guidelines on multicultural education, training, research, practice, and organizational change for psychologists. *American Psychologist, 58*(3), 377–402.

American Psychological Association. (2006). *Guidelines for psychotherapy with lesbian, gay, and bisexual clients.* Washington, DC: Author.

American Psychological Association. (2007). *Disability issues in psychology: Enhancing your interactions with people with disabilities.* Washington, DC: Author.

American Psychological Association. (2007). *Report of the APA task force on socioeconomic status.* Washington, DC: Author.

Ancis, J. R., Sedlacek, W. E., & Mohr, J. J. (2000). Student perceptions of campus cultural climate by race. *Journal of Counseling and Development, 78,* 180–185.

Andersen, A. E. (1986). Males with eating disorders. In F. E. F. Larocca (Ed.), *Eating disorders* (pp. 39–46). San Francisco: Jossey-Bass.

Anderson, N. B. (2003). *Unraveling the mystery of racial and ethnic health disparities: Who, what, when, where, how and especially, why?* Boston, MA: Institute on Urban Health Research, Northeastern University.

Anderson, S. K., & Middleton, V. A. (2004). *Explorations in privilege, oppression, and diversity.* Belmont, CA: Wadsworth.

ANRED. (2006). *Anorexia and related eating disorders.* Retrieved September 28, 2007, from http://www.anred.com/stats.html

Appleby, G. A., Colon, E., & Hamilton, J. (2001). Culture, social class, and social identity development. In G. Appleby, E. Colon, & J. Hamilton (Eds.), *Diversity, oppression and social functioning: Person-in-environment assessment and intervention* (pp. 16–34). Needham Heights, MA: Allyn & Bacon.

Arab American Institute (2006). *Arab Americans.* Retrieved September 15, 2007, from http//www.aaiusa.org/census

Arredondo, P. (1992). *Latina/Latino value orientations: Tape 1. Cultural considerations for working more effectively with Latin Americans.* Amherst, MA: Microtraining and Multicultural Development.

Arredondo, P., & Arciniega, G. M. (2001). Strategies and techniques for counselor training based on the multicultural counseling competencies. *Journal of Multicultural Counseling and Development, 29,* 263–273.

Arredondo, P., Psalti, A., & Cella, K. (1993). The woman factor in multicultural counseling. *Counseling and Human Development, 25*(8), 1–8.

Arredondo, P., & Rodriguez, V. (2005). Working with contemporary Latino immigrants. *Counseling and Human Development, 38,* 1–12.

Arredondo, P., Toporek, R., Brown, S. P., Jones, J., Locke, D. C., Sanchez, J., et al. (1996). Operationalization of the multicultural competencies. *Journal of Multicultural Counseling and Development, 24,* 42–78.

Atkinson, D. R., & Hackett, G. (1995). *Counseling diverse populations.* Madison, WI: Brown and Benchmark.

Atkinson, D. R., Morten, G., & Sue, D. W. (1983). *Counseling American minorities: A cross cultural perspective.* Dubuque, IA: William C. Brown.

Avakian, M. (2002). *Atlas of Asian-American history.* New York: Checkmark Books.

Balch, P. A. (2006). *Prescription for nutritional healing* (4th ed.). Garden City Park, NY: Avery.

Ballentine, B., & Ballentine, I. (1993). *The Native Americans: An illustrated history.* Atlanta, GA: Turner.

Battle, J., Cohen, C. J., Warren, D., Fergerson, G., & Audam, S. (2002). Say it loud. I'm Black and I'm Proud. *Black Pride Survey 2000.* New York: The Policy Institute of the National Gay and Lesbian Task Force. Retrieved August 8, 2003, from http://www.ngltf.org/pi/blackpride.htm

Beals, K. P. M., & Peplau, L. A. (2006). Disclosure patterns within social networks of gay men and lesbians. *Journal of Homosexuality, 51,* 101–117.

Beals, M. J., & Beals, K. L. (1993). Transcultural counseling and the Hispanic community. In J. McFadden (Ed.), *Transcultural counseling: Bilateral and international perspectives* (pp. 213–238). Alexandria, VA: American Counseling Association.

Becerra, R. M. (1988). The Mexican American family. In C. H. Mindel, R. W. Habenstein, & R. Wright (Eds.), *Ethnic families in America: Patterns and variations* (3rd ed., pp. 141–159). New York: Elsevier.

Becvar, S. B., & Becvar, R. (1993). *Family therapy: A systematic integration* (2nd ed.). Boston: Allyn & Bacon.

Begley, S. (1995, February 13). Three is not enough. *Newsweek,* 67–69.

Belgrave, F. Z. (1991, January–March). Psychosocial predictors of adjustment to disability in African Americans. *Journal of Rehabilitation,* 37–40.

Bell, A., & Weinberg, M. (1978). *Homosexuality: A study of human diversity among men and women.* New York: Simon & Schuster.

Bem, S. L. (1993). *The lenses of gender: Transforming the debate on sexuality Inequality.* New Haven, CT: Yale University Press.

Bennett, L., Jr. (1982). *Before the Mayflower: A history of Black America.* Chicago: Johnson.

Berliner, P. M. (1995). Soul healing: A model of feminist therapy. In M. Burke and J. Mirant (Eds.), *Counseling: The spiritual dimension* (pp. 113–125). Thousand Oaks, CA: Sage.

Bernardez, T. (1987). Gender-based countertransference of female therapists in the psychotherapy of women. In M. Braude (Ed.), *Women and therapy* (pp. 25–39). New York: Haworth Press.

Berry, J. W., & Kim, U. (1988). Acculturation and mental health. In P. R. Dasen, J. W. Berry, & N. Sartorius (Eds.), *Health and cross-cultural psychology: Toward applications* (pp. 207–236). Newbury Park, CA: Sage.

Berry, J. W., & Sam, D. L. (1997). Acculturation and adaptation. In J. Berry, M. Segall, & C. Kagitcibasi (Eds.), *Cross-cultural psychology* (Vol. 3, pp. 291–326). Boston: Allyn & Bacon.

Berzon, B. (1988). *Permanent partners: Building gay and lesbian relationships that last.* New York: E. P. Dutton.

Birtchnell, S. A., Lacey, J. H., & Harte, S. (1985). Body image distortion in bulimia nervosa. *British Journal of Psychiatry, 47,* 408–412.

Black, L. (1996). Families of African origin. In M. McGoldrick, J. Giordano, & J. K. Pearce (Eds.), *Ethnicity and family therapy* (pp. 57–65). New York: Guilford Press.

Block, J., & Block, J. H. (2006). Venturing a 30-year longitudinal study. *The American Psychologist, 61,* 315–327.

Bourdieu, P. (1984). *Distinction: A social critique of the judgment of taste.* Cambridge, MA: Harvard University Press.

Bowman, V. E. (1996). Counselor self-awareness and ethnic self-knowledge as a critical component of multicultural training. In. J. L. DeLucia-Waack (Ed.), *Multicultural counseling competencies: Implications for training and practice* (pp. 7–30). Alexandria, VA: Association for Counselor Education and Supervision.

Boyd-Franklin, N. (1989). *Black families in therapy: A multisystems approach.* New York: Guilford Press.

Boyd-Franklin, N. (2003). Race, class, and poverty. In F. Walsh (Ed.), *Normal family process* (pp. 260–279). New York: Guilford Press.

Bradford, J., Barrett, K., & Honnold, J. A. (2002). *The 2000 Census and same-sex households: A user's guide.* New York: The Policy Institute of the National Gay and Lesbian Task Force. Retrieved from http://www.ngltf.org/downloads/Census/CensusFront.pdf

Bradley, C., & Hawkins-Leon, C, G. (2002). The transracial adoption debate: Counseling and legal implications. *Journal of Counseling & Development, 80,* 433–440.

Bradshaw, C. (1994). Asian and Asian American women: Historical and political considerations in psychotherapy. In L. Comas-Diaz & B. Greene (Eds.), *Women of color: Integrating ethnic and gender identities* (pp. 72–113). New York: Guilford Press.

Brantlinger, E. A. (1993). *Politics of social class in secondary schools: Views of affluent and impoverished youth.* New York: Teachers College Press.

Bronstein, P., & Quina, K. (1988). *Teaching a psychology of people.* Washington, DC: American Psychological Association.

Brookins, C. B., & Robinson, T. L. (1995). Rites of passage as resistance to oppression. *Western Journal of Black Studies, 19*(3), 172–185.

Brouwers, M. (1990). Treatment of body image dissatisfaction among women with bulimia nervosa. *Journal of Counseling and Development, 69,* 144–147.

Brown, D. (1981). *Bury my heart at Wounded Knee.* New York: Henry Holt & Company.

Brown, L. (1994). *Subversive dialogues: Theory in feminist therapy.* New York: Basic Books.

Brown, L. M. (2003). *Girlfighting: Betrayal and rejection among girls.* New York: New York University Press.

Brown, L. M., & Gilligan, C. (1992). *Meeting at the crossroads: The landmark book about the turning points in girls' and women's lives.* New York: Ballantine Books.

Browning, C., Reynolds, A. L., & Dworkin, S. H. (1994). Affirmative psychotherapy for lesbian women. *Counseling Psychologist, 19,* 177–196.

Brunsma, D. L. (2006). Mixed messages: Doing race in the color-blind era. In D. Brunsma (Ed.), *Mixed messages: Multiracial identities in the "color-blind" era* (pp. 1–11). Boulder, CO: Lynne Reinner.

Brunsma, D. L., & Rockquemore, K. A. (2001). The new color complex: Appearances and biracial identity. *Identity: An international journal of theory and research, 1,* 225–246.

Bryant, A., & LaFromboise, T. D. (2005). The racial identity and cultural orientation of Lumbee American Indian high school students. *Cultural Diversity and Ethnic Minority Psychology,11,* 82–89.

Burck, C., & Speed, B. (1995). *Gender, power, and relationships.* New York: Routledge.

Burke, M. T., Hackney, H., Hudson, O., Miranti, J., Watts, G. A., & Epp, L. (1999). Spirituality, religion, and CACREP curriculum standards. *Journal of Counseling & Development, 77,* 251–257.

Burke, M. T., & Miranti, J. (2001). The spiritual and religious dimensions of counseling. In D. Locke, J. Myers, & E. Herr (Eds.), *Handbook of counseling* (pp. 601–612). Thousand Oaks, CA: Sage.

Burnett, J. W., Anderson, W. P., & Heppner, P. P. (1995). Gender roles and self-esteem: A consideration of environmental factors. *Journal of Counseling and Development, 73,* 323–326.

Byrd, W. M., & Clayton, L. A. (2003). Racial and ethnic disparities in healthcare: A background and history. In Institute of Medicine (Ed.), *Unequal treatment: Confronting racial and ethnic disparities in healthcare* (pp. 455–527). Washington, DC: National Academies Press.

Cameron, S. C., & turtle-song, i. (2003). Native American mental health: An examination of resilience in the face of overwhelming odds. In F. Harper and J. McFadden (Eds.), *Culture and counseling: New approaches.* Boston: Allyn & Bacon.

Cao, L., & Novas, H. (1996). *Everything you need to know about Asian-American history.* New York: Penguin.

Carballo-Dieguez, A. (1989). Hispanic culture, gay male culture, and AIDS: Counseling implications. *Journal of Counseling and Development, 68,* 26–30.

Cardemil, E. V., & Battle, C. L. (2003). Guess who's coming to therapy? Getting comfortable with conversations about race and ethnicity in psychotherapy. *Professional Psychology: Research and Practice, 34,* 278–286.

Carpenter, K. M., & Addis, M. E. (2000). Alexithymia, gender, and responses to depressive symptoms. *Sex Roles: A Journal of Research, 42,* 629–638.

Carrigan, T., Connell, B., & Lee, J. (1987). Toward a new sociology of masculinity. In H. Brod (Ed.), *The making of masculinities: The new men's studies* (pp. 63–100). Boston: Allen and Unwin.

Carroll, L., & Gilroy, P. J. (2002). Transgender issues in counselor preparation. *Counselor Education & Supervision, 41,* 233–242.

Carter, R. T., & Parks, E. E. (1996). Womanist identity and mental health. *Journal of Counseling and Development, 74,* 484–489.

Cashwell, C. S., & Young, J. S. (2004) Spirituality in counselor training: A content analysis of syllabi from introductory spirituality courses. *Counseling and Values, 48,* 96–109.

Cass, V. C. (1979). Homosexual identity formation: A theoretical model. *Journal of Homosexuality, 4,* 219–235.

Cass, V. C. (1984). Homosexual identity: A concept in need of definition. *Journal of Homosexuality, 9,* 105–126.

Chan, C. S. (1992). Cultural considerations in counseling Asian American lesbians and gay men. In S. H. Dworkin & F. J. Gutierrez (Eds.), *Counseling gay men and lesbians: Journey to the end of the rainbow* (pp. 115–124). Alexandria, VA: American Association for Counseling and Development.

Chang, E. C. (1996). Cultural differences in optimism, pessimism, and coping: Predictors of subsequent adjustment in Asian American and Caucasian American college students. *Journal of Counseling Psychology, 43,* 113–123.

Chang, J., & Sue, S. (2005). Culturally sensitive research: Where have we gone wrong and what do we need to do now? In M. Constantine & D. Sue (Eds.), *Strategies for building multicultural competence in mental health and educational settings* (pp. 229–246). Hoboken, NJ: John Wiley & Sons.

Chang, P. (2000). Treating Asian/Pacific American addicts and their families. In J. Krestan (Ed.), *Bridges to recovery: Addiction, family therapy, and multicultural treatment* (pp. 192–218). New York: Free Press.

Chase, C. (2003). *The child with an intersex condition: Total patient care.* [Video]. Seattle: Intersex Society of North America.

Chen, G. A., LePhuoc, P., Guzman, M. R., Rude, S. S., & Dodd, B. G. (2006). Exploring Asian American racial identity. *Cultural Diversity and Ethnic Minority Psychology, 12,* 461–476.

Chernin, K. (1985). *The hungry self: Women, eating, and identity.* New York: Harper & Row.

Children's Partnership, The. (2000). *Tomorrow's youth: A changing demographic.* Retrieved December 15, 2003, from http://www.childrenspartnership.org/pub/children2000/children_of_2000.pdf

Chin, J. L. (2003). Multicultural competencies in managed health care. In D. Pope-Davis, H. Coleman, W. Liu, & R. Toporek (Eds.), *Handbook of multicultural competencies in counseling & psychology* (pp. 347–364). Thousand Oaks, CA: Sage.

Choi, Y., Harachi, T. W., Gillmore, M. R., & Catalano, R. F. (2006). Are multiracial adolescents at greater risk? Comparisons of rates, patterns, and correlates of substance use and violence between monoracial and multiracial adolescents. *American Journal of Orthopsychiatry, 76,* 86–97.

Chojnacki, J. T., & Gelberg, S. (1995). The facilitation of a gay/lesbian/bisexual support-therapy group by heterosexual counselors. *Journal of Counseling and Development, 73,* 352–354.

Choudhuri, D. (2005). Oppression of the spirit: Complexities in the counseling encounter. In S. Anderson and V. Middleton (Eds.), *Explorations in privilege, oppression, and diversity* (pp. 127–136). Belmont, CA: Thomson Brooks Cole.

Chow, E. N.-L. (1991). The development of feminist consciousness among Asian American women. In J. Lorber & S. A. Farrell (Eds.), *The social construction of gender* (pp. 255–268). Newbury Park, CA: Sage.

Chow, E. N.-L. (1994). The feminist movement: Where are all the Asian American women? In R. Takaki (Ed.), *From different shores: Perspectives on race and ethnicity in America.* New York: Oxford University Press.

Christian, B. (1989). But who do you really belong to—Black studies or women's studies? *Women's Studies, 17,* 17–23.

Christian, C. M. (1995). *Black saga: The African American experience (a chronology).* Boston: Houghton Mifflin.

Chung, R. C.-Y. (2005). Women, human rights, and counseling: Crossing international boundaries. *Journal of Counseling & Development, 82,* 262–268.

Chusmir, L. H. (1990). Men who make nontraditional choices. *Journal of Counseling and Development, 69*(1), 11–16.

Clark, R., Anderson, N. B., Clark, V. R., & Williams, D. R. (2002). Racism as a stressor for African Americans: A biopsychosocial model. In T. LaVeist (Ed.), *Race, ethnicity and health* (pp. 319–339). San Francisco: Jossey-Bass.

Clutter, A. W., & Nieto, R. D. (n.d.). *Understanding the Hispanic culture.* Ohio State University fact sheet. Family and Consumer Sciences. Retrieved September 25, 2007, from http://ohioline.osu.edu/hyg-fact/5000/5237.html

Cokely, K. O. (2001). Gender differences among African American students in the impact of racial identity on academic psychosocial development. *Journal of College Student Development, 42,* 480–487.

Cokely, K. O. (2005). Racial(ized) identity, ethnic identity, and Afrocentric values: Conceptual and methodological challenges in understanding African American identity. *Journal of Counseling Psychology, 52,* 517–526.

Cole, J. B., & Guy-Sheftall, B. (2003). *Gender talk: The struggle for women's equality in African-American communities.* New York: Random House.

Coleman, E. (1982). Developmental stages of the coming out process. *American Behavioral Scientist, 25,* 469–482.

Collins, J. F. (2000). Biracial Japanese American identity: An evolving process. *Cultural Diversity and Ethnic Minority Psychology, 6,* 115–133.

Collins, P. H. (1989). The social construction of Black feminist thought. *Signs, 14,* 745–773.

Comas-Diaz, L. (1993). Hispanic Latino communities: Psychological implications. In D. Atkinson, G. Morten, & D. W. Sue (Eds.), *Counseling American minorities: A cross-cultural perspective* (pp. 245–263). Madison, WI: Brown and Benchmark.

Comas-Diaz, L., & Greene, B. (1994). Overview: An ethnocultural mosaic. In L. Comas-Diaz & B. Greene (Eds.), *Women of color* (pp. 3–9). New York: Guilford Press.

Comas-Diaz, L., & Greene, B. (1994). Women of color with professional status. In L. Comas-Diaz & B. Greene (Eds.), *Women of color: Integrating ethnic and gender identities in psychotherapy* (pp. 347–388). New York: Guilford Press.

Cook, D. A. (1994). Racial identity in supervision. *Counselor Education and Supervision, 34,* 132–241.

Cook, E. P. (1987). Psychological androgyny: A review of the research. *Counseling Psychologist, 15,* 471–513.

Cooper, R. (2002). A note on the biological concept of race and its application in epidemiological research. In T. A. LaVeist (Ed.), *Race, ethnicity, health: A public health reader* (pp. 99–114). San Francisco: Jossey-Bass.

Corey, G. (1991). *Theory and practice of counseling and psychotherapy.* Pacific Grove, CA: Brooks/Cole.

Cornell, S., & Hartmann, D. (1997). *Ethnicity and race: Making identities in a changing world.* Thousand Oaks, CA: Pine Forge Press.

Cose, E. (1993). *The rage of a privileged class.* New York: HarperCollins.

Cosgrove, L. (2006). The unwarranted pathologizing of homeless mothers: Implication for research and social policy. In R. Toporek, L. Gerstein, N. Fouad, G. Roysircar, & T. Israel (Eds.), *Handbook for social justice in counseling psychology* (pp. 200–214). Thousand Oaks, CA: Sage.

Cottone, R. R., & Tarvydas, V. M. (1998). *Ethical and professional issues in counseling.* Upper Saddle River, NJ: Merrill/Prentice Hall.

Crockett, L. J., Iturbide, M. I., Stone, R. A. T., McGinley, M. Raffaelli, M., & Carlo, G. (2007). Acculturative stress, social support, and coping: Relations to psychological adjustment using Mexican American college students. *Cultural Diversity and Ethnic Minority Psychology, 13,* 347–355.

Crose, R., Nicholas, D. R., Gobble, D. C., & Frank, B. (1992). Gender and wellness: A multidimensional systems model for counseling, *Journal of Counseling & Development, 71,* 149–156.

Cross, W. E. (1991). *Shades of black: Diversity in African American identity.* Philadelphia: Temple University Press.

Curtis, R. A., & Juhnke, G. A. (2003). Counseling the client with prostate cancer. *Journal of Counseling & Development, 81,* 160–167.

D'Andrea, M., & Daniels, J. (1991). Exploring the different levels of multicultural counseling training in counselor education. *Journal of Counseling and Development, 70,* 78–85.

Dana, R. H. (1993). *Multicultural assessment perspectives for professional psychology.* Boston: Allyn & Bacon.

Dana, R. H. (2000). The cultural self as locus for assessment and intervention with American Indians/Alaska Natives. *Journal of Multicultural Counseling and Development, 28,* 66–81.

Dana, R. H. (2002). Examining the usefulness of DSM–IV. In K. Kurasaki, S. Okasaki, & S. Sue (Eds.), *Asian American mental health: Assessment theories and methods* (pp. 29–46). New York: Kluwer.

Darwin, C. (1859). *The origin of species by means of natural selection.* New York: Modern Library.

Day-Vines, N. L., Wood, S. M., Grothaus, T., Craigen, L., Holman, A., Dotson-Blake, K., et al. (2007). Broaching the subjects of race, ethnicity, and culture during the counseling process. *Journal of Counseling and Development, 85,* 401–409.

de la Cruz, G., & Brittingham, A. (2003). The Arab population: 2000. *Census 2000 brief.* Washington, DC: U.S. Department of Commerce, Economics and Statistical Administration.

de las Fuentes, C. (2007). Latina/o American populations. In M. Constantine (Ed.), *Clinical practice with people of color: A guide to becoming culturally competent* (pp. 46–60). New York: Teachers College Press.

DeJong, J., & El-Khoury, G. (2006, October 21). Reproductive health of Arab young people. *British Medical Journal, 333,* 849–851.

Delpit, L. (1997). The silenced dialogue: Power and pedagogy in educating other people's children. In A. Halsey, H. Lauder, P. Brown, & A. Wells (Eds.), *Education: Culture, economy, society* (pp. 582–594). Oxford, UK: Oxford University Press.

DeNavas-Walt, C., Proctor, B. D., & Smith, J. (2007). *Income, poverty, and health insurance coverage in the United States: 2006.* Washington, DC: U.S. Department of Commerce, Current Population Reports.

Devoe, D. (1990). Feminist and nonsexist counseling: Implications for the male counselor. *Journal of Counseling and Development, 69,* 33–36.

Dey, J. G., & Hill, C. (2007). *Behind the pay gap.* Washington, DC: American Association of University Women Foundation.

Diaz, R. M., & Ayala, G. (2002). *Social discrimination and health: The case of Latino gay men and HIV risk.* New York: The Policy Institute of the National Gay and Lesbian Task Force.

Retrieved July 31, 2003, from http://www.ngltf.org/downloads/DiazEng.pdf

Dilworth-Anderson, P., Boswell, G., & Cohen, M. D. (2007). Spiritual and religious coping values and beliefs among African American caregivers: A qualitative study. *Journal of Applied Gerontology, 25,* 355–369.

Dines, G., & Humez, J. M. (2002). *Gender, race, and class in media: A text-reader.* Thousand Oaks, CA: Sage.

Dinsmore, J. A., & England, J. T. (1996). A study of multicultural counseling training at CACREP-accredited counselor education programs. *Counseling Education and Supervision, 36*(1), 58–76.

Dion, K., Berschid, E., & Walster, E. (1972). What is beautiful is good. *Journal of Personality and Social Psychology, 14,* 94–108.

Dobbins, J. E., & Skillings, J. H. (1991). The utility of race labeling in understanding cultural identity: A conceptual tool for the social science practitioner. *Journal of Counseling & Development, 70,* 37–44.

Duerk, J. (1994). *Circle of stones: Woman's journey to herself.* San Diego, CA: Lura Media.

Dulany, P. (1990). On becoming empowered. In J. Spurlock & C. Robinowitz (Eds.), *Women's progress: Promises and problems* (pp. 133–142). New York: Plenum Press.

Durby, D. D. (1994). Gay, lesbian, and bisexual youth. *Journal of Gay and Lesbian Social Services, 1*(3/4), 1–37.

Dwairy, M. (2004). Individuation among Bedouin versus urban Arab adolescents: Ethnic and gender differences. *Cultural Diversity and Ethnic Minority Psychology, 10,* 340–350.

Dwairy, M. (2005). *Culturally sensitive counseling and psychotherapy: Working with Arabic and Muslim clients.* New York: Teachers College Press.

Dworkin, S. H., & Gutierrez, F. J. (1991). *Counseling gay men and lesbians: Journey to the end of the rainbow.* Alexandria, VA: American Association for Counseling and Development.

Efthim, P. W., Kenny, M. E., & Mahalik, J. R. (2001). Gender role stress in relation to shame, guilt, and externalization. *Journal of Counseling & Development, 79,* 430–438.

Elder, P. (2000). An entirely routine test. In M. Clark (Ed.), *Beating our breasts: Twenty New Zealand women tell their breast cancer stories* (pp. 29–35). New Zealand: Cape Catley Limited.

Eliason, M. L., & Schope, R. (2007). Shifting sands or solid foundation. Gay, lesbian, bisexual, and transgender identity formation. In I. H. Meyer & M. E. Northridge (Eds.), *The health of sexual minorities: Public health perspective on lesbian, gay, bisexual, and transgender health* (pp. 3–26). New York: Springer.

Ellis, C. M. (2004). Putting race on the table: Counselors addressing race. *Counseling and Human Development, 37*(1), 1–8.

Emmons, L. (1992). Dieting and purging behavior in Black and White high school students. *Journal of the American Dietetic Association, 92,* 306–312.

Enns, C. Z. (1991). The "new" relationship models of women's identity: A review and critique for counselors. *Journal of Counseling and Development, 69,* 209–217.

Enns, C. Z. (1994). On teaching about the cultural relativism of psychological constructs. *Teaching on Psychology, 21,* 205–212.

Equal Employment Opportunity Commission. (1991). *Americans with Disabilities Act handbook.* Washington, DC: Government Printing Office.

Erickson, C. D., & Al-Timimi, N. (2001). Providing mental health services to Arab Americans: Recommendation and considerations. *Cultural Diversity and Ethnic Minority Psychology, 7,* 308–327.

Erikson, E. (1968). *Identity: Youth and crisis.* New York: Norton.

Erwin, T. M. (2006). A qualitative analysis of the *Lesbian Connection's* discussion forum. *Journal of Counseling & Development, 84,* 95–107.

Evans, K. M., Kincade, E. A., Marbley, A. F., & Seem, S. R. (2005). Feminism and feminist therapy: Lessons from the past and hopes for the future. *Journal of Counseling & Development, 83,* 269–277.

Evans, L., & Davies, K. (2000). No sissy boys here: A content analsysis of the representation of masculinity in elementary school reading textbooks. *Sex Roles: Journal of Research, 42,* 255–270.

Exum, H. A., & Moore, Q. L. (1993). Transcultural counseling from African-American perspectives. In J. McFadden (Ed.), *Transcultural counseling: Bilateral and international perspectives* (pp. 193–212). Alexandria, VA: American Counseling Association.

Falbo, T., & De Baessa, Y. (2006). The influence of Mayan education on middle school students in Guatemala. *Cultural Diversity and Ethnic Minority Psychology, 12,* 601–614.

Falco, K. L. (1991). *Psychotherapy with lesbian clients: Theory into practice.* New York: Brunner/ Mazel.

Fauth, J., & Hayes, J. A. (2006). Counselors' stress appraisals as predictors of countertransference behavior with male clients. *Journal of Counseling & Development, 84,* 430–439.

Fenell, D. L., & Weinhold, B. K. (1996). Treating families with special needs. *Counseling and Human Development, 28*(7), 1–10.

Ferdman, B. M., & Gallegos, P. I. (2001). Racial identity development and Latinos in the United States. In C. Wijeyesinghe & B. Jackson III (Eds.), *New perspectives on racial identity development: A theoretical and practical anthology* (pp. 32–66). New York: New York University Press.

Fine, M. (1991). Invisible flood: Notes on the politics of "dropping out" of an urban public high school. *Equity and Choice, 8,* 30–37.

Fine, M. A., & James-Myers, L. (1990). The development and validation of an instrument to assess an optimal Afrocentric worldview. *Journal of Black Psychology, 17*(1), 37–54.

Fischer, A. R., & Holz, K. B. (2007). Perceived discrimination and women's psychological distress: The roles of collective and personal self-esteem. *Journal of Counseling Psychology, 54,* 154–164.

Fowler, C., O'Rourke, B. O., Wadsworth, J., & Harper, D. (1992). Disability and feminism: Models for counselor exploration of personal values and beliefs. *Journal of Applied Rehabilitation Counseling, 23,* 14–19.

Fowler, J., & Keen, S. (1978). *Life maps: Conversations on the journey of faith.* Waco, TX: Word Books.

Frisbie, W. P., Cho, Y., & Hummer, R. A. (2002). Immigration and the health of Asian and Pacific Islander adults in the United States. In T. A. LaVeist (Ed.), *Race, ethnicity, health: A public health reader* (pp. 231–251). San Francisco: Jossey-Bass.

Ganje-Fling, M. A., & McCarthy, P. (1996). Impact of childhood sexual abuse on client spiritual development: Counseling implications. *Journal of Counseling & Development, 74,* 253–262.

Gans, H. J. (1992, January 8). Fighting the biases embedded in social concepts of the poor. *Chronicle of Higher Education,* p. A56.

Garcia-Coll, C. (1997). Building connection through diversity. In J. Jordan (Ed.), *Women's growth in* diversity: More writings from the Stone Center (pp. 176–182). New York: Guilford Press.

Garcia-Preto, N. (1996). Latino families: An overview. In M. McGoldrick, J. Giordano, & J. Pearce (Eds.), *Ethnicity and family therapy* (pp. 141–154). New York: Guilford Press.

Garland-Thomas, R. (2002). Integrating disability, transforming feminist theory. *NWSA, 14,* 1–32.

Garnets, L., Hancock, K. A., Cochran, S. D., Goodchilds, J., & Peplau, L. A. (1991). Issues in psychotherapy with lesbians and gay men: A survey of psychologists. *American Psychologist, 46,* 964–972.

Garrett, J. T., & Garrett, M. W. (1994). The path of good medicine: Understanding and counseling Native American Indians. *Journal of Multicultural Counseling and Development, 22,* 134–144.

Garrett, J. T., & Garrett, M. W. (1996). *Medicine of the Cherokee: The way of right relationship.* Sante Fe, NM: Bear.

Garrett, J. T., & Herring, R. D. (2001). Honoring the power of relation: Counseling Native adults. *Journal of Humanistic Counseling, Education, and Development, 40,* 139–160.

Garrett, J. T., & Pichette, E. C. (2000). Red as an apple: Native American acculturation and counseling with or without reservation. *Journal of Counseling & Development, 78,* 3–13.

Garrett, M. (1998). *Walking on the wind: Cherokee teachings for harmony and balance.* Santa Fe, NM: Bear.

Garrett, M. T., Garrett, J. T., Torres-Rivera, E., Wilbur, M., & Roberts-Wilbur, J. (2005). Laughing it up: Native American humor as spiritual tradition. *Journal of Multicultural Counseling and Development, 33,* 194–204.

Genetic research confirms: There's only 1 human race (2003, July 15). *St. Louis Post-Dispatch.*

Gerschick, T. J., & Miller, A. S. (1994). Gender identities at the crossroads of masculinity and physical disability. *Masculinities, 2,* 34–55.

Gertner, D. M. (1994). Understanding and serving the needs of men. *Counseling and Human Development, 27,* 1–16.

Gibbs, J. T., & Hines, A. M. (1992). Negotiating ethnic identity: Issues for Black-White biracial adolescents. In M. P. P. Root (Ed.), *Racially mixed people in America* (pp. 223–238). Newbury Park, CA: Sage.

Gibbs, J. T., Huang, L. N., & Associates. (1989). *Children of color: Psychological interventions with minority youth.* San Francisco: Jossey-Bass.

Gillem, A. R., Cohn, L. R., & Throne, C. (2001). Black identity in biracial Black/White people: A comparison of Jacqueline who refuses to be exclusively Black and Adolphus who wishes he were. *Cultural Diversity and Ethnic Minority Psychology, 7,* 182–196.

Gilligan, C. (1982). *In a different voice.* Cambridge, MA: Harvard University Press.

Gladding, S. T. (1997). *Community and agency counseling.* Upper Saddle River, NJ: Merrill/Prentice Hall.

Gloria, A. M., & Ho, T. A. (2003). Environmental, social, and psychological experiences of Asian American undergraduates: Examining issues of academic persistence. *Journal of Counseling & Development, 81,* 93–105.

Gloria, A. M., & Peregoy, J. J. (1995). Counseling Latino alcohol and other substance users/abusers: Cultural considerations for counselors. *Journal of Substance Abuse Treatment, 13,* 1–8.

Gloria, A. M., & Peregoy, J. J. (1996). Counseling Latino alcohol and other substance users/abusers: Cultural considerations for counselors. *Journal of Substance Abuse Treatment, 13,* 119–126.

Goldenberg, I., & Goldenberg, H. (1996). *Family therapy: An overview* (4th ed.). Pacific Grove, CA: Brooks/Cole.

Gonzalez, M., Castill-Canez, I., Tarke, H., Soriano, F., Garcia, O., & Velasquez, R. J. (1997). Promoting the culturally sensitive diagnosis of Mexican Americans: Some personal insights. *Journal of Multicultural Counseling and Development, 25,* 156–161.

Good, G. E., Dell, D. M., & Mintz, L. B. (1989). Male role and gender role conflict: Relations to help seeking in men. *Journal of Counseling Psychology, 36,* 295–300.

Good, G. E., & Mintz, L. B. (1990). Gender role conflict and depression in college men: Evidence for compounded risk. *Journal of Counseling and Development, 69*(1), 17–21.

Good, G. E., Robertson, J. M., Fitzgerald, L. F., Stevens, M., & Bartels, K. M. (1996). The relation between masculine role conflict and psychological distress in male university counseling center clients. *Journal of Counseling and Development, 75*(1), 44–49.

Good, G. E., & Wood, P. K. (1995). Male gender role conflict, depression, and help seeking: Do college men face double jeopardy? *Journal of Counseling and Development, 74*(1), 70–75.

Good, M. J. D., James, C., Good, B. J., & Becker, A. E. (2003). The culture of medicine and racial, ethnic, and class disparities in health care. In Institute of Medicine (Ed.), *Unequal treatment: Confronting racial and ethnic disparities in healthcare* (pp. 594–625). Washington, DC: National Academies Press.

Gossett, T. (1963). *Race: The history of an idea in America.* New York: Schocken.

Greene, B. (1994). Ethnic-minority lesbians and gay men: Mental health and treatment issues. *Journal of Consulting and Clinical Psychology, 62,* 243–251.

Greene, B., & Herek, G. M. (1994). *Lesbian and gay psychology: Theory, research, and clinical applications.* Thousand Oaks, CA: Sage.

Grubb, H. J. (1992). Intelligence at the low end of the curve: Where are the racial differences? In A. Burlew, W. Banks, H. McAdoo, & D. Azibo (Eds.), *African American psychology: Theory, research, and practice* (pp. 219–228). Newbury Park, CA: Sage.

Gunn Allen, P. (1992). *The sacred hoop: Recovering the feminine in American Indian traditions.* Boston: Beacon Press.

Gunn Allen, P. (1994). Who is your mother? Red roots of White feminism. In R. Takaki (Ed.), *From different shores: Perspectives on race and ethnicity in America* (2nd ed., pp. 192–198). New York: Oxford University Press.

Gushue, G. V., & Sciarra, D. P. (1995). Culture and families: A multidimensional approach. In J. G. Ponterotto, J. M. Casas, L. A. Suzuki, & C. M. Alexander (Eds.), *Handbook of multicultural counseling* (pp. 586–606). Thousand Oaks, CA: Sage.

Hacker, A. (1992). *Two nations: Black and White, separate, hostile, unequal.* New York: Ballantine Books.

Haddock, S. A., Zimmerman, T. S., & Lyness, K. P. (2003). Changing gender norms: Transitional dilemmas. In F. Walsh (Ed.), *Normal family process* (pp. 301–336). New York: Guilford Press.

Hage, S. M. (2006). Profiles of women survivors: The development of agency in abusive relationships. *Journal of Counseling & Development, 84,* 83–94.

Hahn, H. (1988a, Winter). Can disability be beautiful? *Social Policy,* pp. 26–32.

Hahn, H. (1988b). The politics of physical differences: Disability and discrimination. *Journal of Social Issues, 44*(1), 39–47.

Haider, R. (1995). *Gender and development.* Cairo, Egypt: American University in Cairo Press.

Halbert, C. H., Bary, F. K., Weathers, B., Delmoor, E., Coyne, J., Wileyto, O., et al. (2007). Differences in cultural beliefs and values among African American and European American men with prostate cancer. *Cancer Control, 14,* 277–284.

Hall, C. R., Dixon, W. A., & Mauzey, E. (2004). Spirituality and religion: Implications for counselors. *Journal of Counseling & Development, 82,* 504–507.

Hall, P. C., & Pargament, K. I. (2003). Advances in the conceptualization and measurement of religion and spirituality. *American Psychologist, 58*(1), 64–74.

Hall, R. E. (1992). Bias among African-Americans regarding skin color: Implications for social work practice. *Research on Social Work Practice, 2,* 479–486.

Hall, R. E. (2001). Identity development across the lifespan: a biracial model. *The Social Sciences Journal, 38,* 119–123.

Hall, R. E. (2005). From psychology of race to issues of skin color: Western trivialization and people of African descent. *International Journal of Psychology and Psychological Therapy, 5,* 125–134.

Hall, R. E., & Livingston, J. N. (2006). Mental health practice with Arab families: The implications of spirituality vis-à-vis Islam. *American Journal of Family Therapy, 34*(2), 139–150.

Hamilton, J., Powe, B., Pollard, A. B., Lee, K., & Felton, A. M. (2007). Spirituality among African American cancer survivors: Having a personal relationship with God. *Cancer Nursing, 30,* 309–316.

Hammelman, T. L. (1993). Gay and lesbian youth: Contributing factors to serious attempts or considerations of suicide. *Journal of Gay and Lesbian Psychotherapy, 2*(1), 77–89.

Hanna, S. M., & Brown, J. H. (1995). *The practice of family therapy: Key elements across models.* Pacific Grove, CA: Brooks/Cole.

Hardiman, R. (1982). *White identity development: A process-oriented model for describing the racial consciousness of White Americans.* Unpublished doctoral dissertation, University of Massachusetts, Amherst.

Hardiman, R. (2001). Reflections on White identity development theory. In C. Wijeyesinghe & B. Jackson III (Eds.), *New perspectives on racial identity development: A theoretical and practical anthology* (pp. 108–128). New York: New York University Press.

Hare-Mustin, R. T. (1988). Family change and gender differences: Implications for theory and practice. *Family Relations, 37,* 36–41.

Harper, F. E. (1854). The slave auction. National Endowment for the Arts & Poetry Foundation. Retrieved January 17, 2008, from www.poetryoutloud.org/poems

Harris, D. R., & Sims, J. J. (2002). Who is multiracial? Assessing the complexity of lived race. *American Sociological Review, 67,* 614–627.

Harris, K. (1995). Collected quotes from Albert Einstein. Retrieved September 1, 2007, from http://rescomp.stanford.edu/~cheshire/EinsteinQuotes. html

Harrison, P. M., & Beck, A. J. (2005). Prisoners in 2004. *Bureau of Justice Statistics Bulletin.* Washington, DC: U. S. Department of Justice, Office of Justice Programs.

Harrison, P. M., & Beck, A. J. (2006, November). Prisoners in 2005. *Bureau of Justice Statistics Bulletin.* Washington, DC: U.S. Department of Justice, Office of Justice Programs.

Hartung, P. J. (1996). Transforming counseling courses: From monocultural to multicultural. *Counseling Education and Supervision, 36*(1), 6–13.

Harvey, R. D., LaBeach, N., Pridgen, E., & Gocial, T. M. (2005). The intragroup stigmatization of skin tone among Black Americans. *Journal of Black Psychology, 31,* 237–253.

Hays, D. G., Dean, J. K., & Chang, C. Y. (2007). Addressing privilege and oppression in counselor training and practice: A qualitative analysis. *Journal of Counseling & Development, 85,* 317–324.

Hays, P. A. (1996). Addressing the complexities of culture and gender in counseling. *Journal of Counseling and Development, 74,* 332–338.

Healey, J. F. (1997). *Race, ethnicity, and gender in the United States: Inequality, group conflict, and power.* Thousand Oaks, CA: Pine Forge Press.

Heinrich, R. K., Corbine, J. L., & Thomas, K. R. (1990). Counseling Native Americans. *Journal of Counseling and Development, 69,* 128–133.

Helms, J. E. (1984). Toward a theoretical explanation of the effects of race on counseling: A Black and White model. *Counseling Psychologist, 12*(3), 153–165.

Helms, J. E. (1990). *Black and White racial identity: Theory, research, and practice.* New York: Greenwood Press.

Helms, J. E. (1995). An update of white and people of color racial identity model. In J. G. Ponterotto, J. M. Casa, L. A. Suzuki, & C. M. Alexander (Eds.), *Handbook of multicultural counseling* (pp. 181–198). Thousand Oaks, CA: Sage.

Helms, J. E. (2003). A pragmatic view of social justice. *The Counseling Psychologist, 31,* 305–313.

Helms, J. E. (2007). Some better practices for measuring ethnic and racial identity constructs. *Journal of Counseling Psychology, 54,* 235–246.

Helms, J. E., & Parham, T. A. (1984). *Racial Identity Attitude Scale.* Unpublished manuscript.

Herman, M. (2004). Forced to choose: Some determinants of racial identification in multiracial adolescents. *Child Development, 75,* 740–748.

Hermann, M. A., & Herlighy, B. R. (2006). Legal and ethical implications of refusing to counsel homosexual clients. *Journal of Counseling & Development, 84,* 414–418.

Hernandez, B. (2005). A voice in the chorus: perspectives of young men of color on their disabilities, identities, and peer-mentors. *Disability & Society, 20,* 117–133.

Hernandez, M. (1996). Central American families. In M. McGoldrick, J. Giordano, & J. Pearce (Eds.), *Ethnicity and family therapy* (pp. 214–224). New York: Guilford Press.

Herring, R. D. (1992). Understanding Native American values: Process and content concerns for counselors. *Counseling and Values, 34,* 134–137.

Herrnstein, R. J., & Murray, C. (1994). *The bell curve: Intelligence and class structure in American life.* New York: Free Press.

Hill, V. R., Weglicki, L. S., Thomas, T., & Hammad, A. (2006). Predicators of Arab American adolescent tobacco use. *Merrill-Palmer Quarterly.*

Hines, P. M., & Boyd-Franklin, N. (1996). African American families. In M. McGoldrick, J. Giordano, & J. K. Pearce (Eds.), *Ethnicity and family therapy* (pp. 66–84). New York: Guilford Press.

Hochschild, A. R. (2003). *The second shift.* New York: Penguin Books.

Hoffman, M. A., Phillips, E. L., Noumair, D. A., Shullman, S., Geishler, C., Gray, J., et al. (2005). Toward a feminist and multicultural model of consultation and advocacy. *Journal of Multicultural Counseling & Development, 34,* 116–128.

Hoffman, R. M. (2001). The measurement of masculinity and femininity: Historical perspective and implications for counseling. *Journal of Counseling & Development, 79,* 472–485.

Hoffman, R. M. (2004). Conceptualizing heterosexual identity development: Issues and challenges. *Journal of Counseling & Development, 82,* 375–380.

Holcomb-McCoy, C. C. (2000). Multicultural counseling competencies: An exploratory factor analysis. *Journal of Multicultural Counseling and Development, 28,* 83–97.

Hong, G. L., & Domokos-Cheng Ham, M. (2001). *Psychotherapy and counseling with Asian American clients: A practical guide.* Thousand Oaks, CA: Sage.

hooks, b. (1993). *Sisters of the yam: Black women and self-recovery.* Boston: South End Press.

Hoopes, D. S. (1979). Intercultural communication concepts: Psychology of intercultural experience. In M. D. Psych (Ed.), *Multicultural education: A cross-cultural training approach.* LaGrange Park, IL: Intercultural Network.

Horse, P. G. (2001). Reflections on American Indian identity. In C. Wijeyesinghe & B. Jackson III (Eds.), *New perspectives on racial identity development: A theoretical and practical anthology* (pp. 91–197). New York: New York University Press.

Horst, E. A. (1995). Reexamining gender issues in Erikson's stages of identity. *Journal of Counseling and Development, 73,* 271–278.

Hoxie, F. E. (Ed.). (1996). *Encyclopedia of North American Indians: Native American history, culture, and life from paleo-Indians to the present.* Boston: Houghton Mifflin.

Hsu, F. L. K. (1953). *American and Chinese: Two ways of life.* New York: Abeland-Schuman.

Hughes, E. C. (1945). Dilemmas and contradictions of status. *American Journal of Sociology, 50,* 353–357.

Hunt, B. (1993). What counselors need to know about counseling gay men and lesbians. *Counseling and Human Development, 26*(1), 1–12.

Hunt, B., Matthews, C., Milsom, A., & Lammel, J. A. (2006). Lesbians with physical disabilities: A qualitative study of their experiences with counseling. *Journal of Counseling & Development, 84,* 163–173.

Hutchinson, M. G. (1982). Transforming body image: Your body—friend or foe? In *Current feminist issues in psychotherapy* (pp. 59–67). New York: Haworth Press.

Icard, L. (1986). Black gay men and conflicting social identities: Sexual orientation versus racial identity. In J. Gripton & M. Valentich (Eds.), Social work practice in sexual problems [Special issue]. *Journal of Social Work and Human Sexuality, 4*(1–2), 83–93.

Ingersoll, R. E. (1995). Spirituality, religion, and counseling: Dimensions and relationship. In M. Burke & J. Mirant (Eds.), *Counseling: The spiritual dimension* (pp. 5–18). Thousand Oaks, CA: Sage.

Ingrassia, M. (1993, August 30). Endangered family. *Newsweek,* pp. 17–29.

Institute of Medicine (Ed.). (2003). *Unequal treatment: Confronting racial and ethnic disparities in healthcare.* Washington, DC: National Academies Press.

Ivey, A. E., & Collins, N. M. (2003). Social justice: A long-term challenge for Counseling Psychology. *The Counseling Psychologist, 31,* 290–298.

Ivey, A. E., Ivey, M. B., & Simek-Morgan, L. (1997). *Counseling and psychotherapy: A multicultural perspective* (4th ed.). Boston: Allyn & Bacon.

Jackson, A. (1908). Second annual message. In J. D. Richardson (Ed.), *A compilation of the messages and papers of the presidents 1789–1902,* Volume II. Retrieved January 10, 2003, from http://www.pbs.org/wgbh/aia/part4/4h3437t.html

Jackson, L. A., Sullivan, L. A., & Rostker, R. (1988). Gender, gender role, and body image. *Sex Roles, 19,* 429–443.

Jackson, V. (2005). Robbing Peter to pay Paul: Reflections on feminist therapy with low-wage earning women. In M. Mirkin, J. Suyemoto, & B. Okun (Eds.), *Psychotherapy with women: Exploring diverse contexts and identities* (pp. 237–246). New York: Guilford Press.

Joe, J. R. (2003). The rationing of healthcare and health disparity for the American Indians/Alaskan Natives. In Institute of Medicine (Ed.), *Unequal treatment: Confronting racial and ethnic disparities in healthcare.* Washington, DC: National Academies Press.

John, R. (1988). The Native American family. In C. H. Mindel, R. W. Habenstein, & R. Wright (Eds.), *Ethnic families in America: Patterns and variations* (3rd ed., pp. 325–366). New York: Elsevier.

Jones, H. L., Cross, W. E., & DeFour, D. C. (2007). Race-related stress, racial identity attitudes, and mental health among Black women. *Journal of Black Psychology, 33,* 208–231.

Jones, J. (1985). *Labor of love, labor of sorrow.* New York: Vintage Books.

Jones, N. A. (2005). We the people of more than one race in the United States. *Census 2000 special reports*. Washington, DC: U.S. Department of Commerce, U.S. Census Bureau.

Jones, N. A., & Symens Smith, A. (2001). The two or more races population: 2000. *Census 2000 brief*. U.S. Department of Commerce. Washington, DC: U.S. Department of Commerce, U.S. Census Bureau.

Jordan, J. (1997). Relational development: Therapeutic implications of empathy and shame. In J. Jordan (Ed.), *Women's growth in diversity: More writings from the Stone Center* (pp. 136–161). New York: Guilford Press.

Jordan, J. (1997a). A relational perspective for understanding women's development. In J. Jordan (Ed.), *Women's growth in diversity: More writings from the Stone Center* (pp. 9–24). New York: Guilford Press.

Jordan, J. (1997b). Clarity in connection, empathic knowing, desire, and sexuality. In J. Jordan (Ed.), *Women's growth in diversity: More writings from the Stone Center* (pp. 50–73). New York: Guilford Press.

Jordan, J., & Romney, P. (2005). Women in the workplace: An application of relational-cultural theory. In M. Mirkin, J. Suyemoto, & B. Okun (Eds.), *Psychotherapy with women: Exploring diverse contexts and identities* (pp. 198–214). New York: Guilford Press.

Jourdan, A. (2006). The impact of the family environment on the ethnic identity development of multiethnic college students. *Journal of Counseling & Development, 84,* 328–340.

Kagitcibasi, C. (1997). Individualism and collectivism. In J. Berry, M. Segall, & C. Kagitcibasi (Eds.), *Cross-cultural psychology: Social and behavioral applications* (Vol. 3, pp. 1–49). Boston: Allyn & Bacon.

Kaplan, A. G. (1987). Reflections on gender and psychotherapy. In M. Braude (Ed.), *Women and therapy* (Vol. 6, pp. 11–24). New York: Haworth Press.

Karenga, M. (1980). *Kawaida theory*. Los Angeles: Kawaida.

Kashubeck, S., Walsh, B., & Crowl, A. (1994). College atmosphere and eating disorders. *Journal of Counseling and Development, 72,* 640–645.

Kegan, R. (1982). *The evolving self*. Cambridge, MA: Harvard University Press.

Kenway, J. (1988). *High-status private schooling in Australia and the production of an educational hegemony*. Unpublished doctoral dissertation, Murdoch University, Western Australia.

Kerwin, C., Ponterotto, J. G., Jackson, B. L., & Harris, A. (1993). Racial identity in biracial children: A qualitative investigation. *Journal of Counseling Psychology, 40,* 221–231.

Kich, G. K. (1992). The developmental process of asserting a biracial, bicultural identity. In M. P. P. Root (Ed.), *Racially mixed people in America* (pp. 304–317). Newbury Park, CA: Sage.

Kim, B. S. K., & Lyons, H. Z. (2003). Experiential activities and multicultural counseling competence training. *Journal of Counseling & Development, 81,* 400–408.

Kim, B. S. K., Li, L. C., & Liang, C. T. H. (2002). Effects of Asian American client adherence to Asian cultural values, session goal, and counselor emphasis of client expression on career counseling process. *Journal of Counseling Psychology, 49,* 342–354.

Kim, J. (2001). Asian American identity development theory. In C. Wijeyesinghe & B. Jackson III (Eds.), *New perspectives on racial identity development: A theoretical and practical anthology* (pp. 67–90). New York: New York University Press.

Kimmel, M. S. (2006). Masculinity as homophobia: Fear, shame, and silence in the construction of gender identity. In T. E. Orr (Ed.), *The social construction of difference and inequality: Race, class, gender, and sexuality* (pp. 133–150). Boston: McGraw-Hill.

King, N. (1988). Teaching about lesbians and gays in the psychology curriculum. In P. A. Bronstein & K. Quina (Eds.), *Teaching a psychology of people: Resources for gender and sociocultural awareness* (pp. 168–174). Washington, DC: American Psychological Association.

Kitano, H. H. L. (1988). The Japanese American family. In C. H. Mindel, R. W. Habenstein, & R. Wright (Eds.), *Ethnic families in America: Patterns and variations* (3rd ed., pp. 258–275). New York: Elsevier.

Kitzinger, C. (1999). Intersexuality: Deconstructing the sex/gender binary. *Feminism & Psychology* (pp. 493–498). New York: Guilford Press.

Kliman, J. (2005). Many differences, many voices: Toward social justice in family therapy. In M. Pravder, K. Suyemoto, & B. Okun (Eds.), *Psychotherapy with women: Exploring diverse contexts and identities* (pp. 42–63). New York: Guilford Press.

Kluckhohn, F. R., & Strodtbeck, F. L. (1961). *Variations in value orientations.* Evanston, IL: Row, Peterson.

Kocarek, C. E., Talbot, D. M., Batka, J. C., & Anderson, M. A. (2001). Reliability and validity of three measures of multicultural competence. *Journal of Counseling & Development, 79,* 486–496.

Kochhar, R. (2007). 1995–2005: Foreign-born Latinos make progress on wages. Washington, DC: Pew Hispanic Center.

Kogan, M. (2000, July/August). Course exposes hidden racial prejudices: Students confront their hidden biases to better prepare for psychology practice. *Monitor on Psychology, 31*(7). Retrieved September 1, 2007, from http://www.apa.org/monitor/julaug00/prejudice.html

Kreider, R. (2003). Adopted children and stepchildren 2000. *Census 2000 special reports.* Washington, DC: U.S. Department of Commerce, Economics and Statistics Administration. Retrieved October 20, 2007, from www.census.gov/prod/2003pubs/censr-6.pdf

Ladany, N., Brittan-Powell, C. S., & Pannu, R. K. (1997). The influence of supervisory racial identity interaction and racial matching on the Supervisory Working Alliance and Supervisee Multicultural Competence. *Counselor Education and Supervision, 36,* 284–304.

Laird, J. (2003). Lesbian and gay families. In F. Walsh (Ed.), *Normal family processes* (pp. 176–209). New York: Guilford Press.

Lakoff, R. T., & Scherr, R. L. (1984). *Face value: Politics of beauty.* Boston: Routledge, Kegan, & Paul.

Lamb, M. E. (1982). Parental behavior and child development in nontraditional families. In M. E. Lamb (Ed.), *Nontraditional families: Parenting and child development.* Hillsdale, NJ: Erlbaum.

Lane, J. M., & Addis, M. E. (2005). Male gender role conflict and patterns of help seeking in Costa Rica and the United States. *Psychology of Men & Masculinity, 6,* 155–168.

Lao Tsu. (1972). *Tao Te Ching* (G. F. Feng & J. English, Trans.). New York: Vintage.

Lareau, A. (1997). Social-class differences in family-school relationships: The importance of cultural capital. In A. Halsey, H. Lauder, P. Brown, & A. Wells (Eds.), *Education: Culture, economy, society* (pp. 703–717). Oxford, UK: Oxford University Press.

LaVeist, T. A. (2002). Why we should study race, ethnicity, and health. In T. A. LaVeist (Ed.), *Race,* *ethnicity, health: A public health reader* (pp. 1–7). San Francisco: Jossey-Bass.

Le, C. N. (2007). Interracial dating & marriage. *Asian-Nation: The landscape of Asian America.* Retrieved October 21, 2007, from http://www.asian-nation.org/interracial.shtml

Le, C. N. (2008). Adopted Asian Americans. *Asian-Nation: The landscape of Asian America.* Retrieved January 27, 2008, from http://www.asian-nation.org/adopted/shtml

Leach, M. M., Behrens, J. T., & LaFleur, N. K. (2002). White racial identity and white racial consciousness: Similarities, differences, and recommendations. *Journal of Multicultural Counseling and Development, 30,* 66–80.

Lee, C. (2001). Defining and responding to racial and ethnic diversity. In D. Locke, J. Myers, & E. Herr (Eds.), *Handbook of counseling* (pp. 581–588). Thousand Oaks, CA: Sage.

Lee, R. M. (2003). Do ethnic identity and other-group orientation protect against discrimination for Asian Americans? *Journal of Counseling Psychology, 50,* 131–141.

Lemkau, J. P., & Landau, C. (1986). The "selfless syndrome": Assessment and treatment considerations. *Psychotherapy, 23,* 227–233.

Leong, F. T. L., Wagner, N. S., & Kim, H. H. (1995). Group counseling expectations among Asian American students: The role of culture-specific factors. *Journal of Counseling Psychology, 42,* 217–222.

Lerner, R. M., & Lerner, J. L. (1977). Effects of age, sex, and physical attractiveness on child-peer relations, academic performance, and elementary school adjustment. *Developmental Psychology, 13,* 585–590.

Lesiak, C., & Jones, M. (1991). *In the White man's image* (The American Experience Series), Public Broadcasting Source.

Lester, R., & Petrie, T. A. (1998). Prevalence of disordered eating behaviors and bulimia nervosa in a sample of Mexican American female college students. *Journal of Multicultural Counseling and Development, 26,* 157–165.

Levitt, H., Butler, M., & Travis, H. (2006). What clients find helpful in psychotherapy: Developing priniciples for facilitating moment-to-moment change. *Journal of Counseling Psychology, 53,* 314–324.

Lin, J. C. H. (1994). How long do Chinese Americans stay in psychotherapy? *Journal of Counseling Psychology, 41,* 288–291.

Lipsitz, G. (2005). The possessive investment in Whiteness: Racialized social democracy and the "White problem in American studies." In T. Ore (Ed), *The social construction of difference and inequality: Race, class, gender and sexuality* (pp. 402–413). Boston: McGraw-Hill.

Liu, W. M., & Arguello, J. L. (2006). Using social class and classism in counseling. *Counseling and Human Development, 39,* 1–9.

Liu, W. M., Saba, R. A., Soleck, G., Hopps, J., Dunston, K., & Pickett, T. (2004). Using social class in counseling psychology research. *Journal of Counseling Psychology, 51,* 3–18.

Livneh, H., & Sherwood, A. (1991). Application of personality theories and counseling strategies to clients with physical disabilities. *Journal of Counseling and Development, 69,* 525–538.

Loewen J. W. (1995). *Lies my teacher told me: Everything your American history textbook got wrong.* New York: Simon & Schuster.

Loiacano, D. K. (1989). Gay identity issues among Black Americans: Racism, homophobia, and the need for validation. *Journal of Counseling and Development, 68,* 21–25.

Lorde, A. (1994). Living with cancer. In E. C. White (Ed.), *The Black women's health book: Speaking for ourselves* (pp. 27–37). Seattle, WA: Seal.

Lott, B. (1994). *Women's lives: Themes and variations in gender learning* (2nd ed.). Pacific Grove, CA: Brooks/Cole.

Maffly-Kipp, L. (2000). *African-American religion in the nineteenth century.* University of North Carolina at Chapel Hill. Retrieved January 15, 2004, from http://www.nhc.rtp.nc.us/tserve/nineteen/nkeyinfo/nafrican.htm

Mahalik, J. R., Lagan, H. D., & Morrison, J. A. (2006). Health behaviors and masculinity in Kenyan and U.S. male college students. *Psychology of Men & Masculinity, 7,* 191–202.

Marini, I. (2001). Cross-cultural counseling issues of males who sustain a disability. *Journal of Applied Rehabilitation Counseling, 32,* 36–44.

Martin, M. K., & Voorhies, B. (1975). *Female of the species.* New York: Columbia University Press.

Mass, A. I. (1992). Interracial Japanese Americans: The best of both worlds or the end of the Japanese American community. In M. P. P. Root (Ed.), *Racially mixed people in America* (pp. 265–279). Newbury Park, CA: Sage.

Mastria, M. R. (2002). Ethnicity and eating disorders. *Psychoanalysis and Psychotherapy, 19*(1), 59–77.

McBride, M. (1990). Autonomy and the struggle for female identity: Implications for counseling women. *Journal of Counseling and Development, 69,* 22–26.

McCarthy, J. (2005). Individualism and collectivism: What do they have to do with counseling? *Journal of Multicultural Counseling and Development, 33,* 108–117.

McCarthy, J., & Holliday, E. L. (2004). Help-seeking and counseling within a traditional male gender role: An examination from a multicultural perspective. *Journal of Counseling & Development, 82,* 25–30.

McDonald, A. L. (1990). Living with our deepest differences. *Journal of Law and Religion, 8,* 237–239.

McFadden, J. (1993). *Transcultural counseling: Bilateral and international perspectives.* Alexandria, VA: American Counseling Association.

McIntosh, P. (1988). *White privilege and male privilege: A personal account of coming to see correspondences through work in women's studies* (Working Paper No. 189). Wellesley, MA: Wellesley College Center for Research on Women.

McIntosh, P. (1989, July/August). White privilege: Unpacking the invisible knapsack. *Peace and Freedom,* pp. 10–12.

McIntosh, P. (1990). *Interactive phases of curricular and personal revision with regard to race* (Working Paper No. 219). Wellesley, MA: Wellesley College Center for Research on Women.

McKelley, R. A., & Rochlen, A. B. (2007). The practice of coaching: Exploring alternatives to therapy for counseling-resistant men. *Psychology of Men & Masculinity, 8*(1), 53–65.

McLoyd, V. C., & Wilson, L. (1992). Telling them like it is: The role of economic and environmental factors in single mothers' discussions with their children. *American Journal of Community Psychology, 20,* 419–444.

McWhirter, E. H. (1991). Empowerment in counseling. *Journal of Counseling and Development, 69,* 222–227.

Mencher, J. (1997). Structural possibilities and constraints of mutuality in psychotherapy. In J. Jordan (Ed.), *Women's growth in diversity: More writings from the Stone Center* (pp. 110–119). New York: Guilford Press.

Mercado, M. M. (2000). The invisible family: Counseling Asian American substance abusers and their families. *The Family Journal: Counseling and Therapy for Couples and Families, 8,* 267–272.

Middle East Institute (2004). Retrieved September 10, 2007, from www.mideast.org

Miller, W. R., & Thorensen, C. E. (2003). Spirituality, religion, and health: An emerging research field. *American Psychologist, 58*(1), 24–35.

Min, P. G. (1988). The Korean American family. In C. H. Mindel, R. W. Habenstein, & R. Wright (Eds.), *Ethnic families in America: Patterns and variations* (3rd ed., pp. 199–229). New York: Elsevier.

Mindel, C. H., Habenstein, R. W., & Wright, R. (1988). *Ethnic families in America: Patterns and variations.* New York: Elsevier.

Mintz, L. B., & O'Neil, J. M. (1990). Gender roles, sex, and the process of psychotherapy: Many questions and few answers. *Journal of Counseling and Development, 68,* 381–387.

Minuchin, S. (1974). *Families and family therapy.* Cambridge, MA: Harvard University Press.

Minuchin, S. (1984). *Family kaleidoscope.* Cambridge, MA: Harvard University Press.

Minuchin, S. (1991). The seductions of constructivism. *The Family Networker 15*(5), 47–50.

Mio, J. S. (2005). Academic mental health training settings and the multicultural guidelines. In M. Constantine & D. Sue (Eds.), *Strategies for building multicultural competence in mental health and educational settings* (pp. 129–144). Hoboken, NJ: John Wiley & Sons.

Mishkind, M. E., Rodin, J., Silbersein, L. R., & Striegel-Moore, R. H. (1987). The embodiment of masculinity: Cultural, psychological, and behavioral dimensions. In M. S. Kimmel (Ed.), *Changing men: New directions in research on men and masculinity* (pp. 37–52). Newbury Park, CA: Sage.

Miville, M. L., Constantine, M. G., Baysden, M. F., & So-Lloyd, G. (2005). Chameleon changes: An exploration of racial identity themes of multiracial people. *Journal of Counseling Psychology, 52,* 507–516.

Mohr, J. J. (2002). Heterosexual identity and the heterosexual therapist: An identity perspective on sexual orientation. *The Counseling Psychologist, 30,* 532–566.

Moir, A., & Jessel, D. (1991). *Brain sex: The real difference between men and women.* New York: Delta.

Moradi, B., & Hasan, N. T. (2004). Arab Americans persons' reported experiences of discrimination and mental health: The mediating role of personal control. *Journal of Counseling Psychology, 51,* 418–428.

Moradi, B., van den Berg, J., & Epting, F. R. (2006). Intrapersonal and interpersonal manifestation of antilesbian and gay prejudice: An application of personal construct theory. *Journal of Counseling Psychology, 53,* 57–66.

Mullins, E., & Sites, P. (1984). Famous Black Americans: A three-generational analysis of social origins. *American Sociological Review, 49,* 672.

Murphy, B. C., & Dillon, C. (2008). *Interviewing in action in a multicultural world.* Belmont, CA: Thomson. Brooks Cole.

Myers, J. E., Sweeney, T. J., & Witmer, J. M. (2001). Optimization of behavior: Promotion of wellness. In D. Locke, J. Myers, & E. Herr (Eds), *The handbook of counseling* (pp. 641–652). Thousand Oaks, CA: Sage Publicatiions.

Myers, L. J. (1991). Expanding the psychology of knowledge optimally: The importance of world view revisited. In R. Jones (Ed.), *Black psychology* (3rd ed., pp. 15–28). Berkeley, CA: Cobb and Henry.

Myers, L. J., Speight, S. L., Highlen, P. S., Cox, C. I., Reynolds, A. L., Adams, E. M., et al. (1991). Identity development and worldview: Toward an optimal conceptualization. *Journal of Counseling and Development, 70,* 54–63.

Napholz, L. (1994). Sex role orientation and psychological well-being among working Black women. *Journal of Black Psychology, 20,* 469–482.

Nassar-McMillan, S. C., & Hakim-Larson, J. (2003). Counseling consideration among Arab Americans. *Journal of Counseling & Development, 81,* 150–159.

Neal, A. M., & Wilson, M. I. (1989). The role of skin color and features in the Black community: Implications for Black women and therapy. *Clinical Psychology Review, 9,* 323–333.

Nelson, H. L. (1997). *Feminism and families.* New York: Routledge.

Nelson, M. C. (1996). Separation versus connection: The gender controversy. *Implications for Counseling Women, 74,* 339–344.

Neville, H., Spanierman, L., & Doan, B. (2006). Exploring the association between color-blind racial ideology and multicultural counseling competencies. *Cultural Diversity and Ethnic Minority Psychology, 12,* 275–290.

Newman, D. M. (2007). *Identities and inequalities: Exploring the intersections of race, class, gender, and sexuality.* Boston: McGraw-Hill.

Newman, J. L., Fuqua, D. R., Gray, E. A., & Simpson, D. B. (2006). Gender differences in the relationship of anger and depression in a clinical sample. *Journal of Counseling & Development, 84,* 157–162.

Newman, K. S. (1999). *No shame in my game: The working poor in the inner city.* New York: Vintage Books and Russell Sage Foundation.

Nhat Hanh, T. (1998). *The heart of the Buddha's teaching.* Berkeley, CA: Parallax Press.

Nicholson, L. (1997). The myth of the traditional family. In H. L. Nelson (Ed.), *Feminism and families* (pp. 27–42). New York: Routledge.

Nicolau, S., & Santiestevan, S. (1990). *The Hispanic almanac.* New York: Hispanic Policy Development Project.

Nisbett, R. (1995). Race, IQ, and scientism. In S. Fraser (Ed.), *The bell curve wars: Race, intelligence, and the future of America.* New York: Basic Books.

Nobles, W. (1972). African philosophy: Foundations for Black psychology. In R. H Jones (Ed.), *Black psychology.* New York: Harper & Row.

Novas, H. (1994). *Everything you need to know about Latino history.* New York: Penguin.

Nuessel, F. H. (1982). The language of ageism. *Gerontologist, 22,* 273–276.

Nugent, H. (2007). Race row Nobel scientist James Watson scraps tour after being suspended. Retrieved October 19, 2007, from www.timesonline.co.uk/tollnews/uk/article2694632.ece

O'Connor, M. F. (1992). Psychotherapy with gay and lesbian adolescents. In S. H. Dworkin & F. J. Gutierrez (Eds.), *Counseling gay men and lesbians: Journey to the end of the rainbow* (pp. 3–22). Alexandria, VA: American Association for Counseling and Development.

Obermeyer, C. M. (2006). HIV in the Middle East. *British Medical Journal, 333,* 851–854.

Ogbu, J. U. (1997). Racial stratification and education in the United States: Why inequality persists. In A. Halsey, H. Lauder, P. Brown, & A. Wells (Eds.), *Education: Culture, economy, society* (pp. 765–778). Oxford, UK: Oxford University Press.

Okazawa-Rey, M., Robinson, T. L., & Ward, J. V. (1987). Black women and the politics of skin color and hair. *Women and Therapy, 6,* 89–102.

Olkin, R. (2004). Making research accessible for people with disabilities. *Journal of Multicultural Counseling and Development, 32,* 332–343.

Olkin, R., & Pledger, C. (2003). Can disability studies and psychology join hands? *American Psychologist, 58,* 296–298.

Olson, M. J. (2003). Counselor understanding of Native American spiritual loss. *Counseling and Values, 47,* 109–117.

Omni, M., & Winant, H. (2006). Racial formations. In T. Ore (Ed.), *The social construction of difference and inequality: Race, class, gender, and sexuality* (pp. 19–29). Boston: McGraw-Hill.

Ore, T. E. (2006). Constructing differences. In T. Ore (Ed.), *The social construction of difference and inequality: Race, class, gender, and sexuality* (pp. 1–18). Boston: McGraw-Hill.

Ossana, S. M., Helms, J. E., & Leonard, M. M. (1992). Do "womanist" identity attitudes influence college women's self-esteem and perceptions of environmental bias? *Journal of Counseling and Development, 70,* 402–408.

Pace, C. (1991). *A description of factors affecting attitudes held by mental health professionals and students toward lesbians and gays.* Unpublished master's thesis, University of Florida, Gainesville.

Padilla, A. M. (1984). Synopsis of the history of Chicano psychology. In J. Martinez & R. Mendoza (Eds.), *Chicano psychology* (pp. 1–19). Orlando, FL: Academic Press.

Palmer, P. J. (1999). A vision of education as transformation. In S. Glazer (Ed.), *The heart of learning: Spirituality in education* (pp. 15–32). New York: Putnam.

Parham, T. (Presenter), (1992). *Counseling African Americans* [Video]. Amherst, MA: Microtraining and Multicultural Development.

Parker, M. S. (1985). Identity and the development of religious thinking. In A. S. Waterman (Ed.), *Identity in adolescence* (pp. 43–60). San Francisco: Jossey-Bass.

Parker, W. M., & Schwartz, R. C. (2002). On the experience of shame in multicultural counseling: Implications for White counselors-in-training. *British Journal of Guidance and Counseling, 30,* 311–318.

Paxton, S. J., Wertheim, E. H., Gibbons, K., Szmukler, G. I., Hillier, L., & Petrovich, J. L. (1991). Body image satisfaction, dieting beliefs, and weight-loss behaviors in adolescent girls and boys. *Journal of Youth and Adolescence, 20,* 361–379.

Pedersen, P. (1990). The constructs of complexity and balance in multicultural counseling theory and practice. *Journal of Counseling and Development, 15,* 16–24.

Pedersen, P. B. (1997). The cultural context of the American Counseling Association code of ethics. *Journal of Counseling and Development, 76,* 23–28.

Peregoy, J. J. (1993). Transcultural counseling with American Indians and Alaskan Natives: Contemporary issues for consideration. In J. McFadden (Ed.), *Transcultural counseling: Bilateral and international perspectives* (pp. 163–191). Alexandria, VA: American Counseling Association.

Peterman, L. M., & Dixon, C. G. (2003). Domestic violence between same sex partners: Implication for counseling. *Journal of Counseling & Development, 81,* 40–47.

Phan, T., & Tylka, T. L. (2006). Exploring a model and moderators of disordered eating with Asian American college women. *Journal of Counseling Psychology, 53,* 36–47.

Pharr, S. (1988). *Homophobia: A weapon of sexism.* Little Rock, AR: Chardon.

Phillips, A., & Daniluk, J. C. (2004). Beyond "survivor": How childhood sexual abuse informs the identity of adult women at the end of the therapeutic process. *Journal of Counseling & Development, 82,* 177–184.

Phillips, M. A., & Murrell, S. A. (1994). Impact of psychological and physical health, stressful events, and social support on subsequent mental health help seeking among older adults. *Journal of Consulting and Clinical Psychology, 62,* 270–275.

Phinney, J. (1989). Stages of ethnic identity development in minority group adolescents. *Journal of Early Adolescence, 9,* 34–49.

Phinney, J. (1992). The Multi-group Ethnic Identity Measure: A new scale for use with adolescents and young adults from diverse groups. *Journal of Adolescent Research, 7,* 156–176.

Phinney, J. S. (1990). Ethnic identity in adolescents and adults: Review of research. *Psychological Bulletin, 198,* 499–514.

Phinney, J. S. (1997). Ethnic and American identity as predictors of self-esteem among African American, Latino, and White adolescents. *Journal of Youth and Adolescence, 26,* 165–185.

Phinney, J. S., & Flores, J. (2002). "Unpackaging" acculturation: Aspects of acculturation as predictors of traditional sex role attitudes. *Journal of Cross-Cultural Psychology, 33,* 320–331.

Phinney, J., & Rosenthal, P. A. (1993). Ethnic identity in adolescence: Process, context, and outcome. In F. Adams, R. Montemayor, & T. Oulotta (Eds.), *Advances in adolescent development* (Vol. 4, pp. 145–172). Newbury Park, CA: Sage.

Phornphutkul, C., Fausto-Sterling, A., & Gruppuso, P. A. (2000). Gender self-reassignment in an XY adolescent female born with ambiguous genitalia. *Pediatrics, 106,* 135–137.

Pieterse, A. L., & Carter, R. T. (2007). An examination of the relationship between general life stress, racism-related stress, and psychological health among Black men. *Journal of Counseling Psychology, 54,* 101–109.

Pinderhughes, E. (1989). *Understanding race, ethnicity, and power: The key to efficacy in clinical practice.* New York: Free Press.

Pinderhughes, E. (1995). Empowering diverse populations: Family practice in the 21st century. *Families in Society: The Journal of Contemporary Human Services,* CEU Article No. 50, 131–140.

Pleck, J. H. (1984). Men's power with women, other men, and society: A men's movement analysis. In P. P. Ricker & E. H. Carmen (Eds.), *The gender gap in psychotherapy: Social realities and psychological processes* (pp. 79–89). New York: Plenum Press.

Pledger, C. (2003). Discourse on disability and rehabilitation issues. *American Psychologist, 58,* 279–284.

Ponterotto, J. G., Alexander, C. M., & Grieger, I. (1995). A multicultural competency checklist for counseling training programs. *Journal of Multicultural Counseling and Development, 23,* 11–20.

Ponterotto, J. G., & Casas, J. M. (1991). *Handbook of racial/ethnic minority counseling research.* Springfield, IL: Charles C. Thomas.

Ponzo, Z. (1985). The counselor and physical attractiveness. *Journal of Counseling and Development, 63,* 482–485.

Pope, M. (1995). The "salad bowl" is big enough for us all: An argument for the inclusion of lesbians and gay men in any definition of multiculturalism. *Journal of Counseling and Development, 73,* 301–304.

Pope-Davis, D. B., Liu, W. M., Toporek, R., & Brittan-Powell, C. S. (2001). What's missing from multicultural competency research: Review, introspection, and recommendations? *Cultural Diversity and Ethnic Minority Psychology, 7,* 121–138.

Pope-Davis, D. B., & Ottavi, T. M. (1994). The relationship between racism and racial identity among White Americans: A replication and extension. *Journal of Counseling and Development, 72,* 293–297.

Portman, T. A. A., & Garrett, M. L. (2005). Beloved women: Nurturing the sacred fire of leadership from an American Indian perspective. *Journal of Counseling & Development, 83,* 284–291.

Portman, T. A. A., & Herring, R. D. (2001). Debunking the Pocahontas paradox: The need for a humanistic perspective. *Journal of Humanistic Counseling, Education, and Development, 40,* 185–199.

Poston, W. S. C. (1990). The biracial identity development model: A needed addition. *Journal of Counseling and Development, 69,* 152–155.

Powell, L. H., Shahabi, L., & Thoresen, C. E. (2003). Religion and spirituality: Linkages to physical health. *American Psychologist, 58*(1), 36–52.

Race and the human genome: Researchers definitely trump the notion of race with DNA research. (2004). Retrieved January 30, 2004, from http://racerelations.about.com/library/weekly/aa021501a.htm

Rampage, C., Eovaldi, M., Ma, C., & Weigel-Foy, C. (2003). Adoptive families. In F. Walsh (Ed.), *Normal family processes: Growing diversity and complexity* (pp. 210–232). New York: Guilford Press.

Rankin, S. (2002). *Campus climate for gay, lesbian, bisexual, and transgender people: A national perspective.* New York: The Policy Institute of the National Gay and Lesbian Task Force. Retrieved August 3, 2003, from http://www.ngltf.org/downloads/CampusClimate.pdf

Rayle, A. D., Chee, C., & Sand, J. K. (2006). Honoring their way: Counseling American Indian women. *Journal of Multicultural Counseling and Development, 34,* 66–79.

Rendon, L. I., & Robinson, T. L. (1994). A diverse America: Implications for minority seniors. In W. Hartel, S. Schwartz, S. Blue, & J. Gardner (Eds.), *Ready for the real world: Senior year experience series* (pp. 170–188). Belmont, CA: Wadsworth.

Renzetti, C. M., & Curran, D. J. (1992). *Women, men, and society.* Boston: Allyn & Bacon.

Reynolds, A. L., & Pope, R. L. (1991). The complexities of diversity: Exploring multiple oppressions. *Journal of Counseling and Development, 70,* 174–180.

Rice, V. H., Weglicki, L. S., Thomas, T., & Hammad, A. (2006, April). Predictors of Arab American Adolescent tobacco use. *Merrill-Palmer Quarterly.*

Richardson, T. Q., & Molinaro, K. L. (1996). White counselor self-awareness: A prerequisite for developing multicultural competence. *Journal of Counseling and Development, 71,* 238–242.

Ridley, C. R. (1989). Racism in counseling as an aversive behavioral process. In P. B. Pedersen, J. G. Draguns, W. J. Lonner, & J. E. Trimble (Eds.), *Counseling across cultures* (pp. 55–78). Honolulu: University of Hawaii Press.

Riggs, M. (Producer/Director). (1994). *Black is . . . Black ain't* [Video]. San Francisco: California Newsreel.

Roberts, S. A., Kisselica, M. S., & Fredrickson, S. A. (2002). Quality of life of persons with medical illnesses: Counseling & holistic contribution. *Journal of Counseling & Development, 80,* 422–432.

Robinson, T. L. (1990). Understanding the gap between entry and exit: A cohort analysis of Black student persistence. *Journal of Negro Education, 59,* 207–218.

Robinson, T. L. (1993). The intersections of gender, class, race, and culture: On seeing clients whole. *Journal of Multicultural Counseling and Development, 21,* 50–58.

Robinson, T. L. (1999a). The intersections of dominant discourses across race, gender, and other identities. *Journal of Counseling & Development, 77,* 73–79.

Robinson, T. L. (1999b). The intersections of identity. In A. Garrod, J. V. Ward, T. L. Robinson, & B. Kilkenney (Eds.), *Souls looking back: Stories of growing up Black.* New York: Routledge.

Robinson, T. L. (2001). White mothers of non-White children. *Journal of Humanistic Counseling, Education and Development, 40,* 171–184.

Robinson, T. L., & Howard-Hamilton, M. (1994). An Afrocentric paradigm: Foundation for a healthy self-image and healthy interpersonal relationships. *Journal of Mental Health Counseling, 16,* 327–339.

Robinson, T. L., & Kennington, P. A. D. (2002). Holding up half the sky: Women and psychological resistance. *Journal of Humanistic Counseling, Education and Development, 41,* 164–177.

Robinson, T. L., & Ward, J. V. (1991). A belief in self far greater than anyone's disbelief: Cultivating resistance among African American adolescents. *Women & Therapy, 11,* 87–103.

Robinson, T. L., & Ward, J. V. (1995). African American adolescents and skin color. *Journal of Black Psychology, 21,* 256–274.

Robinson, T. L., & Watt, S. K. (2001). Where no one goes begging: Gender, sexuality, and religious diversity. In D. Locke, J. Myers, & E. Herr

(Eds.), *Handbook of counseling* (pp. 589–599). Thousand Oaks, CA: Sage.

Robinson-Wood, T. L. (in press). Extending culture beyond race and ethnicity. In C. Lee (Ed.), *Elements of culture*. Boston: Allyn & Bacon.

Robinson-Wood, T. L. (in press). Our whole selves: Privileging multiple converging identities. In R. Moodley, R. Walcott, & D. Curling (Eds.), Weaving culture and spirituality into multicultural counseling. Toronto: University of Toronto Press.

Robinson-Wood, T. L., & Braithwaite-Hall, M. (2005). Spirit matters: Women, spirituality, and clinical contexts. In M. Mirkin, J. Suyemoto, & B. Okun (Eds.), *Psychotherapy with women: Exploring diverse contexts and identities* (pp. 280–296). New York: Guilford Press.

Rockquemore, K. A. (1999). Between Black and White: Understanding the "biracial" experience. *Race and Society, 2,* 197–212.

Rockquemore, K. A. (2002). Negotiating the color line: The gendered process of racial identity construction among Black/White biracial women. *Gender and Society, 16,* 485–503.

Rogers, J. A. (1967) *Sex and race*. St. Petersburg, FL: Helga Rogers.

Rogers, R. L., & Petrie, T. A. (2001). Psychological correlates of anorexic and bulimic symptomatology. *Journal of Counseling and Development, 79,* 178–187.

Root, M. P. P. (1990). Disordered eating in women of color. *Sex Roles, 22,* 525–536.

Root, M. P. P. (1992). Within, between, and beyond race. In M. P. P. Root (Ed.), *Racially mixed people in America* (pp. 3–11). Newbury Park, CA: Sage.

Root, M. P. P. (1998). Experiences and processes affecting racial identity development: Preliminary results from the biracial sibling project. *Cultural Diversity and Mental Health, 4,* 237–247.

Rosenblum, K. E., & Travis, T. C. (2005). *The meaning of difference: American constructions of race, sex, and gender, social class, and sexual orientation*. Boston: McGraw-Hill.

Rothblum, E. D. (1994). "I only read about myself on bathroom walls": The need for research on the mental health of lesbians and gay men. *Journal of Consulting and Clinical Psychology, 62,* 213–220.

Roysircar, G. (Ed.). (2003). *Multicultural counseling competencies: 2003*. Alexandria, VA: Association of Multicultural Counseling and Development.

Rudolph, J. (1990). Counselors' attitudes toward homosexuality: Selective review of the literature. *Journal of Counseling and Development, 65,* 165–168.

Ruelas, S. (2003). Objectively measures multicultural competencies: A preliminary study. In D. Pope-Davis, H. Coleman, W. Liu, & R. Toporek (Eds.), *Handbook of multicultural competencies & counseling* (pp. 283–300). Thousand Oaks, CA: Sage.

Russell, G. (1994). *A map of American Indian history*. Phoenix, AZ: Thunderbird Enterprises.

Rust, P. C. (2006). Sexual identity and bisexual identities: the struggle for self-description in a changing sexual landscape. In T. E. Orr (Ed.), *The social construction of difference and inequality: Race, class, gender, and sexuality* (pp. 169–186). Boston: McGraw-Hill.

Sadker, M., Sadker, D., & Long, L. (1993). Gender and educational equity. In J. Banks & C. McGee-Banks (Eds.), *Multicultural education* (pp. 111–128). Boston: Allyn & Bacon.

Salazar, C. F. (2006). Conceptualizing multiple identities and multiple oppressions in clients' lives. *Counseling and Human Development, 39*(1), 1–18.

Sanchez, G. J. (2002). "Y tu, que?" (YzK): Latino history in the new millennium. In M. Suarez-Orozco & M. M. Paez (Eds.), *Latinos: Remaking America* (pp. 45–58). Berkeley: University of California Press.

Sandhu, D. S. (1997). Psychocultural profiles of Asian and Pacific Islander Americans: Implications for counseling and psychotherapy. *Journal of Multicultural Counseling and Development, 25,* 7–22.

Santiago-Rivera, A. (2003). Latinos values and family transitions: Practical considerations for counseling. *Counseling and Human Development, 35,* 1–12.

Santiago-Rivera, A. L., Arredondo, P., & Gallardo-Cooper, M. (2002). *Counseling Latinos and la familia: A practical guide*. Thousand Oaks CA: Sage.

Saucier, M. G. (2004). Midlife and beyond: Issues for aging women. *Journal of Counseling & Development, 82,* 420–425.

Sawy, N. E. (2005). "Yes, I follow Islam, but I'm not a terrorist." In T. E. Ore (Ed.), *The social construction of difference and inequality: Race, class, gender, and sexuality* (pp. 570–571). Boston: McGraw-Hill.

Schliebner, C. T., & Peregoy, J. J. (1994). Unemployment effects on the family and the child: Interventions for counselors. *Journal of Counseling and Development, 72,* 368–372.

Schnitzer, P. K. (1996). "They don't come in." Stories told, lessons taught about poor families in therapy. *American Journal of Orthopsychiatry, 66,* 572–582.

Schofield, W. (1964). *Psychotherapy: The purchase of friendship.* Upper Saddle River, NJ: Prentice Hall.

Scholl, M. B. (2006). Native American identity development and counseling preferences: A study of Lumbee undergraduates. *Journal of College Counseling, 9,* 47–59.

Schulte, E. (2002). More black men in jail than college. Retrieved September 25, 2007, from http://www.socialistworker.org/2002

Schultz-Rooss, R. A., & Gutheil, T. G. (1997). Difficulties in integrating spirituality into psychotherapy practice, *Journal of Psychotherapy Practice and Research, 6,* 130–138.

Schwartz, W. (1998). The identity development of multiracial youth. *Digest,* No.137, EDO-UD-98–7. Eric Clearinghouse on Urban Education.

Scott, D. A., & Robinson, T. L. (2001). White male identity development: The key model. *Journal of Counseling & Development, 79,* 415–421.

Sharfstein, D. J. (2007). Crossing the color line: Racial migration and the one-drop rule, 1600–1860. *Minnesota Law Review, 91,* 592–656.

Shiarev, E., & Levy, D. (2004). *Cross cultural psychology: Critical thinking and contemporary applications.* Boston: Pearson.

Shih, M., Bonam, C., Sanchez, D., & Peck, C. (2007). The social construction of race: Biracial identity and vulnerability to stereotypes. *Cultural Diversity and Ethnic Minority Psychology, 13,* 125–133.

Shih, M., & Sanchez, D. T. (2005). Perspectives and research on the positive and negative implications of having multiple racial identities. *Psychological Bulletin, 131,* 569–591.

Shinn, F. S. (1989). *The wisdom of Florence Scovel Shinn.* New York: A Fireside Book.

Shore, L. I. (1995). *Tending inner gardens: The healing art of feminist therapy.* New York: Harrington Park Press.

Simon, J. P. (1996). Lebanese families. In M. McGoldrick, J. K. Pearce, & J. Giordano (Eds.), *Ethnicity and family therapy* (pp. 364–375). New York: Guilford Press.

Skovholt, T. M. (1993). Counseling and psychotherapy interventions with men. *Counseling and Human Development, 25,* 1–6.

Slater, S. (1997). Contributions of the lesbian experience to mutuality in therapy relationships. In J. Jordan (Ed.), *Women's growth in diversity: More writings from the Stone Center* (pp. 119–126). New York: Guilford Press.

Smart, J. F., & Smart, D. W. (2006). Models on disability: Implications for the counseling profession. *Journal of Counseling and Development, 84,* 29–40.

Smith, B. (1982). Toward a Black feminist criticism. In G. Hull, P. Scott, & B. Smith (Eds.), *All the women are White, all the Blacks are men, but some of us are brave* (pp. 157–175). Old Westbury, NY: Feminist Press.

Smith, L. (2005). Psychotherapy, classism, and the poor. *American Psychologist, 60,* 687–696.

Smits, S. J. (2004). Disability and employment in the U.S.A.: The quest for best practices. *Disability & Society, 19,* 647–662.

Sodowski, G. R., Wai, E. W. M., & Plake, B. (1991). Moderating effects of sociocultural variables on acculturation attitudes of Hispanics and Asian Americans. *Journal of Counseling and Development, 70,* 194–204.

Souter, A., & Murthy, R. S. (2006, October 21). *British Medical Journal, 333,* 861.

Spanierman, L. B., Poteat, V. P., Beer, A. M., & Armstrong, P. I. (2007). Psychosocial costs of racism to Whites: Exploring patterns through cluster analysis. *Journal of Counseling Psychology, 53*(3), 434–441.

Spence, J. T., & Helmreich, R. L. (1978). *Masculinity and femininity: Their psychological dimensions, correlates, and antecedents.* Austin: University of Texas Press.

Spickard, P. R. (1992). The illogic of American racial categories. In M. P. P. Root (Ed.), *Racially mixed people in America* (pp. 12–23). Newbury Park, CA: Sage.

Staples, R. (1988). The Black American family. In C. H. Mindel, R. W. Habenstein, & R. Wright (Eds.), *Ethnic families in America: Patterns and variations* (3rd ed., pp. 303–324). New York: Elsevier.

Stavans, I. (1995). *The Hispanic condition: Reflections on culture and identity in America.* New York: Harper Perennial.

Steinberg, S. (1989). *The ethnic myth: Race, ethnicity, and class in America.* Boston: Beacon Press.

Steinem, G. (1992). *Revolution from within: A book of self-esteem.* Boston: Little, Brown.

Steinmetz, E. (2006). *Americans with disabilities: 2002.* Washington, DC: U.S. Department of Commerce, U.S. Census Bureau.

Sterling, A. F. (1992). *Myths of gender.* New York: Basic Books.

Stevens, M. J., Pfost, K. S., & Potts, M. K. (1990). Sex role orientation and the willingness to confront existential issues. *Journal of Counseling and Development, 68,* 47–49.

Stewart, J. C. (1996). *1001 things everyone should know about African American history.* New York: Doubleday.

Stiver, I. P. (1997). A relational approach to therapeutic impasses. In J. Jordan (Ed.), *Women's growth in diversity* (pp. 288–310). New York: Guilford Press.

Storck, L. E. (1998). Social class divisions in the consulting room: A theory of psychosocial class and depression. *Group Analysis, 31,* 101–115.

Suarez-Orozco, M., & Paez, M. M. (2002). *Latinos: Remaking America.* Berkeley: University of California Press.

Sue, D. (Presenter). (1989). *Cultural identity development* [Video]. Amherst, MA: Microtraining and Multicultural Development.

Sue, D. W., Arredondo, P., & McDavis, R. J. (1992). Multicultural counseling competencies and standards: A call to the profession. *Journal of Counseling and Development, 70,* 477–483.

Sue, D. W., Bernier, J. E., Daran, A., Feinberg, L., Pedersen, P., Smith, C. T., & Vasquez-Nuttale, G. (1982). Cross-cultural counseling competencies. *Counseling Psychologist, 19,* 45–52.

Sue, D. W., Carter, R. T., Caas, J. M., Fouad, N. A., Ivey, A. E., Jensen, M., et al. (1998). *Multicultural counseling competencies: Individual and organizational development.* Thousand Oaks, CA: Sage.

Sue, D. W., Ivey, A. E., & Pedersen, P. B. (1996). *A theory of multicultural counseling and therapy.* Pacific Grove, CA: Brooks/Cole.

Sue, D. W., & Sue, D. (1990). *Counseling the culturally different: Theory and practice.* New York: John Wiley.

Sue, D. W., & Sue, D. (1995). Asian Americans. In N. Vaac, S. B. Devaney, & J. Witmer (Eds.), *Experiences and counseling multicultural and diverse populations* (3rd ed., pp. 63–90). Bristol, PA: Accelerated Development.

Sullivan, P. (1998). Sexual identity development: The importance of target or dominant group membership. In R. C. Sanlo (Ed.), *Working with lesbian, gay, bisexual, and transgender college students: A handbook for faculty and administrators* (pp. 3–12). Westport, CT: Greenwood Press.

Sutton, C. T., & Broken Nose, M. A. (1996). American Indian families: An overview. In M. McGoldrick, J. Giordano, & J. K. Pearce (Eds.), *Ethnicity and family therapy* (pp. 31–44). New York: Guilford Press.

Suzuki-Crumly, J., & Hyers, L. L. (2004). The relationship among ethnic identity, psychological well-being, and intergroup competence: An investigation of two biracial groups. *Cultural Diversity and Ethnic Minority Psychology, 10,* 137–150.

Swanson, B., Cronin-Stubbs, D., & Sheldon, J. A. (1989). The impact of psychosocial factors on adapting to physical disability: A review of the research literature. *Rehabilitation Nursing, 14,* 64–68.

Swanson, J. L. (1993). Sexism strikes men. *American Counselor, 1,* 10–13, 39.

Swinton, J. (2001). *Spirituality and mental health care: Rediscovering a "forgotten" dimension.* London: Jessica Kingsley Publishers.

Takaki, R. (1993). *A different mirror: A history of multicultural America.* Boston: Back Bay Books.

Takaki, R. (1994). *From different shores: Perspectives on race and ethnicity in America.* New York: Oxford University Press.

Takaki, R. (1994). The myth of the "model minority." In R. C. Monk (Ed.), *Taking sides: Clashing views on controversial issues in race and ethnicity* (pp. 55–61). Guilford, CT: Dushkin.

Tate, D. G., & Pledger, C. (2003). An integrative conceptual framework of disability, *American Psychologist, 58,* 289–295.

Tatum, B. D. (1992). Talking about race, learning about racism: The application of racial identity theory in the classroom. *Harvard Educational Review, 61*(1), 1–24.

Tatum, B. D. (1997). Racial identity development and relational theory: The case of Black women in White communities. In J. Jordan (Ed.), *Women's growth in diversity* (pp. 91–106). New York: Guilford Press.

Thomas, K. T. (2004). Old wine in a slightly cracked new bottle, *American Psychologist, 59,* 274–275.

Thomas, M. B. (2006). Navigators guide patients through the continuum: Barriers include language, finance, transportation. *Hospital Case Management, 3,* 191–194.

Thomason, T. C. (2000). Issues in the treatment of Native Americans with alcohol problems. *Journal of Multicultural Counseling and Development, 28,* 243–252.

Toporek, R. L., & Williams, R. A. (2006). Ethics and professional issues related to the practice of social justice in counseling psychology. In R. Toporek, L. Gerstein, N. Fouad, G. Roysircar, & T. Israel. (Eds.), *Handbook for social justice in counseling psychology* (pp. 17–36). Thousand Oaks, CA: Sage.

Towle, E. B., & Morgan, L. M. (2002). Romancing the transgender native: Rethinking the use of the "third gender" concept. *GLQ: A Journal of Lesbian and Gay Studies, 8,* 469–497.

Tran, T. V. (1988). The Vietnamese American family. In C. H. Mindel, R. W. Habenstein, & R. Wright (Eds.), *Ethnic families in America: Patterns and variations* (3rd ed., pp. 276–302). New York: Elsevier.

Troiden, R. R. (1989). The formation of homosexual identities, *Journal of Homosexuality, 17,* 43–73.

Trujillo, A. (2000). Psychotherapy with Native Americans: A view into the role of religion and spirituality. In P. S. Richards & A. E. Bergin (Eds.), *Handbook of psychotherapy and religious diversity.* Washington, DC: American Psychological Association.

Tsai, J. L., & Chensova-Dutton, Y. (2002). Models of cultural orientation: Differences between American-born and overseas-born Asians. In K. Kurasaki, S. Okasaki, & S. Sue (Eds.), *Asian American mental health: Assessment theories and methods* (pp. 95–106). New York: Kluwer Academic.

Tsai, M., & Uemura, A. (1988). Asian Americans: The struggles, the conflicts, and the successes. In P. Bronstein & K. Quina (Eds.), *Teaching a psychology of people* (pp. 125–133). Washington, DC: American Psychological Association.

Turner, C. W. (1997). Clinical applications of the Stone Center theoretical approach to minority women. In J. Jordan (Ed.), *Women's growth in diversity: More writings from the Stone Center* (pp. 74–90). New York: Guilford Press.

Tylka, T. L., & Subich, L. M. (2002). Exploring young women's perceptions of the effectiveness and safety of maladaptive weight control techniques. *Journal of Counseling & Development, 80,* 101–110.

Uba, L. (1994). *Asian Americans: Personality patterns, identity, and mental health.* New York: Guilford Press.

Udry, J. R., Li, R. M., & Hendrickson-Smith, K. (2003). Health and behavior risks of adolescents with mixed-race identity. *American Journal of Public Health, 93,* 1865–1870.

Umaña-Taylor, A. J. (2004). Ethnic identity and self-esteem: examining the role of social context. *Journal of Adolescence, 27,* 139–146.

U.S. Census Bureau. (2000). *America's families and living arrangements.* Washington, DC: U.S. Department of Commerce.

U.S. Census Bureau. (2000). *Population by age, sex, and race and Hispanic origin: Current population survey.* Washington, DC: U.S. Department of Commerce.

U.S. Census Bureau. (2000). *Profile of selected social characteristics: Current population survey.* Washington, DC: U.S. Department of Commerce.

U.S. Census Bureau. (2000). *The Asian population: 2000.* Washington, DC: U.S. Department of Commerce.

U.S. Census Bureau. (2000). U.S. Summary: 2000. *Census 2000 Profile.* Washington, DC: U.S. Department of Commerce.

U.S. Census Bureau. (2001). Labor force participation for mothers with infants declines for first time, Census Bureau reports. *U.S. Department of Commerce News.* Retrieved September 1, 2007, from http://www.census.gov/Press-Release/www/2001/cb01-170.html

U.S. Census Bureau. (2001). *Poverty in the United States.* Washington, DC: U.S. Department of Commerce, Annual Demographic Supplement.

U.S. Census Bureau. (2001). *The Hispanic population in the United States. March 2000.* Washington, DC: U.S. Department of Commerce, Economics and Statistical Administration.

U.S. Census Bureau. (2001). The nuclear family rebounds, Census Bureau reports. *U.S. Department of Commerce News.* Retrieved March 12, 2004, from http://www.census.gov/Press-Release/www/releases/archives/children/000326.html

U.S. Census Bureau. (2002). *Poverty in the United States.* Washington, DC: U.S. Department of Commerce.

U.S. Census Bureau. (2006). Americans with disabilities. *Household Economic Studies.* Washington, DC: U.S. Department of Commerce.

U.S. Census Bureau. (2007). FactFinder, 2006. American community survey data profile highlights. Washington, DC: U.S. Department of Commerce.

U.S. Census Bureau. (2007). The American community—American Indians and Alaska Natives: 2004. *American community survey reports.* Washington, DC: U.S. Department of Commerce.

U.S. Census Bureau. (2007). The American community—Asians: 2004. *American community survey reports*. Washington, DC: U.S. Department of Commerce.

U.S. Census Bureau. (2007). The American community—Blacks: 2004. *American community survey reports*. Washington, DC: U.S. Department of Commerce.

U.S. Census Bureau. (2007). The American community—Hispanics: 2004. *American community survey reports*. Washington, DC: U.S. Department of Commerce.

U.S. Census Bureau. (2007). The American community—Pacific Islanders: 2004. *American community survey reports*. Washington, DC: U.S. Department of Commerce.

U.S. Census Bureau News. (2005). Educational attainment. People 25 years old and over by total money earnings in 2004, work experience in 2004, age, race, Hispanic, origin. Retrieved August 1, 2007, from http://pubdb3.census.gov/macro/032005/perinc/new03_004.htm

U.S. Census Bureau News. (2007). Household income rises, poverty rate declines, number of uninsured up. Washington, DC: U.S. Department of Commerce.

U.S. Centers for Disease Control and Prevention (2004). *HIV/AIDS among Hispanics: The body*. Retrieved September 1, 2007, from www.thebody.com

U.S. Department of Health and Human Services. (2001). *Mental health: Culture, race, and ethnicity—A supplement to mental health: A report to the Surgeon General*. Rockville, MD: U.S. Department of Health and Human Services, Public Health Service.

U.S. Department of the Interior (2002). *Federal Register*. Washington, DC: Bureau of Indian Affairs.

Utsey, S., Walker, R. L., & Kwate, N. A. (2005). Conducting quantitative research in a cultural context: Practical applications for research with ethnic minority populations. In M. Constantine & D. Sue (Eds.) *Strategies for building multicultural competence in mental health and educational settings* (pp. 247–268). Hoboken, NJ: John Wiley & Sons.

VanBoven, A. M., & Espelage, D. L. (2006). Depressive symptoms, coping strategies, and disordered eating among college women. *Journal of Counseling & Development, 84,* 341–348.

Vandiver, B. J. (2001). Psychological nigrescence revisited: Introduction and overview. *Journal of Multicultural Counseling and Development, 29,* 165–173.

Vanzant, I. (1998). *Yesterday I cried*. New York: A Fireside Book.

Vasquez, H., & Magraw, S. (2005). Building relationships across privilege: Becoming an ally in the therapeutic relationship. In M. Mirkin, K. Suyemoto, & B. Okun (Eds.), *Psychotherapy with women: Exploring diverse contexts and identities* (pp. 64–83). New York: Guilford Press.

Vasquez, M. J. T. (1994). *Latinas*. In L. Comas-Dias & B. Greene (Eds.), *Women of color* (pp. 114–138). New York: Guilford Press.

Venner, K. L., Wall, T. L., Lau, P., & Ehlers, C. L. (2006). Testing of an orthogonal measure of cultural identification with adult mission Indians. *Cultural Diversity and Ethnic Minority Psychology, 12,* 632–643.

Vera, E. M., & Speight, S. L. (2003). Multicultural competence, social justice, and counseling psychology: Expanding our roles. *The Counseling Psychologist, 31,* 253–272.

Vernon, I. (2002). *Killing us quietly: Native Americans and HIV/AIDS*. Lincoln, NE: Bison Books.

Vontress, C. E. (1986). Social and cultural foundations. In R. Hayes & J. Lewis (Eds.), *In the counseling profession* (pp. 215–250). Itasca, IL: Peacock Publishers.

Vontress, C. E. (2004). Reactions to the multicultural counseling competencies debate. *Journal of Mental Health Counseling, 24,* 74–80.

Wachtel P. L. (2002). Psychoanalysis and the disenfranchised: From therapy to justice. *Psychoanalytic Psychology, 19,* 199–215.

Waldman, C. (2000). *Atlas of the North American Indian*. New York: Checkmark Books.

Walker, A. (1987). Oppressed hair puts a ceiling on the brain. In *Living by the word: Selected writings, 1973–1983*. Retrieved January 27, 2008, from http://www.geocities.com/Hotsprings/Falls/8860/ceiling.html

Wall, V. A., & Evans, N. J. (1992). Using psychosocial development theories to understand and work with gay and lesbian persons. In N. J. Evans & V. A. Hall (Eds.), *Beyond tolerance: Gays, lesbians, and bisexuals on campus* (pp. 25–28). Alexandria, VA: American College Personnel Association.

Ward, J. V. (1989). Racial identity formation and transformation. In C. Gilligan, N. P. Lyons, & T. J. Hanmer (Eds.), *Making connections: The relational worlds of adolescent girls at Emma Willard School* (pp. 215–232). New York: Troy Press.

Ward, J. V. (2000). *The skin we're in: Teaching our children to be emotionally strong, socially smart, and spiritually connected.* New York: Free Press.

Warren, A. K., & Constantine, M. G. (2007). Social justice issues. In M. Constantine (Ed.), *Clinical practice with people of color* (pp. 231–242). New York: Teachers College Press.

Washington, C. S. (1987). Counseling Black men. In M. Scher, M. Stevens, G. Good, & G. A. Eichenfield (Eds.), *Handbook of counseling and psychotherapy* (pp. 192–202). Newbury Park, CA: Sage.

Watt, S. K., Robinson, T. L., & Lupton-Smith, H. (2002). Building ego and racial identity: Preliminary perspectives on counselors-in-training. *Journal of Counseling and Development, 80,* 94–100.

Webster, M., Jr., & Driskell, J. E., Jr. (1983). Beauty as status. *American Journal of Sociology, 89,* 140–164.

Weedon, C. (1987). *Feminist practice and post-structuralist theory.* New York: Blackwell Publishing.

Wehrly, B. (1995). *Pathways to multicultural counseling competence: A developmental journey.* Pacific Grove, CA: Brooks/Cole.

Weisman, L. K. (1992). *Discrimination by design: A feminist critique of the man-made environment.* Urbana: University of Illinois Press.

Wendell, S. (1989). Toward a feminist theory of disability. *Hypatia, 4,* 63–81.

West, A. E., & Newman, D. L. (2007). Childhood behavioral inhibition and the experience of social anxiety in American Indian adolescents. *Cultural Diversity and Ethnic Minority Psychology, 13,* 197–206.

West, C., & Zimmerman, D. H. (1991). Doing gender. In J. Lorber & S. A. Farrell (Eds.), *The social construction of gender* (pp. 13–37). Newbury Park, CA: Sage.

West, W. (2000). *Psychotherapy and spirituality: Crossing the line between therapy and religion.* London: Sage Publications.

Wester, S. R., Kuo, B. C. H., & Vogel, D. L. (2006). Multicultural coping: Chinese Canadian adolescents, male gender role conflict, and psychological distress. *Psychology of Men & Masculinity, 7,* 83–100.

Wester, S. R., Vogel, D. L., & Archer, J. (2004). Male restricted emotionality and counseling supervision. *Journal of Counseling & Development, 82,* 91–98.

Wester, S. R., Vogel, D. L., Wei, M., & McLain, R. (2006). African American men, gender role conflict, and psychological distress: The role of racial identity. *Journal of Counseling & Development, 84,* 419–429.

Wiggins-Frame, M., & Braun, C. (1996). Counseling African Americans: Integrating spirituality in therapy. *Counseling and Values, 41,* 16–28.

Wijeyesinghe, C. (2001). Racial identity in multiracial people: An alternative paradigm. In C. Wijeyesinghe & B. Jackson III (Eds.), *New perspectives on racial identity development: A theoretical and practical anthology* (pp. 129–152). New York: New York University Press.

Wikipedia. www.en.wikipedia.org/wiki/Queer_theory, retrieved October 5, 2007.

Wilkinson, D. (1997). Reappraising the race, class, gender equation: A critical theoretical perspective. *Smith College Studies in Social Work, 67,* 261–276.

Wilson, T. P. (1992). Blood quantum: Native American mixed bloods. In M. P. P. Root (Ed.), *Racially mixed people in America* (pp. 108–126). Newbury Park, CA: Sage.

Wilson, W. J. (1994). The Black community: Race and class. In R. Takaki (Ed.), *From different shores: Perspectives on race and ethnicity in America* (2nd ed., pp. 243–250). New York: Oxford University Press.

Wise, T. (2005). *White like me: Reflections on race from a privileged son.* Brooklyn, NY: Soft Skull Press.

Witmer, J. M., & Sweeney, T. J. (1992). A holistic model for wellness and prevention over the life span, *Journal of Counseling & Development, 71,* 140–143.

Wong, F., & Halgin, R. (2006). The "model minority": Bane or blessing for Asian Americans? *Journal of Multicultural Counseling and Development, 34,* 38–49.

Wong, M. G. (1988). The Chinese American family. In C. H. Mindel, R. W. Habenstein, & R. Wright (Eds.), *Ethnic families in America: Patterns and variations* (3rd ed., pp. 230–257). New York: Elsevier.

Worell, J., & Remer, P. (1992). *Feminist perspectives in therapy: An empowerment model for women.* New York: Wiley.

World Health Organization. (2005). *Tobacco free initiative.* Retrieved September 1, 2007, from http://www.who.int/tobacco/en/

Worthington, R. L., Dillon, F. R., & Becker-Schutte, A. M. (2005). Development, reliability, and validity of the lesbian, gay, and bisexual knowledge and attitudes scale for heterosexuals. *Journal of Counseling Psychology, 52,* 104–118.

Worthington, R. L., Soth-McNett, A. M., & Moreno, M. V. (2007). Multicultural counseling competencies research: A 20 year content analysis. *The Counseling Psychologist, 54,* 351–361.

Wrenn, C. G. (1962). The culturally encapsulated counselor. *Harvard Educational Review, 32,* 444–449.

Wu, F. (2002). *Yellow: Race in America beyond Black and White.* New York: Basic Books.

Yakushko, O., & Chronister, K. M. (2005). Immigrant women and counseling: The invisible others. *Journal of Counseling & Development, 83,* 292–298.

Yeh, C., & Wang, Y. (2000). Asian American coping attitudes, sources, and practices: Implications for indigenous counseling strategies. *Journal of College Student Development, 41,* 94–103.

Ying, Y. (2002). The conception of depression in Chinese Americans. In K. Kurasaki, S. Okasaki, & S. Sue (Eds.), *Asian American mental health: Assessment theories and methods* (pp. 173–184). New York: Kluwer Academic.

Ying, Y., & Miller, L. S. (1992). Help-seeking behavior and attitude of Chinese Americans regarding psychological problems. *American Journal of Community Psychology, 20,* 549–556.

Young, J. S., Wiggins-Frame, M., & Cashwell, C. S. (2007). Spirituality and counselor competence: A national survey of American Counseling Association members. *Journal of Counseling & Development, 85*(1), 47–52.

Zane, N. W. S., & Huh-Kim, J. (1998). Addictive behaviors. In L. S. Lee & N. Zane (Eds.), *Handbook of Asian American psychology* (pp. 527–554). Thousand Oaks, CA: Sage.

Zetzer, H.A. (2005). White out. Privilege and its problems. In S. Anderson & V. Middleton (Eds.), *Explorations in privilege, oppression, and diversity* (pp. 3–16). Belmont, CA: Thomson, Cole.

Zia, H. (2000). *Asian American dreams: The emergence of an American people.* New York: Farrar, Straus and Giroux.

Zinn, H. (2003). *A people's history of the United States. 1492–present.* New York: HarperCollins.

Zitzelsberger, H (2005). (In)visibility: accounts of embodiment of women with physical disabilities and differences. *Disability & Society, 20,* 389–403.

Zola, I. K. (1991). Bringing our bodies and ourselves back in: Reflections on a past, present, and future "medical sociology." *Journal of Health and Social Behavior, 32,* 1–16.

Zuckerman, M. (1990). Some dubious premises in research and theory on racial differences. *American Psychologist, 45,* 1297–1303.

Zur, O. (2006). Therapeutic boundaries and dual relationships in rural practice: Ethical, clinical and standard of care considerations. *Journal of Rural Community Psychology, V. E9/1* (Online Journal).

NAME INDEX